To Denis with
lov

December 16, 2019
eBay

THE ENGLISH AUDEN

THE ENGLISH
AUDEN

Poems, Essays and Dramatic Writings
1927–1939

EDITED BY
EDWARD MENDELSON

FABER AND FABER
3 Queen Square
London

First published in 1977
by Faber and Faber Limited
3 Queen Square London WC1
Printed in Great Britain by
BAS Printers Limited, Over Wallop, Hampshire
All rights reserved

British Library Cataloguing in Publication Data

Auden, Wystan Hugh
  The English Auden.
  I. Title   II. Mendelson, Edward
  828'.9'1209   PR6001.U4
  ISBN 0-571-10832-6

Contents

PART III: THE ORATORS

PART IV: POEMS 1931–1936

PART V

PART VI: POEMS 1936–1939

PART VII

PART VIII: THEATRE, FILM, RADIO

PART IX: ESSAYS AND REVIEWS

Preface

Auden's adult career began with a rejection from T. S. Eliot. In June 1927, when Auden was twenty, he submitted a book of poems to Faber and Faber. Eliot, who read poetry for the firm, took three months to reply. 'I am very slow to make up my mind', he wrote Auden at last; 'I do not feel that any of the enclosed is quite right, but I should be interested to follow your work.' Although Auden tried to find comfort in this—'On the whole coming from Eliot's reserve I think it is really quite complimentary', he explained to Christopher Isherwood—he soon came to accept Eliot's judgement. None of the poems in his 1927 manuscript survived into the book that Eliot accepted and published in 1930.

Not more than a few weeks before he received Eliot's rejection Auden wrote his first poems in what he would later recognise as his own voice, the first of his poems to occupy his early personal landscape of guarded frontiers and doomed heroics. The earliest poem that he would later (after this twenty-fifth year) want to preserve begins: 'Who stands, the crux left of the watershed'. It was written in August 1927. Later titled 'The Watershed', this poem marks the watershed or divide between Auden's juvenilia and his adult work. (Two slightly earlier poems found their way into the 1930 volume, but Auden decided to reject them by 1932, possibly even earlier.) A poem written a few weeks before 'The Watershed' introduces a frontier into its first line—'On the frontier at dawn getting down,/Hot eyes were soothed with swallows'—but that frontier extended no further into the poem. In contrast 'The Watershed' knows nothing but barriers.

Auden wrote these border-country poems in the long vacation following his second year at Oxford, and wrote more of them during his final year. He went down in July 1928 with a third-class degree and the manuscript of his first long work, 'Paid on Both Sides: A Charade'. 'The country house charade', he wrote a few years later, is among 'the most living drama of to-day.' Having accepted an invitation to a friend's country house for August, he wrote 'Paid on Both Sides' in the hope of seeing it performed there. But instead, as he wrote Isherwood, 'They refuse to do the play, as they say the village won't stand it.' Also in the long vacation he prepared a little book of twenty poems which Stephen Spender tried to print on a hand-press in an edition of about thirty copies. The press wouldn't stand it, and broke down, leaving Spender to take the book to Oxford to be finished and bound by a commercial printer.

By October 1928 Auden had settled into a middle-class suburb of Berlin. In December he moved to a Berlin slum, where he remained until the following June, when he spent a month in the Harz

Mountains before returning to England. In a café shortly after his arrival he met John Layard, an anthropologist and disciple of the American psychologist Homer Lane. Until Auden met Layard he had written only of a world trapped within borders. Now, through Lane's Lawrentian vision of liberated impulse, a cure seemed possible for the stalled conditions of Auden's poems. In December 1928 he finished a rewritten version of 'Paid on Both Sides', to which he had added the curative dream of John Nower, with its possibilities of reconciliation and healing. (Both versions of the charade are printed in this edition.) Auden however sensed the limits of Lane's psychology: he left the charade's tragic ending unchanged.

In the spring of 1929, after a brief visit from Isherwood, Auden began another play with the working title *The Reformatory*. When he returned to England in July he and Isherwood finished it in collaboration. They gave it the title *The Enemies of a Bishop, or, Die When I Say When: A Morality in Four Acts*. The title is unfortunately the play's high point. Its various sketchy plots—a governor of a reformatory becomes infatuated with a boy in drag who escapes from his reformatory and later becomes the target of a white-slave ring; the governor's brother (the central character, accompanied by a Spectre who keeps reciting Auden's poems at inconvenient moments), who is manager of a lead mine, seduces his under-manager's wife and is then ruined by the mine's failure—are resolved by the appearance of Bishop Law, who, the authors seemed to think, was modelled on Homer Lane. Auden and Isherwood made no effort to publish this farrago.

After Auden returned to England he spent a few months tutoring in London. In April 1930, his allowance from his parents at an end, he took a job as master at the Larchfield School, Helensburgh, Dunbarton. Faber accepted his *Poems* at about this time, but wanted to print only a slim volume of thirty short poems, without 'Paid on Both Sides' which Eliot had earlier in the year printed in *The Criterion*. The charade was eventually added when the book was in proof, and when it was published in September—in blue paper covers at 2/6d—Auden had nearly finished a third play, *The Fronny*. Eliot looked at this near the end of the year, but for some reason the other directors of Faber did not. (They read it a year later, when *The Orators* was almost complete, and for a time planned to publish both works in a single volume. Eventually *The Fronny* was dropped. In fact it seems to have disappeared entirely, for the manuscript has never come to light.[1])

Early in 1931 Auden began work on *The Orators*. This book grew in stages. Originally Auden seems to have thought of it only as the present

---

[1]Probably it will turn up the day this book is published. 'Fronny' was the name some German boys gave to Francis Turville-Petre, a Berlin friend of Auden and Isherwood (and the 'Ambrose' of Isherwood's *Down There on a Visit*). His eponymous play apparently began with his departure from England and continued with the search made for him by a young man named Alan—essentially the plot of *The Dog Beneath the Skin*. Two brief manuscript fragments survive, and it is possible to identify some of the poems that served time in the play before moving on to richer pastures: the prothalamion later used in *The Dog*; 'What's in your mind'; 'Between attention and attention'; 'Doom is dark'; and, probably, 'Who will endure'—the latter three presumably as choruses. Isherwood has recently written at length about Fronny, and about Auden's latter months in Berlin, in *Christopher and his Kind*.

first part, 'The Initiates'; then he planned to add the 'Journal of an Airman' to which he referred, while writing it, as the 'second half' of the book; the third part, the Six Odes, he added at the end of the year, although some of the odes were written earlier. While working on the Journal, in August 1931, he wrote a friend that 'In a sense the work is my memorial to Lawrence; i.e., the theme is the failure of the romantic conception of personality.' About seven months later, shortly before the book went to press, he gave a somewhat different account in a preface which he submitted to Eliot as a possible addition to the typescript:

> I feel this book is more obscure than it ought to be. I'm sorry, for obscurity, as a friend once said to me, is mostly swank. The central theme is a revolutionary hero. The first book describes the effect of him and of his failure on those whom he meets; the second book is his own account; and the last some personal reflections on the question of leadership in our time.

Eliot, with more experience in these matters, advised Auden not to apologise for obscurity. The preface was dropped. Five months later Auden's description of the book changed focus once again. 'I am very dissatisfied with this book', he wrote in reply to a reader's letter; 'I didn't take enough trouble over it, and the result is far too obscure and equivocal. It is meant to be a critique of the fascist outlook, but from its reception among some of my contemporaries, and on rereading it myself, I see that it can, most of it, be interpreted as a favourable exposition. The whole Journal ought to be completely rewritten.'[2]

The Orators is less political than Auden's preface and later explanations suggest, but he was beginning to develop his own political theories—or fantasies—while he was writing it. 'I've had a most important vision about groups which is going to destroy the Church', he wrote Isherwood in October 1931. He provided no details, but some traces may have persisted into his essay on 'Writing' the following spring. His poems became explicitly political for the first time during 1932, when he wrote one or two poems in the voice of a communist. In the same year he also began the first of his plays with any political content, *The Dance of Death*, the 'picture of the decline of a class' ('Middle Class', interjected the chorus in the stage production of 1935) whose death Karl Marx announces as the curtain falls. This play was a commission from Rupert Doone who, together with the painter Robert Medley (the friend Auden mentions in 'Letter to Lord Byron' who first asked him if he wrote poetry) and others, had recently organised the Group Theatre. Doone's commission was for two works, a choral ballet on the Orpheus theme and a play based on the *danse macabre*. What Auden wrote was not quite what Doone had asked for, but was more appropriate to the increasingly political concerns the Group would develop during the next few years.

In the autumn and winter of 1932 Auden—now teaching at the Downs School, Colwall—worked on a long poem in cantos, a dream

---

[2] However, when he had the chance to rewrite it in 1934 for a second edition he did little more than drop two of the interpolated poems and re-sex the airman's lover from female to male.

vision in which Gerald Heard as Virgil led Auden as Dante through the hell of England. Auden wrote about a thousand lines of alliterative verse before abandoning it, although he saved a few fragments for later use elsewhere. ('The Witnesses' was an interpolation in this poem, using a different metre.) The poem, which remains unpublished, was unworkable from the start.[3] Unlike his exiled Florentine original, the Auden of this poem makes no response to what he sees—is barred, like everyone in his early poems, from participating in the world beyond the frontiers of the self. After stopping work on the poem, possibly in January 1933, Auden appears to have written no verse at all until April. Then he wrote the first of a group of poems whose order is significant. This first poem is another dream-vision, not about England but about himself, and not grandiose like his cantos, but comic and compact. This poem, printed here for the first time (it begins 'The month was April') portrays the good ship *Wystan Auden Esquire* in search of 'the Islands of Milk and Honey / Where there's neither death nor old age / And the poor have all the money.' But a month later, in May, in the sestina 'Hearing of harvests', Auden renounced the 'dream of islands', hoping instead that the 'sorrow' that induced it might 'melt', enabling us to 'rebuild our cities'.

In this poem Auden did not pretend to know what it would mean if sorrow melted, nor could he say what tasks would be required in rebuilding cities, but a month later an answer came to him. 'One fine summer night in June 1933', he wrote thirty years afterwards in an account of a 'Vision of Agape' (which he did not claim explicitly as his own, although he said it was an account 'for the authenticity of which I can vouch', as he could do only if he had written it himself),

> I was sitting on a lawn after dinner with three colleagues, two women and one man. We liked each other well enough but we were certainly not intimate friends, nor had any one of us a sexual interest in another. Incidentally, we had not drunk any alcohol. We were talking casually about everyday matters when, quite suddenly and unexpectedly, something happened. I felt myself invaded by a power which, though I consented to it, was irresistible and certainly not mine. For the first time in my life I knew exactly—because, thanks to the power, I was doing it—what it means to love one's neighbour as oneself. I was also certain, though the conversation continued to be perfectly ordinary, that my three colleagues were having the same experience. (In the case of one of them, I was able later to confirm this.) My personal feelings towards them were unchanged—they were still colleagues, not intimate friends—but I felt their existence as themselves to be of infinite value and rejoiced in it. . . .
>
> (*Forewords and Afterwords*, p. 69)

This is seen through the resolving lens of hindsight but, whatever the precise nature of the event, certainly, in Auden's phrase, 'something happened'. The poem occasioned by the event, 'Out on the lawn I lie in

[3] The poem is of far more scholarly than literary interest; a transcript of the draft fragment will appear in the *Review of English Studies* in 1978.

bed', presents metrical celebrations unlike anything Auden had written earlier—as well as a vision of cities rebuilding, to fulfil the hopes of his previous poem, with 'sounds of riveting'. Within less than a month he asked Eliot if he could review for *The Criterion* Violet Clifton's *The Book of Talbot*, a book altogether different from anything he had reviewed before, and of which he wrote—after dismissing as without interest its ostensible subject, the life of the explorer Talbot Clifton—'It shows more clearly than anything I have read for a long time that the first criterion of success in any human activity, the necessary preliminary, whether to scientific discovery or to artistic vision, is intensity of attention or, less pompously, love.' The book's value lay in its author's love for her subject, not in the subject itself. There is nothing like this in Auden's earlier prose, nor would he sound so exalted a note again until 1940. It is possible to read almost all his work during the rest of the thirties as a series of attempts to learn—or to evade—the meaning of that summer night in June 1933.

The history of Auden's work during the next few months is unclear. He finished working on *The Dance of Death* (he sent it to Faber at the end of August); and he seems to have begun a sequence of rather detached love sonnets. The following summer, 1934, after composing more of these sonnets, he wrote another play for the Group Theatre, *The Chase*. This he submitted to Faber in October, but withdrew it a month later. Isherwood, to whom he had sent a copy earlier, suggested extensive changes (including the final burial of the reformatory subplot which had survived from *The Enemies of a Bishop*), and the two once again drifted into a collaboration. Auden flew to Copenhagen to visit Isherwood in January 1935, and returned with the nearly complete draft of the rewritten version, *Where is Francis?* Rupert Doone gave the play its final title, *The Dog Beneath the Skin*.

That spring and summer Auden began working on another collective undertaking, documentary film. While still teaching at the Downs School he wrote a lyric for the film *Coal Face* and the first version of his narration for *Night Mail*. Both were set by Benjamin Britten. In September he moved to London to work full time (at £3 a week) for the G.P.O. Film Unit under John Grierson. He worked less as a writer than as an apprentice and odd-jobs man, sometimes carrying cans of film, sometimes serving as assistant director. His colleagues may have hesitated to give him greater responsibility: when he directed a brief shot of a railway guard, the guard dropped dead a minute later. A planned sequel to *Night Mail*, to be called *Air Mail to Australia*, was his most ambitious project. Grierson planned to put him aboard the mail plane, to photograph the stops along the way, but the project never got off the ground.

Auden left the film unit in March 1936, when he visited Isherwood in Portugal where, in a month, they wrote *The Ascent of F6*. Back in England, he signed a contract with Faber for a travel book on Iceland. He sailed there in June, followed by Louis MacNeice and a school party from Bryanston, and returned in September.

Before he sailed he delivered to Faber the manuscript of a book titled *Poems 1936*, with a dedication to Erika Mann whom he had married the year before to provide her with a British passport. When

Faber's sales manager warned that Auden's title would mislead buyers into expecting a complete retrospective collection, Eliot asked Auden to supply another. Eliot's letter reached Auden in Iceland quickly enough, but Auden's reply, in which he suggested the titles *It's a Way* or *The Island* (or, he added, 'On the analogy of *Burnt Norton* I might call it *Piddle-in-the-hole*'), reached England too late to be used. Faber had already devised the title *Look, Stranger!*, and in the absence of Auden's reply they went ahead and used it for the printed book, which they published in October. Auden was not pleased. He wrote his American publisher that 'Faber invented a bloody title while I was away without telling me. It sounds like the work of a vegetarian lady novelist. Will you please call the American edition *On this island.*'

The latter part of 1936 was spent preparing *Letters from Iceland* with MacNeice. In one of the letters Auden printed in the book he mentioned that he had just heard the news of the outbreak of civil war in Spain. In December, with the book nearly finished, he decided to join the International Brigade. He wrote E. R. Dodds: 'I so dislike everyday political activities that I won't do them, but here is something I can do as a citizen and not as a writer, and as I have no dependents, I feel I ought to go.' Shortly afterwards, in another letter to Dodds, he continued:

> I am not one of those who believe that poetry need or even should be directly political, but in a critical period such as ours, I do believe that the poet must have direct knowledge of the major political events. . . .
> I feel I can speak with authority about la condition humaine of only a small clan of English intellectuals and professional people and that the time has come to gamble on something bigger.
> I shall probably be a bloody bad soldier but how can I speak to/for them without becoming one?

But before he went out in January 1937 he had decided not to become a soldier after all. He intended to drive an ambulance instead, but when he got to Valencia the government refused him permission, and put him to work broadcasting propaganda. Apparently he did this only briefly. It is unclear how he spent the rest of his seven weeks in Spain. (Twenty years later he wrote that when he arrived in Barcelona and found the churches closed, 'To my astonishment, this discovery left me profoundly shocked and disturbed. The feeling was far too intense to be the result of a mere liberal dislike of intolerance, the notion that it is wrong to stop people from doing what they like, even if it is something silly like going to church. I could not escape acknowledging that, however I had consciously ignored and rejected the Church for sixteen years, the existence of churches and what went on in them had all the time been very important to me.') When he returned to England he said almost nothing of his visit. He wrote a poem, 'Spain', which is less committed than its first readers may have imagined (its royalties went to Medical Aid for Spain), and, when asked to make a statement on the war, he wrote:

> I support the Valencia Government in Spain because its defeat by

the forces of International Fascism would be a major disaster for Europe. It would make a European war more probable; and the spread of Fascist Ideology and practice to countries as yet comparatively free from them, which would inevitably follow upon a Fascist victory in Spain, would create an atmosphere in which the creative artist and all who care for justice, liberty and culture would find it impossible to work or even exist.

This says nothing about the merits of the Valencia government itself. (The macabre ballads he wrote later this year seem an elliptical rejection of political solutions and of his own public role.)

Auden and Isherwood began planning another play shortly after Auden's return, but they did not write it until August, in Dover, after Auden taught the summer term at the Downs School. The play was *On the Frontier*. During the autumn, while they discussed plans for a production with its chief backer J. M. Keynes, Auden wrote a radio script *Hadrian's Wall* for the BBC and, to the distress of some of his admirers, accepted the King's Gold Medal for Poetry. The plans for *On the Frontier* were put aside while Auden and Isherwood took up work on a commission they had received from their American publisher Random House for a travel book about Asia. They chose to report on the Sino-Japanese War.

They sailed in January 1938, spent three months in China and a few days in Japan, then returned *via* Canada and the United States at the end of July. They brought with them a revised *On the Frontier*, their travel diaries, and some of the sonnets that Auden would extend into a sequence with verse commentary. They lectured frequently on China during the autumn while finishing *Journey to a War*, then visited Brussels for a month at the end of the year.

They had stayed two weeks in New York on their way back from China, and had decided then to move to America. Later Auden said that he had known for more than two years, ever since they wrote *The Ascent of F6*, that he would someday leave England. He had already begun to find intolerable his public role as court poet to the left. (*F6* is in part an allegory of an artist destroyed by the public role that his private terrors tempted him to accept.) Immediately after *F6* Auden's poems, which in earlier years had been unable to cross a border or even move 'from town to town', began to travel all over the map. Their titles referred to Iceland, Spain, Dover, Oxford, Paris (this one unpublished), the Sphinx, Macao, Hongkong, China and Brussels. (In 1937 Auden signed a contract for a travel book about America, to be written in collaboration with Stephen Spender, but the project fell through.) Throughout this period Auden's voyage poems all made a single complaint:

No, he discovers nothing: he does not want to arrive.
The journey is false; the false journey really an illness . . .

Now he hoped to make a different voyage, one in which

maybe the fever shall have a cure, the true journey an end
Where hearts meet and are really true . . .

On January 19, 1939, after a brief stay in England, Auden and Isherwood sailed for New York. Early in April Auden met Chester Kallman for the first time. They would remain together for the rest of his life. A few months later Auden began, for the first time since adolescence, to attend church. Before leaving England he and Isherwood had contracted to write a travel book on America with the title *Address Not Known*. They never began it. By the summer of 1939 Auden had stopped writing poems about places, and turned his attention instead to time. He now gave his poems such titles as 'Another Time', 'Time with Us' (a manuscript title of 'The hour-glass whispers'), 'New Year Letter', 'Spring in Wartime', 'Autumn 1940', 'No Time', 'For the Time Being'.

For a few months his English manner and American matter overlapped. 'September 1, 1939' has a temporal title, and is set firmly in New York, but retains Auden's English accent. One reason he left England, he wrote in later years, 'was precisely to *stop* me writing poems like "September 1, 1939"'. He called the poem 'a hangover from the U.K. It takes time to cure oneself.'

A letter to a friend in England, late in 1939, spoke in more positive terms:

America

The most decisive experience of my life so far. It has taught me the kind of writer I am, i.e. an introvert who can only develop by obeying his introversion. All Americans are introverts. I adore New York as it is the only city in which I find I can work and live quietly. For the first time I am leading a life which remotely approximates to the way I think I ought to live. I have never written nor read so much.

His feelings would change in later years, as would his feelings about England. (In the late forties he hoped to write one of the Shell County Guides.) But in 1939 he felt his departure was irrevocable. 'No, God willing,' he wrote a friend, 'I never wish to see England again. All I want is when this [war] is over, for all of you to come here.'

*　　*　　*

CONTENTS OF THIS EDITION Auden published his poems of 1927–1939 in three collections: *Poems* (1930, second edition with seven substitutions 1933), *Look, Stranger!* (1936, American edition as *On This Island* 1937), and *Another Time* (1940). The present edition contains all the poems in these three books, less some of the poems in *Another Time* written after Auden's arrival in America. Also present are *The Orators* (1932, second edition 1934), the short poems and 'Letter to Lord Byron' from *Letters from Iceland* (1937), and all the poems in *Journey to a War* (1939). I have added most of the poems Auden published only in periodicals or anthologies during this period, and have included four poems that Auden never published in any form. I have also included excerpts from the plays *The Dance of Death* (1933), *The Dog Beneath the Skin* (1935), and *The Ascent of F6* (1936); from an unpublished draft of *On the Frontier* (and from the published version, 1938); and two excerpts from the unpublished plays *The Enemies of a Bishop* and *The Chase*. I have made a selection from Auden's essays and reviews, and have added to this a selection of journal entries from 1929 and the first chapter of an unpublished book written in 1939. The unpublished early version of 'Paid on Both Sides' appears in an appendix; the published version is Part I of the book. Another appendix includes the poems in the privately printed *Poems* (1928) that did not survive into later editions; the two poems from the 1932 edition of *The Orators* that Auden dropped in 1934; and the poems written from 1939 to 1942 that Auden published in book form but did not preserve for later collections. The present edition and the *Collected Poems* thus reprint between them all the separable poems that Auden published in book form. In excerpting from the plays I have followed the example set by Auden in his 1938 *Selected Poems*; a complete edition of the plays and libretti is in preparation.

PROSE SELECTIONS   The versatile and integrated prose style familiar from Auden's later books is a product of his American years. During the thirties he had not yet developed the coherent vision of literature and society that made such a style possible. Therefore any selection—or even a complete reprinting—of Auden's early prose will have a somewhat miscellaneous air. For the present volume I have chosen, for the most part, those essays and reviews that best serve as a commentary on the poems and on Auden's changing ideas of poetry's social role. It is mostly for convenience that these pieces are printed in a single numbered sequence; ideally, perhaps, each piece should be read, not in sequence, but in conjunction with the poems written at about the same time. Some of the essays express the intentions that Auden, with varying success, tried to fulfil in his poems (see, for example, items III, XI, XIII, XV, XVII, XX, XXI, XXII, XXVI); others present the social views which partly determined his problematic relation with his audience (II, IV, V, VI, VII, XII, XIV, XXIII, XXIV, XXV); while others are of biographical interest (VIII, X, XVIII, XXVII). Auden apparently reworked some of his reviews into a book in 1939, but he never published it, and the manuscript is lost.

ORDER OF POEMS   For the shorter poems I have followed, in the main, the chronological order of composition to the extent that I could determine it. The notes in Appendix II list the instances where I have used an order devised by Auden or have otherwise departed slightly from the known order of composition. Part II, Poems 1927–1931, corresponds to the two editions of *Poems*; Part IV, 1931–1936, to *Look, Stranger!*; and Part VI, 1936–1939, to *Another Time*. The order of poems as originally printed in these books is given in Appendix III.

TEXT   I have used the text in the form it reached at the end of 1939. That is to say, I have used the text of the 1933 second edition of *Poems* (although I also reprint the poems that appeared only in 1930), the 1934 edition of *The Orators*, the American edition of *Look, Stranger!—On This Island*—which included Auden's corrections, and the American edition of *Another Time*, which is more accurate than the British. I have incorporated corrections and changes Auden made in friends' copies, and have occasionally amended according to manuscript readings; Appendix II records the most significant of these, and also sets out some of the more interesting readings from early versions (e.g., in 'Spain'). When a poem made its way into one of the plays I have not felt bound to use the latest version, which was often as much the product of stage necessities as of literary ones. I have thus printed the full texts of 'The Witnesses' and 'The soldier loves his rifle', not the fragments that survived into the plays, and in the excerpts from the plays themselves I have twice used versions earlier than the final ones. A few lines and phrases in the uncollected poems and early versions will be found repeated in later texts.

In a few places in *The Orators*, and once in 'Letter to Lord Byron', I have restored manuscript readings changed in the printed editions to avoid libel, obscenity or discourtesy. The most important of these is in Ode IV of *The Orators* where I have restored some proper names concealed in earlier editions by names taken from the Mortmere stories devised by Isherwood and Edward Upward. In the previous editions of 'Journal of an Airman' one of the 'enemy faces' was 'the June bride'; this was Eliot's palliation of 'the fucked hen'.

Auden's punctuation in his early years was erratic or worse. He wrote a reviewer in 1936, 'You are quite right in saying that some of the difficulties in the first book [*Poems*] were due to punctuation. I never have understood that art. Now I make someone else do it for me.' On the whole, I have not, however, interfered with the punctuation of the printed texts except to replace full stops or semi-colons with colons where the sense clearly demands them, and to make a few other changes, recorded in Appendix II, on the basis of manuscript readings. Poems printed here for the first time have been fitted with minimal punctuation.

I have corrected Auden's miscopied quotations from books under review.

TITLES AND DATES I have used the latest titles Auden provided by 1939, except that I have generally followed his own early practice in dropping titles used in periodicals when collecting poems in a book, and also in dropping titles such as 'Song', or titles like 'Prologue' that make sense only in the context of the book where they appear. The titles Auden used in his books are given in Appendix III. The dates appended to each poem are dates of composition, or the date on which a poem related ancestrally to the printed poem was first complete. ('Sir, no man's enemy', for example, was originally a much longer poem; I have given the date of the long version, as the date when Auden trimmed it to its present size cannot now be determined.) For the published prose pieces in Part IX the dates are dates of publication, as only one or two dates of composition could be identified.

*   *   *

Auden's friends and mine have been generous with their help in the preparation of this edition. Thanks are due above all to Christopher Isherwood; also to Alan Ansen, Nicolas Barker, B. C. Bloomfield, Lord Britten, David Bromwich, Professor A. H. Campbell, Professor E. R. Dodds, Mrs. Valerie Eliot (by whose kind permission I have quoted a letter from T. S. Eliot), John Fuller, Margaret Gardiner,

Theodore Hoffman, Professor Samuel Hynes, Professor Wendell S. Johnson, Dr. David Luke, Dr. Lucy McDiarmid, Robert Medley, Charles Monteith, Dr. Alice Prochaska, Julie Rivkin, Professor Peter H. Salus, Dr. M. J. Sidnell, Janet Adam Smith, Stephen Spender, John Whitehead, Robert A. Wilson, T. C. Worsley, and Basil Wright. For courtesies extended when I examined manuscripts in their care I am grateful to the curators of the British Library manuscript room; the libraries of the University of California, Berkeley and Los Angeles; the Columbia University Library; the University of Chicago Library; the library of Exeter College, Oxford; the Houghton Library; the library of King's College, Cambridge; the Lockwood Memorial Library; the University of Minnesota Library; the Berg Collection of the New York Public Library; the Swarthmore College Library; and the Humanities Research Center at the University of Texas. I am happy also to thank the resourceful staff of the National Film Archive.

EDWARD MENDELSON

Part I

Paid on Both Sides

A CHARADE

(TO CECIL DAY-LEWIS)

CHARACTERS

Lintzgarth	*Nattrass*
JOHN NOWER	AARON SHAW*****
DICK	SETH SHAW
GEORGE****	THE SPY—SETH'S BROTHER
WALTER	BERNARD
KURT	SETH'S MOTHER***
CULLEY	ANNE SHAW
STEPHEN**	
ZEPPEL—JOHN NOWER'S SERVANT	
NO. 6	
STURTON	
JOAN—MOTHER OF JOHN NOWER	
TRUDY***	

FATHER XMAS*
THE DOCTOR
BO****
PO*****
THE MAN-WOMAN
THE DOCTOR'S BOY**
THE PHOTOGRAPHER
THE ANNOUNCER*
THE CHIEF GUEST*
THE BUTLER*

THE CHORUS

The starred parts should be doubled

[*No scenery is required. The stage should have a curtained-off recess. The distinction between the two hostile parties should be marked by different coloured arm-bands. The chorus, which should not consist of more than three persons, wear similar and distinctive clothing.*]

[*Enter Trudy and Walter.*]

T.   You've only just heard?
W.   Yes. A breakdown at the Mill needed attention, kept me all morning. I guessed no harm. But lately, riding at leisure, Dick met me, panted disaster. I came here at once. How did they get him?
T.   In Kettledale above Colefangs road passes where high banks overhang dangerous from ambush. To Colefangs had to go, would speak with Layard, Jerry and Hunter with him only. They must have stolen news, for Red Shaw waited with ten, so

I

Jerry said, till for last time unconscious. Hunter was killed at first shot. They fought, exhausted ammunition, a brave defence but fight no more.

W.   Has Joan been told yet?

T.   Yes. It couldn't be helped. Shock, starting birth pangs, caused a premature delivery.

W.   How is she?

T.   Bad, I believe. But here's the doctor.

[*Enter Doctor.*]

Well, Doctor, how are things going?

D.   Better, thanks. We've had a hard fight, but it's going to be all right. She'll pull through and have a fine infant as well. My God, I'm thirsty after all that. Where can I get a drink?

W.   Here in the next room, Doctor.

[*Exeunt. Back curtains draw. Joan with child and corpse.*]

J.   Not from this life, not from this life is any
     To keep; sleep, day and play would not help there
     Dangerous to new ghost; new ghost learns from many
     Learns from old termers what death is, where.

     Who's jealous of his latest company
     From one day to the next final to us,
     A changed one; would use sorrow to deny
     Sorrow, to replace death; sorrow is sleeping thus.

     Unforgetting is not to-day's forgetting
     For yesterday, not bedrid scorning,
     But a new begetting
     An unforgiving morning.

[*Baby squeals.*]

     O see, he is impatient
     To pass beyond this pretty lisping time:
     There'll be some crying out when he's come there.

[*Back curtains close.*]

Chorus. Can speak of trouble, pressure on men
     Born all the time, brought forward into light
     For warm dark moan.
     Though heart fears all heart cries for, rebuffs with mortal beat
     Skyfall, the legs sucked under, adder's bite.
     That prize held out of reach
     Guides the unwilling tread,
     The asking breath,
     Till on attended bed
     Or in untracked dishonour comes to each
     His natural death.

We pass our days
Speak, man to men, easy, learning to point
To jump before ladies, to show our scars:
But no
We were mistaken, these faces are not ours.
They smile no more when we smile back:
Eyes, ears, tongue, nostrils bring
News of revolt, inadequate counsel to
An infirm king.

O watcher in the dark, you wake
Our dream of waking, we feel
Your finger on the flesh that has been skinned,
By your bright day
See clear what we were doing, that we were vile.
Your sudden hand
Shall humble great
Pride, break it, wear down to stumps old systems which await
The last transgression of the sea.

[*Enter John Nower and Dick.*]

J. If you have really made up your mind, Dick, I won't try and persuade you to stop. But I shall be sorry to lose you.

D. I have thought it all over and I think it is the best thing to do. My cousin writes that the ranch is a thoroughly good proposition. I don't know how I shall like the Colonies but I feel I must get away from here. There is not room enough . . . but the actual moving is unpleasant.

J. I understand. When are you thinking of sailing?

D. My cousin is sailing to-morrow. If I am going I am to join him at the Docks.

J. Right. Tell one of the men to go down to the post-office and send a wire for you. If you want anything else, let me know.

D. Thank you.

[*Exit Dick. Enter Zeppel.*]

Z. Number Six wishes to see you, sir.

J. All right, show him in.

[*Enter Number Six.*]

Well, what is it?

6. My area is Rookhope. Last night at Horse and Farrier, drank alone, one of Shaw's men. I sat down friendly next, till muzzed with drink and lateness he was blabbing. Red Shaw goes to Brandon Walls to-day, visits a woman.

J. Alone?

6. No, sir. He takes a few. I got no numbers.

J. This is good news. Here is a pound for you.

6. Thank you very much, sir.

[*Exit Number Six.*]

J.	Zeppel.
Z.	Sir.
J.	Ask George to come here at once.
Z.	Very good sir.

[*John gets a map out. Enter George.*]

J.	Red Shaw is spending the day at Brandon Walls. We must get him. You know the ground well, don't you, George?
G.	Pretty well. Let me see the map. There's a barn about a hundred yards from the house. Yes, here it is. If we can occupy that without attracting attention it will form a good base for operations, commands both house and road. If I remember rightly, on the other side of the stream is a steep bank. Yes, you can see from the contours. They couldn't get out that way, but lower down is marshy ground and possible. You want to post some men there to catch those who try.
J.	Good. Who do you suggest to lead that party?
G.	Send Sturton. He knows the whole district blindfold. He and I as boys fished all those streams together.
J.	I shall come with you. Let's see: it's dark now about five. Fortunately there's no moon and it's cloudy. We'll start then about half-past. Pick your men and get some sandwiches made up in the kitchen. I'll see about the ammunition if you will remember to bring a compass. We meet outside at a quarter past.

[*Exeunt. Enter Kurt and Culley.*]

K.	There's time for a quick one before changing. What's yours?
C.	I'll have a sidecar, thanks.
K.	Zeppel, one sidecar and one C.P.S. I hear Chapman did the lake in eight.
C.	Yes, he is developing a very pretty style. I am not sure though that Pepys won't beat him next year if he can get out of that double kick. Thanks. Prosit.
K.	Cheerio.

[*Enter Walter and Trudy.*]

W.	Two half pints, Zeppel, please. (*To Kurt.*) Can you let me have a match? How is the Rugger going?
K.	All right, thank you. We have not got a bad team this season.
W.	Where do you play yourself?
K.	Wing 3Q.
W.	Did you ever see Warner? No, he'd be before your time. You remember him don't you, Trudy?
T.	He was killed in the fight at Colefangs, wasn't he?
W.	You are muddling him up with Hunter. He was the best three-quarter I have ever seen. His sprinting was marvellous to watch.
Z.	(*producing Christmas turkey*). Not bad eh?
T.	(*feeling it*). Oh a fine one. For to-morrow's dinner?
Z.	Yes. Here, puss . . . gobble, gobble . . .

4

T. (to W.) What have you got Ingo for Christmas?
W.   A model crane. Do you think he will like it?
T.   He loves anything mechanical. He's so excited he can't sleep.
K.   Come on, Culley, finish your drink. We must be getting along.
        (To W.) You must come down to the field on Monday and see
        us.
W.   I will if I can.

[*Exit Kurt and Culley.*]

T.   Is there any news yet?
W.   Nothing has come through. If things are going right they may
        be back any time now.
T.   I suppose they will get him?
W.   It's almost certain. Nower has waited long enough.
T.   I am sick of this feud. What do we want to go on killing each
        other for? We are all the same. He's trash, yet if I cut my finger
        it bleeds like his. But he's swell, keeps double shifts working all
        night by flares. His mother squealed like a pig when he came
        crouching out.
        Sometimes we read a sign, cloud in the sky,
        The wet tracks of a hare, quicken the step
        Promise the best day. But here no remedy
        Is to be thought of, no news but the new death;
        A Nower dragged out in the night, a Shaw
        Ambushed behind the wall. Blood on the ground
        Would welcome fighters. Last night at Hammergill
        A boy was born fanged like a weasel. I am old,
        Shall die before next winter, but more than once shall hear
        The cry for help, the shooting round the house.

W.   The best are gone.

        Often the man, alone shut, shall consider
        The killings in old winters, death of friends.
        Sitting with stranger shall expect no good.

        Spring came, urging to ships, a casting off,
        But one would stay, vengeance not done; it seemed
        Doubtful to them that they would meet again.

        Fording in the cool of the day they rode
        To meet at crossroads when the year was over:
        Dead is Brody, such a man was Maul.

        I will say this not falsely; I have seen
        The just and the unjust die in the day,
        All, willing or not, and some were willing.

        Here they are.

[*Enter Nower, George, Sturton and others. The three speak alternately.*]

Day was gone Night covered sky
Black over earth When we came there
To Brandon Walls Where Red Shaw lay
Hateful and sleeping Unfriendly visit.
I wished to revenge Quit fully
Who my father At Colefangs valley
Lying in ambush Cruelly shot
With life for life.

Then watchers saw They were attacked
Shouted in fear A night alarm
To men asleep Doomed men awoke
Felt for their guns Ran to the doors
Would wake their master Who lay with woman
Upstairs together Tired after love.
He saw then There would be shooting
Hard fight.

Shot answered shot Bullets screamed
Guns shook Hot in the hand
Fighters lay Groaning on ground
Gave up life Edward fell
Shot through the chest First of our lot
By no means refused fight Stephen was good
His first encounter Showed no fear
Wounded many.

Then Shaw knew We were too strong
Would get away Over the moor
Return alive But found at the ford
Sturton waiting Greatest gun anger
There he died Nor any came
Fighters home Nor wives shall go
Smiling to bed They boast no more.

[*Stephen suddenly gets up.*]

S.   A forward forward can never be a backward backward.
G.   Help me put Stephen to bed, somebody. He got tight on the
      way back. Hullo, they've caught a spy.

Voices outside. Look out. There he is. Catch him. Got you.

[*Enter Kurt and others with prisoner.*]

K.   We found this chap hiding in an outhouse.
J.   Bring him here. Who are you?
S.   I know him. I saw him once at Eickhamp. He's Seth Shaw's
      brother.
J.   He is, is he. What do you come here for? You know what we do
      to spies. I'll destroy the whole lot of you. Take him out.
Spy. You may look big, but we'll get you one day, Nower.

[*Exeunt all but John, Stephen following.*]

6

S.   Don't go, darling.

[*John sits. A shot outside followed by cheers. Enter Zeppel.*]

Z.   Will you be wanting anything more to-night, Sir?
J.   No, that will be all thank you.
Z.   Good night, sir.

John.   Always the following wind of history
        Of others' wisdom makes a buoyant air
        Till we come suddenly on pockets where
        Is nothing loud but us; where voices seem
        Abrupt, untrained, competing with no lie
        Our fathers shouted once. They taught us war,
        To scamper after darlings, to climb hills,
        To emigrate from weakness, find ourselves
        The easy conquerors of empty bays:
        But never told us this, left each to learn,
        Hear something of that soon-arriving day
        When to gaze longer and delighted on
        A face or idea be impossible.
        Could I have been some simpleton that lived
        Before disaster sent his runners here;
        Younger than worms, worms have too much to bear.
        Yes, mineral were best: could I but see
        These woods, these fields of green, this lively world
        Sterile as moon.

Chorus. The Spring unsettles sleeping partnerships,
        Foundries improve their casting process, shops
        Open a further wing on credit till
        The winter. In summer boys grow tall
        With running races on the froth-wet sand,
        War is declared there, here a treaty signed;
        Here a scrum breaks up like a bomb, there troops
        Deploy like birds. But proudest into traps
        Have fallen. These gears which ran in oil for week
        By week, needing no look, now will not work;
        Those manors mortgaged twice to pay for love
        Go to another.

                    O how shall man live
        Whose thought is born, child of one farcical night,
        To find him old? The body warm but not
        By choice, he dreams of folk in dancing bunches,
        Of tart wine spilt on home-made benches,
        Where learns, one drawn apart, a secret will
        Restore the dead; but comes thence to a wall.
        Outside on frozen soil lie armies killed
        Who seem familiar but they are cold.
        Now the most solid wish he tries to keep
        His hands show through; he never will look up,

7

Say 'I am good'. On him misfortune falls
More than enough. Better where no one feels,
The out-of-sight, buried too deep for shafts.

[*Enter Father Christmas. He speaks to the audience.*]

X.   Ladies and Gentlemen: I should like to thank you all very
       much for coming here to-night. Now we have a little surprise
       for you. When you go home, I hope you will tell your friends to
       come and bring the kiddies, but you will remember to keep this
       a secret, won't you? Thank you. Now I will not keep you
       waiting any longer.

[*Lights. A trial. John as the accuser. The Spy as accused. Joan as his
warder with a gigantic feeding bottle. Xmas as president, the rest as jury,
wearing school caps.*]

X.   Is there any more evidence?
J.   Yes. I know we have and are making terrific sacrifices, but we
       cannot give in. We cannot betray the dead. As we pass their
       graves can we be deaf to the simple eloquence of their
       inscriptions, those who in the glory of their early manhood
       gave up their lives for us? No, we must fight to the finish.
X.   Very well. Call the witness.

[*Enter Bo.*]

B.   In these days during the migrations, days
       Freshening with rain reported from the mountains,
       By loss of memory we are reborn,
       For memory is death; by taking leave,
       Parting in anger and glad to go
       Where we are still unwelcome, and if we count
       What dead the tides wash in, only to make
       Notches for enemies. On northern ridges
       Where flags fly, seen and lost, denying rumour
       We baffle proof, speakers of a strange tongue.

[*The Spy groans. His cries are produced by jazz instruments at the back of
the stage. Joan brandishes her bottle.*]

Joan. Be quiet, or I'll give you a taste of this.
X.   Next, please.

[*Enter Po.*]

P.   Past victory is honour, to accept
       An island governorship, back to estates
       Explored as child; coming at last to love
       Lost publicly, found secretly again
       In private flats, admitted to a sign.
       An understanding sorrow knows no more,
       Sits waiting for the lamp, far from those hills
       Where rifts open unfenced, mark of a fall,
       And flakes fall softly softly burying
       Deeper and deeper down her loving son.

8

[*The Spy groans. John produces a revolver.*]

J.   Better to get it over.
Joan. This way for the Angel of Peace.
X.   Leave him alone. This fellow is very very ill. But he will get
      well.

[*The Man-Woman appears as a prisoner of war behind barbed wire, in the snow.*]

M.W. Because I'm come it does not mean to hold
      An anniversary, think illness healed,
      As to renew the lease, consider costs
      Of derelict ironworks on deserted coasts.
      Love was not love for you but episodes,
      Traffic in memoirs, views from different sides;
      You thought oaths of comparison a bond,
      And though you had your orders to disband,
      Refused to listen, but remained in woods
      Poorly concealed your profits under wads.
      Nothing was any use; therefore I went
      Hearing you call for what you did not want.
      I lay with you; you made that an excuse
      For playing with yourself, but homesick because
      Your mother told you that's what flowers did,
      And thought you lived since you were bored, not dead,
      And could not stop. So I was cold to make
      No difference, but you were quickly meek
      Altered for safety. I tried then to demand
      Proud habits, protestations called your mind
      To show you it was extra, but instead
      You overworked yourself, misunderstood,
      Adored me for the chance. Lastly I tried
      To teach you acting, but always you had nerves
      To fear performances as some fear knives.
      Now I shall go. No, you, if you come,
      Will not enjoy yourself, for where I am
      All talking is forbidden. . . .

[*The Spy groans.*]

J.   I can't bear it.

[*Shoots him. Lights out.*]

Voices. Quick, fetch a doctor.
      Ten pounds for a doctor.
      Ten pounds to keep him away.
      Coming, coming.

[*Lights. Xmas, John and the Spy remain. The Jury has gone, but there is a Photographer.*]

X.   Stand back there. Here comes the doctor.

9

[*Enter Doctor and his Boy.*]

B.   Tickle your arse with a feather, sir.
D.   What's that?
B.   Particularly nasty weather, sir.
D.   Yes, it is. Tell me, is my hair tidy? One must always be careful with a new client.
B.   It's full of lice, sir.
D.   What's that?
B.   It's looking nice, sir. [*For the rest of the scene the boy fools about.*]
X.   Are you the doctor?
D.   I am.
X.   What can you cure?
D.   Tennis elbow, Graves' Disease, Derbyshire neck and Housemaid's knees.
X.   Is that all you can cure?
D.   No, I have discovered the origin of life. Fourteen months I hesitated before I concluded this diagnosis. I received the morning star for this. My head will be left at death for clever medical analysis. The laugh will be gone and the microbe in command.
X.   Well, let's see what you can do.

[*Doctor takes circular saws, bicycle pumps, etc., from his bag.*]

B.   You need a pill, sir.
D.   What's that.
B.   You'll need your skill, sir. O sir you're hurting.

[*Boy is kicked out.*]
[*John tries to get a look.*]

D.   Go away. Your presence will be necessary at Scotland Yard when the criminals of the war are tried, but your evidence will not be needed. It is valueless. Cages will be provided for some of the more interesting specimens. [*Examines the body.*] Um, yes. Very interesting. The conscious brain appears normal except under emotion. Fancy it. The Devil couldn't do that. This advances and retreats under control and poisons everything round it. My diagnosis is: Adamant will, cool brain and laughing spirit. Hullo, what's this? [*Produces a large pair of pliers and extracts an enormous tooth from the body.*] Come along, that's better. Ladies and Gentlemen, you see I have nothing up my sleeve. This tooth was growing ninety-nine years before his great grandmother was born. If it hadn't been taken out to-day he would have died yesterday. You may get up now.

[*The Spy gets up. The Photographer gets ready.*]

P.   Just one minute, please. A little brighter, a little brighter. No, moisten the lips and start afresh. Hold it.

[*Photographer lets off his flash. Lights out. Xmas blows a whistle.*]

X.   All change.

[*Lights. Spy behind a gate guarded by Xmas. Enter John running.*]

J.   I'm late, I'm late. Which way is it? I must hurry.
X.   You can't come in here, without a pass.

[*John turns back his coat lapel.*]

X.   O I beg your pardon, sir. This way, sir.

[*Exit Xmas. The Accuser and Accused plant a tree.*]

John.   Sometime sharers of the same house
        We know not the builder nor the name of his son.
        Now cannot mean to them; boy's voice among
                                        dishonoured portraits
        To dockside barmaid speaking
        Sorry through wires, pretended speech.
Spy.   Escaped
        Armies pursuit, rebellion and eclipse
        Together in a cart
        After all journeys
        We stay and are not known.

[*Lights out.*]

        Sharers of the same house
        Attendants on the same machine
        Rarely a word, in silence understood.

[*Lights. John alone in his chair. Enter Dick.*]

D.   Hullo. I've come to say good-bye.
        Yesterday we sat at table together
        Fought side by side at enemies' face to face meeting
        To-day we take our leave, time of departure.
        I'm sorry.
J.   Here, give me your knife and take mine. By these
        We may remember each other.
        There are two chances, but more of one
        Parting for ever, not hearing the other
        Though he need help.
        Have you got everything you want?
D.   Yes, thanks. Goodbye, John.
J.   Goodbye.

[*Exit Dick.*]

        There is the city,
        Lighted and clean once, pleasure for builders
        And I
        Letting to cheaper tenants, have made a slum
        Houses at which the passer shakes his fist
        Remembering evil.
        Pride and indifference have shared with me, and I
        Have kissed them in the dark, for mind has dark,

Shaded commemorations, midnight accidents
In streets where heirs may dine.

But love, sent east for peace
From tunnels under those
Bursts now to pass
On trestles over meaner quarters
A noise and flashing glass.

Feels morning streaming down
Wind from the snows
Nowise withdrawn by doubting flinch
Nor joined to any by belief's firm flange
Refreshed sees all
The tugged-at teat
The hopper's steady feed, the frothing leat.

Zeppel.

[*Enter Zeppel.*]

Z.   Sir.
J.   Get my horse ready at once, please. [*Exeunt.*]

Chorus. To throw away the key and walk away
Not abrupt exile, the neighbours asking why,
But following a line with left and right
An altered gradient at another rate
Learns more than maps upon the whitewashed wall
The hand put up to ask; and makes us well
Without confession of the ill. All pasts
Are single old past now, although some posts
Are forwarded, held looking on a new view;
The future shall fulfil a surer vow
Not smiling at queen over the glass rim
Nor making gunpowder in the top room,
Not swooping at the surface still like gulls
But with prolonged drowning shall develop gills.

But there are still to tempt; areas not seen
Because of blizzards or an erring sign
Whose guessed—at wonders would be worth alleging,
And lies about the cost of a night's lodging.
Travellers may meet at inns but not attach,
They sleep one night together, not asked to touch;
Receive no normal welcome, not the pressed lip,
Children to lift, not the assuaging lap.
Crossing the pass descend the growing stream
Too tired to hear except the pulse's strum,
Reach villages to ask for a bed in
Rock shutting out the sky, the old life done.

[*Culley enters right and squats in the centre of the stage, looking left through field glasses. Several shots are heard off. Enter George and Kurt.*]

G.   Are you much hurt?

K.   Nothing much, sir. Only a slight flesh wound. Did you get him, sir?

G.   On ledge above the gulley, aimed at, seen moving, fell; looked down on, sprawls in the stream.

K.   Good. He sniped poor Billy last Easter, riding to Flash.

G.   I have some lint and bandages in my haversack, and there is a spring here. I'll dress your arm.

[*Enter Seth and Bernard, left.*]

S.   Did you find Tom's body?

B.   Yes, sir. It's lying in the Hangs.

S.   Which way did they go?

B.   Down there, sir.

[*Culley observes them and runs right.*]

C.   There are twenty men from Nattrass, sir, over the gap, coming at once.

G.   Have they seen us?

C.   Not yet.

G.   We must get out. You go down to the copse and make for the Barbon road. We'll follow the old tramway. Keep low and run like hell.

[*Exeunt right. Seth watches through field glasses.*]

S.   Yes. No. No. Yes, I can see them. They are making for the Barbon road. Go down and cut them off. There is good cover by the bridge. We've got them now.

[*A whistle. The back curtains draw, showing John, Anne and Aaron and the Announcer grouped. Both sides enter left and right.*]

Aa.   There is a time for peace; too often we
Have gone on cold marches, have taken life,
Till wrongs are bred like flies; the dreamer wakes
Whose beats a smooth door, behind footsteps, on the left
The pointed finger, the unendurable drum,
To hear of horses stolen or a house burned.
Now this shall end with marriage as it ought:
Love turns the wind, brings up the salt smell,
Shadow of gulls on the road to the sea.

Announcer. The engagement is announced of John Nower, eldest son of the late Mr. and Mrs. George Nower of Lintzgarth, Rookhope, and Anne Shaw, only daughter of the late Mr. and Mrs. Joseph Shaw of Nattrass, Garrigill.

All.   Hurrah.

[*George and Seth advance to the centre, shake hands and cross over the stage to their opposite sides. Back curtains close. Exeunt in different directions, talking as they go.*]

G.   It was a close shave that time. We had a lucky escape. How are you feeling?

K.   The arm is rather painful. I owe Bernard one for that.

B.   It's a shame. Just when we had them fixed.

S.   Don't you worry. You'll get your chance.

B.   But what about this peace?

S.   That remains to be seen. Only wait.

[*Exeunt. Back curtains draw. John and Anne alone. John blows on a grass held between the thumbs and listens.*]

J.   On Cautley where a peregrine has nested, iced heather hurt the knuckles. Fell on the ball near time, the forwards stopped. Good-bye now, he said, would open the swing doors. . . . These I remember, but not love till now. We cannot tell where we shall find it, though we all look for it till we do, and what others tell us is no use to us.
Some say that handsome raider still at large,
A terror to the Marches, is truth in love;
And we must listen for such messengers
To tell us daily 'To-day a saint came blessing
The huts.' 'Seen lately in the provinces
Reading behind a tree and people passing.'
But love returns;
At once all heads are turned this way, and love
Calls order—silenced the angry sons—
Steps forward, greets, repeats what he has heard
And seen, feature for feature, word for word.

Anne.   Yes, I am glad this evening that we are together.
The silence is unused, death seems
                 An axe's echo.

The summer quickens all,
Scatters its promises
To you and me no less
Though neither can compel.

J.   The wish to last the year,
The longest look to live,
The urgent word survive
The movement of the air.

A.   But loving now let none
Think of divided days
When we shall choose from ways,
All of them evil, one.

J.   Look on with stricter brows
The sacked and burning town,
The ice-sheet moving down,
The fall of an old house.

A.   John, I have a car waiting. There is time to join Dick before the
      boat sails. We sleep in beds where men have died howling.
J.   You may be right, but we shall stay.
A.   To-night the many come to mind
      Sent forward in the thaw with anxious marrow,
      For such might now return with a bleak face,
      An image pause half-lighted in the door,
      A greater but not fortunate in all;
      Come home deprived of an astonishing end . . .
      Morgan's who took a clean death in the north
      Shouting against the wind, or Cousin Dodds',
      Passed out in her chair, the snow falling.
      The too-loved clays, borne over by diverse drifts,
      Fallen upon the far side of all enjoyment,
      Unable to move closer, shall not speak
      Out of that grave stern on no capital fault;
      Enough to have lightly touched the unworthy thing.
J.   We live still.
A.   But what has become of the dead? They forget.
J.   These. Smilers, all who stand on promontories, slinkers,
      whisperers, deliberate approaches, echoes, time, promises of
      mercy, what dreams or goes masked, embraces that fail,
      insufficient evidence, touches of the old wound.
      But let us not think of things which we hope will be long in
      coming.

Chorus. The Spring will come,
      Not hesitate for one employer who
      Though a fine day and every pulley running
      Would quick lie down; nor save the wanted one
      That, wounded in escaping, swam the lake
      Safe to the reeds, collapsed in shallow water.

      You have tasted good and what is it? For you,
      Sick in the green plain, healed in the tundra, shall
      Turn westward back from your alone success,
      Under a dwindling Alp to see your friends
      Cut down the wheat.
J.   It's getting cold dear, let's go in.

[*Exeunt. Back curtains close.*]

Chorus. For where are Basley who won the Ten,
      Dickon so tarted by the House,
      Thomas who kept a sparrow-hawk?
      The clock strikes, it is time to go,
      The tongue ashamed, deceived by a shake of the hand.

[*Enter Bridal Party left, guests right.*]

Guests. Ssh.

[*The Chief Guest comes forward and presents a bouquet to the bride.*]

15

C.G.   With gift in hand we come
        From every neighbour farm
        To celebrate in wine
        The certain union of
        A woman and a man;
        And may their double love
        Be shown to the stranger's eye
        In a son's symmetry.
        Now hate is swallowed down,
        All anger put away;
        The spirit comes to its own,
        The beast to its play.

[*All clap. The Chief Guest addresses the Audience.*]

Will any lady be so kind as to oblige us with a dance?... Thank you very much ... This way miss.... What tune would you like?

[*Gramophone. A dance. As the dance ends, the back curtains draw and the Butler enters centre.*]

Butler. Dinner is served.

[*Aaron goes to the Dancer.*]

Aa.   You'll dine with us, of course?

[*Exeunt all except Seth and his Mother.*]

Guests, as they go out. It will be a good year for them, I think.
        You don't mean that he ... well, you know what.
        Rather off his form lately.
        The vein is showing good in the Quarry Hazel.
        One of Edward's friends.
        You must come and have a look at the Kennels some day.
        Well it does seem to show.
                [*Etc., etc.*]

[*Back curtains close.*]

Mother. Seth.
S.   Yes, Mother.
M.   John Nower is here.
S.   I know that. What do you want me to do?
M.   Kill him.
S.   I can't do that. There is peace now; besides he is a guest in our house.
M.   Have you forgotten your brother's death ... taken out and shot like a dog? It is a nice thing for me to hear people saying that I have a coward for a son. I am thankful your father is not here to see it.
S.   I'm not afraid of anything or anybody, but I don't want to.
M.   I shall have to take steps.
S.   It shall be as you like. Though I think that much will come of this, chiefly harm.

16

M.   I have thought of that. [*Exit.*]
S.   The little funk. Sunlight on sparkling water, its shades dis-
      solved, reforming, unreal activity where others laughed but he
      blubbed clinging, homesick, an undeveloped form. I'll do it.
      Men point in after days. He always was. But wrongly. He
      fought and overcame, a stern self-ruler. You didn't hear.
      Hearing they look ashamed too late for shaking hands. Of
      course I'll do it. [*Exit.*]

[*A shot. More shots. Shouting.*]

Voices outside. A trap. I might have known.
            Take that, damn you.
            Open the window.
            You swine.
            Jimmy, O my God.

[*Enter Seth and Bernard.*]

B.   The Master's killed. So is John Nower, but some of them got
      away, fetching help, will attack in an hour.
S.   See that all the doors are bolted.

[*Exeunt right and left. The back curtains draw. Anne with the dead.*]

Anne. Now we have seen the story to its end.
        The hands that were to help will not be lifted,
        And bad followed by worse leaves to us tears,
        An empty bed, hope from less noble men.
        I had seen joy
        Received and given, upon both sides, for years.
        Now not.

Chorus. Though he believe it, no man is strong.
          He thinks to be called the fortunate,
          To bring home a wife, to live long.

          But he is defeated; let the son
          Sell the farm lest the mountain fall:
          His mother and her mother won.

          His fields are used up where the moles visit,
          The contours worn flat; if there show
          Passage for water he will miss it:

          Give up his breath, his woman, his team;
          No life to touch, though later there be
          Big fruit, eagles above the stream.

CURTAIN

1928 (see App. I)

17

Part II

Poems 1927–1931

(TO CHRISTOPHER ISHERWOOD)

Let us honour if we can
The vertical man
Though we value none
But the horizontal one.

Part II

Poems 1927–1931

I

Bones wrenched, weak whimper, lids wrinkled, first dazzle known,
World-wonder hardened as bigness, years, brought knowledge, you:
Presence a rich mould augured for roots urged—but gone,
The soul is tetanous; gun-barrel burnishing
In summer grass, mind lies to tarnish, untouched, undoing,
Though body stir to sweat, or, squat as idol, brood,
Infuriate the fire with bellows, blank till sleep
And two-faced dream—'I want', voiced treble as once
Crudely through flowers till dunghill cockcrow, crack at East.
Eyes, unwashed jewels, the glass floor slipping, feel, know Day,
Life stripped to girders, monochrome. Deceit of instinct,
Features, figure, form irrelevant, dismissed
Ought passes through points fair plotted and you conform,
Seen yes or no, too just for weeping argument.

June 1927

II

No trenchant parting this
Of future from the past,
No idol fractured is
Nor bogey scared at last.
Yet still the mind would tease
In local irritation,
And difficult images,
Demand an explanation.
Across this finite space,
Buttressed expensively,
The pointed hand would trace
Error in you, in me;
Eye squiny for a way
To mitigate the stare,
When shadow turns on day,
Find argument too bare,
Till pendulum again
Restore the gravamen.

But standing now I see
The diver's brilliant bow,
His quiet break from the sea,
With one trained movement throw
The hair from his forehead;
And I, stung by the sun,

21

Think, semi-satisfied
That, ere the smile is done,
The eye deliberate
May qualify the joy
And that which we create
We also may destroy.

August 1927

III

Who stands, the crux left of the watershed,
On the wet road between the chafing grass
Below him sees dismantled washing-floors,
Snatches of tramline running to the wood,
An industry already comatose,
Yet sparsely living. A ramshackle engine
At Cashwell raises water; for ten years
It lay in flooded workings until this,
Its latter office, grudgingly performed,
And further here and there, though many dead
Lie under the poor soil, some acts are chosen
Taken from recent winters; two there were
Cleaned out a damaged shaft by hand, clutching
The winch the gale would tear them from; one died '
During a storm, the fells impassable,
Not at his village, but in wooden shape
Through long abandoned levels nosed his way
And in his final valley went to ground.

Go home, now, stranger, proud of your young stock,
Stranger, turn back again, frustrate and vexed:
This land, cut off, will not communicate,
Be no accessory content to one
Aimless for faces rather there than here.
Beams from your car may cross a bedroom wall,
They wake no sleeper; you may hear the wind
Arriving driven from the ignorant sea
To hurt itself on pane, on bark of elm
Where sap unbaffled rises, being Spring;
But seldom this. Near you, taller than grass,
Ears poise before decision, scenting danger.

August 1927

IV

Suppose they met, the inevitable procedure
Of hand to nape would drown the staling cry
Of cuckoos, filter off the day's detritus,
And breach in their continual history.

Yet, spite of this new heroism, they feared
That doddering Jehovah whom they mocked;
Enough for him to show them to their rooms—
They slept apart though doors were never locked.

(The womb began its crucial expulsion.
The fishermen, aching, drenched to the skin,
The ledge cleared, dragged their boat up on the beach.
The survivor dropped, the bayonets closing in.)

In these who saw and never rubbed an eye,
A thousand dancers brought to sudden rest,
Transformed to tiger-lilies by the band,
It was no wonder they were not impressed

By certain curious carving in the porch,
A generous designation of the fate
Of those shut altogether from salvation.
Down they fell; sorrow they had after that.

September 1927

V

The crowing of the cock
Though it may scare the dead,
Call on the fire to strike,
Sever the yawing cloud,
Shall also summon up
The pointed crocus top,
Which smelling of the mould,
Breathes of the underworld.

A god was slain for love,
A god was brought to birth,
There in the sunless grove
Not pierceable by star
Nor spidery moonlight where
The crow may startle us
Back from his foul nest with
A solitary curse.

The chosen in a cave
Forgot old whiffs, alive
Suffered the dizzy calm,
Waited the rising storm,
Prayed through the scorching season
And saw ere daylight set
Blocked conduits in spate,
Delectable horizon.

Such kept back since, done with,
The tired ears prick and beg
An altered pressure, eyes
Look in the glass, confess
The tightening of the mouth,
Know the receding face
A blemished psychogogue:
But symmetry will please.

Now straightway swallowed up
In memory as these,
Its tilting planes disclose
—The snowstorm on the marsh,
The champagne at the lip—
Swung into vision, fresh
By fleeting contact, mind
Sees faculty confined

To breast the final hill,
Thalassa on the tongue,
Snap at the dragon's tail
To find the yelp its own;
Or sit, the doors being shut,
'Twixt coffee and the fruit,
Touching, decline to hear
Sounds of conclusive war.

September 1927

VI

Nor was that final, for about that time
Gannets blown over northward, going home,
Surprised the secrecy beneath the skin.

'Wonderful was that cross and I full of sin.
Approaching, utterly generous, came one
For years expected, born only for me.'

Returned from that dishonest country, we
Awake, yet tasting the delicious lie:
And boys and girls, equal to be, are different still.

No, these bones shall live, while daffodil
And saxophone have something to recall
Of Adam's brow and of the wounded heel.

October 1927

VII

From the very first coming down
Into a new valley with a frown
Because of the sun and a lost way,
You certainly remain: to-day
I, crouching behind a sheep-pen, heard
Travel across a sudden bird,
Cry out against the storm, and found
The year's arc a completed round
And love's worn circuit re-begun,
Endless with no dissenting turn.
Shall see, shall pass, as we have seen
The swallow on the tile, Spring's green
Preliminary shiver, passed
A solitary truck, the last
Of shunting in the Autumn. But now
To interrupt the homely brow,
Thought warmed to evening through and through
Your letter comes, speaking as you,
Speaking of much but not to come.

Nor speech is close nor fingers numb,
If love not seldom has received
An unjust answer, was deceived.
I, decent with the seasons, move
Different or with a different love,
Nor question overmuch the nod,
The stone smile of this country god
That never was more reticent,
Always afraid to say more than it meant.

December 1927

VIII

Control of the passes was, he saw, the key
To this new district, but who would get it?
He, the trained spy, had walked into the trap
For a bogus guide, seduced with the old tricks.

At Greenhearth was a fine site for a dam
And easy power, had they pushed the rail
Some stations nearer. They ignored his wires.
The bridges were unbuilt and trouble coming.

The street music seemed gracious now to one
For weeks up in the desert. Woken by water
Running away in the dark, he often had
Reproached the night for a companion
Dreamed of already. They would shoot, of course,
Parting easily who were never joined.

January 1928

IX

Taller to-day, we remember similar evenings,
Walking together in the windless orchard
Where the brook runs over the gravel, far from the glacier.

Again in the room with the sofa hiding the grate,
Look down to the river when the rain is over,
See him turn to the window, hearing our last
Of Captain Ferguson.

It is seen how excellent hands have turned to commonness.
One staring too long, went blind in a tower,
One sold all his manors to fight, broke through, and faltered.

Nights come bringing the snow, and the dead howl
Under the headlands in their windy dwelling
Because the Adversary put too easy questions
On lonely roads.

But happy now, though no nearer each other,
We see the farms lighted all along the valley;
Down at the mill-shed the hammering stops
And men go home.

Noises at dawn will bring
Freedom for some, but not this peace
No bird can contradict: passing, but is sufficient now
For something fulfilled this hour, loved or endured.

March 1928

X

We made all possible preparations,
Drew up a list of firms,
Constantly revised our calculations
And allotted the farms,

Issued all the orders expedient
In this kind of case:
Most, as was expected, were obedient,
Though there were murmurs, of course;

Chiefly against our exercising
Our old right to abuse:
Even some sort of attempt at rising
But these were mere boys.

For never serious misgiving
Occurred to anyone,

Since there could be no question of living
If we did not win.

The generally accepted view teaches
That there was no excuse,
Though in the light of recent researches
Many would find the cause

In a not uncommon form of terror;
Others, still more astute,
Point to possibilities of error
At the very start.

As for ourselves there is left remaining
Our honour at least,
And a reasonable chance of retaining
Our faculties to the last.

December 1928

XI

Again in conversations
Speaking of fear
And throwing off reserve
The voice is nearer
But no clearer
Than first love
Than boys' imaginations.

For every news
Means pairing off in twos and twos
Another I, another You
Each knowing what to do
But of no use.

Never stronger
But younger and younger
Saying goodbye but coming back, for fear
Is over there
And the centre of anger
Is out of danger.

January 1929

XII

From scars where kestrels hover,
The leader looking over
Into the happy valley,
Orchard and curving river,
May turn away to see
The slow fastidious line
That disciplines the fell,
Hear curlew's creaking call
From angles unforseen,
The drumming of a snipe
Surprise where driven sleet
Had scalded to the bone
And streams are acrid yet
To an unaccustomed lip.
The tall unwounded leader
Of doomed companions, all
Whose voices in the rock
Are now perpetual,
Fighters for no one's sake,
Who died beyond the border.

Heroes are buried who
Did not believe in death
And bravery is now
Not in the dying breath
But resisting the temptations
To skyline operations.
Yet glory is not new;
The summer visitors
Still come from far and wide,
Choosing their spots to view
The prize competitors,
Each thinking that he will
Find heroes in the wood,
Far from the capital
Where lights and wine are set
For supper by the lake,
But leaders must migrate:
'Leave for Cape Wrath to-night',
And the host after waiting
Must quench the lamps and pass
Alive into the house.

January 1929

XIII

Under boughs between our tentative endearments, how should we
                                                                hear
But with flushing pleasure drums distant over difficult country,
            Events not actual
            In time's unlenient will?

Which we shall not avoid, though at a station's chance delay
Lines branch to peace, iron up valleys to a hidden village;
            For we have friends to catch
            And none leave coach.

Sharers of our own day, thought smiling of, but nothing known,
What industries decline, what chances are of revolution,
            What murders flash
            Under composed flesh.

Knowledge no need to us whose wrists enjoy the chafing leash,
Can plunder high nests; who sheer off from old like gull from granite,
            From their mind's constant sniffling,
            Their blood's dulled shuffling.

Who feebling, still have time to wonder at the well-shaped heads
Conforming every day more closely to the best in albums:
            Fathers in sons may track
            Their voices' trick.

But their ancestral curse, jumbled perhaps and put away,
Baffled for years, at last in one repeats its potent pattern
            And blows fall more than once,
            Although he wince:

Who was to moorland market town retired for work or love,
May creep to sumps, pile up against the door, crouching in cases,
            This anger falling
            Opens, empties that filling.

Let each one share our pity, hard to withhold and hard to bear.
None knows of the next day if it be less or more, the sorrow:
            Escaping cannot try;
            Must wait though it destroy.

March 1929

29

XIV

Love by ambition
Of definition
Suffers partition
And cannot go
From yes to no:
For no is not love, no is no,
The shutting of a door
The tightening jaw
A conscious sorrow,
And saying yes
Turns love into success
Views from the rail
Of land and happiness,
Assured of all
The sofas creak
And were this all, love were
But cheek to cheek
And dear to dear.

Voices explain
Love's pleasure and love's pain
Still tap the knee
And cannot disagree
Hushed for aggression
Of full confession
Likeness to likeness
Of each old weakness;
Love is not there
Love has moved to another chair.

Aware already
Of who stands next
And is not vexed
And is not giddy
Leaves the North in place
With a good grace
And would not gather
Another to another,
Designs his own unhappiness
Foretells his own death and is faithless.

March 1929

XV

Before this loved one
Was that one and that one
A family
And history
And ghost's adversity
Whose pleasing name
Was neighbourly shame.
Before this last one
Was much to be done,
Frontiers to cross
As clothes grew worse
And coins to pass
In a cheaper house
Before this last one
Before this loved one.

Face that the sun
Is supple on
May stir but here
Is no new year;
This gratitude for gifts is less
Than the old loss;
Touching is shaking hands
On mortgaged lands;
And smiling of
This gracious greeting
'Good day, good luck'
Is no real meeting
But instinctive look
A backward love.

March 1929

XVI

Watch any day his nonchalant pauses, see
His dextrous handling of a wrap as he
Steps after into cars, the beggar's envy.

'There is a free one', many say, but err.
He is not that returning conqueror,
Nor ever the poles' circumnavigator.

But poised between shocking falls, on razor-edge
Has taught himself this balancing subterfuge
Of the accosting profile, the erect carriage.

The song, the varied action of the blood
Would drown the warning from the iron wood,
Would cancel the inertia of the buried:

31

Travelling by daylight on from house to house
The longest way to the intrinsic peace,
With love's fidelity and with love's weakness.

March 1929

XVII

The strings' excitement, the applauding drum
Are but the initiating ceremony
That out of cloud the ancestral face may come.

And never hear their subaltern mockery,
Graffiti-writers, moss-grown with whimsies,
Loquacious when the watercourse is dry.

It is your face I see, and morning's praise
Of you is ghost's approval of the choice,
Filtered through roots of the effacing grass.

Fear, taking me aside, would give advice
'To conquer her, the visible enemy,
It is enough to turn away the eyes.'

Yet there's no peace in this assaulted city
But speeches at the corners, hope for news,
Outside the watchfires of a stronger army.

And all emotions to expression come,
Recovering the archaic imagery:
This longing for assurance takes the form

Of a hawk's vertical stooping from the sky;
These tears, salt for a disobedient dream,
The lunatic agitation of the sea;

While this despair with hardened eyeballs cries
'A Golden Age, a Silver . . . rather this,
Massive and taciturn years, the Age of Ice.'

April 1929

XVIII

Upon this line between adventure
Prolong the meeting out of good nature
Obvious in each agreeable feature.

Calling of each other by name
Smiling, taking a willing arm
Has the companionship of a game.

But should the walk do more than this
Out of bravado or drunkenness
Forward or back are menaces.

On neither side let foot slip over
Invading Always, exploring Never,
For this is hate and this is fear,

On narrowness stand, for sunlight is
Brightest only on surfaces;
No anger, no traitor, but peace.

June 1929

XIX

Sentries against inner and outer,
At stated interval is feature;
And how shall enemy on these
Make sudden raid or lasting peace?
For bribery were vain to try
Against the incorruptible eye
Too amply paid with tears, the chin
Has hairs to hide its weakness in,
And proud bridge and indignant nostril
Nothing to do but to look noble.
But in between these lies the mouth;
Watch that, that you may parley with:
There strategy comes easiest,
Though it seem stern, was seen compressed
Over a lathe, refusing answer,
It will release the ill-fed prisoner,
It will do murder or betray
For either party equally,
Yielding at last to a close kiss
It will admit tongue's soft advance,
So longed for, given in abandon,
Given long since, had it but known.

June 1929

XX

On Sunday walks
Past the shut gates of works
The conquerors come
And are handsome.

Sitting all day
By the open window
Say what they say

33

Know what to know
Who brought and taught
Unusual images
And new tunes to old cottages,
With so much done
Without a thought
Of the anonymous lampoon
The cellar counterplot,
Though in the night
Pursued by eaters
They clutch at gaiters
That straddle and deny
Escape that way,
Though in the night
Is waking fright.

Father by son
Lives on and on
Though over date
And motto on the gate
The lichen grows
From year to year,
Still here and there
That Roman nose
Is noticed in the villages
And father's son
Knows what they said
And what they did.

Not meaning to deceive,
Wish to give suck
Enforces make-believe
And what was fear
Of fever and bad-luck
Is now a scare
At certain names
A need for charms
For certain words
At certain fords
And what was livelihood
Is tallness, strongness
Words and longness,
All glory and all story
Solemn and not so good.

August 1929

XXI

The silly fool, the silly fool
Was sillier in school
But beat the bully as a rule.

The youngest son, the youngest son
Was certainly no wise one
Yet could surprise one.

Or rather, or rather
To be posh, we gather,
One should have no father.

Simple to prove
That deeds indeed
In life succeed
But love in love
And tales in tales
Where no one fails.

August 1929

XXII

Will you turn a deaf ear
To what they said on the shore,
Interrogate their poises
In their rich houses;

Of stork-legged heaven-reachers
Of the compulsory touchers
The sensitive amusers
And masked amazers?

Yet wear no ruffian badge
Nor lie behind the hedge
Waiting with bombs of conspiracy
In arm-pit secrecy;

Carry no talisman
For germ or the abrupt pain
Needing no concrete shelter
Nor porcelain filter.

Will you wheel death anywhere
In his invalid chair,
With no affectionate instant
But his attendant?

For to be held for friend
By an undeveloped mind
To be joke for children is
Death's happiness:

Whose anecdotes betray
His favourite colour as blue

Colour of distant bells
And boys' overalls.

His tales of the bad lands
Disturb the sewing hands;
Hard to be superior
On parting nausea;

To accept the cushions from
Women against martyrdom,
Yet applauding the circuits
Of racing cyclists.

Never to make signs
Fear neither maelstrom nor zones
Salute with soldiers' wives
When the flag waves;

Remembering there is
No recognised gift for this;
No income, no bounty,
No promised country.

But to see brave sent home
Hermetically sealed with shame
And cold's victorious wrestle
With molten metal.

A neutralising peace
And an average disgrace
Are honour to discover
For later other.

September 1929

XXIII

Sir, no man's enemy, forgiving all
But will his negative inversion, be prodigal:
Send to us power and light, a sovereign touch
Curing the intolerable neural itch,
The exhaustion of weaning, the liar's quinsy,
And the distortions of ingrown virginity.
Prohibit sharply the rehearsed response
And gradually correct the coward's stance;
Cover in time with beams those in retreat
That, spotted, they turn though the reverse were great;
Publish each healer that in city lives
Or country houses at the end of drives;
Harrow the house of the dead; look shining at
New styles of architecture, a change of heart.

October 1929

XXIV

1

It was Easter as I walked in the public gardens
Hearing the frogs exhaling from the pond,
Watching traffic of magnificent cloud
Moving without anxiety on open sky—
Season when lovers and writers find
An altering speech for altering things,
An emphasis on new names, on the arm
A fresh hand with fresh power.
But thinking so I came at once
Where solitary man sat weeping on a bench,
Hanging his head down, with his mouth distorted
Helpless and ugly as an embryo chicken.

So I remember all of those whose death
Is necessary condition of the season's setting forth,
Who sorry in this time look only back
To Christmas intimacy, a winter dialogue
Fading in silence, leaving them in tears.
And recent particulars come to mind:
The death by cancer of a once hated master,
A friend's analysis of his own failure,
Listened to at intervals throughout the winter
At different hours and in different rooms.
But always with success of others for comparison,
The happiness, for instance, of my friend Kurt Groote,
Absence of fear in Gerhart Meyer
From the sea, the truly strong man.

A 'bus ran home then, on the public ground
Lay fallen bicycles like huddled corpses:
No chattering valves of laughter emphasised
Nor the swept gown ends of a gesture stirred
The sessile hush; until a sudden shower
Fell willing into grass and closed the day,
Making choice seem a necessary error.

April 1929

Coming out of me living is always thinking,
Thinking changing and changing living,
Am feeling as it was seeing—
In city leaning on harbour parapet
To watch a colony of duck below
Sit, preen, and doze on buttresses
Or upright paddle on flickering stream,

Casually fishing at a passing straw.
Those find sun's luxury enough,
Shadow know not of homesick foreigner
Nor restlessness of intercepted growth.

All this time was anxiety at night,
Shooting and barricade in street.
Walking home late I listened to a friend
Talking excitedly of final war
Of proletariat against police—
That one shot girl of nineteen through the knees,
They threw that one down concrete stair—
Till I was angry, said I was pleased.

Time passes in Hessen, in Gutensberg,
With hill-top and evening holds me up,
Tiny observer of enormous world.
Smoke rises from factory in field,
Memory of fire: On all sides heard
Vanishing music of isolated larks:
From village square voices in hymn,
Men's voices, an old use.
And I above standing, saying in thinking:

'Is first baby, warm in mother,
Before born and is still mother,
Time passes and now is other,
Is knowledge in him now of other,
Cries in cold air, himself no friend.
In grown man also, may see in face
In his day-thinking and in his night-thinking
Is wareness and is fear of other,
Alone in flesh, himself no friend.'

He say 'We must forgive and forget',
Forgetting saying but is unforgiving
And unforgiving is in his living;
Body reminds in him to loving,
Reminds but takes no further part,
Perfunctorily affectionate in hired room
But takes no part and is unloving
But loving death. May see in dead,
In face of dead that loving wish,
As one returns from Africa to wife
And his ancestral property in Wales.

Yet sometimes man look and say good
At strict beauty of locomotive,
Completeness of gesture or unclouded eye;
In me so absolute unity of evening
And field and distance was in me for peace,

Was over me in feeling without forgetting
Those ducks' indifference, that friend's hysteria,
Without wishing and with forgiving,
To love my life, not as other,
Not as bird's life, not as child's,
'Cannot', I said, 'being no child now nor a bird'.

May 1929

3

Order to stewards and the study of time,
Correct in books, was earlier than this
But joined this by the wires I watched from train,
Slackening of wire and posts' sharp reprimand,
In month of August to a cottage coming.

Being alone, the frightened soul
Returns to this life of sheep and hay
No longer his: he every hour
Moves further from this and must so move,
As child is weaned from his mother and leaves home
But taking the first steps falters, is vexed,
Happy only to find home, a place
Where no tax is levied for being there.

So, insecure, he loves and love
Is insecure, gives less than he expects.
He knows not if it be seed in time to display
Luxuriantly in a wonderful fructification
Or whether it be but a degenerate remnant
Of something immense in the past but now
Surviving only as the infectiousness of disease
Or in the malicious caricature of drunkenness;
Its end glossed over by the careless but known long
To finer perception of the mad and ill.

Moving along the track which is himself,
He loves what he hopes will last, which gone,
Begins the difficult work of mourning,
And as foreign settlers to strange country come,
By mispronunciation of native words
And by intermarriage create a new race
And a new language, so may the soul
Be weaned at last to independent delight.

Startled by the violent laugh of a jay
I went from wood, from crunch underfoot,
Air between stems as under water;
As I shall leave the summer, see autumn come
Focusing stars more sharply in the sky,

See frozen buzzard flipped down the weir
And carried out to sea, leave autumn,
See winter, winter for earth and us,
A forethought of death that we may find ourselves at death
Not helplessly strange to the new conditions.

August 1929

4

It is time for the destruction of error.
The chairs are being brought in from the garden,
The summer talk stopped on that savage coast
Before the storms, after the guests and birds:
In sanatoriums they laugh less and less,
Less certain of cure; and the loud madman
Sinks now into a more terrible calm.

The falling leaves know it, the children,
At play on the fuming alkali-tip
Or by the flooded football ground, know it—
This is the dragon's day, the devourer's:
Orders are given to the enemy for a time
With underground proliferation of mould,
With constant whisper and the casual question,
To haunt the poisoned in his shunned house,
To destroy the efflorescence of the flesh,
The intricate play of the mind, to enforce
Conformity with the orthodox bone,
With organised fear, the articulated skeleton.

You whom I gladly walk with, touch,
Or wait for as one certain of good,
We know it, we know that love
Needs more than the admiring excitement of union,
More than the abrupt self-confident farewell,
The heel on the finishing blade of grass,
The self-confidence of the falling root,
Needs death, death of the grain, our death,
Death of the old gang; would leave them
In sullen valley where is made no friend,
The old gang to be forgotten in the spring,
The hard bitch and the riding-master,
Stiff underground; deep in clear lake
The lolling bridegroom, beautiful, there.

October 1929

XXV

Which of you waking early and watching daybreak
Will not hasten in heart, handsome, aware of wonder
At light unleashed, advancing, a leader of movement,
Breaking like surf on turf, on road and roof,
Or chasing shadow on downs like whippet racing,
Then stilled against stone, halting at eyelash barrier,
Enforcing in face a profile, marks of misuse,
Beating impatient and importunate on boudoir shutters
Where the old life is not up yet, with rays
Exploring through rotting floor a dismantled mill—
The old life never to be born again?

For the dawn of common day is a reminder of birth,
Is as the first day was when truth divided
Light from the original and incoherent darkness:
As after the growth of light comes growth of movement,
When birds have done, the sound of unlocking gates,
The pushing over of important levers, noise
Increasing in volume till it reach a noonday roar
Guttural, the personal cry of a great city,
What man but is reminded? Whistling as he shuts
His door behind him, travelling to work by tube
Or walking through the park to it to ease the bowels,
His morning mind illumined as the plane sea,
No trace there of that midnight fleet of persecutors
Gone down with all hands, will not guess at success,
A fresh rendezvous or unexpected inheritance?

For daily under the disguise of immediate day-dream
Or nightly in direct vision the man is nourished,
Fed through the essential artery of memory
Out of the earth the mother of all life;
And all that were living flesh at any time,
The entire record of change in spirit and structure
Cry in his veins for air, plead to be born,
Enriching life, which if he refuse and abort,
Perishing they poison and he become a cypher
With codified conduct and a vacant vessel for heart.
Yes, she is always with him and will sustain him;
Often he knows it—caught in a storm on fells
And sheltering with horses behind a dripping wall,
Or in prolonged interview with another's eyes
And full length contact he will forget himself
As passion coming to its climax loses identity
And consciousness, is one with all flesh.

As a boy lately come up from country to town
Returns for the day to his village in expensive shoes,
Standing scornful in a ring of old companions
Amazes them with new expressions, with strange hints
And promises, then leaves them never to return,
Who later will never know of his feverish end
In dockland dosshouse or frozen on the Embankment
Under the luminous dial of Big Ben—
So is the fate of the insolent mind that takes
Truth as itself, in homicidal phantasies
Of itself as the divine punisher of the world,
In aphasia and general paralysis of the insane.
Or by opposite error also is man deceived,
Seeking a heaven on earth he chases his shadow,
Loses his capital and his nerve in pursuing
What yachtsmen, explorers, climbers and buggers are after,
Till exhaustion come and homeless he cry for support
In a hot room with the sagging melody of jazz
And the waters of the womb or a blue heaven close over him.

Yet the dawn of each day is still as a promise to man
Of peace and life, that he despair not watching
How heroes have fallen into vats and stewed while men
Drink up their beer unknowing and are soon asleep.
Not immediate peace nor the peace of old men
At rest from mere fatigue of animal desire
And freedom from all anxiety about money,
Leisurely reading the Masters in their rock-gardens,
But truth's assurance of life—that darkness shall die
Desiring at last the perfect security of death,
Shall bless the new life and die; a promise to man
Pushed on like grass-blade into undiscovered air,
Embracing old loves, uncertain, a sailor's farewell,
Of security upon earth and life in heaven.

October 1929

XXVI

It's no use raising a shout.
No, Honey, you can cut that right out.
I don't want any more hugs;
Make me some fresh tea, fetch me some rugs.
Here am I, here are you:
But what does it mean? What are we going to do?

A long time ago I told my mother
I was leaving home to find another:
I never answered her letter
But I never found a better.
Here am I, here are you:
But what does it mean? What are we going to do?

It wasn't always like this?
Perhaps it wasn't, but it is.
Put the car away; when life fails,
What's the good of going to Wales?
Here am I, here are you:
But what does it mean? What are we going to do?

In my spine there was a base,
And I knew the general's face:
But they've severed all the wires,
And I can't tell what the general desires.
Here am I, here are you:
But what does it mean? What are we going to do?

In my veins there is a wish,
And a memory of fish:
When I lie crying on the floor,
It says, 'You've often done this before.'
Here am I, here are you:
But what does it mean? What are we going to do?

A bird used to visit this shore:
It isn't going to come any more.
I've come a very long way to prove
No land, no water, and no love.
Here am I, here are you:
But what does it mean? What are we going to do?

November 1929

XXVII

To have found a place for nowhere
To fall ill after death
Out of breath
And afraid of fear
Is the creation
Of nation from nation.

Once mortal ones
But now they come
With girls and guns
And letters home,
Turn vantage spots
To neighbour plots
While wards and banks
Give many thanks.

And their labours
Are now among neighbours
Leading to tables
Where mortals dwelt,
Enforce their fables
With bending forks
And musical talks,
But stopping anywhere
Pulling the cap down, tightening belt
For famine or to disappear
In a new direction
With honourable mention,
Cross any Alp
To bring their help,
To reach love's side
Though counties divide
But not for the ride.

For each, a mortal's heir
With loathing remembrance
And a growing resemblance,
Neighbours till hair
Turns white with the idea,
Executing for treason
To no good reason,
Making the ending
Promise, putting the unoccurred
Upon its word,
Accounts for the misunderstood
With misunderstanding.

November 1929

XXVIII

Since you are going to begin to-day
Let us consider what it is you do.
You are the one whose part it is to lean,
For whom it is not good to be alone.
Laugh warmly turning shyly in the hall
Or climb with bare knees the volcanic hill,
Acquire that flick of wrist and after strain
Relax in your darling's arms like a stone
Remembering everything you can confess,
Making the most of firelight, of hours of fuss;
But joy is mine not yours—to have come so far,
Whose cleverest invention was lately fur;
Lizards my best once who took years to breed,
Could not control the temperature of blood.
To reach that shape for your face to assume,
Pleasure to many and despair to some,

I shifted ranges, lived epochs handicapped
By climate, wars, or what the young men kept,
Modified theories on the types of dross,
Altered desire and history of dress.

You in the town now call the exile fool
That writes home once a year as last leaves fall,
Think—Romans had a language in their day
And ordered roads with it, but it had to die:
Your culture can but leave—forgot as sure
As place-name origins in favourite shire—
Jottings for stories, some often-mentioned Jack,
And references in letters to a private joke,
Equipment rusting in unweeded lanes,
Virtues still advertised on local lines;
And your conviction shall help none to fly,
Cause rather a perversion on next floor.

Nor even is despair your own, when swiftly
Comes general assault on your ideas of safety:
That sense of famine, central anguish felt
For goodness wasted at peripheral fault,
Your shutting up the house and taking prow
To go into the wilderness to pray,
Means that I wish to leave and to pass on,
Select another form, perhaps your son;
Though he reject you, join opposing team
Be late or early at another time,
My treatment will not differ—he will be tipped,
Found weeping, signed for, made to answer, topped.
Do not imagine you can abdicate;
Before you reach the frontier you are caught;
Others have tried it and will try again
To finish that which they did not begin:
Their fate must always be the same as yours,
To suffer the loss they were afraid of, yes,
Holders of one position, wrong for years.

November 1929

XXIX

Having abdicated with comparative ease
And dismissed the greater part of your friends;
Escaped in a submarine
With a false beard, hoping the ports were watched.
How shall we greet your arrival;
For it isn't snowing
And no one will take you for a spy.

Of course we shall mention
Your annual camp for the Tutbury glass workers
Your bird-photography phase, and the Dream at the Hook,
Even the winter in Prague though not very fully:
Your public refusal of a compass
Is fixed for to-morrow.

Stinker is anxious to meet you;
Came in the other day waving the paper
Asking the question that it asked, 'Am I,
Am I among the living or the dead?'
You heard about Bog-Eyes?
Got into trouble and was asked to leave;
Never the same, poor chap, since the day of the explosion.

But now look at this map.
Here are the first- and the second-class roads,
Crossed swords for battles, and gothic letters
For places of archaeological interest.
The car will take you as far as the forge,
Further than that we fear is impossible.
At Bigsweir look out for the Kelpie.
If you meet Mr. Wren, it is wiser to hide.
Consult before leaving a water doctor.
Do you wish to ask any questions? Good; you may go.

January 1930

XXX

Consider this and in our time
As the hawk sees it or the helmeted airman:
The clouds rift suddenly—look there
At cigarette-end smouldering on a border
At the first garden party of the year.
Pass on, admire the view of the massif
Through plate-glass windows of the Sport Hotel;
Join there the insufficient units
Dangerous, easy, in furs, in uniform
And constellated at reserved tables
Supplied with feelings by an efficient band
Relayed elsewhere to farmers and their dogs
Sitting in kitchens in the stormy fens.

Long ago, supreme Antagonist,
More powerful than the great northern whale
Ancient and sorry at life's limiting defect,
In Cornwall, Mendip, or the Pennine moor
Your comments on the highborn mining-captains,
Found they no answer, made them wish to die
—Lie since in barrows out of harm.

46

You talk to your admirers every day
By silted harbours, derelict works,
In strangled orchards, and the silent comb
Where dogs have worried or a bird was shot.
Order the ill that they attack at once:
Visit the ports and, interrupting
The leisurely conversation in the bar
Within a stone's throw of the sunlit water,
Beckon your chosen out. Summon
Those handsome and diseased youngsters, those women
Your solitary agents in the country parishes;
And mobilise the powerful forces latent
In soils that make the farmer brutal
In the infected sinus, and the eyes of stoats.
Then, ready, start your rumour, soft
But horrifying in its capacity to disgust
Which, spreading magnified, shall come to be
A polar peril, a prodigious alarm,
Scattering the people, as torn-up paper
Rags and utensils in a sudden gust,
Seized with immeasurable neurotic dread.

Financier, leaving your little room
Where the money is made but not spent,
You'll need your typist and your boy no more;
The game is up for you and for the others,
Who, thinking, pace in slippers on the lawns
Of College Quad or Cathedral Close,
Who are born nurses, who live in shorts
Sleeping with people and playing fives.
Seekers after happiness, all who follow
The convolutions of your simple wish,
It is later than you think; nearer that day
Far other than that distant afternoon
Amid rustle of frocks and stamping feet
They gave the prizes to the ruined boys.
You cannot be away, then, no
Not though you pack to leave within an hour,
Escaping humming down arterial roads:
The date was yours; the prey to fugues,
Irregular breathing and alternate ascendancies
After some haunted migratory years
To disintegrate on an instant in the explosion of mania
Or lapse for ever into a classic fatigue.

March 1930

XXXI

Get there if you can and see the land you once were proud to own
Though the roads have almost vanished and the expresses never run:

Smokeless chimneys, damaged bridges, rotting wharves and choked
                                                    canals,
Tramlines buckled, smashed trucks lying on their side across the
                                                    rails;

Power-stations locked, deserted, since they drew the boiler fires;
Pylons fallen or subsiding, trailing dead high-tension wires;

Head-gears gaunt on grass-grown pit-banks, seams abandoned years
                                                    ago;
Drop a stone and listen for its splash in flooded dark below.

Squeeze into the works through broken windows or through damp-
                                                    sprung doors;
See the rotted shafting, see holes gaping in the upper floors;

Where the Sunday lads come talking motor-bicycle and girl,
Smoking cigarettes in chains until their heads are in a whirl.

Far from there we spent the money, thinking we could well afford,
While they quietly undersold us with their cheaper trade abroad;

At the theatre, playing tennis, driving motor-cars we had,
In our continental villas, mixing cocktails for a cad.

These were boon companions who devised the legends for our tombs,
These who have betrayed us nicely while we took them to our rooms.

Newman, Ciddy, Plato, Fronny, Pascal, Bowdler, Baudelaire,
Doctor Frommer, Mrs. Allom, Freud, the Baron, and Flaubert.

Lured with their compelling logic, charmed with beauty of their
                                                    verse,
With their loaded sideboards whispered 'Better join us, life is worse.'

Taught us at the annual camps arranged by the big business men
'Sunbathe, pretty till you're twenty. You shall be our servants then.'

Perfect pater. Marvellous mater. Knock the critic down who dares—
Very well, believe it, copy, till your hair is white as theirs.

Yours you say were parents to avoid, avoid then if you please
Do the reverse on all occasions till you catch the same disease.

When we asked the way to Heaven, these directed us ahead
To the padded room, the clinic and the hangman's little shed.

Intimate as war-time prisoners in an isolation camp,
Living month by month together, nervy, famished, lousy, damp.

On the sopping esplanade or from our dingy lodgings we
Stare out dully at the rain which falls for miles into the sea.

Lawrence, Blake and Homer Lane, once healers in our English land;
These are dead as iron for ever; these can never hold our hand.

Lawrence was brought down by smut-hounds, Blake went dotty as
                                         he sang,
Homer Lane was killed in action by the Twickenham Baptist gang.

Have things gone too far already? Are we done for? Must we wait
Hearing doom's approaching footsteps regular down miles of
                                         straight;

Run the whole night through in gumboots, stumble on and gasp for
                                         breath,
Terrors drawing close and closer, winter landscape, fox's death;

Or, in friendly fireside circle, sit and listen for the crash
Meaning that the mob has realised something's up, and start to
                                         smash;

Engine-drivers with their oil-cans, factory girls in overalls
Blowing sky-high monster stores, destroying intellectuals?

Hope and fear are neck and neck: which is it near the course's end
Crashes, having lost his nerve; is overtaken on the bend?

Shut up talking, charming in the best suits to be had in town,
Lecturing on navigation while the ship is going down.

Drop those priggish ways for ever, stop behaving like a stone:
Throw the bath-chairs right away, and learn to leave ourselves alone.

If we really want to live, we'd better start at once to try;
If we don't it doesn't matter, but we'd better start to die.

April 1930

49

XXXII

Pick a quarrel, go to war,
Leave the hero in the bar.
Hunt the lion, climb the peak,
No one guesses you are weak.

*   *   *

Those who will not reason
Perish in the act.
Those who will not act
Perish for that reason.

*   *   *

Schoolboy, making lonely maps:
Better do it with some chaps.

*   *   *

You're a long way off becoming a saint
As long as you suffer from any complaint:
But if you don't there's no denying
The chances are that you're not trying.

*   *   *

Medicines and Ethics: these
Are like mercenaries.
They join the other side when they
Have made you pay.

*   *   *

The General and the Doctor
    Came walking arm in arm.
They edited the Gospel
    And did the English harm.

The General and the Doctor
    They said love wouldn't do,
In case we loved the enemy.
    They substituted 'flu.

*   *   *

'We take that hill' the colonel cried.
And so they did, though most of them died,
And the enemy were their own side.

                    *   *   *

Where old authority resigns we see
The new small life beginning to be.

                    *   *   *

The pleasures of the English nation:
Copotomy and sodulation.

                    *   *   *

I'm afraid there's many a spectacled sod
Prefers the British Museum to God.

                    *   *   *

The Radcliffe Camera
Has made many a stammerer
And causes friggings
In Oxford diggings.

                    *   *   *

The friends of the born nurse
Are always getting worse.

                    *   *   *

I am beginning to lose patience
With my personal relations.
They are not deep
And they are not cheap.

                    *   *   *

When he is well
She gives him hell.
But she's a brick
When he is sick.

                    *   *   *

Love is not a thing to understand:
In love the cunt is better than the hand.

                    *   *   *

There are two kinds of friendship even in babes:
Two against one and seven against Thebes.

*   *   *

The bird goes up and the bat goes down:
The bird will burn and the bat will drown.

1929–1930

XXXIII

This lunar beauty
Has no history
Is complete and early;
If beauty later
Bear any feature
It had a lover
And is another.

This like a dream
Keeps other time
And daytime is
The loss of this;
For time is inches
And the heart's changes
Where ghost has haunted
Lost and wanted.

But this was never
A ghost's endeavour
Nor finished this,
Was ghost at ease;
And till it pass
Love shall not near
The sweetness here
Nor sorrow take
His endless look.

April 1930

XXXIV

Between attention and attention
The first and last decision
Is mortal distraction
Of earth and air,
Further and nearer,
The vague wants
Of days and nights
And personal error;
And the fatigued face,
Taking the strain
Of the horizontal force

And the vertical thrust,
Makes random answer
To the crucial test;
The uncertain flesh
Scraping back chair
For the wrong train,
Falling in slush,
Before a friend's friends
Or shaking hands
With a snub-nosed winner.

The opening window, closing door
Open, close, but not
To finish or restore;
These wishes get
No further than
The edges of the town,
And leaning asking from the car
Cannot tell us where we are;
While the divided face
Has no grace,
No discretion,
No occupation
But registering
Acreage, mileage,
The easy knowledge
Of the virtuous thing.

May 1930

XXXV

Who will endure
Heat of day and winter danger,
Journey from one place to another,
Nor be content to lie
Till evening upon headland over bay,
Between the land and sea;
Or smoking wait till hour of food,
Leaning on chained-up gate
At edge of wood?

Metals run
Burnished or rusty in the sun
From town to town,
And signals all along are down;
Yet nothing passes
But envelopes between these places,
Snatched at the gate and panting read indoors,
And first spring flowers arriving smashed,
Disaster stammered over wires,

And pity flashed.
For should professional traveller come,
Asked at the fireside he is dumb,
Declining with a small mad smile,
And all the while
Conjectures on the maps that lie
About in ships long high and dry
Grow stranger and stranger.

There is no change of place
But shifting of the head
To keep off glare of lamp from face,
Or climbing over to wall-side of bed;
No one will ever know
For what conversion brilliant capital is waiting,
What ugly feast may village band be celebrating;
For no one goes
Further than railhead or the ends of piers,
Will neither go nor send his son
Further through foothills than the rotting stack
Where gaitered gamekeeper with dog and gun
Will shout 'Turn back'.

? Summer 1930

XXXVI

To ask the hard question is simple;
Asking at meeting
With the simple glance of acquaintance
To what these go
And how these do:
To ask the hard question is simple,
The simple act of the confused will.

But the answer
Is hard and hard to remember:
On steps or on shore
The ears listening
To words at meeting,
The eyes looking
At the hands helping,
Are never sure
Of what they learn
From how these things are done.
And forgetting to listen or see
Makes forgetting easy;
Only remembering the method of remembering,
Remembering only in another way,
Only the strangely exciting lie,
Afraid

To remember what the fish ignored,
How the bird escaped, or if the sheep obeyed.

Till, losing memory,
Bird, fish, and sheep are ghostly,
And ghosts must do again
What gives them pain.
Cowardice cries
For windy skies,
Coldness for water,
Obedience for a master.

Shall memory restore
The steps and the shore,
The face and the meeting place;
Shall the bird live,
Shall the fish dive,
And sheep obey
In a sheep's way;
Can love remember
The question and the answer,
For love recover
What has been dark and rich and warm all over?
? August 1930

XXXVII

Doom is dark and deeper than any sea-dingle.
Upon what man it fall
In spring, day-wishing flowers appearing,
Avalanche sliding, white snow from rock-face,
That he should leave his house,
No cloud-soft hand can hold him, restraint by women;
But ever that man goes
Through place-keepers, through forest trees,
A stranger to strangers over undried sea,
Houses for fishes, suffocating water,
Or lonely on fell as chat,
By pot-holed becks
A bird stone-haunting, an unquiet bird.

There head falls forward, fatigued at evening,
And dreams of home,
Waving from window, spread of welcome,
Kissing of wife under single sheet;
But waking sees
Bird-flocks nameless to him, through doorway voices
Of new men making another love.

Save him from hostile capture,
From sudden tiger's spring at corner;
Protect his house,
His anxious house where days are counted
From thunderbolt protect,
From gradual ruin spreading like a stain;
Converting number from vague to certain,
Bring joy, bring day of his returning,
Lucky with day approaching, with leaning dawn.

August 1930

XXXVIII

What's in your mind, my dove, my coney;
Do thoughts grow like feathers, the dead end of life;
Is it making of love or counting of money,
Or raid on the jewels, the plans of a thief?

Open your eyes, my dearest dallier;
Let hunt with your hands for escaping me;
Go through the motions of exploring the familiar;
Stand on the brink of the warm white day.

Rise with the wind, my great big serpent;
Silence the birds and darken the air;
Change me with terror, alive in a moment;
Strike for the heart and have me there.

November 1930

XXXIX

Look there! The sunk road winding
To the fortified farm.
Listen! The cock's alarm
In the strange valley.

Are we the stubborn athletes;
Are we then to begin
The run between the gin
And bloody falcon?

The horns of the dark squadron
Converging to attack;
The sound behind our back
Of glaciers calving.

In legend all were simple,
And held the straitened spot;
But we in legend not,
Are not simple.

In weakness how much further;
Along what crooked route
By hedgehog's gradual foot,
Or fish's fathom.

Bitter the blue smoke rises
From garden bonfires lit,
To where we burning sit:
Good, if it's thorough.

It won't be us who eavesdrop
In days of luck and heat,
Timing the double beat
At last together.

January 1931

Part III

The Orators

AN ENGLISH STUDY

(TO STEPHEN SPENDER)

Private faces in public places
Are wiser and nicer
Than public faces in private places.

Prologue

By landscape reminded once of his mother's figure
The mountain heights he remembers get bigger and bigger:
With the finest of mapping pens he fondly traces
All the family names on the familiar places.

Among green pastures straying he walks by still waters;
Surely a swan he seems to earth's unwise daughters,
Bending a beautiful head, worshipping not lying,
'Dear' the dear beak in the dear concha crying.

Under the trees the summer bands were playing;
'Dear boy, be brave as these roots', he heard them saying:
Carries the good news gladly to a world in danger,
Is ready to argue, he smiles, with any stranger.

And yet this prophet, homing the day is ended,
Receives odd welcome from the country he so defended:
The band roars 'Coward, Coward', in his human fever,
The giantess shuffles nearer, cries 'Deceiver'.

March 1931

BOOK I

The Initiates

I · ADDRESS FOR A PRIZE-DAY

Commemoration. Commemoration. What does it mean? What does it
mean? Not what does it mean to them, there, then. What does it mean
to us, here now? It's a facer, isn't it boys? But we've all got to answer it.
What were the dead like? What sort of people are we living with now?
Why are we here? What are we going to do? Let's try putting it in
another way.

Imagine to yourselves a picked body of angels, all qualified experts
on the human heart, a Divine Commission, arriving suddenly one day
at Dover. After some weeks in London, they separate, one passing the
petrol pumps along the Great North Road, leaving the dales on his left
hand, to take all rain-wet Scotland for his special province, one to the
furnace-crowded Midlands, another to the plum-rich red-earth valley

61

of the Severn, another to the curious delta-like area round King's Lynn, another to Cornwall where granite resists the sea and our type of thinking ends, and so on. And then when every inch of the ground has been carefully gone over, every house inspected, they return to the Capital again to compare notes, to collaborate in a complete report, which made, they depart as quietly as they came. Beauty of the scenery apart, would you not feel some anxiety as to the contents of that report? Do you consider their statistics as to the average number of lost persons to the acre would be a cause for self-congratulation? Take a look round this hall, for instance. What do you think? What do you think about England, this country of ours where nobody is well?

All of you must have found out what a great help it is, before starting on a job of work, to have some sort of scheme or plan in your mind beforehand. Some of the senior boys, I expect, will have heard of the great Italian poet Dante, who wrote that very difficult but wonderful poem, *The Divine Comedy*. In the second book of this poem, which describes Dante's visit to Purgatory, the sinners are divided into three main groups, those who have been guilty in their life of excessive love towards themselves or their neighbours, those guilty of defective love towards God and those guilty of perverted love. Now this afternoon I want, if I may, to take these three divisions of his and apply them to ourselves. In this way, I hope, you will be able to understand better what I am driving at.

To start with, then, the excessive lovers of self. What are they like? These are they who even in childhood played in their corner, shrank when addressed. Lovers of long walks, they sometimes become bird watchers, crouching for hours among sunlit bushes like a fox, but prefer as a rule the big cities, living voluntarily in a top room, the curiosity of their landlady. Habituees of the mirror, famous readers, they fall in love with historical characters, with the unfortunate queen, or the engaging young assistant of a great detective, even with the voice, of the announcer, maybe, from some foreign broadcasting station they can never identify; unable to taste pleasure unless through the rare coincidence of naturally diverse events, or the performance of a long and intricate ritual. With odd dark eyes like windows, a lair for engines, they pass suffering more and more from cataract or deafness, leaving behind them diaries full of incomprehensible jottings, complaints less heard than the creaking of a wind pump on a moor. The easiest perhaps for you to recognise. They avoid the study fire, at games they are no earthly use. They are not popular. But isn't it up to you to help? Oughtn't you to warn them then against tampering like that with time, against those strange moments they look forward to so? Next time you see one sneaking from the field to develop photographs, won't you ask if you can come too? Why not go out together next Sunday; say, casually, in a wood: 'I suppose you realise you are fingering the levers that control eternity?'

Then the excessive lovers of their neighbours. Dare-devils of the soul, living dangerously upon their nerves. A rich man taking the fastest train for the worst quarters of eastern cities; a private school-mistress in a provincial town, watching the lights go out in another wing, immensely passionate. You will not be surprised to learn that they are both heavy smokers. That one always in hot water with the prefects, that one who will not pass the ball; they are like this. You call them selfish, but no, they care immensely, far too much. They're beginning to go faster. Have you never noticed in them the gradual abdication of central in favour of peripheral control? What if the tiniest stimulus should provoke the full, the shattering response, not just then but all the time? It isn't going to stop unless you stop it. Daring them like that only makes them worse. Try inviting them down in the holidays to a calm house. You can do most for them in the summer. They need love.

Next the defective lovers. Systems run to a standstill, or like those ship-cranes along Clydebank, which have done nothing all this year. Owners of small holdings, they sit by fires they can't make up their minds to light, while dust settles on their unopened correspondence and inertia branches in their veins like a zinc tree. That tomato house blown down by the autumn gales they never rebuilt. Wearers of soiled linen, the cotton wool in their ears unchanged for months. Often they are collectors, but of what? Old tracts, brackets picked up on the road, powders, pieces of wood, uncatalogued, piled anyhow in corners of the room, or hidden under tea-stained saucers. Anaemic, muscularly undeveloped and rather mean. Without servants. Each hour bringing its little barrowful of unacted desires, mounting up day after day, week after week, month after month, year after year has made a slag heap miles high shutting out air and sun. It's getting rather smelly. The effort required for clearance will be immense. Dare they begin? Well, you've got to show them they'd jolly well better dare. Give them regular but easy tasks and see that they do them properly. Hit them in the face if necessary. If they hit back you will know they are saved.

Last and worst, the perverted lovers. So convincing at first, so little apparent cause for anxiety. A slight proneness to influenza, perhaps, a fear of cows, traits easily misunderstood or dismissed. Have a good look at the people you know; at the boy sitting next to you at this moment, at that chum of yours in the Lower School. Think of the holidays, your father, the girl you met at that dance. Is he one? Was she one? Yes, they are charming, but they've lost their nerve. Pray God, boys, you may not have to see them as they will be not so very long from now. 'What have you been up to?' you'd think; 'What did you ask for to be given that?' Faces in suffering so ugly they inspire feelings only of disgust. Their voice toneless, they stoop, their gait wooden like a galvanised doll so that one involuntarily exclaims on meeting, 'You really oughtn't to be out in weather like this.' In some a simple geometrical figure can arouse all the manifestations of extreme alarm. Others haters of life, afraid to die, end in hospitals as incurable cases. These are they who when the saving thought came shot it for a spy. Unable to sleep at nights, they look at watches as the train passes, pushed struggling in towards a protracted deathbed, attended by every circumstance of horror, the hard death of those who never have and never could be loved.

Who have done this? There must be several here. Yes I can see some already. There you sit, who smooth sick pillows, devoted as lice, yet have no daydreams: wince at no curse, are never ill, put kindness, words and sleekness in. You're going to have friends, you're going to bring up children. You're going to be like this for ever, all the time, more terrible than the bursting of the bolted door or the exhausting adverse wind of dreams.

Now, boys, I want you all to promise me that you'll never be like that. Are you just drifting or thinking of flight? You'd better not. No use saying 'The mater wouldn't like it', or 'For my part I prefer to read Charles Lamb'. Need I remind you that you are no longer living in Ancient Egypt? Time's getting on and I must hurry or I shall miss my train. You've got some pretty stiff changes to make. We simply can't afford any passengers or skrimshankers. I should like to see you make a beginning before I go, now, here. Draw up a list of rotters and slackers, of proscribed persons under headings like this. Committees for municipal or racial improvement—the headmaster. Disbelievers in the occult—the school chaplain. The bogusly cheerful—the games master. The really disgusted—the teacher of modern languages. All these have got to die without issue. Unless my memory fails me there's a stoke hole under the floor of this hall, the Black Hole we called it in my day. New boys were always put in it. Ah, I see I am right. Well look to it. Quick, guard that door. Stop that man. Good. Now boys hustle them, ready, steady—go.

? Spring 1931

II · ARGUMENT

I

Lo, I a skull show you, exuded from dyke when no pick was by

Before the forenoon of discussion, as the dawn-gust wrinkles the pools, I waken with an idea of building.

Speak the name only with meaning only for us, meaning Him, a call to our clearing. Secret the meeting in time and place, the time of the off-shore wind, the place where the loyalty is divided. Meeting of seven, each with a talent.

On the concrete banks of baths, in the grassy squares of exercise, we are joined, brave in the long body, under His eye. (Their annual games under the auspices of the dead.) Our bond, friend, is a third party.

Smile inwardly on their day handing round tea. (Their women have the faces of birds.) Walking in the mountains we were persons unknown to our parents, awarded them little, had a word of our own for our better shadow. Crossing ourselves under the arch of a bridge we crucified fear.

Crofter, leader of hay, working in sweat and weathers, tin-streamer, heckler, blow-room major, we are within a vein's distance of your prisoned blood. Stranger who cannot read our letters, you are remembered.

Rooks argue in the clump of elms to the left. Expect what dream

64

above the indented heel, end-on to traffic, down the laurelled drive?

At the frontier getting down, at railhead drinking hot tea waiting for pack-mules, at the box with the three levers watching the swallows. Choosing of guides for the passage through gorges.

The young mother in the red kerchief suckling her child in the doorway, and the dog fleaing itself in the hot dust. Clatter of nails on the inn's flagged floor. The hare-lipped girl sent with as far as the second turning. Talk of generals in a panelled room translated into a bayonet thrust at a sunbrowned throat, wounds among wheat fields. Grit from the robbers' track on goggles, a present from aunts. Interrogation of villagers before a folding table, a verbal trap. Execution of a spy in the nettled patch at the back of the byre. A tale of sexual prowess told at a brazier and followed by a maternal song. The fatty smell of drying clothes, smell of cordite in a wood, and the new moon seen along the barrel of a gun. Establishment of a torpedo base at the head of the loch; where the bye-roads meet, a depot for tractors, with sliding doors. Visit to a tannery in the hill-village where the stream runs under the houses; to the mine with obsolete machinery, an undershot wheel, steam pipes in the open, swaddled in sacking. Designs for the flow sheet of a mill. Sound of our hammers in the solemn beat of a quarry, and the packing of labelled specimens in japanned boxes. Theories inter-relating the system of feudal tenure with metabolic gradients, and arguments from the other side of the lake on the formation of hanging valleys, interrupted by the daughter of the house with a broken doll. Writing reports for Him in the copper-green evenings. (Trunks caught by the grapnel dragged inert towards the spurting saw, ewers of warm milk, the sugary layer under the rind, and pipe-lines clamped to the rock) and at the tiny post-office, His word waiting.

If it were possible, yes, now certain. To meet Him alone on the narrow path, forcing a question, would show our unique knowledge. Would hide Him wounded in a cave, kneeling all night by His bed of bracken, bringing hourly an infusion of bitter herbs; wearing His cloak receive the mistaken stab, deliver His message, fall at His feet, He gripping our moribund hands, smiling. But never for us with note-books there, a league of two or three waiting for low water to execute His will. The tripod shadow falls on the dunes. World of the Spider, not Him.

Rook shadows cross to the right. A schoolmaster cleanses himself at half-term with a vegetable offering; on the north side of the hill, one writes with his penis in a patch of snow 'Resurgam'.

Going abroad to-day? Under a creaking sign, one yellow leg drawn up, he crows, the cock. The dew-wet hare hangs smoking, garotted by gin. The emmet looks at sky through lenses of fallen water. Sound of horns in the moist spring weather, and the women tender. I feel sorry for you I do.

Girls, it is His will just now that we get up early. But watching the morning dredger, picking the afternoon fruit, wait; do not falsify our obedience. When we shuffle at night late round up-country stoves, although in waders, a dance of males, it is your hour; remember. It is your art just now against the inner life. Parting by hangars we are sorry but reborn.

Wrap gifts in clothes, prepare a present for a simpler nation. A heliograph seen from below, a camera with smuggled lenses: a soured drink for the tongue, a douche for the unpopular member, a dream dirt-cheap for the man of action. Leave the corks behind as warning of wires, let the shafts be fenced as before, leave ordinary kindness.

Going abroad to-night? The face lit up by the booking-clerk's window. Poetry of the waiting-room. Is it wise, the short adventure on the narrow ship? The boat-train dives accomplished for the hoop of the tunnel; over the derne cutting lingering, its white excreta. Too late: smelling the first sea-weed we may not linger. The waving handkerchiefs recede and the gulls wheel after screaming for scraps. Throb of turbines below water, passing the mud islands, the recurrent light. Past. Handrail, funnel, oilskins, them, His will. The lasting sky.

II

Remember not what we thought during the frost, what we said in the small hours, what we did in the desert. Spare us, lest of our own volition we draw down the avalanche of your anger: lest we suffer the tragic fate of the insects,
> O Four Just Men, spare us.

From the immense bat-shadow of home; from the removal of land-marks: from appeals for love and from the comfortable words of the devil,
> O Dixon Hawke, deliver us.

From all opinions and personal ties; from pity and shame; and from the wish to instruct,
> O Sexton Blake, deliver us.

From all nervous excitement and follies of the will; from the postponed guilt and the deferred pain; from the oppression of noon and from the terror in the night,
> O Bulldog Drummond, deliver us.

From the surgeon's pioneering hand; from the power of the red lamp; and from the death-will of the Jews,
> O Ferrers Locke, deliver us.

From the encroaching glaciers of despair, from the drought that withers the lower centres: from the star Wormwood, and from the death by burning,
> O Panther Grayle, deliver us.

By the flash of insight in the rears; by the slow influence of natural scenery; by the phrase in the book and by the word overheard on the platform,
>O Poirot, deliver us.

In the moment of vision; in the hour of applause; in the place of defeat, and in the hour of desertion,
>O Holmes, deliver us.

For those who dance in the capitals; for those who handle a saw; those who discuss the problem of style and those aware of the body; for those who have done everything and those who dare not begin,
>O Cat with the Fiddle, hear us.

For those who cannot go to bed; for those in dormitories; for those in pairs; for those who sleep alone,
>O Bull at the Gate, hear us.

For the devoted; for the unfaithful; for those in whom the sexual crisis is delayed; for the two against one, and for the Seven against Thebes,
>O Goat with the Compasses, hear us.

For the virgin afraid of thunder; for the wife obeyed by her husband; for the spinster in love with Africa,
>O Bear with the Ragged Staff, hear us.

For those who grow by division; for those who protest their innocence; for those who decline to die,
>O Blue Boar, hear us.

For those who borrow and for those who lend, for those who are shunned on the towpath; for those regarded in their households as saints,
>O Swan with the Two Necks, hear us.

For sunbathers; for those who dress soberly; for those who expect to be respected, and for those who have been taught to adore,
>O White Horse, hear us.

For those determined to suffer; for those who believe they can control the weather,
>O Jack Straw from your Castle hear us.

For those capable of levitation; for those who have days of collapse; for those whose impulses are negative,
>Fair Maid of Kent, hear us.

For those who elect to live in the bower; for those on the hill; for those who return to the epoch of the poisoner,
>O Man laden with Mischief, hear us.

For those who take vows of silence; for those who do not; for those who visit churches after the death of sons,
O Marquis of Granby, hear us.

For all parasites and carrion feeders, for the double rose and for domesticated animals,
O Green Man, hear us.

And that it may please thee to calm this people,
George, we beseech thee to hear us.

III

Came one after a ruined harvest, with a schoolroom globe, a wizard, sorry. From the nipping North Righteousness running. But where that warm boy of the summer château? Found on wet roads early this morning, patches of oil, the face of an avenger, downwards. Speech of worn tools in a box, thoughts from the trap.

Sound of guns in the city, the voice of the demonstrator, 'Gentlemen, to-morrow we shall tie the carotid.' What memory of self-regard from the locked room, shaken by lorries, from the depressed areas?
Suspicion of one of our number, away for week-ends. Catching sight of Him on the lawn with the gardener, from the upper rooms of a house. His insane dislike of birds. His fondness for verbal puzzles. Friendly joking converting itself into a counterplot, the spore of fear. Then in the hot weeks, the pavement blistering and the press muzzled, the sudden disaster, surprising as a comic turn. Shutting the door on the machines, we stood in the silence, thinking of nothing. (Murder of a rook by weasels.) Some taking refuge in thankful disillusion, others in frank disbelief, the youngest getting drunk. Hysterical attempts of two women to reach Him. The slow seeping in of their sly condolences, of the mass hatred of the villas. A child's sense of failure after burning a slug in a candle.
Daylight, striking at the eye from far-off roofs, why did you blind us, think: we who on the snow-line were in love with death, despised vegetation, we forgot His will; who came to us in an extraordinary dream, calming the plunging dangerous horses, greeting our arrival on a reedy shore. His sharing from His own provisions after the blizzard's march. The thrashing He gave the dishonest contractor who promised marvels in an old boy's tie. The old peasant couple's belief in His magical powers. His ability to smell a wet knife at a distance of half a mile. His refusal to wear anything but silk next to His skin. His reverent stories of the underpaid drunken usher who taught Him all. His tale of the Three Sorb Trees. His words after we had failed Him at the Roman bridge.
Love, that notable forked one, riding away from the farm, the ill word said, fought at the frozen dam, transforms itself to influenza and

guilty rashes. Seduction of a postmistress on the lead roof of a church-tower, and an immature boy wrapping himself in a towel, ashamed at the public baths. From these stony acres, a witless generation, plant-like in beauty.

On the steps of His stone the boys play prisoner's base, turning their backs on the inscription, unconscious of sorrow as the sea of drowning. Passage to music of an unchaste hero from a too-strict country. March, long black piano, silhouetted head; cultured daughter of a greying ironmaster, march through fields. The hammer settles on the white-hot ingot. The telescope focuses accurately upon a recent star. On skyline of detritus, a truck, nose up. Loiterer at carved gates, immune stranger, follow. It is nothing, your loss. The priest's mouth opens in the green graveyard, but the wind is against it.

? Spring 1931

III · STATEMENT

I

Men pass through doors and travel to the sea, stand grouped in attitudes of play or labour, bending to children, raising equal's glass, are many times together, man with woman. To each an award, suitable to his sex, his class and the power.

One charms by thickness of wrist; one by variety of positions; one has a beautiful skin, one a fascinating smell. One has prominent eyes, is bold at accosting. One has water sense; he can dive like a swallow without using his hands. One is obeyed by dogs, one can bring down snipe on the wing. One can do cart wheels before theatre queues; one can slip through a narrow ring. One with a violin can conjure up images of running water; one is skilful at improvising a fugue; the bowel tremors at the pedal-entry. One amuses by pursing his lips; or can imitate the neigh of a randy stallion. One casts metal in black sand; one wipes the eccentrics of a great engine with cotton waste. One jumps out of windows for profit. One makes leather instruments of torture for titled masochists; one makes ink for his son out of oak galls and rusty nails. One makes bedsteads, adorned with carvings, at the request of friends. One in a red-brick villa makes designs for a bridge, creates beauty for a purpose. One is eloquent, persuades committees of the value of spending; one announces weddings in a solemn voice. One is told secrets at night, can stop a young girl biting her nails. One can extirpate a goitre with little risk. One can foretell the migrations of mackerel; one can distinguish the eggs of sea-birds. One is a lightning calculator; he is a young one. One is clumsy but amazes by his knowledge of time-tables. One delivers buns in a van, halting at houses. One can emend a mutilated text; one can estimate the percentage of moisture in a sample of nitre. One decorates a room for a lady in black and silver; one manufactures elephant drums for a circus.

One has an extraordinary capacity for organising study circles. One fosters snowdrops in a green bowl. One does nothing at all but is good.

Summon. And there passed such cursing his father, and the curse was given him.

II

Do not listen at doors.
On lawns in flannels, in garages, in golf clubs, talking, starting slightly at the shooting, the small disaster on the limitless plain, returning from matches after the streets are lit, who can protest at the words from the other room.

One slips on crag, is buried by guides. One gets cramp in the bay, sinks like a stone near crowded tea-shops. One is destroyed in his bath, the geyser exploding. One is arrested for indecent exposure. One suffers from an intestinal worm; men remark on his paleness. One believes himself to be two persons, is restrained with straps. One cannot remember the day of the week. One is impotent from fear of the judgment. One pays for foolishness with the loss of land. One loses his job for an error in long division. One drinks alone in another country. One repels by unsightly facial eruptions; one is despised for wearing stiff collars. The wife of one is unfaithful with schoolboys. One is bullied by an elder sister; one is disappointed in his youngest son.
Always think of the others.
One is saved from drowning by a submerged stake. One healed by drinking from a holy well. One is honoured by a countess with a gift of grapes. One is hailed as the master by monthly reviews. One is known in his club as 'the Skipper'. One discovers in middle age his talent for painting. One is a hero, covered with medals, is greeted by bands. One wins a battle through a change in the weather. One has a unique collection of indigenous insects. One is promoted for his suggestions respecting overhead charges. One makes a fortune out of a locking device for lifts. One receives a grant from a fund for research; one is invited to give a course of lectures on a philosophical subject. One discovers a new variety of sneeze wort; it shall be called by his name. The mayorship of one is commemorated by a public lavatory at the cross-roads. One is famous after his death for his harrowing diary.

Have seen the red bicycle leaning on porches and the cancelling out was complete.

III

An old one is beginning to be two new ones. Two new ones are beginning to be two old ones. Two old ones are beginning to be one new one. A new one is beginning to be an old one. Something that has been done, that something is done again by someone. Nothing is being done but something being done again by someone.

Life is many; in the pine a beam, very still: in the salmon an arrow leaping the ladder. The belly receives; the back rejects; the eye is an experiment of the will. Jelly fish is laziest, cares very little. Tapeworm is most ashamed; he used to be free. Fish is most selfish; snake is most envious, poisoned within; bird is most nervous; he is shot for his spirit. Eagle is proudest. Bull is stupidest, oppressed by blood. Insect is most different; he multiplies for another reason; he is not with us.

The man shall love the work; the woman shall receive him as the divine representative; the child shall be born as the sign of the trust; the friend shall laugh at the joke apparently obscure. The boy and the girl shall not play together; they shall wait for power; the old shall wait in the garden, happy for death. The leader shall be a fear; he shall protect from panic; the people shall reverence the carved stone under the oak-tree. The muscular shall lounge in bars; the puny shall keep diaries in classical Greek. The soldier shall say 'It is a fine day for hurting'; the doctor shall speak of death as of a favourite dog. The glutton shall love with his mouth; to the burglar love shall mean 'Destroy when read'; to the rich and poor the sign for 'our money'; the sick shall say of love 'It's only a phase'; the psychologist, 'That's easy'; the bugger, 'Be fair'. The censor shall dream of knickers, a nasty beast. The murderer shall be wreathed with flowers; he shall die for the people.

Sun is on right, moon on left, powers to earth. The action of light on dark is to cause it to contract. That brings forth.

? Spring 1931

IV · LETTER TO A WOUND

The maid has just cleared away tea and I shall not be disturbed until supper. I shall be quite alone in this room, free to think of you if I choose and believe me, my dear, I do choose. For a long time now I have been aware that you are taking up more of my life every day, but I am always being surprised to find how far this has gone. Why, it was only yesterday, I took down all those photographs from my mantelpiece—Gabriel, Olive, Mrs. Marshall, Molim, and the others. How could I have left them there like that so long, memorials to my days of boasting? As it is, I've still far too many letters. (Vow. To have a grand clearance this week—hotel bills, bus tickets from Damascus, presentation pocket-mirrors, foreign envelopes, etc.)

Looking back now to that time before I lost my 'health' (Was that really only last February?) I can't recognise myself. The discontinuity seems absolute. But of course the change was really gradual. Over and over again in the early days when I was in the middle of writing a newsy letter to M., or doing tricks in the garden to startle R. and C., you showed your resentment by a sudden bout of pain. I had outbursts, wept even, at what seemed to me then your insane jealousy, your bad manners, your passion for spoiling things. What a little idiot I was not to trust your more exquisite judgment, which declined absolutely to let me go on behaving like a child. People would have tried to explain it all. You would not insult me with pity. I think I've learned my lesson now. Thank you, my dear. I'll try my hardest not to let you down again.

Do you realise we have been together now for almost a year? Eighteen months ago, if anyone had foretold this to me I should have asked him to leave the house. Haven't I ever told told you about my first interview with the surgeon? He kept me waiting three quarters of an hour. It was raining outside. Cars passed or drew up squeaking by the curb. I sat in my overcoat, restlessly turning over the pages of back numbers of illustrated papers, accounts of the Battle of Jutland, jokes about special constables and conscientious objectors. A lady came down with a little girl. They put on their hats, speaking in whispers, tight-lipped. Mr. Gangle would see me. A nurse was just coming out as I entered, carrying a white-enamelled bowl containing a pair of scissors, some instruments, soiled swabs of cotton wool. Mr. Gangle was washing his hands. The examination on the hard leather couch under the brilliant light was soon over. Washing again as I dressed he said nothing. Then reaching for a towel turned, 'I'm afraid', he said. . . .

Outside I saw nothing, walked, not daring to think. I've lost everything, I've failed. I wish I was dead. And now, here we are, together, intimate, mature.

Later. At dinner Mrs. T. announced that she'd accepted an in-vitation for me to a whist-drive at the Stewarts' on Wednesday. 'It's so good for you to get out in the evenings sometimes. You're as bad as Mr. Bedder.' She babbled on, secretly disappointed, I think, that I did not make more protest. Certainly six months ago she couldn't have brought it off, which makes me think what a great change has come over us recently. In what I might call our honeymoon stage, when we had both realised what we meant to each other (how slow I was, wasn't I?) and that this would always be so, I was obsessed (You too a little? No?) by what seemed my extraordinary fortune. I pitied everybody. Little do you know, I said to myself, looking at my neighbour on the bus, what has happened to the little man in the black hat sitting next to you. I was always smiling. I mortally offended Mrs. Hunter, I remember, when she was describing her son's career at Cambridge. She thought I was laughing at her. In restaurants I used to find myself drawing pictures of you on the bottom of the table mats. 'Who'll ever guess what that is?' Once, when a whore accosted me, I bowed, 'I deeply regret it, Madam, but I have a friend.' Once I carved on a seat in the park 'We have sat here. You'd better not.'

Now I see that all that sort of thing is juvenile and silly, merely a reaction against insecurity and shame. You as usual of course were the first to realise this, making yourself felt whenever I had been particularly rude or insincere.

Thanks to you, I have come to see a profound significance in relations I never dreamt of considering before, an old lady's affection for a small boy, the Waterhouses and their retriever, the curious bond between Offal and Snig, the partners in the hardware shop on the front. Even the close-ups on the films no longer disgust nor amuse me. On the contrary they sometimes make me cry; knowing you has made me understand.

It's getting late and I have to be up betimes in the morning. You are so quiet these days that I get quite nervous, remove the dressing. No I am safe, you are still there. The wireless this evening says that the frost is coming. When it does, we know what to expect, don't we? But I am calm. I can wait. The surgeon was dead right. Nothing will ever part us. Good-night and God bless you, my dear.

Better burn this.

? July 1931

BOOK II

Journal of an Airman

A system organises itself, if interaction is undisturbed. Organisation owes nothing to the surveyor. It is in no sense pre-arranged. The surveyor provides just news.

The effect of the enemy is to introduce inert velocities into the system (called by him laws or habits) interfering with organisation. These can only be removed by friction (war). Hence the enemy's interest in peace societies.

Nothing shows the power of the enemy more than that while the fact that a state of tension seeks to relieve itself seems to us perfectly obvious, an orderly arrangement, the natural result of such an effort, is inexplicable to us without introducing first causes and purposive ends.

The second law of thermodynamics—self-care or minding one's own business.

But—
(1) It is a sure sign of a busybody if he talks of *laissez-faire*.
(2) Self-care is not to be confused with self-regard. Self-care is care-free. Self-regard is the treating of news as a private poem; it is the consequence of eavesdropping.

Note—Self-regard, in origin a mere accident of overcrowding, like haemophilia is a sex-linked disease. Man is the sufferer, woman the carrier. 'What a wonderful woman she is!' Not so fast: wait till you see her son.

73

A Sure Test.

FIG. 1

Give the party you suspect the above figure and ask him to pick out a form from it.

If he picks out either of the two crosses below (Fig. 2)

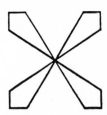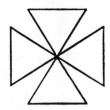

FIG. 2

you may accept him as a friend, but if he chooses such a form as Fig. 3

FIG. 3

it is wiser to shoot at once.

THE ENEMY IS A LEARNED NOT A NAÏVE OBSERVER

Note—Naïve observation—insight.
Introspection   —spying.

The Circle.

FIG. 4

There is a centre and a circumference, and between them is awareness of interdependence—sympathy.

The enemy attempts to disturb this awareness by theories of partial priority.

The Two Circles.

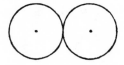

FIG. 5

Between circumference and circumference, awareness of likeness—kindness. Between centre and centre, awareness of difference—love.

THE AIRMAN IS THE AGENT OF THIS CENTRAL AWARENESS

Note 1—The relation between the centres of circles lying on the same axis—ancestor worship. This has nothing to do with history, which is the circle's after-image of itself exploited for private ends.

> After the death of their proud master, who
> Stood man-high in his socks and paid his debts,
> The clumsy pilferer whose back was sore,
> The nasty lave-eared pop-eyed bitch
> Out of their envy of the ordinary
> And dreading the imitations of the Boots,
> Started their legends in the servants' hall,
> Denying weakness by believing legends,
> Lacking not only in the Master's wit
> But the Boots' habit just to use his eyes.
> 'He was an ogre taller than a mill
> Who slew all comers greedy for their brass—
> We dared not leave our houses after dark.
> No, he had bat's wings, dog's head, scorpion's tail.
> A dragon living in the marsh, that stole
> My lovely Maggie on her fourteenth birthday.'
>
> But now these offspring of their lukewarm bed,
> Reared in a tidy nursery, poops and smarties,
> Who pilfer always but are never whipped,
> Who have not seen a body undiseased,
> Denying legends, believe weakness pride,
> Rifle the giant's grave but cannot sleep,
> Drain out the Dragon's Pond but die from dropsy.

The true ancestral line is not necessarily a straight or continuous one. Take a simple biological analogy, black and white colour, with white recessive to black.

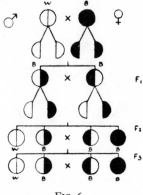

Fig. 6

In the F_3 generation the true ancestor of the pure white is his uncle or his great grandfather.

My mother's dislike of my uncle, the people's satisfaction at crashes. 'If the Lord had intended people to fly He'd have given them wings', compared with their day-dreams of looping the loop, the falling leaf, dragging their chum from blazing fuselage—signs of a mixed character. Most people mixed characters—the two-faced, the obscure and amazed, the touch-line admirers.

Note 2—The aeroplane has only recently become necessary, owing to the progress of enemy propaganda, and even now not for flying itself, but as a guarantee of good faith to the people, frightened by ghost stories, the enemy's distorted vision of the airman's activities.

*   *   *

Vadill of Urafirth, Stubba, Smirnadale, Hamar and Sullom, all possible bases: particularly at Hubens or Gluss. Survey to be completed by Monday.

At Grind of the Navir to-day watching skuas.

You are a man, or haven't you heard
That you keep on trying to be a bird?

*   *   *

Of the enemy as philosopher. Talking of intellect-will-sensation as real and separate entities. The Oxford Don: 'I don't feel quite happy about pleasure.'

*   *   *

We have brought you, they said, a map of the country;
Here is the line that runs to the vats,
This patch of green on the left is the wood,
We've pencilled an arrow to point out the bay.
No thank you, no tea; why look at the clock.
Keep it? Of course. It goes with our love.

We shall watch your future and send our love.
We lived for years, you know, in the country,
Remember at week-ends to wind up the clock.
We've wired to our manager at the vats.
The tides are perfectly safe in the bay
But whatever you do don't go to the wood.

There's a flying trickster in that wood,
And we shan't be there to help with our love.
Keep fit by bathing in the bay,
You'll never catch fever then in the country.
You're sure of a settled job at the vats
If you keep their hours and live by the clock.

He arrived at last; it was time by the clock,
He crossed himself as he passed the wood
Black against evening sky the vats
Brought tears to his eyes as he thought of their love;
Looking out over the darkening country
He saw the pier in the little bay.

At the week-ends the divers in the bay
Distracted his eyes from the bandstand clock;
When down with fever and in the country
A skein of swans above the wood
Caused him no terror; he came to love
The moss that grew on the derelict vats.

And he has met sketching at the vats
Guests from the new hotel in the bay;
Now curious following his love,
His pulses differing from the clock,
Finds consummation in the wood
And sees for the first time the country.

Sees water in the wood and trees by the bay,
Hears a clock striking near the vats:
This is your country and the hour of love.

*   *   *

The terrible rat-courage of the enemy. The stout clergyman at our hotel estimating on the back of an envelope the height of the waterfall for the hydraulic engineer.

*　　*　　*

The Enemy as Observer.

His remarks, like those of invalids and precocious children half-true. His accuracy of description of symptoms compared with his prescription.

'The dog is sick. You see, the hind legs are paralysed. We must get him to walk. Give him a tablespoonful of this arsenic three times a day.' But, doctor, he is suffering from arsenical poisoning.

The antithesis between the passions and reason. The passions are nothing, but the unreal parts as seen by his learned reason (see Fig. 1) of the unity of passion of which nothing can be said but that it is the effort of a thing to realise its own nature. (*N.B.*, however, that the whole has its *real* parts.)

Man miserable without diversion. But diversion is human activity. A man doing nothing is not a man.

Their extraordinary idea that man's only glory is to think.

The misery of a dispossessed king. Who should know that better than the usurper?

The enemy's sense of humour—verbal symbolism. Private associations (rhyming slang), but note that he is serious, the associations are constant. He means what *he* says.

Practical jokes consist in upsetting these associations. They are in every sense contradictory and public, e.g. my bogus lecture to the London Truss Club. Derek's seduction of Mrs. Solomon by pretending to have been blessed by the Pope.

*　　*　　*

We leave to-morrow. Uncle Sam is arranging the final sing-song with all the assurance of a non-airman. Catching the largest fish, sieving the funniest story for the ladies, abrogating to oneself the right of feeding the hotel gull, such are the sole manifestations reserved for the spirit when all the risks are known. After tea Bob and Stan, the boy fishermen, will give an exhibition of Japanese wrestling on the floor of the lounge. Community singing of wartime songs will lull for a moment all awareness of lost contacts. At dinner an imaginary telegram of regret from a guest who has left the hotel to die may amuse. In the hall a Highland reel will, of course, be attempted, lit up by pocket torches fetched hurriedly from the bedrooms. Yes, but all the time distant but distinct as the eyepiece image in field-glasses, the thought 'What is to be done? Punch was mistaken; we ought never to have come.' Trapped. Gangrene has already set in.

Only once here, quite at the beginning, and I put it back. Uncle Sam, is he one too? He has the same backward-bending thumb that I have. I wonder. It's going to be alright. Courage. The daily exercise of the will in trivial tasks.

The Airman's Alphabet.

ACE—
Pride of parents
and photographed person
and laughter in leather.

BOMB—
Curse from cloud
and coming to crook
and saddest to steeple.

COCKPIT—
Soft seat
and support of soldier
and hold for hero.

DEATH—
Award for wildness
and worst in the west
and painful to pilots.

ENGINE—
Darling of designers
and dirty dragon
and revolving roarer.

FLYING—
Habit of hawks
and unholy hunting
and ghostly journey.

GAUGE—
Informer about oil
and important to eye
and graduated glass.

HANGAR—
Mansion of machine
and motherly to metal
and house of handshaking.

INSTRUMENT—
Dial on dashboard
and destroyer of doubt
and father of fact.

JOYSTICK—
Pivot of power
and responder to pressure
and grip for the glove.

KISS—	Touch taking off and tenderness in time and firmness on flesh.
LOOPING—	Flying folly and feat at fairs and brave to boys.
MECHANIC—	Owner of overalls and interested in iron and trusted with tools.
NOSE-DIVE—	Nightmare to nerves and needed by no one and dash toward death.
OBSERVER—	Peeper through periscope and peerer at pasture and eye in the air.
PROPELLER—	Wooden wind-oar and twisted whirler and lifter of load.
QUIET—	Absent from airmen and easy to horses and got in the grave.
RUDDER—	Deflector of flight and flexible fin and pointer of path.
STORM—	Night from the north and numbness nearing and hail ahead.
TIME—	Expression of alarm and used by the ill and personal space.
UNDERCARRIAGE—	Softener of shock and seat on the soil and easy to injure.
VICTIM—	Corpse after crash and carried through country and atonement for aircraft.
WIRELESS—	Sender of signal and speaker of sorrow and news from nowhere.

X—	Mark upon map and meaning mischief and lovers' lingo.
YOUTH—	Daydream of devils and dear to the damned and always to us.
ZERO—	Love before leaving and touch of terror and time of attack.

Three signs of an airman—practical jokes—nervousness before taking off—rapid healing after injury.

Of the Enemy.

> His collar was spotless; he talked very well,
> He spoke of our homes and duty and we fell.

Three kinds of enemy walk—the grandiose stunt—the melancholic stagger—the paranoic sidle.

Three kinds of enemy bearing—the condor stoop—the toad stupor—the robin's stance.

Three kinds of enemy face—the fucked hen—the favourite puss—the stone in the rain.

Three kinds of enemy eye—the lobster—the boot-button—the submarine.

Three kinds of enemy hand—the marsh—the claw—the dead yam.

Three kinds of enemy clothing—fisherman's pockets—Dickens' waistcoats—adhesive trousers.

Three enemy traits—refusal to undress in public—proficiency in modern languages—inability to travel back to the engine.

Three enemy occupations—playing cards—collecting—talking to animals.

Three terms of enemy speech—I mean—quite frankly—speaking as a scientist, etc.

Three signs of an enemy letter—underlining—parentheses in brackets—careful obliteration of cancelled expressions.

Three enemy questions—Am I boring you?—Could you tell me the time?—Are you sure you're fit enough?

Three enemy catchwords—insure now—keep smiling—safety first.

Three enemy don'ts—don't kiss your baby on the mouth—don't lean out of the carriage window—don't miss this.

Three signs of an enemy country—licensed hours—a national art—nursery schools.

Three signs of an enemy house—old furniture—a room called the Den—photographs of friends.

Three warnings of enemy attack—depression in the mornings—rheumatic twinges—blips on the face.

Three symptoms in convalescence—nail-biting—nightmares—short-sight.

Three results of an enemy victory—impotence—cancer—paralysis.

Three counter attacks—complete mastery of the air—ancestor worship—practical jokes.

*   *   *

Monday—Interviewed A about his report.
Tuesday—Pamphlet dropping in Bridgnorth area.
Wednesday—Address at Waterworm College.
Thursday—The Hollies, 7.30.
Friday—See M about the gin to be introduced into the lemonade at the missionary whist-drive.
Saturday—Committee meeting.
Sunday—Break up the Mimosa's lecture on blind flying.

*   *   *

As I thought, A tells me they have been in Kettlewell and most of the outlying farms. A doesn't believe they intend to move before October, which should give us time if only B will move. We know for a fact that tanks are being built at Cockshutt Forge. Can't B see what this means?

Trains keep stopping regular as dogs by certain posts. The red dormitory wing of the Academy extrudes a succession of white and black particles which, obedient to laws of attraction and repulsion, quickly assume group patterns, and caught by a northerly current, stream slowly toward the green square. Nurse-maids pause on the esplanade for mutual investigations. The band is leaving the Winter Gardens by an emergency exit. A lady has fainted. Time for lunch. There isn't going to be very much lunch unless you all wake up. The group snapped at the fifth tee against a background of Scotch firs, frowning, conscious of their pipes, cellular underwear, the train whistle in the valley, the tall capless one in the back row deliberately

82

half-hidden, are taken for ambassadors. In the crowded marquee near the front windows the vicar presents the beautiful spy with a handsome eight-day clock, the first prize in the ladies' croquet competition, signs for a registered package brought him by the gardener, with a nickel-plated fountain pen, the gift of his parishioners after twenty years of services. 'A treaty has been arranged', say the people, and are reassured. The agents smile for a moment then turn back to their charming companions.

Another is afraid and would be safe. Every day his journeys to escape the danger extend further, get more and more dangerous. Circling anxiously for a landing over icy tundras, firing the last drum against frenzied tribes, he can remember a time when a five-minute walk to an aunt's house was quite sufficient. On maps his red-ink line crossing and re-crossing, sweeps ever wider, to end in a cross marking his approximate position when the last wireless was received, or to be stopped by heart failure at a branch line station among kindly but inconvenienced officials.

Last day but ten
It's moving again.
Last day but nine
I've forgotten the sign.
Last day but eight
And it's getting late.
Last day but seven
Why aren't there eleven?
Last day but six
I don't like its tricks.
Last day but five
O God, it's alive.
Last day but four
I can't live any more.
Last day but three
Now it's looking at me
Last day but two
What shall I do?
Last day but one
I think I'll run.
Last day of all
It's here and I fall.

But are there not after all some houses to which all this does not apply? Cases of immunity, queer to research, but quite authentic?

Here a home, rather than name which the enemy will employ any circumlocution; there a figure he will cross the street to avoid, assume an interest in a barber's window rather than meet that incorruptible eye. The Hollies, for instance, their most intrepid would steer clear of though disobeying the most urgent order. So far I have said nothing to E. How could he understand a danger more remote from him than the crouching of a sabre-tooth tiger for a Bronze-Age huntsman, or the unsheathing of a knife in a Shanghai bar?

By October:

All Siskins to be replaced by Bulldogs.
3 Short Gurnards for reconnaissance.
2 Vickers 163 for troop conveyance.
3 Gloster s.s.19 for fast fighting.
1 Moth trainer fully equipped for advanced training.
Secure Harvey for first aid classes.
Darling to replace ffennell (who is perfectly useless) at Hawes.

HURRY. NO MORE GRATE GAZING.

*   *   *

Dawn 13,000 ft. Shadows of struts falling across the cockpit. Perfect calm, light, strength. Yesterday positively the last time. Hands to remember please, always.

*   *   *

Continuity and Discontinuity.

Both true. Continuity in that the *existence* of a whole results from the sum of its parts. Discontinuity in that its *nature* cannot be *inferred* from theirs. The enemy's two waves of attack.

(1) Flux-mongers (shock-troops for destruction).
(2) Order-doctrinaires (establishment of martial law).

The latter of course do not admit collusion into the former, claim rather to come as redeemers.

One must draw the line somewhere. Theory of numbers. Dedekind's section. Not to confuse the real line with that drawn for personal convenience, to remember the margin of safety. By denying the existence of the real line, the enemy offers relief, at a price, from their own imaginary one. Their exploitation of this fear—building societies—summer camps.

*   *   *

Fourteenth anniversary of my Uncle's death. Fine. Cleaned the air-gun as usual. But what have I done to avenge, to disprove the boy's faked evidence at the inquest? NOTHING (never reloaded since it was found discharged by your untasted coffee). Give me time. I PROMISE.

Only those in the last stage of disease could believe that children are true judges of character. The child's life is intermittent, isolated desultory jerks now and then, which scandalise and alarm its parents, but for the most part it is a motor run off their accumulators. My first memories of my Uncle were like images cast on the screen of a television set, maternally induced. My fascinated fear of his red sealing ring, his slightly protruding eyes with which he used to look at our house in a way that always made me feel ashamed of it. I could never make up my mind about their colour. Sometimes they seemed brown, sometimes blue, and sometimes a terrifying sea-green. I thought I hated him but I was always eager to please him or run errands, and a word of approval from him made me happy for the rest of the day.

He didn't come very often, but I can remember when I was about thirteen a letter from him coming at breakfast. 'Of course I know he's very clever', my mother sniffed, and then there was a silence.

It wasn't till I was sixteen and a half that he invited me to his flat. We had champagne for dinner. When I left I knew who and what he was— my real ancestor.

Dream Last Night.

I was on the bank of a deep river. On the further bank were B and a whole crowd standing round E who was tied to the rails of a railway track. An express was racing towards him. I knew that E was being executed on a charge of sabotage and that I had the evidence to save him if I could get there in time. Moored to the other bank was a ferry boat in which stood the ferryman, a tall fair young man who I feel I have met before, but not in real life. His back was turned to me as he was watching the proceedings. Behind me a football match was in progress and the spectators were crying my name. I screamed to the ferryman, but their row drowned my voice completely. As the engine reached E the driver leant out with a disgusting leer, dangling a large old-fashioned fob and I saw the time was 6.0 a.m.

Everything disappeared as a newsboy touched my arm holding out a news-sheet bordered with black. At the top was a photograph of my Uncle Henry, the one which actually appeared at the time, but under it the words 'I have crossed it'. I woke hearing voices as if the battle were lost.

*   *   *

Thursday.

The Hollies. Some blazers lounge beneath the calming tree; they talk in birds' hearing; girls come with roses, servants with a tray, skirting the sprinkler preaching madly to the grass, where mower worries in the afternoons; draw not you leagues away, Too-much-alone.

Between box-edges, past the weathering urns, walk, acquire their ruses. Visit enough till coat-stand in their hall seem arsenal stocked against a lifetime's harm.

These also dogs follow, are loved by grooms; milder than hawks have conquered fear of ledges, sailed over fishes swaying with the sea; have looked in ponds but not for reassurance; bathing in front of inattentive weasels, a tan-armed gonsil or a first-of-May.

O turn your head this way, be faithful here. The working mouth, the flimsy flexing knee, the leap in summer in the rubber shoes, these signal in their only codes. There is no other rendezvous for you to keep before the simple night (at night elopement is potty from the private drome. The little train will halt to pick up flowers.) There are no other agents if these were cads. You stand in time's nick now with all to lose. The spies have gone to phone for their police—locked behind mirrors in his study, his secret heroes ragging round the fire, Death swots ungraceful, keen on his career; notes in his journal 'I have never lived—left-handed and ironic, but have loved'.

Again. Always the same weakness. No progress against this terrible thing. What would E say if he knew? Dare I tell him? Does Derek suspect? He looked at me very strangely at dinner. No; no one must ever know. If the enemy ever got to hear of it, my whole work would be nullified. I must be careful to avoid sitting up with E alone to late hours. The signed confession in my pocket shall remain unread, always.

A cold bath every morning. Never to funk but to return everything, no matter how distasteful the explanations. (The Hollies this evening, mind.) Whenever temptation is felt go at once to do mechanical drawing.

Hands, in the name of my Uncle, I command you, or . . .

*   *   *

Of the Enemy Gambits.

Hygiene against the awareness of likeness.

Newspapers against the awareness of difference.

To-day 'Seven-round contest against Worry. Distinguished pyschologist as referee'. On the football page—'Hearts humbled by Queens'.

> Beethameer, Beethameer, bully of Britain,
> With your face as fat as a farmer's bum;
> Though you pose in private as a playful kitten
> Though the public you poison are pretty well dumb,
> They shall turn on their betrayer when the time is come.
> The cousins you cheated shall recover their nerve
> And give you the thrashing you richly deserve.
>
> In kitchen, in cupboard, in club-room, in mews,
> In palace, in privy, your paper we meet
> Nagging at our nostrils with its nasty news,
> Suckling the silly from a septic teat,
> Leading the lost with lies to defeat;
> But defeat shall force them to find the nerve
> To give you the thrashing you richly deserve.

To your yoke, you suggest, we should offer our necks,
We should learn from your lips the laws to spell
Of Art, of Religion, of Science, of Sex,
You appear as the prophet, your periods swell.
Are you sure you're our Saviour? We're certain you smell:
All of us itching in every nerve
To give you the thrashing you richly deserve.

Each talented contributor tells what he thinks.
A lady novelist has given her view,
A father of fourteen, a professor of stinks,
A beater, a bone-setter, a curate from Kew;
So you take us for trees, so you think, do you,
We'll forget your games and forgive your nerve?
No, we'll give you the thrashing you richly deserve.

Heathcliffe before you was a newspaper peer:
I'm the sea-dog, he said, who shall steer this ship;
I advertise idiocy, uplift, and fear,
I succour the State, I shoot from the hip;
He grasped at God but God gave him the slip.
Life gave him one look and he lost his nerve,
So you'll get the thrashing you richly deserve.

10,000 Cyclostyle copies of this for aerial distribution.

*   *   *

To return to the interest we were discussing,
You were saying:

I'm afraid it sounds more like a fairy story.
There was a family called Do:
There were Do–a, Do–ee, and other Do–s
And Uncle Dick and Uncle Wiz had come to stay with them
(Nobody slept that night).
Now Do–a loved to bathe before his breakfast
With Uncle Dick, but Uncle Wiz . . .

Well?

As a matter of fact the farm was in Pembrokeshire.
The week the Labour Cabinet resigned
Dick had returned from Germany in love.
I hate cold water and am very fond of potatoes. . . .
You're wondering about these scratches?

Well, I thought perhaps . . .

Merely the gorse between Stumble Head and Llwndda.
Gabriel was entertaining a young couple, so . . .

Gabriel?

O I hadn't meant to let the name out;
To explain all that I shall have to go a long way back.
There was an economics Don called Harrod
(Now Junior Censor)
Who asked me to call on a young scholar.
I stayed with Bill often after that,
He came from the same school but not till a year later.
There is a lot about the Essay Club and Stephen,
But I shall have to leave that out.
The point I want to make clear is . . .

But Tennyson, remember, thought trains ran in grooves;
The Queen believed cigars were all one price.

Precisely! I'm certain, just because I do remember.
Someone had coined the phrase 'a cheat of bursars',
And that was laughed at.
We gambled away our shirts on the last evening;
There must have been something, don't you see,
There must have been, to have these memories about.
And then this morning at the dentist's they gave me gas.
Going under I heard a cry
Under that sea, a hydrocephalic cry,
'Keep calm,' I tried to shout, 'I'm coming'; I was almost there.
Light broke.
Someone was giving me a glass of water;
Something had just been done to me without my knowledge.
Had I arrived in time?
I should have said the word by now to have convinced you.

Yes, but the interest.

*   *   *

The new batch of recruits arrived this morning, looking tired after
the night journey but very excited about to-morrow. Poor little
buggers. I'm afraid half of them won't get through the medical. Sands
is too rough.

*   *   *

There is something peculiarly horrible about the idea of women
pilots.

*   *   *

Derek was killed this afternoon. Went into a barrel roll at 8000 ft.
and never came out. His collar bone was sticking through his navel. Of

88

course the mechanics swear the machine was all right when it left the hangar, but I know better. When I saw the driver of that Renault wearing sphagnum moss in his cap, I ought to have realised. I ought never to have let him go up. Greath in March, Bronx last month, and now Derek. Yet B is still only half convinced.

*　*　*

Enemy messages to be decoded—'The little apples will grow again.' 'Don't touch me or I'll spill.'

*　*　*

Another awful night. Cabbage water very little good now. Waking early after night terrors. The faint tang of irretrievable disaster; as if Lake Constance were outside the window and had destroyed all countries and human beings. Solitude. Among the gooseberry bushes in the kitchen garden he crouches, scratched, holding his breath as the noisy steps approach. 'I bet he's here somewhere.' In the greenhouse they loiter, imagine coiled shapes, malignant, phosphorescent, in the zinc darkness of a tank. Come on you chaps! After their change of heart, a desert silence, shadows of wool-white clouds. A caterpillar, lacking compass or guides, crosses the vast uplands of his shoe, whom bees ignore. They have all gone in to tea. No one will look for you again.

Derek buried to-day. A choir of quarrymen and boys. Imagining one's death-bed; universal understanding and forgiveness; lines produced to meet at infinity; the eternised moment.

*　*　*

Conference at Arncliffe in the old water tower. B looking ill; Allen and Page like two rival railway companies—jealous and un-accommodating. Got Absalom through, but they still haggle about the cost of Lot's Wife (this operation is essential). Percy is not to be trusted and should be watched. The enemy's strength lies in the people's disbelief in his existence. If they believed he would be powerless. To convince them—unrelaxed attention—demonstration—sacred abuse.

*　*　*

Tea to-day at the Cardross Golf Club. A hot-bed. Far too many monks in Sinclair Street.

*　*　*

There are some birds in these valleys
Who flutter round the careless
With intimate appeal,
By seeming kindness trained to snaring,
They feel no falseness.

Under the spell completely
They circle can serenely,
And in the tricky light
The masked hill has a purer greenness.
Their flight looks fleeter.

But fowlers, O, like foxes,
Lie ambushed in the rushes.
Along the harmless tracks
The madman keeper crawls through brushwood,
Axe under oxter.

Alas, the signal given,
Fingers on trigger tighten.
The real unlucky dove
Must smarting fall away from brightness
Its love from living.

*   *   *

Of the Enemy's Definitions by Negation.

Unless you do well you will *not* be loved.
I'm *afraid* of death (instead of I *want* to live).
Pleasure is the *decrease* of pain (olives—whisky).

To him glory is only a reversal of rôle—the rejected lover's phantasy—to be cold and to be desired, e.g. the Mimosa's affair with the parachute jumper.

*   *   *

Day-dreams of victory. Bomb fragment exposed by share set up on mantelpiece, a wonder to the new children. Renewal of work at my monograph on Professional Jealousy. Aerial photography of earthworks in a harvest season.

In hours of gentleness always to remember my Uncle, the connection between the last desperate appeals of the lost for help scribbled on the walls of public latrines and such a letter as this.

'The wound is healing and we can now look back to the war, not forgetting a sacrifice, and all the miseries which it caused, but without such very painful memories.
'Some people say "Why does anyone want to think about war at all?" and accuse those who do of militarist ideas. We weren't thinking about war in 1914, except for a small body of thinking soldiers and statesmen, who saw it inevitably approaching. The British nation as a whole had no thought or idea of war—and yet in a matter of days it was upon us, and we entered it as thoughtlessly and light-heartedly as we would send off a team for a cricket match. I must say that the team—in this case the British Expeditionary Force—went into the game just as

cheerfully and light-heartedly, if not more so—but that was their job as soldiers. The people who committed them to the greatest war in history, and who afterwards backed them up and took their turn so nobly, were the British public, the British nation.'

After Victory.

Few executions except for the newspaper peers—Viscount Stuford certainly. The Rev. McFarlane?
Duchess of Holbrook for the new human zoo.
Tom to have the Welsh Marches.
Ian a choice of Durham and Norfolk.
Edward for films.
Gabriel to Foreign department.
B something he can't spoil.
Other posts to be decided as quickly as possible.
Monthly firework displays.

Much more research needed into the crucial problem—group organisation (the real parts).

*   *   *

Very little progress this year. Never quite as bad as that dreadful spring of 1927, but still generally at week-ends. So much better when seeing E. The rosebowl from Ardencaple still unreturned. Weak. Weak. Weak. No sooner do we succeed a little against the enemy than I let us all down, dishonour my Uncle. Look what happened after my fighting speech at Preston. Little did they guess when they chaired me what kind of a person it was to whom they were awarding that honour.

*   *   *

August 23rd, 3 p.m.
We are lost. A cart has just passed carrying the plaster eagle. The enemy are going to attack.

*   *   *

The enemy orders communicated to-night of August 23rd–24th—
1st Army: 15 attack divisions, 2 ordinary divisions.
2nd Army: 15 attack divisions, 3 ordinary divisions.
3rd Army: 19 attack divisions, 5 ordinary divisions.
Reserve: 3 attack divisions,
    To Norna, Dudley, Arno, Niagara—each a corps.

G.H.Q. Commands.

    1. That the attack take place on Aug. 28th. First penetration of the hostile position, 7.10 a.m.
    2. A feint landing by pleasure paddle-steamers near the bathing-machines on Beach V.

3. A flank attack in an E.N.-E. direction by troops carrying special golf-ball grenades, to secure the heights above the club-house and to cut the York road.

4. A main frontal attack. Divisions to be concentrated in the Shenly brick-fields and moved forward to the battle zone in bakers' vans, disguised as nuns.

5. G.H.Q. retains command of 2nd Guard and 26th Nuthatchers.

6. Remaining Armies to act in accordance with the operation order 6925, dated July 26th.

First Day of Mobilisation.

At the pre-arranged zero hour the widow bent into a hoop with arthritis gives the signal for attack by unbending on the steps of St. Philip's. A preliminary bombardment by obscene telephone messages for not more than two hours destroys the *morale* already weakened by predictions of defeat made by wireless-controlled crows and card-packs. Shock troops equipped with wire-cutters, spanners and stinkbombs, penetrating the houses by infiltration, silence all alarm clocks, screw down the bathroom taps, and remove plugs and paper from the lavatories. The *Courier* Offices are the first objective. A leading article accusing prominent citizens of arson, barratry, coining, dozing in municipal offices, espionage, family skeletons, getting and bambling, heresy, issuing or causing to be issued false statements with intent to deceive, jingoism, keeping disorderly houses, loitering, mental cruelty, nepotism, onanism, piracy on the high seas, quixotry, romping at forbidden hours, sabotage, tea-drinking, unnatural offences against minors, vicious looks, will-burning, a yellow streak, is on the table of every householder in time for a late breakfast.

Conversion of hotels and boarding houses into private nursing-homes is carried out as rapidly as possible. Major operations without anaesthetics begin at noon. At 6 p.m. passages of unprepared translation from dead dialects are set to all non-combatants. The papers are collected at 6.10. All who fail to obtain 99% make the supreme sacrifice. Candidates must write on three sides of the paper.

Second Day.

The nine o'clock business train leaves on a mystery trip through the more remote upland valleys; there is no refreshment car. Packed excursions at five-minute intervals, jumping the points, enter the sea from Craigendoran Pier. Slight modifications in the trams connecting the electric circuit with the seat buttons shrivel the lolling parcel-carriers. Banks make payments in fairy gold; girl-guides, nocturnally stimulated, mob vicars at the climax of their sermons; organists light pipes at the moment of consecration; at evensong choirs sing hymns in hesitation waltz time. Form-masters find crude graffiti on their blackboards; the boys, out of control, imbibe Vimto through india-rubber tubing, openly pee into the ink-pots.

A white-faced survivor informs the prison governor that the convicts, loosed, storming the execution shed, are calculating the drop formula by practical experiment, employing warders of varying weights.

Third Day.

Secret catalysts introduced into the city reservoirs convert the entire drinking supply into tepid urine. Adulterated milk drawn by order of the military from consumptive gentlewomen is only procurable by those who are fortunate enough to possess attractive daughters. The factories, structurally altered, reduce all raw products to an irritant filter-passing dust. Eyeballs of ravished virgins, black puddings made from the blood of the saints, sucking children already flyblown, are exposed for sale at famine prices. For those who desire an honourable release, typhoid lice, three in a box, price twopence, are peddled in the streets by starving corner boys.

Fourth Day.

All menstruation ceases. Vampires are common in the neighbourhood of the Cathedral, epidemics of lupus, halitosis, and superfluous hair.

Fifth Day.

Pressure of ice, falling fire. The last snarl of families beneath the toppling column. Biting at wounds as the sutures tear.

24th.

Four days. What's the use of counting them now?

25th.

Why, the words in my dream under Uncle's picture, 'I HAVE CROSSED IT'. To have been told the secret that will save everything and not to have listened; and now less than three days in which to prepare myself. My whole life has been mistaken, progressively more and more complicated, instead of finally simple.

My incredible blindness, with all the facts staring me in the face, not to have realised these elementary truths.

1. The power of the enemy is a function of our resistance, therefore

2. The only efficient way to destroy it—self-destruction, the sacrifice of all resistance, reducing him to the state of a man trying to walk on a frictionless surface.

3. Conquest can only proceed by absorption of, i.e. infection by, the conquered. The true significance of my hands. 'Do not imagine that you, no more than any other conqueror, escape the mark of grossness.' They stole to force a hearing.

To begin at once.

To my Uncle, perpetual gratitude and love for this crowning mercy. For myself, absolute humility.

I know that I am I, living in a small way in a temperate zone, blaming father, jealous of son, confined to a few acts often repeated, easily attracted to a limited class of physique, yet envying the simple life of the gut, desiring the certainty of the breast or prison, happiest sawing wood, only knowledge of the real, disturbances in the general law of the dream; the quick blood fretting against the slowness of the hope; a unit of life, needing water and salt, that looks for a sign.

93

What have I written? Thoughts suitable to a sanatorium. Three days to break a lifetime's pride.

26th.
Two days.

Read Mifflin on Air Currents.
A complete course for the commercial flying licence.
The life of Count Zeppelin (obtainable in Air and Airways Library).
Remember to pay Bryden's Bill.
To answer C's letter.
The £100 for Tom's holiday.
Destroy all letters, snapshots, lockets, etc., of E.
Further purification.
Deep breathing exercises instead of smoking.
A clean shirt, collar and handkerchief each morning till the end.

27th.
Supper at The Hollies. E alone. Salmon fresh from the loch. O understand, darling. God just loves us all, but means to be obeyed; and unaffecting is our solid tear. Thank you for your share in this, but good-bye. Uncle, save them all, make me worthy.

28th.
3.40 a.m. Pulses and reflexes, normal.
Barometric reading, 30.6.
Mean temperature, 34°F.
Fair. Some cumulus cloud at 10,000 feet. Wind easterly and moderate.
Hands in perfect order.

August–November 1931 (see App. II)

BOOK III

Six Odes

I

Watching in three planes from a room overlooking the courtyard
                That year decaying,
Stub-end of year that smoulders to ash of winter,
                The last day dropping;
Lo, a dream met me in middle night, I saw in a vision
Life pass as a gull, as a spy, as a dog-hated dustman:
Heard a voice saying—'Wystan, Stephen, Christopher, all of you,
                Read of your losses'.

Shaped me a Lent scene first, a bed, hard, surgical,
              And a wound hurting;
The hour in the night when Lawrence died and I came
              Round from the morphia.
A train went clanking over the bridges leaving the city;
A sleep-walker pushed on groaning down the velvet passage;
The night-nurse visited—'We shall not all sleep, dearie',
              She said, and left me.

Felt sap collecting anon in unlighted cylinders
              For birdward facing;
The flat snake moving again in the pit, the schoolboy
              From home migrating.
After a night of storm was a lawn in sunlight,
A colleague bending for measurements there at the rain-gauge,
Gritting his teeth after breakfast, the Headmaster muttered
              'Call no man happy'.

Came summer like a flood, did never greediest gardener
              Make blossoms flusher:
Sunday meant lakes for many, a browner body,
              Beauty from burning:
Far out in the water two heads discussed the position,
Out of the reeds like a fowl jumped the undressed German,
And Stephen signalled from the sand dunes like a wooden madman
              'Destroy this temple'.

It did fall. The quick hare died to the hounds' hot breathing,
              The Jewess fled Southwards;
The drunken Scotsman, regarding the moon's hedge-rising,
              Shook and saluted:
And in cold Europe, in the middle of Autumn destruction,
Christopher stood, his face grown lined with wincing
In front of ignorance—'Tell the English', he shivered,
              'Man is a spirit'.

What I saw further was general but in sorrow,
              Many together
Forgiving each other in the dark of the picture palaces
              But past forgiveness;
The pair walking out on the mole, getting ready to quarrel;
The exile from superb Africa, employed in a laundry;
Deserters, mechanics, conjurers, delicate martyrs,
              Yes, self-regarders.

I saw the brain-track perfected, laid for conveying
                    The fatal error,
Sending the body to islands or after its father,
                    Cold with a razor:
One sniffed at a root to make him dream of a woman,
One laid his hands on the heads of dear little pages;
Neither in the bed nor on the *arête* was there shown me
                    One with power.

'Save me!' the voice commanded, but as I paused hesitant
                    A troop rushed forward
Of all the healers, granny in mittens, the Mop, the white surgeon,
                    And loony Layard.
The captains grouped round the flagstaff shut up their glasses,
Broke yelping over the gravel—as I stood a spectator;
One tapped my shoulder and asked me 'How did you fall, sir?'
                    Whereat I awakened.

Roof-line sharpens, intense in the New Year morning;
                    Far down in courtyard
Beggar addresses the earth on the state of East Europe:
                    'Won't you speak louder?
Have you heard of someone swifter than Syrian horses?
Has he thrown the bully of Corinth in the sanded circle?
Has he crossed the Isthmus already? Is he seeking brilliant
                    Athens and us?'

January 1931

II

(TO GABRIEL CARRITT, CAPTAIN OF SEDBERGH SCHOOL XV,
SPRING, 1927)

Walk on air do we? And how!
With the panther's pad, with his lightness
Never did members conspire till now
                    In such whole gladness:
Currents of joy incalculable in ohms
Wind from the spine along the moving arms
Over the great alkali wastes of the bowel, calming them too.

Success my dears—Ah!
Rounding the curve of the drive
Standing up, waving, cheering from car,
                    The time of their life:
The fags are flushed, would die at their heroes' feet;
Quick, someone, tug at that handle, get
At them shouting, shoulder them high, who won by their pluck and
                    their dare.

Tudor from the tram-lined town,
Self-confident under the moor;
Scott from the chalk-pitted horse-taming down,
        And otter-smooth Kerr:
Sure-footed MacColl from the life-hostile gabbros of Skye,
Red-bush Abrahall, diving Gray,
Waters from dykes of the Wash, and Fagge from the bird-singing
        plain.

    The Bryants, major and minor,
    —Surely their pater the Dean
    Sings as he waters his roses like a soldier—
        Proud of each son:
Lanky-legged Lloyd, and Morgan from Aberdovey,
Peacock and long-skulled Cornish Davy
Not least, though we mention him last: we ought to have mentioned
        him sooner.

    Symondson—praise him at once!—
    Our right-wing three-quarter back
    Sergy, bulwark of every defence,
        Mainspring of attack:
When aligned like a squadron of bombers they flew downfield
Over and over again we yelled
'Let the ball out to Sergy!' They did, he scored, and we dance.

    That rush when he fell on the ball,
    The surprised applause was so loud
    That the horses galloped to look over wall
        At delirious crowd.
Strangers smiled at each other, off their English guard
And watching weak from hospital ward,
Propped-up cases felt ever so well when he dropped that goal.

    Sandroyd—what of their side?—
    In jerseys of chocolate and white
    Prancing for prowess, posh in their pride,
        Unbeaten last night:
No changing-room clapping for them, no welcoming dazzle,
But a hushed school receives them in a drizzle,
Clambering, sodden, from a maundering chara., licked to the wide.

    Easy for us to tell,
    Defeats on them like lavas
    Have fallen, fell, kept falling, fell
        On them, poor lovies:
Regents have ranted, and flash-talk in a quarry plotted
To burn down barns, but both were noughted;
On purse-proud, swank-limb, cock-wit has it fallen, and so it will.

Heart of the heartless world
Whose pulse we count upon;
Alive, the live on which you have called
   Both pro and con,
Good to a gillie, to an elver times out of mind
Tender, to work-shy and game-shy kind
Does he think? Not as kind as all that; he shall find one fine day he is
                 sold.

  From darkness your roses came
  In one little week of action
  By fortunate prejudice to delighting form
    And profuse production;
  Now about these boys as keen as mustard to grow
  Give you leave for that, sir, well in them, flow,
Deep in their wheel-pits may they know you foaming and feel you
                warm.

  With the change in the breathing, the hair
  Clustering at the sensitised nodes,
  Charge them in shock after shock, make them 'ware
    The eternal needs:
  Whether at lathe-work, loading, reading, to resist
  Rather! the torsion, the tension, the list:
Fellows you well may be proud of, no matter when or where,

  Whom we shall like to remember
  We welcomed once as a team
  With bands under beeches, tubas by timber,
    The cup brought home:
  Not, as the desperate need to, do we clutch at arm,
  Dark-fearers, dreading December's harm,
Not now. Joy docked in every duct, we to the right sleep come.
              April 1931

III

(TO EDWARD UPWARD, SCHOOLMASTER)

  What siren zooming is sounding our coming
  Up frozen fjord forging from freedom
    What shepherd's call
    When stranded on hill,
    With broken axle
    On track to exile?

With labelled luggage we alight at last
Joining joking at the junction on the moor
        With practised smile
        And harmless tale
        Advance to meet
        Each new recruit.

Expert from uplands, always in oilskins,
Recliner from library, laying down law,
        Owner from shire,
        All meet on this shore
        Facing each prick
        With ginger pluck.

Our rooms are ready, the register signed,
There is time to take a turn before dark,
        See the blistered paint
        On the scorching front,
        Or icicles sombre
        On pierhead timber.

To climb the cliff path to the coastguard's point
Past the derelict dock deserted by rats,
        Look from concrete sill
        Of fort for sale
        To the bathers' rocks
        The lovers' ricks.

Our boots will be brushed, our bolsters pummelled,
Cupboards are cleared for keeping our clothes.
        Here we shall live
        And somehow love
        Though we only master
        The sad posture.

Picnics are promised and planned for July
To the wood with the waterfall, walks to find,
        Traces of birds,
        A mole, a rivet,
        In factory yards
        Marked strictly private.

There will be skating and curling at Christmas—indoors
Charades and ragging; then riders pass
        Some afternoons
        In snowy lanes
        Shut in by wires
        Surplus from wars.

In Spring we shall spade the soil on the border
For blooming of bulbs; we shall bow in Autumn
         When trees make passes,
         As high gale pushes,
         And bewildered leaves
         Fall on our lives.

We are here for our health, we have not to fear
The fiend in the furze or the face at the manse;
         Proofed against shock
         Our hands can shake;
         The flag at the golf-house flutters
         And nothing matters.

We shall never need another new outfit;
These grounds are for good, we shall grow no more,
         But lose our colour
         With scurf on collar
         Peering through glasses
         At our own glosses.

This life is to last, when we leave we leave all,
Though vows have no virtue, though voice is in vain,
         We live like ghouls
         On posts from girls
         What the spirit utters
         In formal letters.

Watching through windows the wastes of evening,
The flare of foundries at fall of the year.
         The slight despair
         At what we are,
         The marginal grief
         Is source of life.

In groups forgetting the gun in the drawer
Need pray for no pardon, are proud till recalled
         By music on water
         To lack of stature
         Saying Alas
         To less and less.

Till holding our hats in our hands for talking
Or striding down streets for something to see
         Gas-light in shops
         The fate of ships
         And the tide-wind
         Touch the old wound.

Till the town is ten and the time is London
And nerves grow numb between north and south
            Hear last in corner
            The pffwungg of burner
            Accepting dearth
            The shadow of death.

October 1930

IV

(TO JOHN WARNER, SON OF REX AND FRANCES WARNER)

Roar Gloucestershire, do yourself proud;
The news I tell you should make you move
As a pride of lions or an exaltation of larks.
Not who you are but whom you foster
At Amberley near Stroud
Shall give you full marks.
I cannot state it too clearly, I shall not refrain,
It is John, son of Warner, has pulled my chain.

John Bull, John Bull, I understand well;
I know, Bull, I know what you want me to tell.
Calm, Bull, calm, news coming in time;
News coming, Bull; calm, Bull,
Fight it down, fight it down,
That terrible hunger; calm, Bull; first
We must have a look round, we must know the worst.

England our cow
Once was a lady—is she now?

Walk through her cities, walk with a pal
Through the streets between the power-house and green canal
And see what they're at—our proletariat.
O my, what peeps
At disheartened sweeps—
Fitters and moulders,
Wielders and welders,
Dyers and bakers
And boiler-tube makers,
Poufs and ponces,
All of them dunces.
Those over thirty,
Ugly and dirty,
What are they doing
Except just stewing?
Content for the year
With food out of tins and very small beer—
Flaking the rust off obsolete plant

Slacking at the corners, thinking 'I can't'.
Sloping up the hill, for they've nowhere else to go—
To the park and the platforms where the windbags blow
Spying on athletes playing on a green,
Spying on kisses shown on a screen,
Their minds as pathic as a boxer's face,
A shamed, uninteresting, and hopeless race.

As for our upper class:
Let's be frank a moment, fellows—they won't pass.
Majors, Vicars, Lawyers, Doctors, Advertisers, Maiden Aunts,
They're all in a funk but they daren't do a bunk,
Either rufflers or mousers, they haven't a chance.
'I shall have to be careful until I see,
But I'll like you if you'll love me.'
'Careful, careful; can we afford it?'
'Careful, careful; till we've insured it.'
'Careful, careful; don't kiss me please.
Don't you know there's such a thing as disease?'
'The Duchess of Atholl with a *lorgnette*
Is observing the dunes; we can't bathe yet.'
'If she or the Bishop of London caught us,
They'd be certain to report us.'
'Hush! not a word of the beast with two backs
Or Mead and Muskett will be on our tracks!'
Wakeful at night, in the morning fagged;
They feel like angels, but they look just shagged.
Kind to their women, indeed too kind,
It's a pity their women go out of their mind.

Who will save?
Who will teach us how to behave?

O yes, MacDonald's a giant,
President Hoover's a giant.
Baldwin and Briand are giants—
Haven't they told us?
But why have they sold us?
They said they were winners,
They were only beginners.
Pygmies, poor dears,
Beside the Giant Sloths and the Giant Despairs.
Mussolini, Pilsudski and Hitler have charm
But they make such a noise:
We're getting a little tired of boys,
Of the ninny, the mawmet and the false alarm.

These had stopped seeking
But went on speaking,
Have not contributed,
But have diluted.

102

These ordered light
But had no right,
And handed on
War and a son

Wishing no harm.
But to be warm
These went to sleep
On the burning heap.

Who will save?
Who will teach us how to behave?

'Youth's on the march' says Jocker to Prushun.
Youth's the solution of every good scout.
Youth has the secret Toc H has found out.
Youth's a success.
Youth has the blessing of the *Sunday Express*.
Youth says the teacher.
Youth says the bishop.
Youth says the bumslapper.
'Strewth, says I,
They're most of them dummies who want their mummies,
In Rolls or on bicycle they bolt for mama,
Let them scorch as they like for they won't get far.
Look at them now,
Sooner or later it'll come to the pater,
Sooner or later there'll be a row.

Who believes them, wants to choose
Between their efforts to amuse.
Attractions for the coming week
Are Masters Wet, Dim, Drip and Bleak:
Master Wet will show his pet,
Master Drip will crack his whip,
Master Bleak will speak in Greek,
Master Dim will sing a hymn.

Who'll save, who—
Who'll save John Bull
From losing his wool?
Now, Bull, now
I'll tell you who,
I'll tell you how
The flying stationer flies round the corner.
Here it is, look! John, son of Warner,
John, son of Warner, shall rescue you.

You awkward pairs in studios upstairs
Spending a secret hour in learning
The One-step, the Two-step, the Tango, the Blues,
Stumbling, tripping, practising, turning,
Aching, blushing, almost in tears,
Relax completely now at my news:
A different teacher is born to this nation
He'll teach you deportment and co-ordination.
Because of this boy
You shall dance without difficulty, you shall dance for joy.

A birthday, yes, a day without rain,
A cake but no candles, we're born again;
The church cat is ordering cocktail glasses,
The general's arranging the ensemble classes,
The cissy is going for cross-country runs,
We haven't much time, get ready at once
For John
Goal-getter, holer-in-one,
Hurdler, high-jumper, hope of our side,
Our hush-hush engine, our wonder liner,
Our gadget, our pride,
Our steel-piercing bullet, our burglar-proof safe,
Will
Save.

Wanted by John
Brains and nerve
Some for shock-troops, some for reserve,
For propaganda, for section-commander,
For transport, dispatches—there're posts to fill.
The son from the bungalow up the hill
With the crazy paving and the squash-court,
He shall report.
The girl from Ivydene if she's alive,
Descend its dreary drive.
To-day may mean division for the newly-weds,
To-day although American Pillar
Fertilise Dorothy Perkins and kill her,
Rose-lovers also must leave their beds,
Caddies and kiddies leave colonel and kitchen
For John, son of Warner, shall find you your pigeon.

Spring again
In the buds, in the birds, in the bowels, and the brain,
Spring in the bedroom ventilator.
Spring in the bearing of the hotel waiter,
At every corner
News of Warner,
His march on London,
His enemies undone.

Now Cods the curate coughs in the church,
With Ballocks the rector he's left in the lurch.
In the neo-Tudor club-house the captains frown,
The poor old colonel is red to the ears
'Phoning the Army and Navy for chairs
(He's only got a bayonet and he wants to sit down).
Dear me! Where is that darling dreamer,
That piss-proud prophet, that pooty redeemer
The bugger magician with his Polish lad,
The aesthetic, the ascetic, the malicious and the mad?
Wouldn't they like to stop the cheering?
Hearing the arrival of his special train,
Hearing the fireworks, the saluting and the guns,
Middleton Murry's looking in pain,
Robert and Laura spooning in Spain,
Where is Lewis? Under the sofa.
Where is Eliot? Dreaming of nuns.
Their day is over, they shall decorate the Zoo
With Professor Jeans and Bishop Barnes at 2d a view,
Or be ducked in a gletcher, as they ought to be,
With the Simonites, the Mosleyites and the I.L.P.

Queer to these birds: yes, very queer,
But to the tryers such a dear,
Only hard
On smugging, smartness, and self-regard,
See him take off his coat and get down with a spanner
To each unhappy Joseph and repressed Diana,
Say Bo to the invalids and take away their rugs,
The war-memorials decorate with member-mugs,
The gauche and the lonely he will introduce of course
To the smaller group, the right field of force;
The few shall be taught who want to understand,
Most of the rest shall live upon the land;
Living in one place with a satisfied face
All of the women and most of the men
Shall work with their hands and not think again.

This is the season of the change of heart,
The final keeping of the ever-broken vow,
The official re-marriage of the whole and part,
The poor in employment and the country sound,
Over is the tension, over the alarms,
The falling wage, and the flight from the pound,
The privates are returning now to the farms,
The silo is full, the marsh under plough,
The two worlds in each other's arms.
Falcon is poised over fell in the cool,
Salmon draws
Its lovely quarrons through the pool.
A birthday, a birth

On English earth
Restores, restore will, has restored
To England's story
The directed calm, the actual glory.

Go south, lovey, south by the Royal Scot,
    Or hike if you like it, or hire a Ford.
But however, you travel, be careful not
        To offend County Council or Fisheries Board,
        From the Clyde to the Thames where the punts are moored.
Off to tell Frances and Rex you are come
With a greeting from me and Derek my chum.

In the Helensburgh streets the used leaf falls;
    On my way to the field for football I pass
Bonfires crackling behind back walls,
        Affectionate fathers washing their cars.
        In the Hermitage Park they're cutting the grass.
Scotland is stirring: in Scotland they say
That Compton Mackenzie will be king one day.

We live in the north where the sun is soon gone;
    At six the lamps of Greenock are clear,
In uncurtained windows the lights go on,
        White in the dining-room, red on the stair;
        Night is ahead of London here.
We make ourselves cosy when the weather is wet
With a shocker, a spaniel and a crystal set.

The taps are turned off and the boys are in bed:
    Drowsing I droop like a dying flower,
But I'm going to sleep, not going to be dead:
        The couples are coming now out of The Tower,
        Love has its licence, the darkmans its power,
Linking their arms they pass up the hill
Motions their own though not what they will.

                                    October 1931

V

(TO MY PUPILS)

Though aware of our rank and alert to obey orders,
Watching with binoculars the movement of the grass for an ambush,
The pistol cocked, the code-word committed to memory;
                The youngest drummer
Knows all the peace-time stories like the oldest soldier,
                Though frontier-conscious,

About the tall white gods who landed from their open boat,
Skilled in the working of copper, appointing our feast-days,
Before the islands were submerged, when the weather was calm,
             The maned lion common,
An open wishing-well in every garden;
             When love came easy.

Perfectly certain, all of us, but not from the records,
Not from the unshaven agent who returned to the camp;
The pillar dug from the desert recorded only
             The sack of a city,
The agent clutching his side collapsed at our feet,
             'Sorry! They got me!'

Yes, they were living here once but do not now,
Yes, they are living still but do not here;
Lying awake after Lights Out a recruit may speak up:
             'Who told you all this?'
The tent-talk pauses a little till a veteran answers
             'Go to sleep, Sonny!'

Turning over he closes his eyes, and then in a moment
Sees the sun at midnight bright over cornfield and pasture,
Our hope. . . . Someone jostles him, fumbling for boots,
             Time to change guard:
Boy, the quarrel was before your time, the aggressor
             No one you know.

Your childish moments of awareness were all of our world,
At five you sprang, already a tiger in the garden,
At night your mother taught you to pray for our Daddy
             Far away fighting,
One morning you fell off a horse and your brother mocked you:
             'Just like a girl!'

You've got their names to live up to and questions won't help,
You've a very full programme, first aid, gunnery, tactics,
The technique to master of raids and hand-to-hand fighting;
             Are you in training?
Are you taking care of yourself? Are you sure of passing
             The endurance test?

Now we're due to parade on the square in front of the Cathedral,
When the bishop has blessed us, to file in after the choir-boys,
To stand with the wine-dark conquerors in the roped-off pews,
             Shout ourselves hoarse:
'They ran like hares; we have broken them up like firewood;
             They fought against God'.

While in a great rift in the limestone miles away
At the same hour they gather, tethering their horses beside them;
A scarecrow prophet from a boulder foresees our judgment,
        Their oppressors howling;
And the bitter psalm is caught by the gale from the rocks:
        'How long shall they flourish?'

What have we all been doing to have made from Fear
That laconic war-bitten captain addressing them now
'Heart and head shall be keener, mood the more
        As our might lessens':
To have caused their shout 'We will fight till we lie down beside
        The Lord we have loved'?

There's Wrath who has learnt every trick of guerilla warfare,
The shamming dead, the night-raid, the feinted retreat;
Envy their brilliant pamphleteer, to lying
        As husband true,
Expert impersonator and linguist, proud of his power
        To hoodwink sentries.

Gluttony living alone, austerer than us,
Big simple Greed, Acedia famed with them all
For her stamina, keeping the outposts, and somewhere Lust
        With his sapper's skill,
Muttering to his fuses in a tunnel 'Could I meet here with Love,
        I would hug him to death'.

There are faces there for which for a very long time
We've been on the look-out, though often at home we imagined,
Catching sight of a back or hearing a voice through a doorway,
        We had found them at last;
Put our arms round their necks and looked in their eyes and
                             discovered
        We were unlucky.

And some of them, surely, we seem to have seen before:
Why, that girl who rode off on her bicycle one fine summer evening
And never returned, she's there; and the banker we'd noticed
        Worried for weeks;
Till he failed to arrive one morning and his room was empty,
        Gone with a suitcase.

They speak of things done on the frontier we were never told,
The hidden path to their squat Pictish tower
They will never reveal though kept without sleep, for their code is
        'Death to the squealer':
They are brave, yes, though our newspapers mention their bravery
        In inverted commas.

But careful; back to our lines; it is unsafe there,
Passports are issued no longer; that area is closed;
There's no fire in the waiting-room now at the climbers' junction,
      And all this year
Work has been stopped on the power-house; the wind whistles under
      The half-built culverts.

Do you think that because you have heard that on Christmas Eve
In a quiet sector they walked about on the skyline,
Exchanged cigarettes, both learning the words for 'I love you'
      In either language,
You can stroll across for a smoke and a chat any evening?
      Try it and see.

That rifle-sight you're designing; is it ready yet?
You're holding us up; the office is getting impatient;
The square munition works out on the old allotments
      Needs stricter watching;
If you see any loiterers there you may shoot without warning,
      We must stop that leakage.

All leave is cancelled to-night; we must say good-bye.
We entrain at once for the North; we shall see in the morning
The headlands we're doomed to attack; snow down to the tide-line:
      Though the bunting signals
'Indoors before it's too late; cut peat for your fires',
      We shall lie out there.

November 1931

VI

Not, Father, further do prolong
   Our necessary defeat;
Spare us the numbing zero-hour,
   The desert-long retreat.

Against your direct light, displayed,
   Regardant, absolute,
In person stubborn and oblique
   Our maddened set we foot.

These nissen huts if hiding could
   Your eye inseeing from
Firm fenders were, but look! to us
   Your loosened angers come.

Against your accusations
   Though ready wit devise,
Nor magic countersigns prevail
   Nor airy sacrifice.

Weaker we are, and strict within
　　Your organised blockade,
And from our desperate shore the last
　　Few pallid youngsters fade.

Be not another than our hope;
　　Expect we routed shall
Upon your peace; with ray disarm,
　　Illumine, and not kill.

June 1931

Epilogue

'O where are you going?' said reader to rider,
'That valley is fatal where furnaces burn,
Yonder's the midden whose odours will madden,
That gap is the grave where the tall return.'

'O do you imagine', said fearer to farer,
'That dusk will delay on your path to the pass,
Your diligent looking discover the lacking
Your footsteps feel from granite to grass?'

'O what was that bird', said horror to hearer,
'Did you see that shape in the twisted trees?
Behind you swiftly the figure comes softly,
The spot on your skin is a shocking disease?'

'Out of this house'—said rider to reader
'Yours never will'—said farer to fearer
'They're looking for you'—said hearer to horror
As he left them there, as he left them there.

October 1931

Part IV

Poems 1931–1936

(TO ERIKA MANN)

Since the external disorder, and extravagant lies,
The baroque frontiers, the surrealist police;
What can truth treasure, or heart bless,
But a narrow strictness?

I

For what as easy
For what though small
For what is well
Because between
To you simply
From me I mean.

Who goes with who
The bedclothes say
And I and you
Go kissed away
The data given
The senses even.

Fate is not late
Nor the ghost houseless
Nor the speech re-written
Nor the tongue listless
Nor the word forgotten
Said at the start
About heart
By heart, for heart.

October 1931

II

That night when joy began
Our narrowest veins to flush
We waited for the flash
Of morning's levelled gun.

But morning let us pass
And day by day relief
Outgrew his nervous laugh;
Grows credulous of peace

As mile by mile is seen
No trespasser's reproach
And love's best glasses reach
No fields but are his own.

November 1931

III

Enter with him
These legends, love,
For him assume
Each diverse form
As legend simple
As legend queer
That he may do
What these require
Be, love, like him
To legend true.

When he to ease
His heart's disease
Must cross in sorrow
Corrosive seas
As dolphin go,
As cunning fox
Guide through the rocks,
Tell in his ear
The common phrase
Required to please
The guardians there.
And when across
The livid marsh
Big birds pursue
Again be true
Between his thighs
As pony rise
As swift as wind
Bear him away
Till cries and they
Are left behind.

But when at last
These dangers past
His grown desire
Of legends tire
O then, love, standing
At legends' ending,
Claim your reward
Submit your neck
To the ungrateful stroke
Of his reluctant sword
That starting back
His eyes may look
Amazed on you
Find what he wanted
Is faithful too
But disenchanted
Your simplest love.

December 1931

114

IV

Now from my window-sill I watch the night.
The church clock's yellow face, the green pier light
Burn for a new imprudent year;
The silence buzzes in my ear;
The jets in both the dormitories are out.

Under the darkness nothing seems to stir;
The lilac bush like a conspirator
Shams dead upon the lawn and there
Above the flagstaff the Great Bear
Hangs as a portent over Helensburgh.

But deaf to prophecy or China's drum
The blood moves strangely in its moving home,
Diverges, loops to travel further
Than the long still shadow of the father,
Though to the valley of regret it come.

Now in this season when the ice is loosened,
In scrubbed laboratories research is hastened
And cameras at the growing wood
Are pointed; for the long lost good,
Desire like a police-dog is unfastened.

O Lords of Limit, training dark and light
And setting a tabu 'twixt left and right:
The influential quiet twins
From whom all property begins,
Look leniently upon us all to-night.

Oldest of masters, whom the schoolboy fears
Failing to find his pen, to keep back tears,
Collecting stamps and butterflies
Hoping in some way to appease
The malice of the erratic examiners.

No one has seen you. None can say 'Of late,
Here—you can see the marks—they lay in wait'.
But in my thought to-night you seem
Forms which I saw once in a dream,
The stocky keepers of a wild estate.

With guns beneath your arms, in sun and wet
At doorways posted or on ridges set,
By copse or bridge we know you there
Whose sleepless presences endear
Our peace to us with a perpetual threat.

We know you moody, silent, sensitive,
Quick to be offended, slow to forgive,
But to your discipline the heart
Submits when we have fallen apart
Into the isolated personal life.

Look not too closely, be not over-quick;
We have no invitation, but we are sick,
Using the mole's device, the carriage
Of peacock or rat's desperate courage,
For we shall only pass you by a trick.

At the end of my corridor are boys who dream
Of a new bicycle or winning team;
On their behalf guard all the more
This late-maturing Northern shore,
Who to their serious season must shortly come.

Give them spontaneous skill at holding rein,
At twisting dial, or at making fun,
That these may never need our craft,
Who, awkward, pasty, feeling the draught,
Have health and skill and beauty on the brain.

The clocks strike ten: the tea is on the stove;
And up the stair come voices that I love.
Love, satisfaction, force, delight,
To these players of Badminton to-night,
To Favel, Holland, sprightly Alexis give.

Deeper towards the summer the year moves on.
And what if the starving visionary have seen
The carnival within our gates,
Your bodies kicked about the streets,
We need your power still: use it, that none

O from this table break uncontrollably away
Lunging, insensible to injury,
Dangerous in the room, or out wild-
-ly spinning like a top in the field,
Mopping and mowing through the sleepless day.

February 1932

V

The chimneys are smoking, the crocus is out in the border;
The mountain ranges are massive in the blue March day;
Like a sea god the political orator lands at the pier;
But, O, my magnet, my pomp, my beauty
More telling to heart than the sea,

Than Europe or my own home town
To-day is parted from me
And I stand on our world alone.

Over the town now, in for an hour from the desert
A hawk looks down on us all; he is not in this;
Our kindness is hid from the eye of the vivid creature;
     Sees only the configuration of field,
     Copse, chalk-pit, and fallow,
     The distribution of forces,
     The play of sun and shadow
     On upturned faces.

For the game is in progress which tends to become like a war,
The contest of the Whites with the Reds for the carried thing
Divided in secret among us, a portion to each:
     That power which gave us our lives
     Gave us, we found when we met,
     Out of the complex to be reassembled
     Pieces that fit,
     Whereat with love we trembled.

Last week we embraced on the dunes and thought they were
                             pleased;
Now lakes and holes in the mountains remind us of error,
Strolling in the valley we are uncertain of the trees:
     Their shadow falls upon us;
     Are they spies on the human heart
     Motionless, tense in the hope
     Of catching us out? Are they hostile, apart
     From the belovèd group?

For our hour of unity makes us aware of two worlds:
That one was revealed to us then in our double-shadow,
Which for the masters of harbours, the colliers, and us,
     For our calculating star,
     Where the divided feel
     Tears in their eyes
     And time and doctors heal,
     Eternally sighs.

Yes, the white death, friendless, has his own idea of us;
We're something far more exciting than just friends.
He has his private saga he tells himself at night,
     Which starts with the handsome couple
     Estranged by a mistake,
     Follows their lifetime curses,
     Ends with the fruitless rescue from the lake,
     Their death-bed kisses.

Then lightly, my darling, leave me and slip away
Playful, betraying him nothing, allaying suspicion:
His eye is on all these people about us, leading
       Their quiet horrified lives,
       But if we can trust we are free,
       Though alone among those
       Who within earshot of the ungovernable sea
       Grow set in their ways.

We ride a turning globe, we stand on a star;
It has thrust us up together; it is stronger than we.
In it our separate sorrows are a single hope,
       It's in its nature always to appear
       Behind us as we move
       With linked arms through our dreams,
       Wherefore, apart, we love
       Its sundering streams.

And since our desire cannot take that route which is straightest,
Let us choose the crooked, so implicating these acres,
These millions in whom already the wish to be one
       Like a burglar is stealthily moving,
       That these, on the new façade of a bank
       Employed, or conferring at health resort,
       May, by circumstance linked,
       More clearly act our thought.

Then dance, the boatmen, virgins, camera-men and us
Round goal-post, wind-gauge, pylon or bobbing buoy;
For our joy abounding is, though it hide underground,
       As insect or camouflaged cruiser
       For fear of death sham dead,
       Is quick, is real, is quick to answer
       The bird-like sucking tread
       Of the quick dancer.

April 1932

VI

O Love, the interest itself in thoughtless Heaven,
Make simpler daily the beating of man's heart; within,
There in the ring where name and image meet,

Inspire them with such a longing as will make his thought
Alive like patterns a murmuration of starlings
Rising in joy over wolds unwittingly weave;

Here too on our little reef display your power,
This fortress perched on the edge of the Atlantic scarp,
The mole between all Europe and the exile-crowded sea;

And make us as Newton was, who in his garden watching
The apple falling towards England, became aware
Between himself and her of an eternal tie.

For now that dream which so long has contented our will,
I mean, of uniting the dead into a splendid empire,
Under whose fertilising flood the Lancashire moss

Sprouted up chimneys, and Glamorgan hid a life
Grim as a tidal rock-pool's in its glove-shaped valleys,
Is already retreating into her maternal shadow;

Leaving the furnaces gasping in the impossible air,
The flotsam at which Dumbarton gapes and hungers;
While upon wind-loved Rowley no hammer shakes

The cluster of mounds like a midget golf course, graves
Of some who created these intelligible dangerous marvels;
Affectionate people, but crude their sense of glory.

Far-sighted as falcons, they looked down another future;
For the seed in their loins were hostile, though afraid of their pride,
And, tall with a shadow now, inertly wait.

In bar, in netted chicken-farm, in lighthouse,
Standing on these impoverished constricting acres,
The ladies and gentlemen apart, too much alone,

Consider the years of the measured world begun,
The barren spiritual marriage of stone and water.
Yet, O, at this very moment of our hopeless sigh

When inland they are thinking their thoughts but are watching these
                                                                islands,
As children in Chester look to Moel Fammau to decide
On picnics by the clearness or withdrawal of her treeless crown,

Some possible dream, long coiled in the ammonite's slumber
Is uncurling, prepared to lay on our talk and kindness
Its military silence, its surgeon's idea of pain;

And out of the Future into actual History,
As when Merlin, tamer of horses, and his lords to whom
Stonehenge was still a thought, the Pillars passed

And into the undared ocean swung north their prow,
Drives through the night and star-concealing dawn
For the virgin roadsteads of our hearts an unwavering keel.

May 1932

VII

The sun shines down on the ships at sea,
It shines on you and it shines on me
Whatever we are or are going to be.

To-morrow if everything goes to plan,
To-morrow morning you'll be a man:
Let wishes be horses as fast as they can.

   The dogs are barking, the crops are growing,
   But nobody knows how the wind is blowing:
   Gosh, to look at we're no great catch;
   History seems to have struck a bad patch.

   We haven't the time—it's been such a rush—
   Except to attend to our own little push:
   The teacher setting examinations,
   The journalist writing his falsifications,

   The poet reciting to Lady Diana
   While the footmen whisper 'Have a banana',
   The judge enforcing the obsolete law,
   The banker making the loan for the war,

   The expert designing the long-range gun
   To exterminate everyone under the sun,
   Would like to get out but can only mutter:—
   'What can I do? It's my bread and butter.'

In your house to-night you are flushed and gay;
Twenty-one years have passed away;
To-morrow morning's another day.

If we can't love, though miles apart,
If we can't trust with all our heart,
If we can't do that, then we're in the cart.

July 1932

VIII

   Brothers, who when the sirens roar
   From office, shop and factory pour
      'Neath evening sky;
   By cops directed to the fug
   Of talkie-houses for a drug,
   Or down canals to find a hug
      Until you die:

We know, remember, what it is
That keeps you celebrating this
      Sad ceremonial;
We know the terrifying brink
From which in dreams you nightly shrink.
'I shall be sacked without', you think,
      'A testimonial.'

We cannot put on airs with you
The fears that hurt you hurt us too
      Only we say
That like all nightmares these are fake
If you would help us we could make
Our eyes to open, and awake
      Shall find night day.

On you our interests are set
Your sorrow we shall not forget
      While we consider
Those who in every county town
For centuries have done you brown,
But you shall see them tumble down
      Both horse and rider.

O splendid person, you who stand
In spotless flannels or with hand
      Expert on trigger;
Whose lovely hair and shapely limb
Year after year are kept in trim
Till buffers envy as you swim
      Your Grecian figure:

You are not jealous yet, we know,
But we must warn you, even so
      So pray be seated:
It isn't cricket, but it's true
The lady who admires us, you
Have thought you're getting off with too,
      For you're conceited.

Your beauty's a completed thing.
The future kissed you, called you king,
      Did she? Deceiver!
She's not in love with you at all
No feat of yours can make her fall,
She will not answer to your call
      Like your retriever.

Dare-devil mystic who bear the scars
Of many spiritual wars
        And smoothly tell
The starving that their one salvation
Is personal regeneration
By fasting, prayer and contemplation;
        Is it? Well,

Others have tried it, all delight
Sustained in that ecstatic flight
        Could not console
When through exhausting hours they'd flown
From the alone to the Alone,
Nothing remained but the dry-as-bone
        Night of the soul.

Coward; for all your goodness game
Your dream of Heaven is the same
        As any bounder's;
You hope to corner as reward
All that the rich can here afford:
Love and music and bed and board
        While the world flounders.

And you, the wise man, full of humour
To whom our misery's a rumour
        And slightly funny;
Proud of your nicely balanced view
You say as if it were something new
The fuss we make is mostly due
        To lack of money.

Ah, what a little squirt is there
When of your aren't-I-charming air
        You stand denuded.
Behind your subtle sense of humour
You hide the boss's simple stuma,
Among the foes which we enumer
        You are included.

Because you saw but were not indignant
The invasion of the great malignant
        Cambridge ulcer
That army intellectual
Of every kind of liberal
Smarmy with friendship but of all
        There are none falser.

A host of columbines and pathics
Who show the poor by mathematics
        In their defence
That wealth and poverty are merely
Mental pictures, so that clearly
Every tramp's a landlord really
        In mind-events.

Let fever sweat them till they tremble
Cramp rack their limbs till they resemble
        Cartoons by Goya:
Their daughters sterile be in rut,
May cancer rot their herring gut,
The circular madness on them shut,
        Or paranoia.

Their splendid people, their wiseacres,
Professors, agents, magic-makers,
        Their poets and apostles,
Their bankers and their brokers too,
And ironmasters shall turn blue
Shall fade away like morning dew
        With club-room fossils.

August 1932

IX

I have a handsome profile
I've been to a great public school
I've a little money invested
Then why do I feel such a fool
As if I owned a world that has had its day?

You certainly have a good reason
For feeling as you do
No wonder you are anxious
Because it's perfectly true
You own a world that has had its day.

I'll throw my money in the gutter
I'll throw it all away
I'll throw it where the workmen can pick it up
Then nobody can say
I own a world that has had its day.

The workmen will never get it
Though you throw it all over the town
The armament firms will collect it all
And use it for shooting them down
To save a world that has had its day.

I'll get a job in a factory
I'll live with working boys
I'll play them at darts in the public house
I'll share their sorrows and joys
Not live in a world that has had its day.

They won't tell you their secrets
Though you pay for their drinks in the bar
They'll tell you lies for your money
For they know you for what you are
That you live in a world that has had its day.

I'll book a berth on a liner
I'll sail away out to sea
I'll settle down on an island
Where the natives shall set me free
I'll leave a world that has had its day.

Most of the natives are dying
They've sampled your sort before
It gave them no satisfaction
They're in no mood for more
Who come from a world that has had its day.

I'll hire a furnished attic
A room on the top floor
I'll spend my mornings writing
A book that will cause a furore
About a world that has had its day.

You may be a little genius
You may be doing your best
To tell us about yours truly
But where is the interest
It's just a world that has had its day.

I'll attend when the parson is preaching
I'll tell all my sins to the priest
I'll do exactly as they ask
I'll go to heaven at least
After this world has had its day.

You may sit down under the pulpit
You may go down on your knees
But you don't believe them any more
And they won't give you ease
They're of this world that has had its day.

I'll go down to the brothel
Stick a syringe in my arm
I'll go out poaching on my own estate

Then I shall feel perfectly calm
About my world that has had its day.

It's no use turning nasty
It's no use turning good
You're what you are and nothing you do
Will get you out of the wood
Out of a world that has had its day.

Remember you're no old soldier
Remember that you are afraid
Remember you'd be no use at all
Behind the barricade
You belong to your world that has had its day.

Your son may be a hero
Carry a great big gun
Your son may be a hero
But you will not be one
Go down with your world that has had its day.

                                          September 1932

X

O what is that sound which so thrills the ear
    Down in the valley drumming, drumming?
Only the scarlet soldiers, dear,
        The soldiers coming.

O what is that light I see flashing so clear
    Over the distance brightly, brightly?
Only the sun on their weapons, dear,
        As they step lightly.

O what are they doing with all that gear;
    What are they doing this morning, this morning?
Only the usual manœuvres, dear,
        Or perhaps a warning.

O why have they left the road down there;
    Why are they suddenly wheeling, wheeling?
Perhaps a change in the orders, dear;
        Why are you kneeling?

O haven't they stopped for the doctor's care;
    Haven't they reined their horses, their horses?
Why, they are none of them wounded, dear,
        None of these forces.

O is it the parson they want with white hair;
   Is it the parson, is it, is it?
No, they are passing his gateway, dear,
      Without a visit.

O it must be the farmer who lives so near;
   It must be the farmer so cunning, so cunning?
They have passed the farm already, dear,
      And now they are running.

O where are you going? stay with me here!
   Were the vows you swore me deceiving, deceiving?
No, I promised to love you, dear,
      But I must be leaving.

O it's broken the lock and splintered the door,
   O it's the gate where they're turning, turning;
Their feet are heavy on the floor
      And their eyes are burning.

October 1932

XI · The Witnesses

I

You dowagers with Roman noses
Sailing along between banks of roses
      well dressed,
You Lords who sit at committee tables
And crack with grooms in riding stables
      your father's jest;

Solicitors with poker faces,
And doctors with black bags to cases
      hurried,
Reporters coming home at dawn
And heavy bishops on the lawn
      by sermons worried;

You stokers lit by furnace-glare,
And you, too, steeplejacks up there
      singing,
You shepherds wind-blown on the ridges,
Tramps leaning over village bridges
      your eardrums ringing;

On land, on sea, in field, in town
Attend: Musician put them down,
        those trumpets;
Let go, young lover, of her hand
Come forward both of you and stand
        as still as limpets

Close as you can and listen well:
My companion here is about to tell
        a story;
Peter, Pontius Pilate, Paul
Whoever you are, it concerns you all
        and human glory.

2

Call him Prince Alpha if you wish
He was born in a palace, his people were swish;
        his christening
Was called by the Tatler the event of the year,
All the photographed living were there
        and the dead were listening.

You would think I was trying to foozle you
If I told you all that kid could do;
        enough
To say he was never afraid of the dark
He climbed all the trees in his pater's park;
        his nurse thought him rough.

At school his brilliance was a mystery,
All languages, science, maths, and history
        he knew;
His style at cricket was simply stunning
At rugger, soccer, hockey, running
        and swimming too.

The days went by, he grew mature;
He was a looker you may be sure,
        so straight
Old couples cried 'God bless my soul
I thought that man was a telegraph pole'
        when he passed their gate.

His eyes were blue as a mountain lake,
He made the hearts of the girls to ache;
        he was strong;
He was gay, he was witty, his speaking voice
Sounded as if a large Rolls-Royce
        had passed along.

He kissed his dear old mater one day,
He said to her 'I'm going away,
       good-bye'.
No sword nor terrier by his side
He set off through the world so wide
       under the sky.

Where did he travel? Where didn't he travel?
Over the ice and over the gravel
       and the sea;
Up the fevered jungle river,
Through haunted forests without a shiver
       he wandered free.

What did he do? What didn't he do,
He rescued maidens, overthrew
       ten giants
Like factory chimneys, slaughtered dragons,
Though their heads were larger than railway waggons
       tamed their defiance.

What happened, what happened? I'm coming to that;
He came to a desert and down he sat
       and cried,
Above the blue sky arching wide
Two tall rocks as black as pride
       on either side.

There on a stone he sat him down,
Around the desert stretching brown
       like the tide,
Above the blue sky arching wide
Two black rocks on either side
       and, O how he cried.

'I thought my strength could know no stemming
But I was foolish as a lemming;
       for what
Was I born, was it only to see
I'm as tired of life as life of me?
       let me be forgot.

'Children have heard of my every action
It gives me no sort of satisfaction
       and why?
Let me get this as clear as I possibly can
No, I am not the truly strong man,
       O let me die.'

There in the desert all alone
He sat for hours on a long flat stone
        and sighed;
Above the blue sky arching wide
Two black rocks on either side,
        and then he died.

Now ladies and gentlemen, big and small,
This story of course has a morale;
        again
Unless like him you wish to die
Listen, while my friend and I
        proceed to explain.

3

What had he done to be treated thus?
If you want to know, he'd offended us:
        for yes,
We guard the wells, we're handy with a gun,
We've a very special sense of fun,
        we curse and bless.

You are the town, and we are the clock,
We are the guardians of the gate in the rock,
        the Two;
On your left, and on your right
In the day, and in the night
        we are watching you.

Wiser not to ask just what has occurred
To them that disobeyed our word;
        to those
We were the whirlpool, we were the reef,
We were the formal nightmare, grief,
        and the unlucky rose.

Climb up the cranes, learn the sailors' words
When the ships from the islands, laden with birds
        come in;
Tell your stories of fishing and other men's wives,
The expansive moments of constricted lives,
        in the lighted inn.

By all means say of the peasant youth
'That person there is in the truth'
        we're kind,
Tire of your little rut and look it,
You have to obey but you don't have to like it,
        we do not mind:

But do not imagine we do not know
Or that what you hide with care won't show
              at a glance;
Nothing is done, nothing is said
But don't make the mistake of thinking us dead;
              I shouldn't dance

For I'm afraid in that case you'll have a fall;
We've been watching you over the garden wall
              for hours,
The sky is darkening like a stain,
Something is going to fall like rain
              and it won't be flowers.

When the green field comes off like a lid
Revealing what were much better hid,
              unpleasant;
And look! behind you without a sound
The woods have come up and are standing round
              in deadly crescent.

The bolt is sliding in its groove,
Outside the window is the black remov-
              ers' van,
And now with sudden swift emergence
Come the women in dark glasses, the hump-backed surgeons
              and the scissor-man.

This might happen any day
So be careful what you say
              or do
Be clean, be tidy, oil the lock,
Trim the garden, wind the clock:
              Remember the Two.

? late 1932

XII

The month was April, the year
   Nineteen hundred and thirty-three,
The place a philosopher's garden
   In Oxford, the person me.
The weather was mild and sunny
   As prophesied by Old Moore;
I fell asleep in a deck-chair
   And this is what I saw.

I found myself a seagull
    Looking down on the wide blue ocean;
Directly below was a ship
    Evidently in motion.
I didn't have to be told
    That she was looking for land,
But her steering was so peculiar
    I couldn't quite understand.

So down there flew yours truly
    To get a closer view
Of the ship and all her fittings
    And to have a look at the crew.
She was flying the Union Jack,
    And strike me dead if I'm a liar,
The name painted on her bows
    Was *Wystan Auden Esquire*.

Nobody took any notice
    As I circled and perched on the deck;
I can recommend my disguise
    To any young amateur tec.
Surprises were waiting for me
    In what I saw and heard;
I'd better tell the whole story,
    Beginning with the people on board.

The captain was pacing the bridge
    Like a polar bear in a cage;
I was startled to find him a woman
    Of rather uncertain age.
Her bottle-green mac was too big
    For she was as thin as a biscuit;
She was wearing waders and carried
    On her shoulder an old-fashioned musket.

Just then the first mate came up
    Bringing her a cup of tea;
He was rather bald and bow-legged
    And his trousers bagged at the knee.
As he bent to put down the tray
    I noticed his broad behind,
But his manner was very gentle
    And his mouth and eyes were kind.

'Six bells, my dear', he said,
    'Won't you let me take a turn?'
But she barked 'Once is enough
    And it cost us much to learn.
Coming out of the harbour mouth

We gave you the ship to steer;
You ran in straight at the breakwater,
    You'd have sunk her if I'd not been there.

'Fetch me the chart, if you please,
    That's hanging there on the wall.'
As he laid it out I flitted
    To where I could see it all.
The course of the ship was plotted
    Across it in a perfect straight line;
There were plenty of notes in the margin
    But of land there wasn't a sign.

The captain put on sunglasses
    And studied the chart a lot;
She measured the course with a ruler
    And with a pencil marked a dot.
Then she turned to the mate and said
    'Go and call the crew together,
The meaning of the chart is clear:
    There's going to be stormy weather.

'Now go and tell the wireless
    Operator I'd like a word.'
He disappeared down a hatchway
    And presently I heard
A light step quickly approaching
    And a voice saying 'Evening, miss.'
The captain picked up a paper
    And cried 'What nonsense is this?

'What do you mean by stating
    You received a message last night
From a ship three miles to the west
    Saying everything was quite all right?
All right, indeed! Look here—
    In her position the chart marks a reef.
If you're getting disloyal, my friend,
    You'll very soon come to grief.

'I want the truth remember.'
    The young man said with a grin,
Looking at his shark-skin shoes,
    'I must have been taken in.'
'Well, be more careful next time,
    Now go and join the crew.'
They were gathered on the lower deck,
    I had a splendid view.

There was the engineer and the stoker,
    The cabin boy and the cook,
The mate and the wireless man;
    The passengers were the Duke
And—busy doing cat's cradles—
    The one they all called the Professor.
Except for him they looked up
    At the captain and began to address her.

The engineer who was wiping
    His hands on some waste looked cross:
'O can't you cut this cackle?
    My engines need me, boss.'
The stoker, who'd only one eye,
    Glared at the company and swore,
'If anyone's looking for trouble
    I'll sock his bloody jaw.'

The cook was clasping his hands
    Across a mountainous belly:
'Where do that sandwich go to?'
    He sang, and shook like a jelly.
The cabin boy threw me a fish head
    And gave me a meaning wink,
The Duke put his arm round his shoulder,
    Said, 'A lovely cweature, I think.'

The captain shouted 'Silence!
    I brought you here to inform
You all that the course of the ship
    Is about to enter a storm.'
(The Professor went on muttering,
    'I was right: at Position A
Navaho index strings—
    Yes, this must be the way.')

'I would remind you we are sailing
    To the Islands of Milk and Honey
Where there's neither death nor old age
    And the poor have all the money.
The wells are full of wine,
    New bread grows on the trees,
And roasted pigs run about
    Crying "Eat me, if you please."

'So if it's a little rough
    It's well worth while, you see.'
(The cook cried, licking his lips,
    'It sounds all right to me.'
The Duke pinched the cabin boy's ear,
    'It'll be amusin' there with you.'

The engineer said 'I'm going,
   I've got some work to do.')

'The sky is already darker,
   Everyone to their stations;
Until the storm is over
   You'll have to go without rations.'
The cook's face fell, the stoker
   Spat into the sea,
The mate said 'I'll go below
   And make them all cups of tea.'

The wireless operator
   Now comes to the captain and says
'Excuse me, Ma'am, but you know
   I've received some messages
Which suggest that there's calmer water
   If we steer our course to the east.
Of course it's not perfectly certain
   But we ought to try it at least.

'The ship's not as young as she was
   And it's getting very rough;
You surely don't want to sink her.'
   But the captain shouted 'Enough!
Liar, reformist, traitor,
   You've the impudence to start
Insulting our ship, and worse,
   Contradicting the chart.'

She signed to the stoker, who conked him
   One on the nut with a spanner,
And dragged him away to the hold
   Like a small child trailing a banner.
The lighting flashed, the thunder
   Roared and the hailstorm caught us.
Waterspouts skated like flies
   Upon the face of the waters.

The Professor, quite forgotten,
   Was sitting still on the deck
Holding his string above him
   For the water was up to his neck.
Except for him and the captain
   There was no one to be found,
The engineer was below
   Watching his wheels go round.

The cook had gone to his galley
    And locked himself in alone;
He was evidently being seasick
    For I could hear him moan.
The mate with a spirit stove
    Was keeping a kettle hot;
The Duke and the boy had retired
    To do—well, you know what.

Alone on her bridge the captain,
    While the gale whirled shriller and colder,
Was eating the chart, and now
    Took the musket from her shoulder,
Loaded it and began to fire
    Wildly at sky and sea,
Then suddenly she turned round
    And levelled it straight at me.

'Saboteur, spy', she hissed,
    'I've got you.' The musket spoke.
There was a sudden flash,
    A roar in my ears, and I woke.
The book I was reading had fallen,
    Someone was calling me.
I got up, and on the verandah
    The table was laid for tea.

April 1933

XIII

Hearing of harvests rotting in the valleys,
Seeing at end of street the barren mountains,
Round corners coming suddenly on water,
Knowing them shipwrecked who were launched for islands,
We honour founders of these starving cities,
Whose honour is the image of our sorrow.

Which cannot see its likeness in their sorrow
That brought them desperate to the brink of valleys;
Dreaming of evening walks through learned cities,
They reined their violent horses on the mountains,
Those fields like ships to castaways on islands,
Visions of green to them that craved for water.

They built by rivers and at night the water
Running past windows comforted their sorrow;
Each in his little bed conceived of islands
Where every day was dancing in the valleys,
And all the year trees blossomed on the mountains,
Where love was innocent, being far from cities.

135

But dawn came back and they were still in cities;
No marvellous creature rose up from the water,
There was still gold and silver in the mountains,
And hunger was a more immediate sorrow;
Although to moping villagers in valleys
Some waving pilgrims were describing islands.

'The gods', they promised, 'visit us from islands,
Are stalking head-up, lovely through the cities;
Now is the time to leave your wretched valleys
And sail with them across the lime-green water;
Sitting at their white sides, forget your sorrow,
The shadow cast across your lives by mountains.'

So many, doubtful, perished in the mountains
Climbing up crags to get a view of islands;
So many, fearful, took with them their sorrow
Which stayed them when they reached unhappy cities;
So many, careless, dived and drowned in water;
So many, wretched, would not leave their valleys.

It is the sorrow; shall it melt? Ah, water
Would gush, flush, green these mountains and these valleys
And we rebuild our cities, not dream of islands.

May 1933

XIV

(TO GEOFFREY HOYLAND)

Out on the lawn I lie in bed,
Vega conspicuous overhead
   In the windless nights of June;
Forests of green have done complete
The day's activity; my feet
   Point to the rising moon.

Lucky, this point in time and space
Is chosen as my working place;
   Where the sexy airs of summer,
The bathing hours and the bare arms,
The leisured drives through a land of farms,
   Are good to the newcomer.

Equal with colleagues in a ring
I sit on each calm evening,
   Enchanted as the flowers
The opening light draws out of hiding
From leaves with all its dove-like pleading
   Its logic and its powers.

That later we, though parted then
May still recall these evenings when
   Fear gave his watch no look;
The lion griefs loped from the shade
And on our knees their muzzles laid,
   And Death put down his book.

Moreover, eyes in which I learn
That I am glad to look, return
   My glances every day;
And when the birds and rising sun
Waken me, I shall speak with one
   Who has not gone away.

Now North and South and East and West
Those I love lie down to rest;
   The moon looks on them all:
The healers and the brilliant talkers,
The eccentrics and the silent walkers,
   The dumpy and the tall.

She climbs the European sky;
Churches and power stations lie
   Alike among earth's fixtures:
Into the galleries she peers,
And blankly as an orphan stares
   Upon the marvellous pictures.

To gravity attentive, she
Can notice nothing here; though we
   Whom hunger cannot move,
From gardens where we feel secure
Look up, and with a sigh endure
   The tyrannies of love:

And, gentle, do not care to know,
Where Poland draws her Eastern bow,
   What violence is done;
Nor ask what doubtful act allows
Our freedom in this English house,
   Our picnics in the sun.

The creepered wall stands up to hide
The gathering multitudes outside
   Whose glances hunger worsens;
Concealing from their wretchedness
Our metaphysical distress,
   Our kindness to ten persons.

And now no path on which we move
But shows already traces of
 Intentions not our own,
Thoroughly able to achieve
What our excitement could conceive,
 But our hands left alone.

For what by nature and by training
We loved, has little strength remaining:
 Though we would gladly give
The Oxford colleges, Big Ben,
And all the birds in Wicken Fen,
 It has no wish to live.

Soon through the dykes of our content
The crumpling flood will force a rent,
 And, taller than a tree,
Hold sudden death before our eyes
Whose river-dreams long hid the size
 And vigours of the sea.

But when the waters make retreat
And through the black mud first the wheat
 In shy green stalks appears;
When stranded monsters gasping lie,
And sounds of riveting terrify
 Their whorled unsubtle ears:

May this for which we dread to lose
Our privacy, need no excuse
 But to that strength belong;
As through a child's rash happy cries
The drowned voices of his parents rise
 In unlamenting song.

After discharges of alarm,
All unpredicted may it calm
 The pulse of nervous nations;
Forgive the murderer in his glass,
Tough in its patience to surpass
 The tigress her swift motions.

June 1933

XV

What was the weather on Eternity's worst day? And where was that
Son of God during the fatal second: pausing before a mirror in an
anteroom, or in the Supreme Presence Itself, in the middle of an awful
crescendo of praise, or again, withdrawn apart, regarding pensively
the unspeakable beauties of the heavenly landscape?

The divinest of books says nothing. Of the primary crises of the soul no history is ever written. Yon citizen crossing the street while the policeman holds up the traffic like the Red Sea: he leaves one curb an honest man; but, ah, quickly, Constable, handcuffs out! Roll on, you heavy lorries! He is Pharaoh! Mercifully exterminate this pest! Too late, the warning cannot be given. It's done, the poison administered, the soul infected. The other curb is reached and our John Bull, honest-seeming, unsuspected is free to walk away, within a few years to involve widows in financial ruin or a party of school children in some frightful accident.

So, on this inconceivably more catastrophic occasion, no door banged, no dog barked. There was no alarm of any kind. But consider its importance! No judge's sentence had yet been passed. Basedow's Disease had not occurred. Love. Joy. Peace. God. No words but these. No population but angels. And after . . . the whole lexicon of sin: the sullen proletariat of hell!

What, then, of the central figure in the tragedy: First among the Sons of God? Power? No Caliph or Mikado had one grain of it. Beauty? Alcibiades beside him were extraordinarily plain. Wits? Einstein were a stammerer. But for him it was not enough. For him, nothing was enough, but the unique majority of God. That or nothing! That or (ah, had he reckoned with the dread alternative!) unqualified ruin. Alas, for us he raised the question; but the answer was to lie with another!

O, even then, when the first thought tempted, was all irrevocably lost? Was there not still time, wonderful creature, to cast it from you with a phew of disgust? It doesn't matter now. Altered for ever and for the worse, he went out to corrupt others, to form his notorious and infamous societies. Gone for ever was the frank handshake, the obvious look, the direct and simple speech. The Golden Age was definitely over. Language had become symbolic, gesture a code of signals. The arrangement of books on a table conveyed a shame-faced message: flowers in a vase expressed some unsavoury *double entendre*.

Personalities acquired a new and sinister significance, lost all but that. For or against: On this side of the ledger or on that. Gabriel and Michael: Out of the question. What glorious praise! Demogorgon: Safe. What a shameful comment! Abdiel and Azazael: Perhaps. Oh, beware, you unsuspecting pair! This is a terrible examination, decisive of your everlasting career. This is your only chance. Here are but two colours from which to choose, the whitest white or the blackest black; salvation or damnation at one hundred per cent. Azazael chooses. What? The Black. Miserable, unlucky he! He's failed. Now, Abdiel! You hesitate? Quick, man, the White! Bravissimo, he passes! Baffled, they slink away to make their preparations. Too late for diplomacy or apologetic telegrams. It is war.

On the details of that appalling combat, History is mercifully silent. To the vanquished, unable to consider such reminiscences without a shudder, the subject is tabu: And the victors, to whom all boasting is by nature abhorrent, have been content to leave the matter in a decent obscurity. Remember, they were divine, and therefore omniscient, omnipotent. No new-fangled auxiliary arm, the value of which is realised only by the few enthusiastic subalterns, no depth-charges or detectors, no camouflage, no poison-gas which in times of peace even generals do not see how they could bring themselves to use, no technique of deployment or barrage can have been unknown to them. It was conflict on an astronomical scale and with the gloves off. Here were no Quakers, strikers or International Red Cross, no questions of colonies or reparations. Where all were committed absolutely, there could be no ironic misgivings.

Every schoolboy knows the result. For the rebels it was destruction. The reservoirs of the Divine Wrath were inexhaustible. Nothing was signed. There was no one left to discharge so unnecessary an office. Into the fosse of Hell they fell like water. Hurrah! Hurrah! Hurrah!

Yet, my friends, you know and I know, don't we, that the events I have just narrated were not the last. Would God they had been! The scene of operations was transferred to another front, to us. Impotent to attack Him directly, the defeated sought to strike at God through His creatures, to wound where it was most tender, His artist's love. And, to our shame, they succeeded. The world became an everlasting invalid. Of course, God could have dismissed us with a snap of His fingers. One little stellar collision and . . . no more trouble for him. Why not? All reason was for it. It would have been quite cricket. But God is no eugenist. There was no talk of sterilisation, euthanasia. Only the treatment of a very merciful and loving physician. He set over us a kindly strictness, appointed His authorities, severe but just, a kind of martial law. He gave them power to govern in His name and access to His presence in their prayers, to make their reports and ask for help and guidance, that through them the people might learn His primary will.

And so, to-day, we are here for a very good reason. His enemies have launched another offensive, on the grandest scale, perhaps, that this poor planet of ours has yet witnessed. As on the first awful occasion in Eden, so now: under the same deluding banner of Freedom. For their technique of propaganda has never varied—it has been far too successful for them to need to change it—to suggest that it is in the human interest to destroy God. In silk-clad China or the naked archipelagos, in the Bermudas or Brighton, in the stone hamlet among the beechwoods or the steel flats of the metropolis, that three-syllable whisper: 'You are God', has been, is and, alas, will be sufficient to convert in an instant the chapped-handed but loyal ploughboy, the patient sufferer from incurable disease, the tired economical student or the beautiful juvenile mama into a very spiteful maniac indeed, into whose hands modern science has placed an all-too-efficient axe.

I should like just to try and imagine for one moment what the world would be like if this lunacy with its grim fanatic theories were to spread over the civilised globe. I tell you there would exist a tyranny compared with which a termite colony would seem dangerously lax. No family love. Sons would inform against fathers, cheerfully send them to the execution cellars. Mothers send their daughters to the mines. No romance. Even the peasant must beget that standard child under laboratory conditions. Motherhood would be by licence. Truth and Beauty would be proscribed as dangerously obstructive. To be beautiful would be treason against the State, Thought a sabotage deadly to the thinker. No books, no art, no music. A year of this, I say, and even the grass would cease to grow, flowers would not risk appearance, heifers would not dare to calve.

So you see our job. To those to whom danger in God's cause makes exclaim, like a schoolboy comforted with an ice: 'How lush!' this is a lucky day. God has given them extraordinary privileges, but if there be any doubters, cowards wavering like the cowl on an oast-house, to these I say: 'Go out of that door before it is too late!' Only those whose decisions are swift as the sirocco, senses keen as the finest mirror galvanometer, will constant as the standard inch and of a chemical purity need apply. And to these I say: 'Remember, God is behind you: Nelson, Henry the Fifth, Shackleton, Julius Caesar.' As for the enemy, those rats! they shall skedaddle like a brook. Nature herself is on our side. Their boasts are vain. You cannot threaten a thunderstorm with a revolver. They shall be trapped by the stalks of flowers. Sheep shall chase them away. Useless for them to imitate natural objects: a boulder or a tree. Even the spade-handed moles shall declare their folly!

But mind, God first! To God the glory and let Him reward! God is no summer tourist. We're more than scenery to Him. He has a farmer's eye for ergot and tares. Oh delight higher than Everest and deeper than the Challenger Gulf! His commodores come into His council and His lieutenants know His love. Lord, I confess! I confess! I am all too weak and utterly unworthy. There is no other want. All actions and diversions of the people, their greyhound races, their football competitions, their clumsy acts of love, what are they but the pitiful, maimed expression of that entire passion, the positive tropism of the soul to God?

Oh Father, I am praising Thee, I have always praised Thee, I shall always praise Thee! Listen to the wooden sabots of Thy eager child running to Thy arms! Admit him to the fairs of that blessed country where Thy saints move happily about their neat, clean houses under the blue sky! O windmills, O cocks, O clouds and ponds! Mother is waving from the tiny door! The quilt is turned down in my beautiful blue and gold room! Father, I thank Thee in advance! Everything has been grand! I am coming home!

1933

XVI

Here on the cropped grass of the narrow ridge I stand,
A fathom of earth, alive in air,
Aloof as an admiral on the old rocks,
 England below me:
Eastward across the Midland plains
An express is leaving for a sailors' country;
 Westward is Wales
Where on clear evenings the retired and rich
From the french windows of their sheltered mansions
See the Sugarloaf standing, an upright sentinel
 Over Abergavenny.

When last I stood here I was not alone; happy
Each thought the other, thinking of a crime,
And England to our meditations seemed
    The perfect setting:
But now it has no innocence at all;
It is the isolation and the fear,
    The mood itself;
It is the body of the absent lover,
An image to the would-be hero of the soul,
The little area we are willing to forgive
    Upon conditions.

For private reasons I must have the truth, remember
These years have seen a boom in sorrow;
The presses of idleness issued more despair
    And it was honoured,
Gross Hunger took on more hands every month,
Erecting here and everywhere his vast
    Unnecessary workshops;
Europe grew anxious about her health,
Combines tottered, credits froze,
And business shivered in a banker's winter
    While we were kissing.

To-day no longer occupied like that, I give
The children at the open swimming pool
Lithe in their first and little beauty
    A closer look;
Follow the cramped clerk crooked at his desk,
The guide in shorts pursuing flowers
    In their careers;
A digit of the crowd, would like to know
Them better whom the shops and trams are full of,
The little men and their mothers, not plain but
    Dreadfully ugly.

Deaf to the Welsh wind now, I hear arising
From lanterned gardens sloping to the river
Where saxophones are moaning for a comforter,
    From Gaumont theatres
Where fancy plays on hunger to produce
The noble robber, ideal of boys,
    And from cathedrals,
Luxury liners laden with souls,
Holding to the east their hulls of stone,
The high thin rare continuous worship
    Of the self-absorbed.

Here, which looked north before the Cambrian alignment,
Like the cupped hand of the keen excavator
Busy with bones, the memory uncovers
    The hopes of time;
Of empires stiff in their brocaded glory,
The luscious lateral blossoming of woe
    Scented, profuse;
And of intercalary ages of disorder
When, as they prayed in antres, fell
Upon the noblest in the country night
    Angel assassins.

Small birds above me have the grace of those who founded
The civilisation of the delicate olive,
Learning the laws of love and sailing
    On the calm Aegean;
The hawk is the symbol of the rule by thirst,
The central state controlling the canals;
    And the blank sky
Of the womb's utter peace before
The cell, dividing, multiplied desire,
And raised instead of death the image
    Of the reconciler.

And over the Cotswolds now the thunder mutters:
'What little of the truth your seers saw
They dared not tell you plainly but combined
    Assertion and refuge
In the common language of collective lying,
In codes of a bureau, laboratory slang
    And diplomats' French.
The relations of your lovers were, alas, pictorial;
The treasure that you stole, you lost; bad luck
It brought you, but you cannot put it back
    Now with caresses.

'Already behind you your last evening hastens up
And all the customs your society has chosen
Harden themselves into the unbreakable
    Habits of death.
Has not your long affair with death
Of late become increasingly more serious;
    Do you not find
Him growing more attractive every day?
You shall go under and help him with the crops,
Be faithful to him, and to your friends
    Remain indifferent.'

And out of the turf the bones of the war continue:
'Know then, cousin, the major cause of our collapse
Was a distortion in the human plastic by luxury produced,

'Never higher than in our time were the vital advantages;
To matter entire, to the unbounded vigours of the instrument,
To all logical precision we were the rejoicing heirs.

'But pompous, we assumed their power to be our own,
Believed machines to be our hearts' spontaneous fruit,
Taking our premises as shoppers take a tram.

'While the disciplined love which alone could have employed
these engines
Seemed far too difficult and dull, and when hatred promised
An immediate dividend, all of us hated.

'Denying the liberty we knew quite well to be our destiny,
It dogged our steps with its accusing shadow
Until in every landscape we saw murder ambushed.

'Unable to endure ourselves, we sought relief
In the insouciance of the soldier, the heroic sexual pose
Playing at fathers to impress the little ladies.

'Call us not tragic; falseness made farcical our death:
Nor brave; ours was the will of the insane to suffer
By which since we could not live we gladly died:
And now we have gone for ever to our foolish graves.'

The Priory clock chimes briefly and I recollect
I am expected to return alive
My will effective and my nerves in order
    To my situation.
'The poetry is in the pity', Wilfred said,
And Kathy in her journal, 'To be rooted in life,
    That's what I want.'
These moods give no permission to be idle,
For men are changed by what they do;
And through loss and anger the hands of the unlucky
    Love one another.

                                                      1933

XVII

The earth turns over, our side feels the cold,
And life sinks choking in the wells of trees;
The ticking heart comes to a standstill, killed,
The icing on the pond waits for the boys.
Among the holly and the gifts I move,
The carols on the piano, the glowing hearth,
All our traditional sympathy with birth,
Put by your challenge to the shifts of love.

144

Your portrait hangs before me on the wall
And there what view I wish for, I shall find,
The wooded or the stony—though not all
The painter's gifts can make its flatness round—
Through the blue irises the heaven of failures,
The mirror world where logic is reversed,
Where age becomes the handsome child at last,
The glass sea parted for the country sailors.

There move the enormous comics, drawn from life;
My father as an Airedale and a gardener,
My mother chasing letters with a knife:
You are not present as a character.
—Only the family have speaking parts—
You are a valley or a river bend,
The one an aunt refers to as a friend,
The tree from which the weasel racing starts.

False; but no falser than the world it matches,
Love's daytime kingdom which I say you rule,
The total state where all must wear your badges,
Keep order perfect as a naval school:
Noble emotions organised and massed
Line the straight flood-lit tracks of memory
To cheer your image as it flashes by;
All lust at once informed on and suppressed.

Yours is the only name expressive there,
And family affection the one in cypher;
Lay-out of hospital and street and square
That comfort to the homesick children offer:
As I, their author, stand between these dreams,
Son of a nurse and doctor, loaned a room,
Your would-be lover who has never come
In the great bed at midnight to your arms.

Such dreams are amorous; they are indeed:
But no one but myself is loved in these,
And time flies on above the dreamer's head,
Flies on, flies on, and with your beauty flies.
All things he takes and loses but conceit,
The Alec who can buy the life within,
License no liberty except his own,
Order the fireworks after the defeat.

Language of moderation cannot hide;
My sea is empty and the waves are rough:
Gone from the map the shore where childhood played
Tight-fisted as a peasant, eating love;
Lost in my wake the archipelago,
Islands of self through which I sailed all day,

Planting a pirate's flag, a generous boy;
And lost the way to action and to you.

Lost if I steer. Gale of desire may blow
Sailor and ship past the illusive reef,
And I yet land to celebrate with you
Birth of a natural order and of love;
With you enjoy the untransfigured scene,
My father down the garden in his gaiters,
My mother at her bureau writing letters,
Free to our favours, all our titles gone.

December 1933

XVIII

I

Turn not towards me lest I turn to you:
Stretch not your hands towards your harm and me
Lest, waking, you should feel the need I do
To offer love's preposterous guarantee
That the stars watch us, that there are no poor,
No boyish weakness justifying scorn,
To cancel off from the forgotten score
The foiled caresses from which thought was born.

Yes, sleep: how easily may we do good
To those we have no wish to see again;
Love knows he argues with himself in vain,
He means to do no mischief but he would.
Love would content us: that is untrue.
Turn not towards me, lest I turn to you.

? Summer 1933

2

On the provincial lawn I watch you play,
To me and to your brothers a success
Upon whose charm the world has still to lay
Her suffocating motherly caress,
The future like a promised picnic still:
I stand where luck may vary, out or in,
The barrage never. Soon enough you will
Enter the zone where casualties begin.

O will time falter at your tone of voice
Or will the wretched at attention wait
To treat you as a stranger when you pass
Nor make their special claims upon your face;

Will love refuse the power to exploit
Or you the power which corrupts the heart?

? Summer 1934

3

At the far end of the enormous room
An orchestra is playing to the rich,
The drumtaps nagging like a nervous twitch,
The fiddle soaring like a flying dream:
At tables round me all the winners sit,
Lean over talking to a lovely prize,
And I imagine you before my eyes
Flushed with the wine I order and my wit.

It is an enemy that sighs for you:
Love has one wish and that is, not to be.
Had you been never beautiful nor true
He would not have been born and I were free
From one whose whispers shall go on and on
Till you are false and all your beauties gone.

? Summer 1933

4

The latest ferrule now has tapped the curb
And the night's tiny noises everywhere
Beat vivid on the owl's developed ear,
Vague in the watchman's, and in wards disturb
The cases counting sheep. Blessing this moon
Like treasures touching sides, how many lie,
Successful lovers who were once as I;
But in your northern house you sleep alone.

All the hot stars beyond me and the sun,
Down the great trackways where our tribe is nothing
And meaningless a change from love to loathing,
Their vast involuntary errands run:
And I find nothing sensible to do,
But, shivering, look towards the north and you.

? Summer 1933

5

One absence closes other lives to him
Like Sunday; his self-pity falls like rain
And keeps the pasty household all indoors;
Up in the poky nursery of the brain

The thoughts grow tired of story and charade
And start to pinch each other; with inertion
His head aches; petted senses at his side
Exasperate him with their dumb devotion.

Let him then learn from this that he's a dreamer:
To him the wretched are a race apart,
He is not yet their indifferent redeemer
For only beauty still can make him kind,
Make teachers from the errors of his mind
Or surgeons from the vices of his heart.

May 1934

6

The fruit in which your parents hid you, boy,
Their death, is summer perfect: at its core
You grow already; soon you will not be
One of the young for whom all wish to care
Having at last the matter for a story
For you will know what people mean by looking:
Some you will beckon closer and be sorry,
You will not have to guess at what is lacking.

But you are death this summer, we the hurt
For whose profoundest sigh you give no penny
Though, calmer than us all, you move our lives;
Send back the writer howling to his art,
And the rich driver pulling on his gloves
Start in a snowstorm on his deadly journey.

? Spring 1933

7

Just as his dream foretold, he met them all:
The smiling grimy boy at the garage
Ran out before he blew his horn; the tall
Professor in the mountains with his large
Tweed pockets full of plants addressed him hours
Before he would have dared; the deaf girl too
Seemed to expect him at the green chateau;
The meal was laid, the guest room full of flowers.

More, the talk always took the wished-for turn,
Dwelt on the need for stroking and advice;
Yet, at each meeting, he was forced to learn,
The same misunderstanding would arise.
Which was in need of help? Were they or he
The physician, bridegroom and incendiary?

May 1934

8

Fleeing the short-haired mad executives,
The subtle useless faces round my home,
Upon the mountains of our fear I climb;
Above, the breakneck scorching rock, the caves;
No col, no water; with excuse concocted,
Soon on a lower alp I fall and pant,
Cooling my face there in the faults that flaunt
The life which they have stolen and perfected.

Climbing with you was easy as a vow;
We reached the top not hungry in the least;
But it was eyes we looked at, not the view;
Saw nothing but ourselves, left-handed, lost:
Returned to shore, the rich interior still
Unknown. Love gave the power, but took the will.

? Summer 1933

9

To lie flat on the back with the knees flexed
And sunshine on the soft receptive belly,
Or face down, the insolent spine relaxed,
No more compelled to cower or to bully,
Is good; and good to see them passing by
Below on the white sidewalk in the heat,
The dog, the lady with parcels, and the boy:
There is the casual life outside the heart.

Yes, we are out of sight and earshot here.
Are you aware what weapon you are loading,
To what that teasing talk is quietly leading?
Our pulses count but do not judge the hour.
Who are you with, from whom you turn away,
At whom you dare not look? Do you know why?

? 1933

10

Dear to me now and longer than a summer,
Not like an ugly cousin starved for love
Or prisoned in the tower of a stammer,
Through sharpened senses peer into my life
With insight and loathing; but sigh and sign
Interpret simply like an animal
That finds the fenced-in pasture very green,
No hint of malice in the trainer's call.

Elsewhere these hands have hurt, these lips betrayed,
This will has quarrelled under different names,
The proofs of love have had to be destroyed
Or lost their whole assurance many times.
See in my eyes the look you look to see;
I may be false but O be true to me.

? 1933

11

A shilling life will give you all the facts:
How Father beat him, how he ran away,
What were the struggles of his youth, what acts
Made him the greatest figure of his day:
Of how he fought, fished, hunted, worked all night,
Though giddy, climbed new mountains; named a sea:
Some of the last researchers even write
Love made him weep his pints like you and me.

With all his honours on, he sighed for one
Who, say astonished critics, lived at home;
Did little jobs about the house with skill
And nothing else; could whistle; would sit still
Or potter round the garden; answered some
Of his long marvellous letters but kept none.

? 1934

12

Love had him fast, but though he fought for breath
He struggled only to possess Another,
The snare forgotten in the little death;
Till You, the seed, to which he was a mother,
That never heard of Love, through Love was free,
While he within his arms a world was holding,
To take the all-night journey under sea,
Work west and northward, set up building.

Cities and years constricted to your scope,
All sorrow simplified, though almost all
Shall be as subtle when you are as tall:
Yet clearly in that 'almost' all his hope
That hopeful falsehood cannot stem with love
The flood on which all move and wish to move.

? Summer 1933

XIX

To settle in this village of the heart,
My darling, can you bear it? True, the hall
With its yews and famous dovecote is still there
Just as in childhood, but the grand old couple
Who loved us all so equally are dead;
And now it is a licensed house for tourists,
None too particular. One of the new
Trunk roads passes the very door already,
And the thin cafés spring up over night.
The sham ornamentation, the strident swimming pool,
The identical and townee smartness,
Will you really see as home, and not depend
For comfort on the chance, the shy encounter
With the irresponsible beauty of the stranger?
O can you see precisely in our gaucheness
The neighbour's strongest wish, to serve and love?

May 1934

XX

Our hunting fathers told the story
    Of the sadness of the creatures,
Pitied the limits and the lack
    Set in their finished features;
Saw in the lion's intolerant look,
Behind the quarry's dying glare,
Love raging for the personal glory
    That reason's gift would add,
The liberal appetite and power,
    The rightness of a god.

Who nurtured in that fine tradition
    Predicted the result,
Guessed love by nature suited to
    The intricate ways of guilt?
That human ligaments could so
His southern gestures modify,
And make it his mature ambition
    To think no thought but ours,
To hunger, work illegally,
    And be anonymous?

? May 1934

XXI

May with its light behaving
Stirs vessel, eye, and limb;
The singular and sad
Are willing to recover,
And to the swan-delighting river
The careless picnics come,
The living white and red.

The dead remote and hooded
In their enclosures rest; but we
From the vague woods have broken,
Forests where children meet
And the white angel-vampires flit;
We stand with shaded eye,
The dangerous apple taken.

The real world lies before us;
Animal motions of the young,
The common wish for death,
The pleasured and the haunted;
The dying master sinks tormented
In the admirers' ring,
The unjust walk the earth.

And love that makes impatient
The tortoise and the roe, and lays
The blonde beside the dark,
Urges upon our blood,
Before the evil and the good
How insufficient is
The endearment and the look.

1934

XXII

Easily, my dear, you move, easily your head
And easily as through the leaves of a photograph album I'm led
Through the night's delights and the day's impressions,
Past the tall tenements and the trees in the wood;
Though sombre the sixteen skies of Europe
       And the Danube flood.

Looking and loving our behaviours pass
The stones, the steels and the polished glass;
Lucky to Love the new pansy railway,
The sterile farms where his looks are fed,
And in the policed unlucky city
       Lucky his bed.

He from these lands of terrifying mottoes
Makes worlds as innocent as Beatrix Potter's;
Through bankrupt countries where they mend the roads
Along the endless plains his will is
Intent as a collector to pursue
      His greens and lilies.

Easy for him to find in your face
The pool of silence and the tower of grace,
To conjure a camera into a wishing rose;
Simple to excite in the air from a glance
The horses, the fountains, the sidedrum, the trombone
      And the dance, the dance.

Summoned by such a music from our time,
Such images to audience come
As vanity cannot dispel nor bless:
Hunger and love in their variations
Grouped invalids watching the flight of the birds
      And single assassins.

Ten thousand of the desperate marching by
Five feet, six feet, seven feet high:
Hitler and Mussolini in their wooing poses
Churchill acknowledging the voters' greeting
Roosevelt at the microphone, Van der Lubbe laughing
      And our first meeting.

But love, except at our proposal,
Will do no trick at his disposal;
Without opinions of his own, performs
The programme that we think of merit,
And through our private stuff must work
      His public spirit.

Certain it became while we were still incomplete
There were certain prizes for which we would never compete;
A choice was killed by every childish illness,
The boiling tears among the hothouse plants,
The rigid promise fractured in the garden,
      And the long aunts.

And every day there bolted from the field
Desires to which we could not yield;
Fewer and clearer grew the plans,
Schemes for a life and sketches for a hatred,
And early among my interesting scrawls
      Appeared your portrait.

You stand now before me, flesh and bone
These ghosts would like to make their own.
Are they your choices? O, be deaf
When hatred would proffer her immediate pleasure,
And glory swap her fascinating rubbish
        For your one treasure.

Be deaf too, standing uncertain now,
A pine tree shadow across your brow,
To what I hear and wish I did not:
The voice of love saying lightly, brightly—
'Be Lubbe, Be Hitler, but be my good
        Daily, nightly.'

The power that corrupts, that power to excess
The beautiful quite naturally possess:
To them the fathers and the children turn:
And all who long for their destruction,
The arrogant and self-insulted, wait
        The looked instruction.

Shall idleness ring then your eyes like the pest?
O will you unnoticed and mildly like the rest,
Will you join the lost in their sneering circles,
Forfeit the beautiful interest and fall
Where the engaging face is the face of the betrayer,
        And the pang is all?

Wind shakes the tree; the mountains darken;
And the heart repeats though we would not hearken:
'Yours is the choice, to whom the gods awarded
The language of learning and the language of love,
Crooked to move as a moneybug or a cancer
        Or straight as a dove.'

November 1934

XXIII

O for doors to be open and an invite with gilded edges
To dine with Lord Lobcock and Count Asthma on the platinum
                                                benches,
With the somersaults and fireworks, the roast and the smacking
                                                kisses—
        Cried the six cripples to the silent statue,
        The six beggared cripples.

And Garbo's and Cleopatra's wits to go astraying,
In a feather ocean with me to go fishing and playing
Still jolly when the cock has burst himself with crowing—
        Cried the six cripples to the silent statue,
        The six beggared cripples.

And to stand on green turf among the craning yellow faces,
Dependent on the chestnut, the sable, and Arabian horses,
And me with a magic crystal to foresee their places—
     Cried the six cripples to the silent statue,
     The six beggared cripples.

And this square to be a deck, and these pigeons sails to rig
And to follow the delicious breeze like a tantony pig
To the shaded feverless islands where the melons are big—
     Cried the six cripples to the silent statue,
     The six beggared cripples.

And these shops to be turned to tulips in a garden bed,
And me with my stick to thrash each merchant dead
As he pokes from a flower his bald and wicked head—
     Cried the six cripples to the silent statue,
     The six beggared cripples.

And a hole in the bottom of heaven, and Peter and Paul
And each smug surprised saint like parachutes to fall,
And every one-legged beggar to have no legs at all—
     Cried the six cripples to the silent statue,
     The six beggared cripples.

? Spring 1935

XXIV

(TO CHRISTOPHER ISHERWOOD)

August for the people and their favourite islands.
Daily the steamers sidle up to meet
The effusive welcome of the pier, and soon
The luxuriant life of the steep stone valleys,
The sallow oval faces of the city
Begot in passion or good-natured habit,
Are caught by waiting coaches, or laid bare
Beside the undiscriminating sea.

Lulled by the light they live their dreams of freedom;
May climb the old road twisting to the moors,
Play leap-frog, enter cafés, wear
The tigerish blazer and the dove-like shoe.
The yachts upon the little lake are theirs,
The gulls ask for them, and to them the band
Makes its tremendous statements; they control
The complicated apparatus of amusement.

All types that can intrigue the writer's fancy,
Or sensuality approves, are here.
And I, each meal-time with the families,
The animal brother and his serious sister,
Or after breakfast on the urned steps watching
The defeated and disfigured marching by,
Have thought of you, Christopher, and wished beside me
Your squat spruce body and enormous head.

Nine years ago, upon that southern island
Where the wild Tennyson became a fossil,
Half-boys, we spoke of books and praised
The acid and austere, behind us only
The stuccoed suburb and expensive school.
Scented our turf, the distant baying
Nice decoration to the artist's wish;
Yet fast the deer was flying through the wood.

Our hopes were set still on the spies' career,
Prizing the glasses and the old felt hat,
And all the secrets we discovered were
Extraordinary and false; for this one coughed
And it was gasworks coke, and that one laughed
And it was snow in bedrooms; many wore wigs,
The coastguard signalled messages of love,
The enemy were sighted from the Norman tower.

Five summers pass and now we watch
The Baltic from a balcony: the word is love.
Surely one fearless kiss would cure
The million fevers, a stroking brush
The insensitive refuse from the burning core.
Was there a dragon who had closed the works
While the starved city fed it with the Jews?
Then love would tame it with his trainer's look.

Pardon the studied taste that could refuse
The golf-house quick one and the rector's tea;
Pardon the nerves the thrushes could not soothe,
Yet answered promptly the no-subtler lure
To private joking in a panelled room,
The solitary vitality of tramps and madmen;
Believed the whisper in the double bed:
Pardon for these and every flabby fancy.

For now the moulding images of growth
That made our interest and us, are gone.
Louder to-day the wireless roars
Its warnings and its lies, and it's impossible
Among the well-shaped cosily to flit,
Or longer to desire about our lives

The beautiful loneliness of the banks, or find
The stoves and resignation of the frozen plains.

The close-set eyes of mother's boy
Saw nothing to be done; we look again:
See Scandal praying with her sharp knees up,
And Virtue stood at Weeping Cross,
The green thumb to the ledger knuckled down,
And Courage to his leaking ship appointed,
Slim Truth dismissed without a character,
And gaga Falsehood highly recommended.

Greed showing shamelessly her naked money,
And all Love's wondering eloquence debased
To a collector's slang, Smartness in furs,
And Beauty scratching miserably for food,
Honour self-sacrificed for Calculation,
And Reason stoned by Mediocrity,
Freedom by Power shockingly maltreated,
And Justice exiled till Saint Geoffrey's Day.

So in this hour of crisis and dismay,
What better than your strict and adult pen
Can warn us from the colours and the consolations,
The showy arid works, reveal
The squalid shadow of academy and garden,
Make action urgent and its nature clear?
Who give us nearer insight to resist
The expanding fear, the savaging disaster?

This then my birthday wish for you, as now
From the narrow window of my fourth-floor room
I smoke into the night, and watch reflections
Stretch in the harbour. In the houses
The little pianos are closed, and a clock strikes.
And all sway forward on the dangerous flood
Of history, that never sleeps or dies,
And, held one moment, burns the hand.

August 1935

XXV

Look, stranger, at this island now
The leaping light for your delight discovers,
Stand stable here
And silent be,
That through the channels of the ear
May wander like a river
The swaying sound of the sea.

Here at the small field's ending pause
Where the chalk wall falls to the foam, and its tall ledges
Oppose the pluck
And knock of the tide,
And the shingle scrambles after the suck-
ing surf, and the gull lodges
A moment on its sheer side.

Far off like floating seeds the ships
Diverge on urgent voluntary errands;
And the full view
Indeed may enter
And move in memory as now these clouds do,
That pass the harbour mirror
And all the summer through the water saunter.

November 1935

XXVI · The Creatures

They are our past and our future: the poles between which our desire
unceasingly is discharged.

A desire in which love and hatred so perfectly oppose themselves that
we cannot voluntarily move; but await the extraordinary
compulsion of the deluge and the earthquake.

Their affections and indifferences have been a guide to all reformers
and tyrants.

Their appearances amid our dreams of machinery have brought a
vision of nude and fabulous epochs.

O Pride so hostile to our Charity.

But what their pride has retained, we may by charity more generously
recover.

? February 1936

XXVII

Let the florid music praise,
    The flute and the trumpet,
Beauty's conquest of your face:
In that land of flesh and bone,
Where from citadels on high
Her imperial standards fly,
    Let the hot sun
    Shine on, shine on.

O but the unloved have had power,
    The weeping and striking,
Always; time will bring their hour:
Their secretive children walk
Through your vigilance of breath
To unpardonable death,
    And my vows break
    Before his look.

February 1936

XXVIII

Now the leaves are falling fast,
Nurse's flowers will not last;
Nurses to the graves are gone,
And the prams go rolling on.

Whispering neighbours, left and right,
Pluck us from the real delight;
And the active hands must freeze
Lonely on the separate knees.

Dead in hundreds at the back
Follow wooden in our track,
Arms raised stiffly to reprove
In false attitudes of love.

Starving through the leafless wood
Trolls run scolding for their food;
And the nightingale is dumb,
And the angel will not come.

Cold, impossible, ahead
Lifts the mountain's lovely head
Whose white waterfall could bless
Travellers in their last distress.

March 1936

XXIX

The soldier loves his rifle,
    The scholar loves his books,
The farmer loves his horses,
    The film star loves her looks.
There's love the whole world over
    Wherever you may be;
Some lose their rest for gay Mae West,
    But you're my cup of tea.

Some talk of Alexander
　　And some of Fred Astaire,
Some like their heroes hairy
　　Some like them debonair,
Some prefer a curate
　　And some an A.D.C.,
Some like a tough to treat 'em rough,
　　But you're my cup of tea.

Some are mad on Airedales
　　And some on Pekinese,
On tabby cats or parrots
　　Or guinea pigs or geese.
There are patients in asylums
　　Who think that they're a tree;
I had an aunt who loved a plant,
　　But you're my cup of tea.

Some have sagging waistlines
　　And some a bulbous nose
And some a floating kidney
　　And some have hammer toes,
Some have tennis elbow
　　And some have housemaid's knee,
And some I know have got B.O.,
　　But you're my cup of tea.

The blackbird loves the earthworm,
　　The adder loves the sun,
The polar bear an iceberg,
　　The elephant a bun,
The trout enjoys the river,
　　The whale enjoys the sea,
And dogs love most an old lamp-post,
　　But you're my cup of tea.

March 1936

XXX

(FOR BENJAMIN BRITTEN)

Underneath the abject willow,
　　Lover, sulk no more;
Act from thought should quickly follow:
　　What is thinking for?
Your unique and moping station
　　Proves you cold;
　　Stand up and fold
Your map of desolation.

Bells that toll across the meadows
　　From the sombre spire,
Toll for those unloving shadows
　　Love does not require.
All that lives may love; why longer
　　Bow to loss
　　With arms across?
Strike and you shall conquer.

Geese in flocks above you flying
　　Their direction know;
Brooks beneath the thin ice flowing
　　To their oceans go;
Coldest love will warm to action,
　　Walk then, come,
　　No longer numb,
Into your satisfaction.

March 1936

XXXI

Dear, though the night is gone,
The dream still haunts to-day
That brought us to a room,
Cavernous, lofty as
A railway terminus,
And crowded in that gloom
Were beds, and we in one
In a far corner lay.

Our whisper woke no clocks,
We kissed and I was glad
At everything you did,
Indifferent to those
Who sat with hostile eyes
In pairs on every bed,
Arms round each other's necks,
Inert and vaguely sad.

O but what worm of guilt
Or what malignant doubt
Am I the victim of;
That you then, unabashed,
Did what I never wished,
Confessed another love;
And I, submissive, felt
Unwanted and went out?

March 1936

XXXII

(FOR BENJAMIN BRITTEN)

Night covers up the rigid land
  And ocean's quaking moor,
And shadows with a tolerant hand
  The ugly and the poor.

The wounded pride for which I weep
  You cannot staunch, nor I
Control the moments of your sleep,
  Nor hear the name you cry,

Whose life is lucky in your eyes,
  And precious is the bed
As to his utter fancy lies
  The dark caressive head.

For each love to its aim is true,
  And all kinds seek their own;
You love your life and I love you,
  So I must lie alone.

O hurry to the fêted spot
  Of your deliberate fall;
For now my dream of you cannot
  Refer to you at all.

March 1936

XXXIII

Fish in the unruffled lakes
The swarming colours wear,
Swans in the winter air
A white perfection have,
And the great lion walks
Through his innocent grove;
Lion, fish, and swan
Act, and are gone
Upon Time's toppling wave.

We till shadowed days are done,
We must weep and sing
Duty's conscious wrong,
The devil in the clock,
The Goodness carefully worn
For atonement or for luck;
We must lose our loves,
On each beast and bird that moves
Turn an envious look.

Sighs for folly said and done
Twist our narrow days;
But I must bless, I must praise
That you, my swan, who have
All gifts that to the swan
Impulsive Nature gave,
The majesty and pride,
Last night should add
Your voluntary love.

March 1936

XXXIV

Stop all the clocks, cut off the telephone,
Prevent the dog from barking with a juicy bone,
Silence the pianos and with muffled drum
Bring out the coffin, let the mourners come.

Let aeroplanes circle moaning overhead
Scribbling on the sky the message He Is Dead,
Put crêpe bows round the white necks of the public doves,
Let the traffic policemen wear black cotton gloves.

He was my North, my South, my East and West,
My working week and my Sunday rest,
My noon, my midnight, my talk, my song;
I thought that love would last for ever: I was wrong.

The stars are not wanted now; put out every one,
Pack up the moon and dismantle the sun,
Pour away the ocean and sweep up the wood;
For nothing now can ever come to any good.

April 1936

XXXV

As it is, plenty;
As it's admitted
The children happy
And the car, the car
That goes so far
And the wife devoted:
To this as it is,
To the work and the banks
Let his thinning hair
And his hauteur
Give thanks, give thanks.

All that was thought
As like as not, is not;
When nothing was enough
But love, but love
And the rough future
Of an intransigent nature
And the betraying smile,
Betraying, but a smile:
That that is not, is not;
Forget, forget.

Let him not cease to praise
Then his spacious days;
Yes, and the success
Let him bless, let him bless:
Let him see in this
The profits larger
And the sins venial,
Lest he see as it is
The loss as major
And final, final.

? April 1936

XXXVI · Casino

Only the hands are living; to the wheel attracted,
Are moved, as deer trek desperately towards a creek
   Through the dust and scrub of the desert, or gently
   As sunflowers turn to the light.

And as the night takes up the cries of feverish children,
The cravings of lions in dens, the loves of dons,
   Gathers them all and remains the night, the
   Great room is full of their prayers.

To the last feast of isolation, self-invited,
They flock, and in the rite of disbelief are joined;
   From numbers all their stars are recreated,
   The enchanted, the world, the sad.

Without, the rivers flow among the wholly living,
Quite near their trysts; and the mountains part them; and
                                                    the bird,
   Deep in the greens and moistures of summer,
   Sings towards their work.

But here no nymph comes naked to the youngest shepherd,
The fountain is deserted, the laurel will not grow;
   The labyrinth is safe but endless, and broken
   Is Ariadne's thread.

As deeper in these hands is grooved their fortune: 'Lucky
Were few, and it is possible that none were loved;
    And what was godlike in this generation
    Was never to be born.'

April 1936

XXXVII

Certainly our city—with the byres of poverty down to
The river's edge, the cathedral, the engines, the dogs;
    Here is the cosmopolitan cooking
    And the light alloys and the glass.

Built by the conscious-stricken, the weapon-making,
By us. The rumours woo and terrify the crowd,
    Woo us. The betrayers thunder at, blackmail
    Us. But where now are They

Who without reproaches shewed us what our vanity has chosen,
Who pursued understanding with patience like a sex, had unlearnt
    Our hatred, and towards the really better
    World had turned their face?

There was Nansen in the north, in the hot south Schweitzer, and
                     the neat man
To their east who ordered Gorki to be electrified;
    There were Freud and Groddeck at their candid studies
    Of the mind and body of man.

Nor was every author both a comforter and a liar;
Lawrence revealed the sensations hidden by shame,
    The sense of guilt was recorded by Kafka,
    There was Proust on the self-regard.

Who knows? The peaked and violent faces are exalted,
The feverish prejudiced lives do not care, and lost
    Their voice in the flutter of bunting, the glittering
    Brass of the great retreat,

And the malice of death. For the wicked card is dealt, and
The sinister tall-hatted botanist stoops at the spring
    With his insignificant phial, and looses
    The plague on the ignorant town.

Under their shadows the pitiful subalterns are sleeping;
The moon is usual; the necessary lovers touch:
    The river is alone and the trampled flower,
    And through years of absolute cold

The planets rush towards Lyra in the lion's charge. Can
Hate so securely bind? Are They dead here? Yes.
      And the wish to wound has the power. And to-morrow
      Comes. It's a world. It's a way.

Spring 1936

Part V

Letter to Lord Byron

PART I

Excuse, my lord, the liberty I take
    In thus addressing you. I know that you
Will pay the price of authorship and make
    The allowances an author has to do.
    A poet's fan-mail will be nothing new.
And then a lord—Good Lord, you must be peppered,
Like Gary Cooper, Coughlin, or Dick Sheppard,

With notes from perfect strangers starting, 'Sir,
    I liked your lyrics, but *Childe Harold's* trash',
'My daughter writes, should I encourage her?'
    Sometimes containing frank demands for cash,
    Sometimes sly hints at a platonic pash,
And sometimes, though I think this rather crude,
The correspondent's photo in the rude.

And as for manuscripts—by every post . . .
    I can't improve on Pope's shrill indignation,
But hope that it will please his spiteful ghost
    To learn the use in culture's propagation
    Of modern methods of communication:
New roads, new rails, new contacts, as we know
From documentaries by the G.P.O.

For since the British Isles went Protestant
    A church confession is too high for most.
But still confession is a human want,
    So Englishmen must make theirs now by post
    And authors hear them over breakfast toast.
For, failing them, there's nothing but the wall
Of public lavatories on which to scrawl.

So if ostensibly I write to you
    To chat about your poetry or mine,
There're many other reasons; though it's true
    That I have, at the age of twenty-nine
    Just read *Don Juan* and I found it fine.
I read it on the boat to Reykjavik
Except when eating or asleep or sick.

The fact is, I'm in Iceland all alone
    —MacKenzie's prints are not unlike the scene—
Ich hab' zu Haus, ein Gra, ein Grammophon.
    Les gosses anglais aiment beaucoup les machines.

Τὸ καλὸν. glubit. che . . . what this may mean
I do not know, but rather like the sound
Of foreign languages like Ezra Pound.

And home is miles away, and miles away
    No matter who, and I am quite alone
And cannot understand what people say,
    But like a dog must guess it by the tone;
    At any language other than my own
I'm no great shakes, and here I've found no tutor
Nor sleeping lexicon to make me cuter.

The thought of writing came to me to-day
    (I like to give these facts of time and space);
The bus was in the desert on its way
    From Möthrudalur to some other place:
    The tears were streaming down my burning face;
I'd caught a heavy cold in Akureyri,
And lunch was late and life looked very dreary.

Professor Housman was I think the first
    To say in print how very stimulating
The little ills by which mankind is cursed,
    The colds, the aches, the pains are to creating;
    Indeed one hardly goes too far in stating
That many a flawless lyric may be due
Not to a lover's broken heart, but 'flu.

But still a proper explanation's lacking;
    Why write to you? I see I must begin
Right at the start when I was at my packing.
    The extra pair of socks, the airtight tin
    Of China tea, the anti-fly were in;
I asked myself what sort of books I'd read
In Iceland, if I ever felt the need.

I can't read Jefferies on the Wiltshire Downs,
    Nor browse on limericks in a smoking-room;
Who would try Trollope in cathedral towns,
    Or Marie Stopes inside his mother's womb?
    Perhaps you feel the same beyond the tomb.
Do the celestial highbrows only care
For works on Clydeside, Fascists, or Mayfair?

In certain quarters I had heard a rumour
    (For all I know the rumour's only silly)
That Icelanders have little sense of humour.
    I knew the country was extremely hilly,
    The climate unreliable and chilly;
So looking round for something light and easy
I pounced on you as warm and civilisé.

There is one other author in my pack:
    For some time I debated which to write to.
Which would least likely send my letter back?
    But I decided that I'd give a fright to
    Jane Austen if I wrote when I'd no right to,
And share in her contempt the dreadful fates
Of Crawford, Musgrove, and of Mr. Yates.

Then she's a novelist. I don't know whether
    You will agree, but novel writing is
A higher art than poetry altogether
    In my opinion, and success implies
    Both finer character and faculties.
Perhaps that's why real novels are as rare
As winter thunder or a polar bear.

The average poet by comparison
    Is unobservant, immature, and lazy.
You must admit, when all is said and done,
    His sense of other people's very hazy,
    His moral judgments are too often crazy,
A slick and easy generalisation
Appeals too well to his imagination.

I must remember, though, that you were dead
    Before the four great Russians lived, who brought
The art of novel writing to a head;
    The Book Society had not been bought.
    But now the art for which Jane Austen fought,
Under the right persuasion bravely warms
And is the most prodigious of the forms.

She was not an unshockable blue-stocking;
    If shades remain the characters they were,
No doubt she still considers you as shocking.
    But tell Jane Austen, that is, if you dare,
    How much her novels are beloved down here.
She wrote them for posterity, she said;
'Twas rash, but by posterity she's read.

You could not shock her more than she shocks me;
    Beside her Joyce seems innocent as grass.
It makes me most uncomfortable to see
    An English spinster of the middle-class
    Describe the amorous effects of 'brass',
Reveal so frankly and with such sobriety
The economic basis of society.

So it is you who is to get this letter.
    The experiment may not be a success.
There're many others who could do it better,
    But I shall not enjoy myself the less.
    Shaw of the Air Force said that happiness
Comes in absorption: he was right, I know it;
Even in scribbling to a long-dead poet.

Every exciting letter has enclosures,
    And so shall this—a bunch of photographs,
Some out of focus, some with wrong exposures,
    Press cuttings, gossip, maps, statistics, graphs;
    I don't intend to do the thing by halves.
I'm going to be very up to date indeed.
It is a collage that you're going to read.

I want a form that's large enough to swim in,
    And talk on any subject that I choose,
From natural scenery to men and women,
    Myself, the arts, the European news:
    And since she's on a holiday, my Muse
Is out to please, find everything delightful
And only now and then be mildly spiteful.

Ottava Rima would, I know, be proper,
    The proper instrument on which to pay
My compliments, but I should come a cropper;
    Rhyme-royal's difficult enough to play.
    But if no classics as in Chaucer's day,
At least my modern pieces shall be cheery
Like English bishops on the Quantum Theory.

Light verse, poor girl, is under a sad weather;
    Except by Milne and persons of that kind
She's treated as démodé altogether.
    It's strange and very unjust to my mind
    Her brief appearances should be confined,
Apart from Belloc's *Cautionary Tales*,
To the more bourgeois periodicals.

'The fascination of what's difficult',
    The wish to do what one's not done before,
Is, I hope, proper to Quicunque Vult,
    The proper card to show at Heaven's door.
    'Gerettet' not 'Gerichtet' be the Law,
Et cetera, et cetera. O curse,
That is the flattest line in English verse.

Parnassus after all is not a mountain,
    Reserved for A.1. climbers such as you;
It's got a park, it's got a public fountain.
        The most I ask is leave to share a pew
        With Bradford or with Cottam, that will do:
To pasture my few silly sheep with Dyer
And picnic on the lower slopes with Prior.

A publisher's an author's greatest friend,
    A generous uncle, or he ought to be.
(I'm sure we hope it pays him in the end.)
        I love my publishers and they love me,
        At least they paid a very handsome fee
To send me here. I've never heard a grouse
Either from Russell Square or Random House.

But now I've got uncomfortable suspicions,
    I'm going to put their patience out of joint.
Though it's in keeping with the best traditions
        For Travel Books to wander from the point
        (There is no other rhyme except anoint),
They well may charge me with—I've no defences—
Obtaining money under false pretences.

I know I've not the least chance of survival
    Beside the major travellers of the day.
I am no Lawrence who, on his arrival,
        Sat down and typed out all he had to say;
        I am not even Ernest Hemingway.
I shall not run to a two-bob edition,
So just won't enter for the competition.

And even here the steps I flounder in
    Were worn by most distinguished boots of old.
Dasent and Morris and Lord Dufferin,
        Hooker and men of that heroic mould
        Welcome me icily into the fold;
I'm not like Peter Fleming an Etonian,
But, if I'm Judas, I'm an old Oxonian.

The Haig Thomases are at Myvatn now,
    At Hvitarvatn and at Vatnajökull
Cambridge research goes on, I don't know how:
        The shades of Asquith and of Auden Skökull
        Turn in their coffins a three-quarter circle
To see their son, upon whose help they reckoned,
Being as frivolous as Charles the Second.

So this, my opening chapter, has to stop
    With humbly begging everybody's pardon.
From Faber first in case the book's a flop,
        Then from the critics lest they should be hard on
        The author when he leads them up the garden,
Last from the general public he must beg
Permission now and then to pull their leg.

July 1936

PART II

I'm writing this in pencil on my knee,
    Using my other hand to stop me yawning,
Upon a primitive, unsheltered quay
        In the small hours of a Wednesday morning.
        I cannot add the summer day is dawning;
In Seythisfjördur every schoolboy knows
That daylight in the summer never goes.

To get to sleep in latitudes called upper
    Is difficult at first for Englishmen.
It's like being sent to bed before your supper
        For playing darts with father's fountain-pen,
        Or like returning after orgies, when
Your breath's like luggage and you realise
You've been more confidential than was wise.

I've done my duty, taken many notes
    Upon the almost total lack of greenery,
The roads, the illegitimates, the goats:
        To use a rhyme of yours, there's handsome scenery
        But little agricultural machinery;
And with the help of Sunlight Soap the Geysir
Affords to visitors le plus grand plaisir.

The North, though, never was your cup of tea;
    'Moral' you thought it so you kept away.
And what I'm sure you're wanting now from me
        Is news about the England of the day,
        What sort of things La Jeunesse do and say.
Is Brighton still as proud of her pavilion,
And is it safe for girls to travel pillion?

I'll clear my throat and take a Rover's breath
    And skip a century of hope and sin—
For far too much has happened since your death.
        Crying went out and the cold bath came in,
        With drains, bananas, bicycles, and tin,
And Europe saw from Ireland to Albania
The Gothic revival and the Railway Mania.

We're entering now the Eotechnic Phase
Thanks to the Grid and all those new alloys;
That is, at least, what Lewis Mumford says.
A world of Aertex underwear for boys,
Huge plate-glass windows, walls absorbing noise,
Where the smoke nuisance is utterly abated
And all the furniture is chromium-plated.

Well, you might think so if you went to Surrey
And stayed for week-ends with the well-to-do,
Your car too fast, too personal your worry
To look too closely at the wheeling view.
But in the north it simply isn't true.
To those who live in Warrington or Wigan,
It's not a white lie, it's a whacking big 'un.

There on the old historic battlefield,
The cold ferocity of human wills,
The scars of struggle are as yet unhealed;
Slattern the tenements on sombre hills,
And gaunt in valleys the square-windowed mills
That, since the Georgian house, in my conjecture
Remain our finest native architecture.

On economic, health, or moral grounds
It hasn't got the least excuse to show;
No more than chamber pots or otter hounds:
But let me say before it has to go,
It's the most lovely country that I know;
Clearer than Scafell Pike, my heart has stamped on
The view from Birmingham to Wolverhampton.

Long, long ago, when I was only four,
Going towards my grandmother, the line
Passed through a coal-field. From the corridor
I watched it pass with envy, thought 'How fine!
Oh how I wish that situation mine.'
Tramlines and slagheaps, pieces of machinery,
That was, and still is, my ideal scenery.

Hail to the New World! Hail to those who'll love
Its antiseptic objects, feel at home.
Lovers will gaze at an electric stove,
Another poésie de départ come
Centred round bus-stops or the aerodrome.
But give me still, to stir imagination
The chiaroscuro of the railway station.

Preserve me from the Shape of Things to Be;
    The high-grade posters at the public meeting,
The influence of Art on Industry,
    The cinemas with perfect taste in seating;
    Preserve me, above all, from central heating.
It may be D. H. Lawrence hocus-pocus,
But I prefer a room that's got a focus.

But you want facts, not sighs. I'll do my best
    To give a few; you can't expect them all.
To start with, on the whole we're better dressed;
    For chic the difference to-day is small
    Of barmaid from my lady at the Hall.
It's sad to spoil this democratic vision
With millions suffering from malnutrition.

Again, our age is highly educated;
    There is no lie our children cannot read,
And as MacDonald might so well have stated
    We're growing up and up and up indeed.
    Advertisements can teach us all we need;
And death is better, as the millions know,
Than dandruff, night-starvation, or B.O.

We've always had a penchant for field sports,
    But what do you think has grown up in our towns?
A passion for the open air and shorts;
    The sun is one of our emotive nouns.
    Go down by chara' to the Sussex Downs,
Watch the manœuvres of the week-end hikers
Massed on parade with Kodaks or with Leicas.

These movements signify our age-long rule
    Of insularity has lost its powers;
The cult of salads and the swimming pool
    Comes from a climate sunnier than ours,
    And lands which never heard of licensed hours.
The south of England before very long
Will look no different from the Continong.

You lived and moved among the best society
    And so could introduce your hero to it
Without the slightest tremor of anxiety;
    Because he was your hero and you knew it,
    He'd know instinctively what's done, and do it.
He'd find our day more difficult than yours
For Industry has mixed the social drawers.

We've grown, you see, a lot more democratic,
    And Fortune's ladder is for all to climb;
Carnegie on this point was most emphatic.
    A humble grandfather is not a crime,
    At least, if father made enough in time!
To-day, thank God, we've got no snobbish feeling
Against the more efficient modes of stealing.

The porter at the Carlton is my brother,
    He'll wish me a good evening if I pay,
For tips and men are equal to each other.
    I'm sure that *Vogue* would be the first to say
    Que le Beau Monde is socialist to-day;
And many a bandit, not so gently born
Kills vermin every winter with the Quorn.

Adventurers, though, must take things as they find them
    And look for pickings where the pickings are.
The drives of love and hunger are behind them,
    They can't afford to be particular:
    And those who like good cooking and a car,
A certain kind of costume or of face,
Must seek them in a certain kind of place.

Don Juan was a mixer and no doubt
    Would find this century as good as any
For getting hostesses to ask him out,
    And mistresses that need not cost a penny.
    Indeed our ways to waste time are so many,
Thanks to technology, a list of these
Would make a longer book than *Ulysses*.

Yes, in the smart set he would know his way
    By second nature with no tips from me.
Tennis and Golf have come in since your day;
    But those who are as good at games as he
    Acquire the back-hand quite instinctively,
Take to the steel-shaft and hole out in one,
Master the books of Ely Culbertson.

I see his face in every magazine.
    'Don Juan at lunch with one of Cochran's ladies.'
'Don Juan with his red setter May MacQueen.'
    'Don Juan, who's just been wintering in Cadiz,
    Caught at the wheel of his maroon Mercedes.'
'Don Juan at Croydon Aerodrome.' 'Don Juan
Snapped in the paddock with the Agha Khan.'

But if in highbrow circles he would sally
        It's just as well to warn him there's no stain on
Picasso, all-in-wrestling, or the Ballet.
        Sibelius is the man. To get a pain on
        Listening to Elgar is a sine qua non.
A second-hand acquaintance of Pareto's
Ranks higher than an intimate of Plato's.

The vogue for Black Mass and the cult of devils
        Has sunk. The Good, the Beautiful, the True
Still fluctuate about the lower levels.
        Joyces are firm and there there's nothing new.
        Eliots have hardened just a point or two.
Hopkins are brisk, thanks to some recent boosts.
There's been some further weakening in Prousts.

I'm saying this to tell you who's the rage,
        And not to loose a sneer from my interior.
Because there's snobbery in every age,
        Because some names are loved by the superior,
        It does not follow they're the least inferior:
For all I know the Beatific Vision's
On view at all Surrealist Exhibitions.

Now for the spirit of the people. Here
        I know I'm treading on more dangerous ground:
I know there're many changes in the air,
        But know my data too slight to be sound.
        I know, too, I'm inviting the renowned
Retort of all who love the Status Quo:
'You can't change human nature, don't you know!'

We've still, it's true, the same shape and appearance,
        We haven't changed the way that kissing's done;
The average man still hates all interference,
        Is just as proud still of his new-born son:
        Still, like a hen, he likes his private run,
Scratches for self-esteem, and slyly pecks
A good deal in the neighbourhood of sex.

But he's another man in many ways:
        Ask the cartoonist first, for he knows best.
Where is the John Bull of the good old days,
        The swaggering bully with the clumsy jest?
        His meaty neck has long been laid to rest,
His acres of self-confidence for sale;
He passed away at Ypres and Passchendaele.

Turn to the work of Disney or of Strube;
    There stands our hero in his threadbare seams;
The bowler hat who straphangs in the tube,
    And kicks the tyrant only in his dreams,
    Trading on pathos, dreading all extremes;
The little Mickey with the hidden grudge;
Which is the better, I leave you to judge.

Begot on Hire-Purchase by Insurance,
    Forms at his christening worshipped and adored;
A season ticket schooled him in endurance,
    A tax collector and a waterboard
    Admonished him. In boyhood he was awed
By a matric, and complex apparatuses
Keep his heart conscious of Divine Afflatuses.

'I am like you', he says, 'and you, and you,
    I love my life, I love the home-fires, have
To keep them burning. Heroes never do.
    Heroes are sent by ogres to the grave.
    I may not be courageous, but I save.
I am the one who somehow turns the corner,
I may perhaps be fortunate Jack Horner.

'I am the ogre's private secretary;
    I've felt his stature and his powers, learned
To give his ogreship the raspberry
    Only when his gigantic back is turned.
    One day, who knows, I'll do as I have yearned.
The short man, all his fingers on the door,
With repartee shall send him to the floor.'

One day, which day? O any other day,
    But not to-day. The ogre knows his man.
To kill the ogre—that would take away
    The fear in which his happy dreams began,
    And with his life he'll guard dreams while he can.
Those who would really kill his dream's contentment
He hates with real implacable resentment.

He dreads the ogre, but he dreads yet more
    Those who conceivably might set him free,
Those the cartoonist has no time to draw.
    Without his bondage he'd be all at sea;
    The ogre need but shout 'Security',
To make this man, so lovable, so mild,
As madly cruel as a frightened child.

Byron, thou should'st be living at this hour!
      What would you do, I wonder, if you were?
Britannia's lost prestige and cash and power,
      Her middle classes show some wear and tear,
      We've learned to bomb each other from the air;
I can't imagine what the Duke of Wellington
Would say about the music of Duke Ellington.

Suggestions have been made that the Teutonic
      Führer-Prinzip would have appealed to you
As being the true heir to the Byronic—
      In keeping with your social status too
      (It has its English converts, fit and few),
That you would, hearing honest Oswald's call,
Be gleichgeschaltet in the Albert Hall.

'Lord Byron at the head of his storm-troopers!'
      Nothing, says science, is impossible:
The Pope may quit to join the Oxford Groupers,
      Nuffield may leave one farthing in his Will,
      There may be someone who trusts Baldwin still,
Someone may think that Empire wines are nice,
There may be people who hear Tauber twice.

You liked to be the centre of attention,
      The gay Prince Charming of the fairy story,
Who tamed the Dragon by his intervention.
      In modern warfare, though it's just as gory,
      There isn't any individual glory;
The Prince must be anonymous, observant,
A kind of lab-boy, or a civil servant.

You never were an Isolationist;
      Injustice you had always hatred for,
And we can hardly blame you, if you missed
      Injustice just outside your lordship's door:
      Nearer than Greece were cotton and the poor.
To-day you might have seen them, might indeed
Have walked in the United Front with Gide,

Against the ogre, dragon, what you will;
      His many shapes and names all turn us pale,
For he's immortal, and to-day he still
      Swinges the horror of his scaly tail.
      Sometimes he seems to sleep, but will not fail
In every age to rear up to defend
Each dying force of history to the end.

Milton beheld him on the English throne,
　　And Bunyan sitting in the Papal chair;
The hermits fought him in their caves alone,
　　At the first Empire he was also there,
　　Dangling his Pax Romana in the air:
He comes in dreams at puberty to man,
To scare him back to childhood if he can.

Banker or landlord, booking-clerk or Pope,
　　Whenever he's lost faith in choice and thought,
When a man sees the future without hope,
　　Whenever he endorses Hobbes' report
　　'The life of man is nasty, brutish, short',
The dragon rises from his garden border
And promises to set up law and order.

He that in Athens murdered Socrates,
　　And Plato then seduced, prepares to make
A desolation and to call it peace
　　To-day for dying magnates, for the sake
　　Of generals who can scarcely keep awake,
And for that doughy mass in great and small
That doesn't want to stir itself at all.

Forgive me for inflicting all this on you,
　　For asking you to hold the baby for us;
It's easy to forget that where you've gone, you
　　May only want to chat with Set and Horus,
　　Bored to extinction with our earthly chorus:
Perhaps it sounds to you like a trunk-call,
Urgent, it seems, but quite inaudible.

Yet though the choice of what is to be done
　　Remains with the alive, the rigid nation
Is supple still within the breathing one;
　　Its sentinels yet keep their sleepless station,
　　And every man in every generation,
Tossing in his dilemma on his bed,
Cries to the shadows of the noble dead.

We're out at sea now, and I wish we weren't;
　　The sea is rough, I don't care if it's blue;
I'd like to have a quick one, but I daren't.
　　And I must interrupt this screed to you,
　　For I've some other little jobs to do;
I must write home or mother will be vexed,
So this must be continued in our next.

August 1936

PART III

My last remarks were sent you from a boat.
    I'm back on shore now in a warm bed-sitter,
And several friends have joined me since I wrote;
    So though the weather out of doors is bitter,
    I feel a great deal cheerier and fitter.
A party from a public school, a poet,
Have set a rapid pace, and make me go it.

We're starting soon on a big expedition
    Into the desert, which I'm sure is corking:
Many would like to be in my position.
    I only hope there won't be too much walking.
    Now let me see, where was I? We were talking
Of Social Questions when I had to stop;
I think it's time now for a little shop.

In setting up my brass-plate as a critic,
    I make no claim to certain diagnosis,
I'm more intuitive than analytic,
    I offer thought in homoeopathic doses
    (But someone may get better in the process).
I don't pretend to reasoning like Pritchard's
Or the logomachy of I. A. Richards.

I like your muse because she's gay and witty,
    Because she's neither prostitute nor frump,
The daughter of a European city,
    And country houses long before the slump;
    I like her voice that does not make me jump:
And you I find sympatisch, a good townee,
Neither a preacher, ninny, bore, nor Brownie.

A poet, swimmer, peer, and man of action,
    —It beats Roy Campbell's record by a mile—
You offer every possible attraction.
    By looking into your poetic style
    And love-life on the chance that both were vile,
Several have earned a decent livelihood,
Whose lives were uncreative but were good.

You've had your packet from the critics, though:
    They grant you warmth of heart, but at your head
Their moral and aesthetic brickbats throw.
    A 'vulgar genius' so George Eliot said,
    Which doesn't matter as George Eliot's dead,
But T. S. Eliot, I am sad to find,
Damns you with: 'an uninteresting mind'.

A statement which I must say I'm ashamed at;
    A poet must be judged by his intention,
And serious thought you never said you aimed at.
    I think a serious critic ought to mention
    That one verse style was really your invention,
A style whose meaning does not need a spanner,
You are the master of the airy manner.

By all means let us touch our humble caps to
    La poésie pure, the epic narrative;
But comedy shall get its round of claps, too.
    According to his powers, each may give;
    Only on varied diet can we live.
The pious fable and the dirty story
Share in the total literary glory.

There's every mode of singing robe in stock,
    From Shakespeare's gorgeous fur coat, Spenser's muff,
Or Dryden's lounge suit to my cotton frock,
    And Wordsworth's Harris tweed with leathern cuff.
    Firbank, I think, wore just a just-enough;
I fancy Whitman in a reach-me-down,
But you, like Sherlock, in a dressing-gown.

I'm also glad to find I've your authority
    For finding Wordsworth a most bleak old bore,
Though I'm afraid we're in a sad minority
    For every year his followers get more,
    Their number must have doubled since the war.
They come in train-loads to the Lakes, and swarms
Of pupil-teachers study him in *Storms*.

'I hate a pupil-teacher' Milton said,
    Who also hated bureaucratic fools;
Milton may thank his stars that he is dead,
    Although he's learnt by heart in public schools,
    Along with Wordsworth and the list of rules;
For many a don while looking down his nose
Calls Pope and Dryden classics of our prose.

And new plants flower from that old potato.
    They thrive best in a poor industrial soil,
Are hardier crossed with Rousseaus or a Plato;
    Their cultivation is an easy toil.
    William, to change the metaphor, struck oil;
His well seems inexhaustible, a gusher
That saves old England from the fate of Russia.

The mountain-snob is a Wordsworthian fruit;
    He tears his clothes and doesn't shave his chin,
He wears a very pretty little boot,
    He chooses the least comfortable inn;
    A mountain railway is a deadly sin;
His strength, of course, is as the strength of ten men,
He calls all those who live in cities wen-men.

I'm not a spoil-sport, I would never wish
    To interfere with anybody's pleasures;
By all means climb, or hunt, or even fish,
    All human hearts have ugly little treasures;
    But think it time to take repressive measures
When someone says, adopting the 'I know' line,
The Good Life is confined above the snow-line.

Besides, I'm very fond of mountains, too;
    I like to travel through them in a car;
I like a house that's got a sweeping view;
    I like to walk, but not to walk too far.
    I also like green plains where cattle are,
And trees and rivers, and shall always quarrel
With those who think that rivers are immoral.

Not that my private quarrel gives quietus to
    The interesting question that it raises;
Impartial thought will give a proper status to
    This interest in waterfalls and daisies,
    Excessive love for the non-human faces,
That lives in hearts from Golders Green to Teddington;
It's all bound up with Einstein, Jeans, and Eddington.

It is a commonplace that's hardly worth
    A poet's while to make profound or terse,
That now the sun does not go round the earth,
    That man's no centre of the universe;
    And working in an office makes it worse.
The humblest is acquiring with facility
A Universal-Complex sensibility.

For now we've learnt we mustn't be so bumptious
    We find the stars are one big family,
And send out invitations for a scrumptious
    Simple, old-fashioned, jolly romp with tea
    To any natural objects we can see.
We can't, of course, invite a Jew or Red
But birds and nebulae will do instead.

The Higher Mind's outgrowing the Barbarian,
    It's hardly thought hygienic now to kiss;
The world is surely turning vegetarian;
    And as it grows too sensitive for this,
    It won't be long before we find there is
A Society of Everybody's Aunts
For the Prevention of Cruelty to Plants.

I dread this like the dentist, rather more so:
    To me Art's subject is the human clay,
And landscape but a background to a torso;
    All Cézanne's apples I would give away
    For one small Goya or a Daumier.
I'll never grant a more than minor beauty
To pudge or pilewort, petty-chap or pooty.

Art, if it doesn't start there, at least ends,
    Whether aesthetics like the thought or not,
In an attempt to entertain our friends;
    And our first problem is to realise what
    Peculiar friends the modern artist's got;
It's possible a little dose of history
May help us in unravelling this mystery.

At the Beginning I shall *not* begin,
    Not with the scratches in the ancient caves;
Heard only knows the latest bulletin
    About the finds in the Egyptian graves;
    I'll skip the war-dance of the Indian braves;
Since, for the purposes I have in view,
The English eighteenth century will do.

We find two arts in the Augustan age:
    One quick and graceful, and by no means holy,
Relying on his lordship's patronage;
    The other pious, sober, moving slowly,
    Appealing mainly to the poor and lowly.
So Isaac Watts and Pope, each forced his entry
To lower middle class and landed gentry.

Two arts as different as Jews and Turks,
    Each serving aspects of the Reformation,
Luther's division into faith and works:
    The God of the unique imagination,
    A friend of those who have to know their station;
And the Great Architect, the Engineer
Who keeps the mighty in their higher sphere.

The important point to notice, though, is this:
    Each poet knew for whom he had to write,
Because their life was still the same as his.
    As long as art remains a parasite,
    On any class of persons it's alright;
The only thing it must be is attendant,
The only thing it mustn't, independent.

But artists, though, are human; and for man
    To be a scivvy is not nice at all:
So everyone will do the best he can
    To get a patch of ground which he can call
    His own. He doesn't really care how small,
So long as he can style himself the master:
Unluckily for art, it's a disaster.

To be a highbrow is the natural state:
    To have a special interest of one's own,
Rock gardens, marrows, pigeons, silver plate,
    Collecting butterflies or bits of stone;
    And then to have a circle where one's known
Of hobbyists and rivals to discuss
With expert knowledge what appeals to us.

But to the artist this is quite forbidden:
    On this point he must differ from the crowd,
And, like a secret agent, must keep hidden
    His passion for his shop. However proud,
    And rightly, of his trade, he's not allowed
To etch his face with his professional creases,
Or die from occupational diseases.

Until the great Industrial Revolution
    The artist had to earn his livelihood:
However much he hated the intrusion
    Of patron's taste or public's fickle mood,
    He had to please or go without his food;
He had to keep his technique to himself
Or find no joint upon his larder shelf.

But Savoury and Newcomen and Watt
    And all those names that I was told to get up
In history preparation and forgot,
    A new class of creative artist set up,
    On whom the pressure of demand was let up:
He sang and painted and drew dividends,
But lost responsibilities and friends.

Those most affected were the very best:
        Those with originality of vision,
Those whose technique was better than the rest,
        Jumped at the chance of a secure position
        With freedom from the bad old hack tradition,
Leave to be sole judges of the artist's brandy,
Be Shelley, or Childe Harold, or the Dandy.

So started what I'll call the Poet's Party:
        (Most of the guests were painters, never mind)—
The first few hours the atmosphere was hearty,
        With fireworks, fun, and games and every kind;
        All were enjoying it, no one was blind;
Brilliant the speeches improvised, the dances,
And brilliant, too, the technical advances.

How nice at first to watch the passers-by
        Out of the upper window, and to say
'How glad I am that though I have to die
        Like all those cattle, I'm less base than they!'
        How we all roared when Baudelaire went fey.
'See this cigar', he said, 'it's Baudelaire's.
What happens to perception? Ah, who cares?'

To-day, alas, that happy crowded floor
        Looks very different: many are in tears:
Some have retired to bed and locked the door;
        And some swing madly from the chandeliers;
        Some have passed out entirely in the rears;
Some have been sick in corners; the sobering few
Are trying hard to think of something new.

I've made it seem the artist's silly fault,
        In which case why these sentimental sobs?
In fact, of course, the whole tureen was salt.
        The soup was full of little bits of snobs.
        The common clay and the uncommon nobs
Were far too busy making piles or starving
To look at pictures, poetry, or carving.

I've simplified the facts to be emphatic,
        Playing Macaulay's favourite little trick
Of lighting that's contrasted and dramatic;
        Because it's true Art feels a trifle sick,
        You mustn't think the old girl's lost her kick.
And those, besides, who feel most like a sewer
Belong to Painting not to Literature.

You know the terror that for poets lurks
  Beyond the ferry when to Minos brought.
Poets must utter their Collected Works,
  Including Juvenilia. So I thought
  That you might warn him. Yes, I think you ought,
In case, when my turn comes, he shall cry 'Atta boys,
Off with his bags, he's crazy as a hatter, boys!'

The clock is striking and it's time for lunch;
  We start at four. The weather's none too bright.
Some of the party look as pleased as Punch.
  We shall be travelling, as they call it, light;
  We shall be sleeping in a tent to-night.
You know what Baden-Powell's taught us, don't you,
Ora pro nobis, please, this evening, won't you?

            August 1936

PART IV

A ship again; this time the *Dettifoss*.
  Grierson can buy it; all the sea I mean,
All this Atlantic that we've now to cross
  Heading for England's pleasant pastures green.
  Pro tem I've done with the Icelandic scene;
I watch the hills receding in the distance,
I hear the thudding of an engine's pistons.

I hope I'm better, wiser for the trip:
  I've had the benefit of northern breezes,
The open road and good companionship,
  I've seen some very pretty little pieces;
  And though the luck was almost all MacNeice's,
I've spent some jolly evenings playing rummy—
No one can talk at Bridge, unless it's Dummy.

I've learnt to ride, at least to ride a pony,
  Taken a lot of healthy exercise,
On barren mountains and in valleys stony,
  I've tasted a hot spring (a taste was wise),
  And foods a man remembers till he dies.
All things considered, I consider Iceland,
Apart from Reykjavik, a very nice land.

The part can stand as symbol for the whole:
  So ruminating in these last few weeks,
I see the map of all my youth unroll,
  The mental mountains and the psychic creeks,
  The towns of which the master never speaks,
The various parishes and what they voted for,
The colonies, their size, and what they're noted for.

A child may ask when our strange epoch passes,
    During a history lesson, 'Please, sir, what's
An intellectual of the middle classes?
    Is he a maker of ceramic pots
    Or does he choose his king by drawing lots?'
What follows now may set him on the rail,
A plain, perhaps a cautionary, tale.

My passport says I'm five feet and eleven,
    With hazel eyes and fair (it's tow-like) hair,
That I was born in York in 1907,
    With no distinctive markings anywhere.
    Which isn't quite correct. Conspicuous there
On my right cheek appears a large brown mole;
I think I don't dislike it on the whole.

My name occurs in several of the sagas,
    Is common over Iceland still. Down under
Where Das Volk order sausages and lagers
    I ought to be the prize, the living wonder,
    The really pure from any Rassenschänder,
In fact I am the great big white barbarian,
The Nordic type, the too too truly Aryan.

In games which mark for beauty out of twenty,
    I'm doing well if my friends give me eight
(When played historically you still score plenty);
    My head looks like an egg upon a plate;
    My nose is not too bad, but isn't straight;
I have no proper eyebrows, and my eyes
Are far too close together to look nice.

Beauty, we're told, is but a painted show,
    But still the public really likes that best;
Beauty of soul should be enough, I know,
    The golden ingot in the plain deal chest.
    But mine's a rattle in a flannel vest;
I can't think what my It had on It's mind,
To give me flat feet and a big behind.

Apart from lyrics and poetic dramma,
    Which Ervine seems more angered by than sad at,
While Sparrow fails to understand their grammar,
    I have some harmless hobbies; I'm not bad at
    Reading the slower movements, and may add that
Out of my hours of strumming most of them
Pass playing hymn tunes out of A. and M.

Read character from taste. Who seem to me
    The great? I know that one as well as you.
'Why, Daunty, Gouty, Shopkeeper, the three
    Supreme Old Masters.' You must ask me who
    Have written just as I'd have liked to do.
I stop to listen and the names I hear
Are those of Firbank, Potter, Carroll, Lear.

Then phantasies? My anima, poor thing,
    Must take the dreams my Alter Ego sends her,
And he's a marvellous diver, not a king.
    But when I'm sickening for influenza,
    I play concertos with my own cadenza;
And as the fever rises find it properer
To sing the love duet from a grand opera.

My vices? I've no wish to go to prison.
    I am no Grouper, I will never share
With any prig who thinks he'd like to listen.
    At answering letters I am well aware
    I'm very slack; I ought to take more care
Over my clothes; my promise always fails
To smoke much less, and not to bite my nails.

I hate pompositas and all authority;
    Its air of injured rightness also sends
Me shuddering from the cultured smug minority.
    'Perpetual revolution', left-wing friends
    Tell me, 'in counter-revolution ends.
Your fate will be to linger on outcast
A selfish pink old Liberal to the last.'

'No, I am that I am, and those that level
    At my abuses reckon up their own.
I may be straight though they, themselves, are bevel.'
    So Shakespeare said, but Shakespeare must have known.
    I daren't say that except when I'm alone,
Must hear in silence till I turn my toes up,
'It's such a pity Wystan never grows up.'

So I sit down this fine September morning
    To tell my story. I've another reason.
I've lately had a confidential warning
    That Isherwood is publishing next season
    'A book about us all. I call that treason.
I must be quick if I'm to get my oar in
Before his revelations bring the law in.

My father's forbears were all Midland yeomen
        Till royalties from coal mines did them good;
I think they must have been phlegmatic slowmen.
        My mother's ancestors had Norman blood,
        From Somerset I've always understood;
My grandfathers on either side agree
In being clergymen and C. of E.

Father and Mother each was one of seven,
        Though one died young and one was not all there;
Their fathers both went suddenly to Heaven
        While they were still quite small and left them here
        To work on earth with little cash to spare;
A nurse, a rising medico, at Bart's
Both felt the pangs of Cupid's naughty darts.

My home then was professional and 'high'.
        No gentler father ever lived, I'll lay
All Lombard Street against a shepherd's pie.
        We imitate our loves: well, neighbours say
        I grow more like my mother every day.
I don't like business men. I know a Prot
Will never really kneel, but only squat.

In pleasures of the mind they both delighted;
        The library in the study was enough
To make a better boy than me short-sighted;
        Our cook Ada surely knew her stuff;
        My elder brothers did not treat me rough;
We lived at Solihull, a village then;
Those at the gasworks were my favourite men.

My earliest recollection to stay put
        Is of a white stone doorstep and a spot
Of pus where father lanced the terrier's foot;
        Next, stuffing shag into the coffee pot
        Which nearly killed my mother, but did not;
Both psycho-analyst and Christian minister
Will think these incidents extremely sinister.

With northern myths my little brain was laden,
        With deeds of Thor and Loki and such scenes;
My favourite tale was Andersen's *Ice Maiden*;
        But better far than any kings or queens
        I liked to see and know about machines:
And from my sixth until my sixteenth year
I thought myself a mining engineer.

The mine I always pictured was for lead,
	Though copper mines might, faute de mieux, be sound.
To-day I like a weight upon my bed;
	I always travel by the Underground;
	For concentration I have always found
A small room best, the curtains drawn, the light on;
Then I can work from nine till tea-time, right on.

I must admit that I was most precocious
	(Precocious children rarely grow up good).
My aunts and uncles thought me quite atrocious
	For using words more adult than I should;
	My first remark at school did all it could
To shake a matron's monumental poise:
'I like to see the various types of boys.'

The Great War had begun: but masters' scrutiny
	And fists of big boys were the war to us;
It was as harmless as the Indian Mutiny,
	A beating from the Head was dangerous.
	But once when half the form put down *Bellus*
We were accused of that most deadly sin,
Wanting the Kaiser and the Huns to win.

The way in which we really were affected
	Was having such a varied lot to teach us.
The best were fighting, as the King expected,
	The remnant either elderly grey creatures,
	Or characters with most peculiar features.
Many were raggable, a few were waxy,
One had to leave abruptly in a taxi.

Surnames I must not write—O Reginald,
	You at least taught us that which fadeth not,
Our earliest visions of the great wide world;
	The beer and biscuits that your favourites got,
	Your tales revealing you a first-class shot,
Your riding breeks, your drama called *The Waves*,
A few of us will carry to our graves.

'Half a lunatic, half a knave'. No doubt
	A holy terror to the staff at tea;
A good headmaster must have soon found out
	Your moral character was all at sea;
	I question if you'd got a pass degree:
But little children bless your kind that knocks
Away the edifying stumbling blocks.

How can I thank you? For it only shows
    (Let me ride just this once my hobby-horse),
There're things a good headmaster never knows.
        There must be sober schoolmasters, of course,
        But what a prep school really puts across
Is knowledge of the world we'll soon be lost in:
To-day it's more like Dickens than Jane Austen.

I hate the modern trick, to tell the truth.
        Of straightening out the kinks in the young mind,
Our passion for the tender plant of youth,
        Our hatred for all weeds of any kind.
        Slogans are bad: the best that I can find
Is this: 'Let each child have that's in our care
As much neurosis as the child can bear.'

In this respect, at least, my bad old Adam is
        Pigheadedly against the general trend;
And has no use for all these new academies
        Where readers of the better weeklies send
        The child they probably did not intend,
To paint a lampshade, marry, or keep pigeons,
Or make a study of the world religions.

Goddess of bossy underlings, Normality!
        What murders are committed in thy name!
Totalitarian is thy state Reality,
        Reeking of antiseptics and the shame
        Of faces that all look and feel the same.
Thy Muse is one unknown to classic histories,
The topping figure of the hockey mistress.

From thy dread Empire not a soul's exempted:
        More than the nursemaids pushing prams in parks,
By thee the intellectuals are tempted,
        O, to commit the treason of the clerks,
        Bewitched by thee to literary sharks.
But I must leave thee to thy office stool,
I must get on now to my public school.

Men had stopped throwing stones at one another,
        Butter and Father had come back again;
Gone were the holidays we spent with Mother
        In furnished rooms on mountain, moor, and fen;
        And gone those summer Sunday evenings, when
Along the seafronts fled a curious noise,
'Eternal Father', sung by three young boys.

Nation spoke Peace, or said she did, with nation;
  The sexes tried their best to look the same;
Morals lost value during the inflation,
    The great Victorians kindly took the blame;
    Visions of Dada to the Post-War came,
Sitting in cafés, nostrils stuffed with bread,
Above the recent and the straight-laced dead.

I've said my say on public schools elsewhere:
  Romantic friendship, prefects, bullying,
I shall not deal with, c'est une autre affaire.
    Those who expect them, will get no such thing,
    It is the strictly relevant I sing.
Why should they grumble? They've the Greek Anthology,
And all the spicier bits of Anthropology.

We all grow up the same way, more or less;
  Life is not known to give away her presents;
She only swops. The unself-consciousness
    That children share with animals and peasants
    Sinks in the *Sturm und Drang* of Adolescence.
Like other boys I lost my taste for sweets,
Discovered sunsets, passion, God, and Keats.

I shall recall a single incident
  No more. I spoke of mining engineering
As the career on which my mind was bent,
    But for some time my fancies had been veering;
    Mirages of the future kept appearing;
Crazes had come and gone in short, sharp gales,
For motor-bikes, photography, and whales.

But indecision broke off with a clean-cut end
  One afternoon in March at half-past three
When walking in a ploughed field with a friend;
    Kicking a little stone, he turned to me
    And said, 'Tell me, do you write poetry?'
I never had, and said so, but I knew
That very moment what I wished to do.

Without a bridge passage this leads me straight
  Into the theme marked 'Oxford' on my score
From pages twenty-five to twenty-eight.
    Aesthetic trills I'd never heard before
    Rose from the strings, shrill poses from the cor;
The woodwind chattered like a pre-war Russian,
'Art' boomed the brass, and 'Life' thumped the percussion.

A raw provincial, my good taste was tardy,
    And Edward Thomas I as yet preferred;
I was still listening to Thomas Hardy
    Putting divinity about a bird;
    But Eliot spoke the still unspoken word;
For gasworks and dried tubers I forsook
The clock at Grantchester, the English rook.

All youth's intolerant certainty was mine as
    I faced life in a double-breasted suit;
I bought and praised but did not read Aquinas,
    At the *Criterion*'s verdict I was mute,
    Though Arnold's I was ready to refute;
And through the quads dogmatic words rang clear,
'Good poetry is classic and austere.'

So much for Art. Of course Life had its passions too;
    The student's flesh like his imagination
Makes facts fit theories and has fashions too.
    We were the tail, a sort of poor relation
    To that debauched, eccentric generation
That grew up with their fathers at the War,
And made new glosses on the noun Amor.

Three years passed quickly while the Isis went
    Down to the sea for better or for worse;
Then to Berlin, not Carthage, I was sent
    With money from my parents in my purse,
    And ceased to see the world in terms of verse.
I met a chap called Layard and he fed
New doctrines into my receptive head.

Part came from Lane, and part from D. H. Lawrence;
    Gide, though I didn't know it then, gave part.
They taught me to express my deep abhorrence
    If I caught anyone preferring Art
    To Life and Love and being Pure-in-Heart.
I lived with crooks but seldom was molested;
The Pure-in-Heart can never be arrested.

He's gay; no bludgeonings of chance can spoil it,
    The Pure-in-Heart loves all men on a par,
And has no trouble with his private toilet;
    The Pure-in-Heart is never ill; catarrh
    Would be the yellow streak, the brush of tar;
Determined to be loving and forgiving,
I came back home to try and earn my living.

The only thing you never turned your hand to
    Was teaching English in a boarding school.
To-day it's a profession that seems grand to
    Those whose alternative's an office stool;
    For budding authors it's become the rule.
To many an unknown genius postmen bring
Typed notices from Rabbitarse and String.

The Head's M.A., a bishop is a patron,
    The assistant staff is highly qualified;
Health is the care of an experienced matron,
    The arts are taught by ladies from outside;
    The food is wholesome and the grounds are wide;
The aim is training character and poise,
With special coaching for the backward boys.

I found the pay good and had time to spend it,
    Though others may not have the good luck I did:
For you I'd hesitate to recommend it;
    Several have told me that they can't abide it.
    Still, if one tends to get a bit one-sided,
It's pleasant as it's easy to secure
The hero worship of the immature.

More, it's a job, and jobs to-day are rare:
    All the ideals in the world won't feed us
Although they give our crimes a certain air.
    So barons of the press who know their readers
    Employ to write their more appalling leaders,
Instead of Satan's horned and hideous minions,
Clever young men of liberal opinions.

Which brings me up to nineteen-thirty-five;
    Six months of film work is another story
I can't tell now. But, here I am, alive
    Knowing the true source of that sense of glory
    That still surrounds the England of the Tory,
Come only to the rather tame conclusion
That no man by himself has life's solution.

I know—the fact is really not unnerving—
    That what is done is done, that no past dies,
That what we see depends on who's observing,
    And what we think on our activities.
    That envy warps the virgin as she dries
But *Post coitum, homo tristis* means
The lover must go carefully with the greens.

The boat has brought me to the landing-stage,
 Up the long estuary of mud and sedges;
The line I travel has the English gauge;
  The engine's shadow vaults the little hedges;
  And summer's done. I sign the usual pledges
To be a better poet, better man;
I'll really do it this time if I can.

I'm home again, and goodness knows to what,
 To read the papers and to earn my bread;
I'm home to Europe where I may be shot;
  'I'm home again', as William Morris said,
  'And nobody I really care for's dead.'
I've got a round of visits now to pay,
So I must finish this another day.

September 1936

PART V

Autumn is here. The beech leaves strew the lawn;
 The power stations take up heavier loads;
The massive lorries shake from dusk till dawn
  The houses on the residential roads;
  The shops are full of coming winter modes.
Dances have started at the Baths next door;
Stray scraps of MS strew my bedroom floor.

I read that there's a boomlet on in Birmingham,
 But what I hear is not so reassuring;
Rumours of War, the B.B.C. confirming 'em,
  The prospects for the future aren't alluring;
  No one believes Prosperity enduring,
Not even Wykehamists, whose golden mean
Maintains the All Souls' Parish Magazine.

The crack between employees and employers
 Is obvious already as the nose on
John Gielgud's face; the keels of new destroyers
  Get laid down somehow though all credit's frozen;
  The Pope's turned protestant at last and chosen,
Thinking it safer in the temporal circs,
The Italian faith against the Russian works.

England, my England—you have been my tutrix—
 The Mater, on occasions, of the free,
Or, if you'd rather, Dura Virum Nutrix,
  Whatever happens I am born of Thee;
  And Englishmen, all foreigners agree,
Taking them by and large, and as a nation,
All suffer from an Oedipus fixation.

With all thy faults, of course we love thee still;
    We'd better for we have to live with you,
From Rhondda Valley or from Bredon Hill,
    From Rotherhithe, or Regent Street, or Kew
    We look you up and down and whistle 'Phew!
Mother looks odd to-day dressed up in peers,
Slums, aspidistras, shooting-sticks, and queers.'

Cheer up! There're several singing birds that sing.
    There's six feet six of Spender for a start;
Eliot has really stretched his eagle's wing,
    And Yeats has helped himself to Parnell's heart;
    This book has samples of MacNeice's art;
There's Wyndham Lewis fuming out of sight,
That lonely old volcano of the Right.

I'm marking time because I cannot guess
    The proper place to which to send this letter,
c/o Saint Peter or The Infernal Press?
    I'll try the Press. World-culture is its debtor;
    It has a list that Faber's couldn't better.
For Heaven gets all the lookers for her pains,
But Hell, I think, gets nearly all the brains.

The congregation up there in the former
    Are those whose early upbringing was right,
Who never suffered from a childish trauma;
    As babies they were Truby King's delight;
    They're happy, lovely, but not overbright.
For no one thinks unless a complex makes him,
Or till financial ruin overtakes him.

Complex or Poverty; in short The Trap.
    Some set to work to understand the spring;
Others sham dead, pretend to take a nap;
    'It is a motor-boat', the madmen sing;
    The artist's action is the queerest thing:
He seems to like it, couldn't do without it,
And only wants to tell us all about it.

While Rome is burning or he's out of sorts
    'Causons, causons, mon bon,' he's apt to say,
'What does it matter while I have these thoughts?'
    Or so I've heard, but Freud's not quite O.K.
    No artist works a twenty-four-hour day.
In bed, asleep or dead, it's hard to tell
The highbrow from l'homme moyen sensuel.

'Es neigen die Weisen zu Schönem sich.'
        Your lordship's brow that never wore a hat
Should thank your lordship's foot that did the trick.
        Your mother in a temper cried, 'Lame Brat!'
        Posterity should thank her much for that.
Had she been sweet she surely would have taken
Juan away and saved your moral bacon.

The match of Hell and Heaven was a nice
        Idea of Blake's, but won't take place, alas.
You can choose either, but you can't choose twice;
        You can't, at least in this world, change your class;
        Neither is alpha plus though both will pass:
And don't imagine you can write like Dante,
Dive like your nephew, crochet like your auntie.

The Great Utopia, free of all complexes,
        The Withered State is, at the moment, such
A dream as that of being both the sexes.
        I like Wolf's *Goethe-Lieder* very much,
        But doubt if *Ganymede's* appeal will touch
—That marvellous cry with its ascending phrases—
Capitalism in its later phases.

Are Poets saved? Well, let's suppose they are,
        And take a peep. I don't see any books.
Shakespeare is lounging grandly at the bar,
        Milton is dozing, judging by his looks,
        Shelley is playing poker with two crooks,
Blake's adding pince-nez to an ad. for Players,
Chaucer is buried in the latest Sayers.

Lord Alfred rags with Arthur on the floor,
        Housman, all scholarship forgot at last,
Sips up the stolen waters through a straw,
        Browning's complaining that Keats bowls too fast,
        And you have been composing as they passed
A clerihew on Wordsworth and his tie,
A rather dirty limerick on Pye.

I hope this reaches you in your abode,
        This letter that's already far too long,
Just like the Prelude or the Great North Road;
        But here I end my conversational song.
        I hope you don't think mail from strangers wrong.
As to its length, I tell myself you'll need it,
You've all eternity in which to read it.

October 1936

Part VI

Poems 1936–1939

The drums tap out sensational bulletins;
Frantic the efforts of the violins
To drown the song behind the guarded hill :
The dancers do not listen; but they will.

I · Journey to Iceland

And the traveller hopes: 'Let me be far from any
Physician'; and the ports have names for the sea;
    The citiless, the corroding, the sorrow;
    And North means to all: 'Reject!'

And the great plains are for ever where the cold fish is hunted,
And everywhere; the light birds flicker and flaunt;
    Under the scolding flag the lover
    Of islands may see at last,

Faintly, his limited hope; and he nears the glitter
Of glaciers, the sterile immature mountains intense
    In the abnormal day of this world, and a river's
    Fan-like polyp of sand.

Then let the good citizen here find natural marvels:
The horse-shoe ravine, the issue of steam from a cleft
    In the rock, and rocks, and waterfalls brushing the
    Rocks, and among the rocks birds.

And the student of prose and conduct, places to visit;
The site of a church where a bishop was put in a bag,
    The bath of a great historian, the rock where
    An outlaw dreaded the dark.

Remember the doomed man thrown by his horse and crying:
'Beautiful is the hillside, I will not go';
    The old woman confessing: 'He that I loved the
    Best, to him I was worst',

For Europe is absent. This is an island and therefore
Unreal. And the steadfast affections of its dead may be bought
    By those whose dreams accuse them of being
    Spitefully alive, and the pale

From too much passion of kissing feel pure in its deserts.
Can they? For the world is, and the present, and the lie.
    And the narrow bridge over the torrent,
    And the small farm under the crag

Are the natural setting for the jealousies of a province;
And the weak vow of fidelity is formed by the cairn;
    And within the indigenous figure on horseback
    On the bridle path down by the lake

The blood moves also by crooked and furtive inches,
Asks all your questions: 'Where is the homage? When
 Shall justice be done? O who is against me?
 Why am I always alone?'

Present then the world to the world with its mendicant shadow;
Let the suits be flash, the Minister of Commerce insane;
 Let jazz be bestowed on the huts, and the beauty's
 Set cosmopolitan smile.

For our time has no favourite suburb; no local features
Are those of the young for whom all wish to care;
 The promise is only a promise, the fabulous
 Country impartially far.

Tears fall in all the rivers. Again the driver
Pulls on his gloves and in a blinding snowstorm starts
 Upon his deadly journey; and again the writer
 Runs howling to his art.

July 1936

II · Detective Story

For who is ever quite without his landscape,
The straggling village street, the house in trees,
All near the church, or else the gloomy town house,
The one with the Corinthian pillars, or
The tiny workmanlike flat: in any case
A home, the centre where the three or four things
That happen to a man do happen? Yes,
Who cannot draw the map of his life, shade in
The little station where he meets his loves
And says good-bye continually, and mark the spot
Where the body of his happiness was first discovered?

An unknown tramp? A rich man? An enigma always
And with a buried past—but when the truth,
The truth about our happiness comes out
How much it owed to blackmail and philandering.

The rest's traditional. All goes to plan:
The feud between the local common sense
And that exasperating brilliant intuition
That's always on the spot by chance before us;
All goes to plan, both lying and confession,
Down to the thrilling final chase, the kill.

Yet on the last page just a lingering doubt
That verdict, was it just? The judge's nerves,
That clue, that protestation from the gallows,
And our own smile . . . why yes . . .

But time is always killed. Someone must pay for
Our loss of happiness, our happiness itself.

July 1936

III

O who can ever praise enough
The world of his belief?
Harum-scarum childhood plays
In the meadows near his home;
In his woods love knows no wrong;
Travellers ride their placid ways;
In the cool shade of the tomb
Age's trusting footfalls ring.
O who can paint the vivid tree
And grass of phantasy?

But to create it and to guard
Shall be his whole reward.
He shall watch and he shall weep,
All his father's love deny,
To his mother's womb be lost.
Eight nights with a wanton sleep,
But upon the ninth shall be
Bride and victim to a ghost,
And in the pit of terror thrown
Shall bear the wrath alone.

July 1936

IV

'O who can ever gaze his fill',
    Farmer and fisherman say,
'On native shore and local hill,
Grudge aching limb or callus on the hand?
Fathers, grandfathers stood upon this land,
And here the pilgrims from our loins shall stand.'
    So farmer and fisherman say
    In their fortunate heyday:
    But Death's soft answer drifts across
    Empty catch or harvest loss
        Or an unlucky May:
The earth is an oyster with nothing inside it
    Not to be born is the best for man
The end of toil is a bailiff's order
    Throw down the mattock and dance while you can.

'O life's too short for friends who share',
        Travellers think in their hearts,
'The city's common bed, the air,
The mountain bivouac and the bathing beach,
Where incidents draw every day from each
Memorable gesture and witty speech.'
        So travellers think in their hearts,
        Till malice or circumstance parts
        Them from their constant humour:
        And slyly Death's coercive rumour
            In the silence starts:
A friend is the old old tale of Narcissus
        Not to be born is the best for man
An active partner in something disgraceful
        Change your partner, dance while you can.

'O stretch your hands across the sea',
        The impassioned lover cries,
'Stretch them towards your harm and me.
Our grass is green, and sensual our brief bed,
The stream sings at its foot, and at its head
The mild and vegetarian beasts are fed.'
        So the impassioned lover cries
        Till his storm of pleasure dies:
        From the bedpost and the rocks
        Death's enticing echo mocks,
            And his voice replies:
The greater the love, the more false to its object
        Not to be born is the best for man
After the kiss comes the impulse to throttle
        Break the embraces, dance while you can.

'I see the guilty world forgiven',
        Dreamer and drunkard sing,
'The ladders let down out of heaven;
The laurel springing from the martyr's blood;
The children skipping where the weepers stood;
The lovers natural, and the beasts all good.'
        So dreamer and drunkard sing
        Till day their sobriety bring:
        Parrotwise with death's reply
        From whelping fear and nesting lie,
            Woods and their echoes ring:
The desires of the heart are as crooked as corkscrews
        Not to be born is the best for man
The second best is a formal order
        The dance's pattern, dance while you can.
Dance, dance, for the figure is easy
        The tune is catching and will not stop
Dance till the stars come down with the rafters
        Dance, dance, dance till you drop.

September 1936

V

Lay your sleeping head, my love,
Human on my faithless arm;
Time and fevers burn away
Individual beauty from
Thoughtful children, and the grave
Proves the child ephemeral:
But in my arms till break of day
Let the living creature lie,
Mortal, guilty, but to me
The entirely beautiful.

Soul and body have no bounds:
To lovers as they lie upon
Her tolerant enchanted slope
In their ordinary swoon,
Grave the vision Venus sends
Of supernatural sympathy,
Universal love and hope;
While an abstract insight wakes
Among the glaciers and the rocks
The hermit's sensual ecstasy.

Certainty, fidelity
On the stroke of midnight pass
Like vibrations of a bell,
And fashionable madmen raise
Their pedantic boring cry:
Every farthing of the cost,
All the dreaded cards foretell,
Shall be paid, but from this night
Not a whisper, not a thought,
Not a kiss nor look be lost.

Beauty, midnight, vision dies:
Let the winds of dawn that blow
Softly round your dreaming head
Such a day of sweetness show
Eye and knocking heart may bless,
Find the mortal world enough;
Noons of dryness see you fed
By the involuntary powers,
Nights of insult let you pass
Watched by every human love.

January 1937

VI

It's farewell to the drawing-room's civilised cry,
The professor's sensible whereto and why,
The frock-coated diplomat's social aplomb,
Now matters are settled with gas and with bomb.

The works for two pianos, the brilliant stories
Of reasonable giants and remarkable fairies,
The pictures, the ointments, the frangible wares
And the branches of olive are stored upstairs.

For the Devil has broken parole and arisen,
He has dynamited his way out of prison,
Out of the well where his Papa throws
The rebel angel, the outcast rose,

Like influenza he walks abroad,
He stands by the bridge, he waits by the ford,
As a goose or a gull he flies overhead,
He hides in the cupboard and under the bed.

Assuming such shapes as may best disguise
The hate that burns in his big blue eyes;
He may be a baby that croons in its pram,
Or a dear old grannie boarding a tram.

A plumber, a doctor, for he has skill
To adopt a serious profession at will;
Superb at ice-hockey, a prince at the dance,
He's fierce as the tigers, secretive as plants.

O were he to triumph, dear heart, you know
To what depths of shame he would drag you low;
He would steal you away from me, yes, my dear,
He would steal you and cut off your beautiful hair.

Millions already have come to their harm,
Succumbing like doves to his adder's charm;
Hundreds of trees in the wood are unsound:
I'm the axe that must cut them down to the ground.

For I, after all, am the Fortunate One,
The Happy-Go-Lucky, the spoilt Third Son;
For me it is written the Devil to chase
And to rid the earth of the human race.

The behaving of man is a world of horror,
A sedentary Sodom and slick Gomorrah;
I must take charge of the liquid fire
And storm the cities of human desire.

The buying and selling, the eating and drinking,
The disloyal machines and irreverent thinking,
The lovely dullards again and again
Inspiring their bitter ambitious men.

I shall come, I shall punish, the Devil be dead,
I shall have caviare thick on my bread,
I shall build myself a cathedral for home
With a vacuum cleaner in every room.

I shall ride the parade in a platinum car,
My features shall shine, my name shall be Star,
Day-long and night-long the bells I shall peal,
And down the long street I shall turn the cartwheel.

So Little John, Long John, Peter and Paul,
And poor little Horace with only one ball,
You shall leave your breakfast, your desk and your play
On a fine summer morning the Devil to slay.

For it's order and trumpet and anger and drum
And power and glory command you to come;
The graves shall fly open and let you all in,
And the earth shall be emptied of mortal sin.

The fishes are silent deep in the sea,
The skies are lit up like a Christmas tree,
The star in the West shoots its warning cry:
'Mankind is alive, but Mankind must die.'

So good-bye to the house with its wallpaper red,
Good-bye to the sheets on the warm double bed,
Good-bye to the beautiful birds on the wall,
It's good-bye, dear heart, good-bye to you all.

January 1937

VII · Blues

(FOR HEDLI ANDERSON)

Ladies and gentlemen, sitting here,
Eating and drinking and warming a chair,
Feeling and thinking and drawing your breath,
Who's sitting next to you? It may be Death.

As a high-stepping blondie with eyes of blue
In the subway, on beaches, Death looks at you;
And married or single or young or old,
You'll become a sugar daddy and do as you're told.

Death is a G-man. You may think yourself smart,
But he'll send you to the hot-seat or plug you through the heart;
He may be a slow worker, but in the end
He'll get you for the crime of being born, my friend.

Death as a doctor has first-class degrees;
The world is on his panel; he charges no fees;
He listens to your chest, says—'You're breathing. That's bad.
But don't worry; we'll soon see to that, my lad.'

Death knocks at your door selling real estate,
The value of which will not depreciate;
It's easy, it's convenient, it's old world. You'll sign,
Whatever your income, on the dotted line.

Death as a teacher is simply grand;
The dumbest pupil can understand.
He has only one subject and that is the Tomb;
But no one ever yawns or asks to leave the room.

So whether you're standing broke in the rain,
Or playing poker or drinking champagne,
Death's looking for you, he's already on the way,
So look out for him to-morrow or perhaps to-day.

? early 1937

VIII · Spain 1937

Yesterday all the past. The language of size
Spreading to China along the trade-routes; the diffusion
        Of the counting-frame and the cromlech;
Yesterday the shadow-reckoning in the sunny climates.

Yesterday the assessment of insurance by cards,
The divination of water; yesterday the invention
        Of cart-wheels and clocks, the taming of
Horses; yesterday the bustling world of the navigators.

Yesterday the abolition of fairies and giants;
The fortress like a motionless eagle eyeing the valley,
        The chapel built in the forest;
Yesterday the carving of angels and of frightening gargoyles;

The trial of heretics among the columns of stone;
Yesterday the theological feuds in the taverns
        And the miraculous cure at the fountain;
Yesterday the Sabbath of Witches. But to-day the struggle.

Yesterday the installation of dynamos and turbines;
The construction of railways in the colonial desert;

Yesterday the classic lecture
On the origin of Mankind. But to-day the struggle.

Yesterday the belief in the absolute value of Greek;
The fall of the curtain upon the death of a hero;
            Yesterday the prayer to the sunset,
And the adoration of madmen. But to-day the struggle.

As the poet whispers, startled among the pines
Or, where the loose waterfall sings, compact, or upright
            On the crag by the leaning tower:
'O my vision. O send me the luck of the sailor.'

And the investigator peers through his instruments
At the inhuman provinces, the virile bacillus
            Or enormous Jupiter finished:
'But the lives of my friends. I inquire, I inquire.'

And the poor in their fireless lodgings dropping the sheets
Of the evening paper: 'Our day is our loss. O show us
            History the operator, the
Organiser, Time the refreshing river.'

And the nations combine each cry, invoking the life
That shapes the individual belly and orders
            The private nocturnal terror:
'Did you not found once the city state of the sponge,

'Raise the vast military empires of the shark
And the tiger, establish the robin's plucky canton?
            Intervene. O descend as a dove or
A furious papa or a mild engineer: but descend.'

And the life, if it answers at all, replies from the heart
And the eyes and the lungs, from the shops and squares of the city:
            'O no, I am not the Mover,
Not to-day, not to you. To you I'm the

'Yes-man, the bar-companion, the easily-duped:
I am whatever you do; I am your vow to be
            Good, your humorous story;
I am your business voice; I am your marriage.

'What's your proposal? To build the Just City? I will.
I agree. Or is it the suicide pact, the romantic
            Death? Very well, I accept, for
I am your choice, your decision: yes, I am Spain.'

Many have heard it on remote peninsulas,
On sleepy plains, in the aberrant fishermen's islands,
            In the corrupt heart of the city;
Have heard and migrated like gulls or the seeds of a flower.

They clung like burrs to the long expresses that lurch
Through the unjust lands, through the night, through the alpine
                                                            tunnel;
        They floated over the oceans;
They walked the passes: they came to present their lives.

On that arid square, that fragment nipped off from hot
Africa, soldered so crudely to inventive Europe,
        On that tableland scored by rivers,
Our fever's menacing shapes are precise and alive.

To-morrow, perhaps, the future: the research on fatigue
And the movements of packers; the gradual exploring of all the
        Octaves of radiation;
To-morrow the enlarging of consciousness by diet and breathing.

To-morrow the rediscovery of romantic love;
The photographing of ravens; all the fun under
        Liberty's masterful shadow;
To-morrow the hour of the pageant-master and the musician.

To-morrow for the young the poets exploding like bombs,
The walks by the lake, the winter of perfect communion;
        To-morrow the bicycle races
Through the suburbs on summer evenings: but to-day the struggle.

To-day the inevitable increase in the chances of death;
The conscious acceptance of guilt in the fact of murder;
        To-day the expending of powers
On the flat ephemeral pamphlet and the boring meeting.

To-day the makeshift consolations; the shared cigarette;
The cards in the candle-lit barn and the scraping concert,
        The masculine jokes; to-day the
Fumbled and unsatisfactory embrace before hurting.

The stars are dead; the animals will not look:
We are left alone with our day, and the time is short and
        History to the defeated
May say Alas but cannot help or pardon.

                                                    April 1937

IX · Orpheus

What does the song hope for? And the moved hands
A little way from the birds, the shy, the delightful?
        To be bewildered and happy,
        Or most of all the knowledge of life?

But the beautiful are content with the sharp notes of the air;
The warmth is enough. O if winter really
        Oppose, if the weak snowflake,
        What will the wish, what will the dance do?

April 1937

X · Johnny

O the valley in the summer where I and my John
Beside the deep river would walk on and on
While the flowers at our feet and the birds up above
Argued so sweetly on reciprocal love,
And I leaned on his shoulder; 'O Johnny, let's play':
But he frowned like thunder and he went away.

O that Friday near Christmas as I well recall
When we went to the Charity Matinee Ball,
The floor was so smooth and the band was so loud
And Johnny so handsome I felt so proud;
'Squeeze me tighter, dear Johnny, let's dance till it's day':
But he frowned like thunder and he went away.

Shall I ever forget at the Grand Opera
When music poured out of each wonderful star?
Diamonds and pearls they hung dazzling down
Over each silver or golden silk gown;
'O John I'm in heaven', I whispered to say:
But he frowned like thunder and he went away.

O but he was as fair as a garden in flower,
As slender and tall as the great Eiffel Tower,
When the waltz throbbed out on the long promenade
O his eyes and his smile they went straight to my heart;
'O marry me, Johnny, I'll love and obey':
But he frowned like thunder and he went away.

O last night I dreamed of you, Johnny, my lover,
You'd the sun on one arm and the moon on the other,
The sea it was blue and the grass it was green,
Every star rattled a round tambourine;
Ten thousand miles deep in a pit there I lay:
But you frowned like thunder and you went away.

April 1937

XI · Miss Gee

Let me tell you a little story
  About Miss Edith Gee;
She lived in Clevedon Terrace
  At Number 83.

She'd a slight squint in her left eye,
  Her lips they were thin and small,
She had narrow sloping shoulders
  And she had no bust at all.

She'd a velvet hat with trimmings,
  And a dark-grey serge costume;
She lived in Clevedon Terrace
  In a small bed-sitting room.

She'd a purple mac for wet days,
  A green umbrella too to take,
She'd a bicycle with shopping basket
  And a harsh back-pedal brake.

The Church of Saint Aloysius
  Was not so very far;
She did a lot of knitting,
  Knitting for that Church Bazaar.

Miss Gee looked up at the starlight
  And said: 'Does anyone care
That I live in Clevedon Terrace
  On one hundred pounds a year?'

She dreamed a dream one evening
  That she was the Queen of France
And the Vicar of Saint Aloysius
  Asked Her Majesty to dance.

But a storm blew down the palace,
  She was biking through a field of corn,
And a bull with the face of the Vicar
  Was charging with lowered horn.

She could feel his hot breath behind her,
  He was going to overtake;
And the bicycle went slower and slower
  Because of that back-pedal brake.

Summer made the trees a picture,
  Winter made them a wreck;
She bicycled to the evening service
  With her clothes buttoned up to her neck.

She passed by the loving couples,
    She turned her head away;
She passed by the loving couples
    And they didn't ask her to stay.

Miss Gee sat down in the side-aisle,
    She heard the organ play;
And the choir it sang so sweetly
    At the ending of the day.

Miss Gee knelt down in the side-aisle,
    She knelt down on her knees;
'Lead me not into temptation
    But make me a good girl, please.'

The days and nights went by her
    Like waves round a Cornish wreck;
She bicycled down to the doctor
    With her clothes buttoned up to her neck.

She bicycled down to the doctor,
    And rang the surgery bell;
'O, doctor, I've a pain inside me,
    And I don't feel very well.'

Doctor Thomas looked her over,
    And then he looked some more;
Walked over to his wash-basin,
    Said: 'Why didn't you come before?'

Doctor Thomas sat over his dinner,
    Though his wife was waiting to ring;
Rolling his bread into pellets,
    Said: 'Cancer's a funny thing.

'Nobody knows what the cause is,
    Though some pretend they do;
It's like some hidden assassin
    Waiting to strike at you.

'Childless women get it,
    And men when they retire;
It's as if there had to be some outlet
    For their foiled creative fire.'

His wife she rang for the servant,
    Said: 'Don't be so morbid, dear';
He said: 'I saw Miss Gee this evening
    And she's a goner, I fear.'

They took Miss Gee to the hospital,
    She lay there a total wreck,
Lay in the ward for women
    With the bedclothes right up to her neck.

They laid her on the table,
    The students began to laugh;
And Mr. Rose the surgeon
    He cut Miss Gee in half.

Mr. Rose he turned to his students,
    Said: 'Gentlemen, if you please,
We seldom see a sarcoma
    As far advanced as this.'

They took her off the table,
    They wheeled away Miss Gee
Down to another department
    Where they study Anatomy.

They hung her from the ceiling,
    Yes, they hung up Miss Gee;
And a couple of Oxford Groupers
    Carefully dissected her knee.

April 1937

XII · Schoolchildren

Here are all the captivities; the cells are as real:
But these are unlike the prisoners we know
Who are outraged or pining or wittily resigned
        Or just wish all away.

For they dissent so little, so nearly content
With the dumb play of the dog, the licking and rushing;
The bars of love are so strong, their conspiracies
        Weak like the vows of drunkards.

Indeed their strangeness is difficult to watch:
The condemned see only the fallacious angels of a vision;
So little effort lies behind their smiling,
        The beast of vocation is afraid.

But watch them, O, set against our size and timing
The almost neuter, the slightly awkward perfection;
For the sex is there, the broken bootlace is broken,
        The professor's dream is not true.

Yet the tyranny is so easy. The improper word
Scribbled upon the fountain, is that all the rebellion?
The storm of tears shed in the corner, are these
      The seeds of the new life?

                           May 1937

XIII

Wrapped in a yielding air, beside
    The flower's soundless hunger,
Close to the tree's clandestine tide,
    Close to the bird's high fever,
    Loud in his hope and anger,
Erect about his skeleton,
    Stands the expressive lover,
    Stands the deliberate man.

Beneath the hot incurious sun,
    Past stronger beasts and fairer
He picks his way, a living gun,
    With gun and lens and bible,
    A militant enquirer,
The friend, the rash, the enemy,
    The essayist, the able,
    Able at times to cry.

The friendless and unhated stone
    Lies everywhere about him,
The Brothered-One, the Not-Alone,
    The brothered and the hated
    Whose family have taught him
To set against the large and dumb,
    The timeless and the rooted,
    His money and his time.

For mother's fading hopes become
    Dull wives to his dull spirits
Soon dulled by nurse's moral thumb,
    That dullard fond betrayer,
    And, childish, he inherits,
So soon by legal father tricked,
    The tall and gorgeous tower,
    Gorgeous but locked, but locked.

And ruled by dead men never met,
    By pious guess deluded,
Upon the stool of madness set
    Or stool of desolation,
    Sits murderous and clear-headed;

Enormous beauties round him move,
    For grandiose is his vision
    And grandiose his love.

Determined on Time's honest shield
    The lamb must face the tigress,
Their faithful quarrel never healed
    Though, faithless, he consider
    His dream of vaguer ages,
Hunter and victim reconciled,
    The lion and the adder,
    The adder and the child.

Fresh loves betray him, every day
    Over his green horizon
A fresh deserter rides away,
    And miles away birds mutter
    Of ambush and of treason;
To fresh defeats he still must move,
    To further griefs and greater,
    And the defeat of grief.

May 1937

XIV · Victor

Victor was a little baby,
    Into this world he came;
His father took him on his knee and said:
    'Don't dishonour the family name.'

Victor looked up at his father
    Looked up with big round eyes;
His father said: 'Victor, my only son,
    Don't you ever ever tell lies.'

Victor and his father went riding
    Out in a little dog-cart;
His father took a Bible from his pocket and read:
    'Blessed are the pure in heart.'

It was a frosty December,
    It wasn't the season for fruits;
His father fell dead of heart disease
    While lacing up his boots.

It was a frosty December
    When into his grave he sank;
His uncle found Victor a post as cashier
    In the Midland Counties Bank.

It was a frosty December
        Victor was only eighteen,
But his figures were neat and his margins straight
        And his cuffs were always clean.

He took a room at the Peveril,
        A respectable boarding-house;
And Time watched Victor day after day
        As a cat will watch a mouse.

The clerks slapped Victor on the shoulder;
        'Have you ever had a woman?' they said,
'Come down town with us on Saturday night.'
        Victor smiled and shook his head.

The manager sat in his office,
        Smoked a Corona cigar;
Said: 'Victor's a decent fellow but
        He's too mousey to go far.'

Victor went up to his bedroom,
        Set the alarum bell;
Climbed into bed, took his Bible and read
        Of what happened to Jezebel.

It was the First of April,
        Anna to the Peveril came;
Her eyes, her lips, her breasts, her hips
        And her smile set men aflame.

She looked as pure as a schoolgirl
        On her First Communion day,
But her kisses were like the best champagne
        When she gave herself away.

It was the Second of April,
        She was wearing a coat of fur;
Victor met her upon the stairs
        And he fell in love with her.

The first time he made his proposal,
        She laughed, said: 'I'll never wed';
The second time there was a pause,
        Then she smiled and shook her head.

Anna looked into her mirror,
        Pouted and gave a frown;
Said: 'Victor's as dull as a wet afternoon
        But I've got to settle down.'

The third time he made his proposal,
    As they walked by the Reservoir,
She gave him a kiss like a blow on the head,
    Said: 'You are my heart's desire.'

They were married early in August,
    She said: 'Kiss me, you funny boy';
Victor took her in his arms and said:
    'O my Helen of Troy.'

It was the middle of September,
    Victor came to the office one day;
He was wearing a flower in his buttonhole,
    He was late but he was gay.

The clerks were talking of Anna,
    The door was just ajar;
One said: 'Poor old Victor, but where ignorance
    Is bliss, etcetera.'

Victor stood still as a statue,
    The door was just ajar;
One said: 'God, what fun I had with her
    In that Baby Austin car.'

Victor walked out into the High Street,
    He walked to the edge of the town;
He came to the allotments and the rubbish heaps
    And his tears came tumbling down.

Victor looked up at the sunset
    As he stood there all alone;
Cried: 'Are you in Heaven, Father?'
    But the sky said 'Address not known.'

Victor looked up at the mountains,
    The mountains all covered with snow;
Cried: 'Are you pleased with me, Father?'
    And the answer came back, 'No.'

Victor came to the forest,
    Cried: 'Father, will she ever be true?'
And the oaks and the beeches shook their heads
    And they answered: 'Not to you.'

Victor came to the meadow
    Where the wind went sweeping by;
Cried: 'O Father, I love her so',
    But the wind said: 'She must die.'

Victor came to the river
       Running so deep and so still;
Crying: 'O Father, what shall I do?'
       And the river answered: 'Kill.'

Anna was sitting at table,
       Drawing cards from a pack;
Anna was sitting at table
       Waiting for her husband to come back.

It wasn't the Jack of Diamonds
       Nor the Joker she drew at first;
It wasn't the King or the Queen of Hearts
       But the Ace of Spades reversed.

Victor stood in the doorway,
       He didn't utter a word;
She said: 'What's the matter, darling?'
       He behaved as if he hadn't heard.

There was a voice in his left ear,
       There was a voice in his right,
There was a voice at the base of his skull
       Saying: 'She must die to-night.'

Victor picked up a carving-knife,
       His features were set and drawn,
Said: 'Anna, it would have been better for you
       If you had not been born.'

Anna jumped up from the table,
       Anna started to scream,
But Victor came slowly after her
       Like a horror in a dream.

She dodged behind the sofa,
       She tore down a curtain rod,
But Victor came slowly after her,
       Said: 'Prepare to meet Thy God.'

She managed to wrench the door open,
       She ran and she didn't stop.
But Victor followed her up the stairs
       And he caught her at the top.

He stood there above the body,
       He stood there holding the knife;
And the blood ran down the stairs and sang:
       'I'm the Resurrection and the Life.'

They tapped Victor on the shoulder,
   They took him away in a van;
He sat as quiet as a lump of moss
   Saying: 'I am the Son of Man.'

Victor sat in a corner
   Making a woman of clay,
Saying: 'I am Alpha and Omega, I shall come
   To judge the earth one day.'

         June 1937

XV · Dover

Steep roads, a tunnel through the downs, are the approaches;
A ruined pharos overlooks a constructed bay;
The sea-front is almost elegant; all this show
Has, somewhere inland, a vague and dirty root:
   Nothing is made in this town.

But the dominant Norman castle floodlit at night
And the trains that fume in the station built on the sea
Testify to the interests of its regular life:
Here live the experts on what the soldiers want
   And who the travellers are,

Whom the ships carry in and out between the lighthouses
That guard for ever the made privacy of this bay
Like twin stone dogs opposed on a gentleman's gate:
Within these breakwaters English is spoken; without
   Is the immense improbable atlas.

The eyes of the departing migrants are fixed on the sea,
To conjure their special fates from the impersonal water:
'I see an important decision made on a lake,
An illness, a beard, Arabia found in a bed,
   Nanny defeated, Money.'

And filled with the tears of the beaten or calm with fame,
The eyes of the returning thank the historical cliffs:
'The heart has at last ceased to lie, and the clock to accuse;
In the shadow under the yew, at the children's party
   Everything will be explained.'

And the old town with its keep and its Georgian houses
Has built its routine upon these unusual moments;
The vows, the tears, the slight emotional signals
Are here eternal and unremarkable gestures
   Like ploughing or soldiers' songs:

Soldiers who swarm in the pubs in their pretty clothes,
As fresh and silly as girls from a high-class academy:
The Lion, the Rose or the Crown will not ask them to die,
Not here, not now. All they are killing is time,
            Their pauper civilian future.

Above them, expensive and lovely as a rich child's toy,
The aeroplanes fly in the new European air,
On the edge of that air that makes England of minor importance;
And the tides warn bronzing bathers of a cooling star,
            With half its history done.

High over France the full moon, cold and exciting
Like one of those dangerous flatterers one meets and loves
When one is very unhappy, returns the human stare:
The night has many recruits; for thousands of pilgrims
            The Mecca is coldness of heart.

And the cry of the gulls at dawn is sad like work:
The soldier guards the traveller who pays for the soldier;
Each one prays in the dusk for himself, and neither
Controls the years. Some are temporary heroes:
            Some of these people are happy.

August 1937

XVI · James Honeyman

James Honeyman was a silent child
He didn't laugh or cry;
He looked at his mother
With curiosity.

Mother came up to the nursery,
Peeped through the open door,
Saw him striking matches
Sitting on the nursery floor.

He went to the children's party,
The buns were full of cream;
Sat dissolving sugar
In his teacup in a dream.

On his eighth birthday
Didn't care that the day was wet
For by his bedside
Lay a ten-shilling chemistry set.

Teacher said: 'James Honeyman's
The cleverest boy we've had,
But he doesn't play with the others
And that, I think, is sad.'

While the other boys played football
He worked in the laboratory
Got a scholarship to college,
And a first-class degree.

Kept awake with black coffee,
Took to wearing glasses,
Writing a thesis
On the toxic gases.

Went out into the country,
Went by a Green Line Bus,
Walked on the Chilterns,
Thought about Phosphorus.

Said: 'Lewisite in its day
Was pretty decent stuff,
But under modern conditions
It's not nearly strong enough.'

His Tutor sipped his port,
Said: 'I think it's clear
That young James Honeyman's
The most brilliant man of his year.'

He got a job in research
With Imperial Alkali,
Said to himself while shaving:
'I'll be famous before I die.'

His landlady said: 'Mr. Honeyman,
You've only got one life,
You ought to have some fun, Sir.
You ought to find a wife.'

At Imperial Alkali
There was a girl called Doreen,
One day she cut her finger,
Asked him for iodine.

'I'm feeling faint', she said.
He led her to a chair,
Fetched her a glass of water,
Wanted to stroke her hair.

They took a villa on the Great West Road,
Painted green and white;
On their left a United Dairy,
A cinema on their right.

At the bottom of his garden
He built a little shed.
'He's going to blow us up',
All the neighbours said.

Doreen called down at midnight:
'Jim dear, it's time for bed.'
'I'll finish my experiment
And then I'll come', he said.

Caught influenza at Christmas,
The Doctor said: 'Go to bed.'
'I'll finish my experiment
And then I'll go', he said.

Walked out on Sundays,
Helped to push the pram,
Said: 'I'm looking for a gas, dear;
A whiff will kill a man.

'I'm going to find it,
That's what I'm going to do.'
Doreen squeezed his hand and said:
'Jim, I believe in you.'

In the hot nights of summer
When the roses all were red
James Honeyman was working
In his little garden shed.

Came upstairs at midnight,
Kissed his sleeping son,
Held up a sealed glass test-tube,
Said: 'Look, Doreen, I've won!'

They stood together by the window,
The moon was bright and clear.
He said: 'At last I've done something
That's worthy of you, dear.'

Took a train next morning,
Went up to Whitehall
With the phial in his pocket
To show it to them all.

Sent in his card,
The officials only swore:
'Tell him we're very busy
And show him the door.'

Doreen said to the neighbours:
'Isn't it a shame?
My husband's so clever
And they didn't know his name.'

One neighbour was sympathetic,
Her name was Mrs. Flower.
She was the agent
Of a foreign power.

One evening they sat at supper,
There came a gentle knock:
'A gentleman to see Mr. Honeyman.'
He stayed till eleven o'clock.

They walked down the garden together,
Down to the little shed:
'We'll see you, then, in Paris.
Good night', the gentleman said.

The boat was nearing Dover,
He looked back at Calais:
Said: 'Honeyman's N.P.C.
Will be heard of, some day.'

He was sitting in the garden
Writing notes on a pad,
Their little son was playing
Round his mother and dad.

Suddenly from the east
Some aeroplanes appeared,
Somebody screamed: 'They're bombers!
War must have been declared!'

The first bomb hit the Dairy,
The second the cinema,
The third fell in the garden
Just like a falling star.

'Oh kiss me, Mother, kiss me,
And tuck me up in bed
For Daddy's invention
Is going to choke me dead!'

'Where are you, James, where are you?
Oh put your arms round me,
For my lungs are full
Of Honeyman's N.P.C.!'

'I wish I were a salmon
Swimming in the sea,
I wish I were the dove
That coos upon the tree.'

'Oh you are not a salmon,
Oh you are not a dove;
But you invented the vapour
That is killing those you love.'

'Oh hide me in the mountains,
Oh drown me in the sea.
Lock me in the dungeon
And throw away the key.'

'Oh you can't hide in the mountains,
Oh you can't drown in the sea,
But you must die, and you know why,
By Honeyman's N.P.C.!'

August 1937

XVII

As I walked out one evening,
 Walking down Bristol Street,
The crowds upon the pavement
 Were fields of harvest wheat.

And down by the brimming river
 I heard a lover sing
Under an arch of the railway:
 'Love has no ending.

'I'll love you, dear, I'll love you
 Till China and Africa meet
And the river jumps over the mountain
 And the salmon sing in the street.

'I'll love you till the ocean
 Is folded and hung up to dry
And the seven stars go squawking
 Like geese about the sky.

'The years shall run like rabbits
 For in my arms I hold
The Flower of the Ages
 And the first love of the world.'

227

But all the clocks in the city
    Began to whirr and chime:
'O let not Time deceive you,
    You cannot conquer Time.

'In the burrows of the Nightmare
    Where Justice naked is,
Time watches from the shadow
    And coughs when you would kiss.

'In headaches and in worry
    Vaguely life leaks away,
And Time will have his fancy
    To-morrow or to-day.

'Into many a green valley
    Drifts the appalling snow;
Time breaks the threaded dances
    And the diver's brilliant bow.

'O plunge your hands in water,
    Plunge them in up to the wrist;
Stare, stare in the basin
    And wonder what you've missed.

'The glacier knocks in the cupboard,
    The desert sighs in the bed,
And the crack in the tea-cup opens
    A lane to the land of the dead.

'Where the beggars raffle the banknotes
    And the Giant is enchanting to Jack,
And the Lily-white Boy is a Roarer
    And Jill goes down on her back.

'O look, look in the mirror,
    O look in your distress;
Life remains a blessing
    Although you cannot bless.

'O stand, stand at the window
    As the tears scald and start;
You shall love your crooked neighbour
    With your crooked heart.'

It was late, late in the evening,
    The lovers they were gone;
The clocks had ceased their chiming
    And the deep river ran on.

November 1937

XVIII · Oxford

Nature is so near: the rooks in the college garden
Like agile babies still speak the language of feeling;
By the tower the river still runs to the sea and will run,
        And the stones in that tower are utterly
        Satisfied still with their weight.

And the minerals and creatures, so deeply in love with their lives
Their sin of accidie excludes all others,
Challenge the nervous students with a careless beauty,
        Setting a single error
        Against their countless faults.

O in these quadrangles where Wisdom honours herself
Does the original stone merely echo that praise
Shallowly, or utter a bland hymn of comfort,
        The founder's equivocal blessing
        On all who worship Success?

Promising to the sharp sword all the glittering prizes,
The cars, the hotels, the service, the boisterous bed,
Then power to silence outrage with a testament,
        The widow's tears forgotten,
        The fatherless unheard.

Whispering to chauffeurs and little girls, to tourists and dons,
That Knowledge is conceived in the hot womb of Violence
Who in a late hour of apprehension and exhaustion
        Strains to her weeping breast
        That blue-eyed darling head.

And is that child happy with his box of lucky books
And all the jokes of learning? Birds cannot grieve:
Wisdom is a beautiful bird; but to the wise
        Often, often is it denied
        To be beautiful or good.

Without are the shops, the works, the whole green county
Where a cigarette comforts the guilty and a kiss the weak;
There thousands fidget and poke and spend their money:
        Eros Paidagogos
        Weeps on his virginal bed.

Ah, if that thoughtless almost natural world
Would snatch his sorrow to her loving sensual heart!
But he is Eros and must hate what most he loves;
        And she is of Nature; Nature
        Can only love herself.

And over the talkative city like any other
Weep the non-attached angels. Here too the knowledge of death
Is a consuming love: And the natural heart refuses
      The low unflattering voice
      That rests not till it find a hearing.

December 1937

XIX

Some say that Love's a little boy
      And some say he's a bird,
Some say he makes the world go round
      And some say that's absurd:
But when I asked the man next door
      Who looked as if he knew,
His wife was very cross indeed
      And said it wouldn't do.

Does it look like a pair of pyjamas
      Or the ham in a temperance hotel,
Does its odour remind one of llamas
      Or has it a comforting smell?
Is it prickly to touch as a hedge is
      Or soft as eiderdown fluff,
Is it sharp or quite smooth at the edges?
      O tell me the truth about love.

The history books refer to it
      In cryptic little notes,
And it's a common topic on
      The Trans-Atlantic boats;
I've found the subject mentioned in
      Accounts of suicides,
And even seen it scribbled on
      The backs of railway guides.

Does it howl like a hungry Alsatian
      Or boom like a military band,
Could one give a first-class imitation
      On a saw or a Steinway Grand,
Is its singing at parties a riot,
      Does it only like Classical stuff,
Will it stop when one wants to be quiet?
      O tell me the truth about love.

I looked inside the summer-house,
      It wasn't ever there,
I've tried the Thames at Maidenhead
      And Brighton's bracing air;

I don't know what the blackbird sang
Or what the roses said,
But it wasn't in the chicken-run
Or underneath the bed.

Can it pull extraordinary faces,
Is it usually sick on a swing,
Does it spend all its time at the races
Or fiddling with pieces of string,
Has it views of its own about money,
Does it think Patriotism enough,
Are its stories vulgar but funny?
O tell me the truth about love.

Your feelings when you meet it, I
Am told you can't forget,
I've sought it since I was a child
But haven't found it yet;
I'm getting on for thirty-five,
And still I do not know
What kind of creature it can be
That bothers people so.

When it comes, will it come without warning
Just as I'm picking my nose,
Will it knock on my door in the morning
Or tread in the bus on my toes,
Will it come like a change in the weather,
Will its greeting be courteous or bluff,
Will it alter my life altogether?
O tell me the truth about love.

January 1938

XX · The Voyage

Where does the journey look which the watcher upon the quay,
Standing under his evil star, so bitterly envies?
When the mountains swim away with slow calm strokes, and the gulls
Abandon their vow? Does it still promise the Juster Life?

And, alone with his heart at last, does the traveller find
In the vaguer touch of the wind and the fickle flash of the sea
Proofs that somewhere there exists, really, the Good Place,
As certain as those the children find in stones and holes?

No, he discovers nothing: he does not want to arrive.
The journey is false; the false journey really an illness
On the false island where the heart cannot act and will not suffer:
He condones the fever; he is weaker than he thought; his weakness is
real.

But at moments, as when the real dolphins with leap and abandon
Cajole for recognition, or, far away, a real island
Gets up to catch his eye, the trance is broken: he remembers
The hours, the places where he was well; he believes in joy.

And maybe the fever shall have a cure, the true journey an end
Where hearts meet and are really true: and away this sea that parts
The hearts that alter, but is the same, always; and goes
Everywhere, joining the false and the true, but cannot suffer.

January 1938

XXI · The Sphinx

Did it once issue from the carver's hand
Healthy? Even the earliest conquerors saw
The face of a sick ape, a bandaged paw,
A Presence in the hot invaded land.

The lion of a tortured stubborn star,
It does not like the young, nor love, nor learning:
Time hurt it like a person; it lies, turning
A vast behind on shrill America,

And witnesses. The huge hurt face accuses,
And pardons nothing, least of all success.
The answers that it utters have no uses

To those who face akimbo its distress:
'Do people like me?' No. The slave amuses
The lion: 'Am I to suffer always?' Yes.

January 1938

XXII · The Ship

The streets are brightly lit; our city is kept clean:
The third class have the greasiest cards, the first play high;
The beggars sleeping in the bows have never seen
What can be done in staterooms; no one asks why.

Lovers are writing letters, sportsmen playing ball;
One doubts the honour, one the beauty, of his wife;
A boy's ambitious; perhaps the captain hates us all;
Someone perhaps is leading the civilised life.

It is our culture that with such calm progresses
Over the barren plains of a sea; somewhere ahead
The septic East, a war, new flowers and new dresses.

Somewhere a strange and shrewd To-morrow goes to bed
Planning the test for men from Europe; no one guesses
Who will be most ashamed, who richer, and who dead.

January 1938

XXIII · Passenger Shanty

The ship weighed twenty thousand ton
    Parlez-vous
The ship weighed twenty thousand ton
    Parlez-vous
She left Marseille at a quarter-to-one
For the China War and the tropical sun.
    Inky-pinky-parlez-vouz.

The passengers are rather *triste*,
There's many a fool, and many a beast,
Who ought to go west, but is bound for the East.

Mr. Jackson buys rubber and sells it again,
He paints in oils and he drinks champagne,
Says: 'I should have been born in Elizabeth's reign.'

His wife learns astrology out of a book,
Says: 'Your horoscope's queer and I don't like its look.
With the Moon against Virgo you might be a crook.'

The planter tells us: 'In Malay
We play rugger in March and cricket in May
But feel starved for sex at the end of the day.'

The journalist Capa plays dicing games,
He photographed Teruel Town in flames,
He pinches the bottoms of all the dames.

The Dominican monks get up with the sun,
They're as fond of their dinner as anyone,
And they have their own mysterious fun.

The belle of the boat-deck laughs like a jay,
She models her face upon *Ta Beauté*
And her eyebrows are shifted every day.

Her rival, the bitch from Aix-les-Bains,
Has a Pekingese *nez* and monkey's *mains*
And her *buste*, it would seem, has been flattened by *trains*.

Alphonse is a student who talks a lot,
When he walks upstairs, he waggles his bot.
He says: 'France may go left, but Annam must not.'

The idiot child stole a cigarette;
The father looks at his wife with regret
And thinks of that night at the *Bal Musette*.

The Siamese doctor is plump and tan,
He thinks shouting a mark of the Westernised Man.
But he cures V.D.—which is more than you can.

The beautiful *matelots* and *mousses*
Would be no disgrace to the Ballets Russes,
But I can't see their presence is very much use.

It's the engineers who run the ship
And the stewards who bring us our tots to sip
Without which we'd never get through the trip.

Christopher sends off letters by air,
He longs for Someone who isn't there,
But Wystan says: 'Love is exceedingly rare.'

The sea is *blau*, the sea is *tief*
    Parlez-vous
The sea is *blau*, the sea is *tief*
    Parlez-vous
C'est le cimetière du Château d'If.
No doubt. But it's dull beyond belief.
    Inky-pinky-parlez vous.

January 1938

XXIV · The Traveller

Holding the distance up before his face
And standing under the peculiar tree,
He seeks the hostile unfamiliar place,
It is the strangeness that he tries to see

Of lands where he will not be asked to stay;
And fights with all his powers to be the same,
The One who loves Another far away,
And has a home, and wears his father's name.

Yet he and his are always the Expected:
The harbours touch him as he leaves the steamer,
The Soft, the Sweet, the Easily-Accepted;

The cities hold his feeling like a fan;
And crowds make room for him without a murmur,
As the earth has patience with the life of man.

January 1938

XXV · Macao

A weed from Catholic Europe, it took root
Between the yellow mountains and the sea,
And bore these gay stone houses like a fruit,
And grew on China imperceptibly.

Rococo images of Saint and Saviour
Promise her gamblers fortunes when they die;
Churches beside the brothels testify
That faith can pardon natural behaviour.

This city of indulgence need not fear
The major sins by which the heart is killed,
And governments and men are torn to pieces:

Religious clocks will strike; the childish vices
Will safeguard the low virtues of the child;
And nothing serious can happen here.

December 1938

XXVI · Hongkong

The leading characters are wise and witty;
Substantial men of birth and education
With wide experience of administration,
They know the manners of a modern city.

Only the servants enter unexpected;
Their silence has a fresh dramatic use:
Here in the East the bankers have erected
A worthy temple to the Comic Muse.

Ten thousand miles from home and What's-her-name,
The bugle on the Late Victorian hill
Puts out the soldier's light; off-stage, a war

Thuds like the slamming of a distant door:
We cannot postulate a General Will;
For what we are, we have ourselves to blame.

December 1938

XXVII · The Capital

Quarter of pleasures where the rich are always waiting,
Waiting expensively for miracles to happen,
O little restaurant where the lovers eat each other,
Café where exiles have established a malicious village;

You with your charm and your apparatus have abolished
The strictness of winter and the spring's compulsion;
Far from your lights the outraged punitive father,
The dullness of mere obedience here is apparent.

Yet with orchestras and glances, O, you betray us
To belief in our infinite powers; and the innocent
Unobservant offender falls in a moment
Victim to the heart's invisible furies.

In unlighted streets you hide away the appalling;
Factories where lives are made for a temporary use
Like collars or chairs, rooms where the lonely are battered
Slowly like pebbles into fortuitous shapes.

But the sky you illumine, your glow is visible far
Into the dark countryside, the enormous, the frozen,
Where, hinting at the forbidden like a wicked uncle,
Night after night to the farmer's children you beckon.

December 1938

XXVIII · Brussels in Winter

Wandering the cold streets tangled like old string,
Coming on fountains silent in the frost,
The city still escapes you; it has lost
The qualities that say 'I am a Thing.'

Only the homeless and the really humbled
Seem to be sure exactly where they are,
And in their misery are all assembled;
The winter holds them like the Opera.

Ridges of rich apartments rise to-night
Where isolated windows glow like farms:
A phrase goes packed with meaning like a van,

A look contains the history of man,
And fifty francs will earn the stranger right
To warm the heartless city in his arms.

December 1938

XXIX · Gare du Midi

A nondescript express in from the South,
Crowds round the ticket barrier, a face
To welcome which the mayor has not contrived
Bugles or braid: something about the mouth

Distracts the stray look with alarm and pity.
Snow is falling. Clutching a little case,
He walks out briskly to infect a city
Whose terrible future may have just arrived.

December 1938

XXX · Musée des Beaux Arts

About suffering they were never wrong,
The Old Masters: how well they understood
Its human position; how it takes place
While someone else is eating or opening a window or just walking
           dully along;
How, when the aged are reverently, passionately waiting
For the miraculous birth, there always must be
Children who did not specially want it to happen, skating
On a pond at the edge of the wood:
They never forgot
That even the dreadful martyrdom must run its course
Anyhow in a corner, some untidy spot
Where the dogs go on with their doggy life and the torturer's horse
Scratches its innocent behind on a tree.

In Brueghel's *Icarus*, for instance: how everything turns away
Quite leisurely from the disaster; the ploughman may
Have heard the splash, the forsaken cry,
But for him it was not an important failure; the sun shone
As it had to on the white legs disappearing into the green
Water; and the expensive delicate ship that must have seen
Something amazing, a boy falling out of the sky,
Had somewhere to get to and sailed calmly on.

December 1938

XXXI · Rimbaud

The nights, the railway-arches, the bad sky,
His horrible companions did not know it;
But in that child the rhetorician's lie
Burst like a pipe: the cold had made a poet.

Drinks bought him by his weak and lyric friend
His senses systematically deranged,
To all accustomed nonsense put an end;
Till he from lyre and weakness was estranged.

Verse was a special illness of the ear;
Integrity was not enough; that seemed
The hell of childhood: he must try again.

Now, galloping through Africa, he dreamed
Of a new self, the son, the engineer,
His truth acceptable to lying men.

December 1938

XXXII · A. E. Housman

No one, not even Cambridge, was to blame;
—Blame if you like the human situation—
Heart-injured in North London, he became
The leading classic of his generation.

Deliberately he chose the dry-as-dust,
Kept tears like dirty postcards in a drawer;
Food was his public love, his private lust
Something to do with violence and the poor.

In savage footnotes on unjust editions
He timidly attacked the life he led.
And put the money of his feelings on

The uncritical relations of the dead,
Where purely geographical divisions
Parted the coarse hanged soldier from the don.

December 1938

XXXIII · The Novelist

Encased in talent like a uniform,
The rank of every poet is well known;
They can amaze us like a thunderstorm,
Or die so young, or live for years alone.

They can dash forward like hussars: but he
Must struggle out of his boyish gift and learn
How to be plain and awkward, how to be
One after whom none think it worth to turn.

For, to achieve his lightest wish, he must
Become the whole of boredom, subject to
Vulgar complaints like love, among the Just

Be just, among the Filthy filthy too,
And in his own weak person, if he can,
Must suffer dully all the wrongs of Man.

December 1938

XXXIV · The Composer

All the others translate: the painter sketches
A visible world to love or reject;
Rummaging into his living, the poet fetches
The images out that hurt and connect,

From Life to Art by painstaking adaption,
Relying on us to cover the rift;
Only your notes are pure contraption,
Only your song is an absolute gift.

Pour out your presence, O delight, cascading
The falls of the knee and the weirs of the spine,
Our climate of silence and doubt invading;

You alone, alone, O imaginary song,
Are unable to say an existence is wrong,
And pour out your forgiveness like a wine.

December 1938

XXXV · Epitaph on a Tyrant

Perfection, of a kind, was what he was after,
And the poetry he invented was easy to understand;
He knew human folly like the back of his hand,
And was greatly interested in armies and fleets;
When he laughed, respectable senators burst with laughter,
And when he cried the little children died in the streets.

January 1939

XXXVI · Edward Lear

Left by his friend to breakfast alone on the white
Italian shore, his Terrible Demon arose
Over his shoulder; he wept to himself in the night,
A dirty landscape-painter who hated his nose.

The legions of cruel inquisitive They
Were so many and big like dogs; he was upset
By Germans and boats; affection was miles away:
But guided by tears he successfully reached his Regret.

How prodigious the welcome was. Flowers took his hat
And bore him off to introduce him to the tongs;
The demon's false nose made the table laugh; a cat
Soon had him waltzing madly, let him squeeze her hand;
Words pushed him to the piano to sing comic songs;

And children swarmed to him like settlers. He became a land.

January 1939

XXXVII · Voltaire at Ferney

Perfectly happy now, he looked at his estate.
An exile making watches glanced up as he passed,
And went on working; where a hospital was rising fast
A joiner touched his cap; an agent came to tell
Some of the trees he'd planted were progressing well.
The white alps glittered. It was summer. He was very great.

Far off in Paris, where his enemies
Whispered that he was wicked, in an upright chair
A blind old woman longed for death and letters. He would write
'Nothing is better than life.' But was it? Yes, the fight
Against the false and the unfair
Was always worth it. So was gardening. Civilise.

Cajoling, scolding, scheming, cleverest of them all,
He'd led the other children in a holy war
Against the infamous grown-ups; and, like a child, been sly
And humble when there was occasion for
The two-faced answer or the plain protective lie,
But patient like a peasant waited for their fall.

And never doubted, like D'Alembert, he would win:
Only Pascal was a great enemy, the rest
Were rats already poisoned; there was much, though, to be done,
And only himself to count upon.
Dear Diderot was dull but did his best;
Rousseau, he'd always known, would blubber and give in.

Night fell and made him think of women: Lust
Was one of the great teachers; Pascal was a fool.
How Emilie had loved astronomy and bed;
Pimpette had loved him too like scandal; he was glad.
He'd done his share of weeping for Jerusalem: As a rule
It was the pleasure-haters who became unjust.

Yet, like a sentinel, he could not sleep. The night was full of wrong,
Earthquakes and executions. Soon he would be dead,
And still all over Europe stood the horrible nurses
Itching to boil their children. Only his verses
Perhaps could stop them: He must go on working. Overhead
The uncomplaining stars composed their lucid song.

February 1939

XXXVIII · Matthew Arnold

His gift knew what he was—a dark disordered city;
Doubt hid it from the father's fond chastising sky;
Where once the mother-farms had glowed protectively,
Stood the haphazard alleys of the neighbours' pity.

—Yet would have gladly lived in him and learned his ways,
And grown observant like a beggar, and become
Familiar with each square and boulevard and slum,
And found in the disorder a whole world to praise.

But all his homeless reverence, revolted, cried:
'I am my father's forum and he shall be heard,
Nothing shall contradict his holy final word,
Nothing.' And thrust his gift in prison till it died,

And left him nothing but a jailor's voice and face,
And all rang hollow but the clear denunciation
Of a gregarious optimistic generation
That saw itself already in a father's place.

February 1939

XXXIX · In Memory of W. B. Yeats

(d. Jan. 1939)

I

He disappeared in the dead of winter:
The brooks were frozen, the air-ports almost deserted,
And snow disfigured the public statues;
The mercury sank in the mouth of the dying day.
O all the instruments agree
The day of his death was a dark cold day.

Far from his illness
The wolves ran on through the evergreen forests,
The peasant river was untempted by the fashionable quays;
By mourning tongues
The death of the poet was kept from his poems.

But for him it was his last afternoon as himself,
An afternoon of nurses and rumours;
The provinces of his body revolted,
The squares of his mind were empty,
Silence invaded the suburbs,
The current of his feeling failed: he became his admirers.

Now he is scattered among a hundred cities
And wholly given over to unfamiliar affections;
To find his happiness in another kind of wood
And be punished under a foreign code of conscience.
The words of a dead man
Are modified in the guts of the living.

But in the importance and noise of to-morrow
When the brokers are roaring like beasts on the floor of the Bourse,
And the poor have the sufferings to which they are fairly accustomed,
And each in the cell of himself is almost convinced of his freedom;
A few thousand will think of this day
As one thinks of a day when one did something slightly unusual.

O all the instruments agree
The day of his death was a dark cold day.

2

You were silly like us: your gift survived it all;
The parish of rich women, physical decay,
Yourself; mad Ireland hurt you into poetry.
Now Ireland has her madness and her weather still,
For poetry makes nothing happen: it survives
In the valley of its saying where executives
Would never want to tamper; it flows south
From ranches of isolation and the busy griefs,
Raw towns that we believe and die in; it survives,
A way of happening, a mouth.

3

Earth, receive an honoured guest;
William Yeats is laid to rest:
Let the Irish vessel lie
Emptied of its poetry.

Time that is intolerant
Of the brave and innocent,
And indifferent in a week
To a beautiful physique,

Worships language and forgives
Everyone by whom it lives;
Pardons cowardice, conceit,
Lays its honours at their feet.

Time that with this strange excuse
Pardoned Kipling and his views,

And will pardon Paul Claudel,
Pardons him for writing well.

In the nightmare of the dark
All the dogs of Europe bark,
And the living nations wait,
Each sequestered in its hate;

Intellectual disgrace
Stares from every human face,
And the seas of pity lie
Locked and frozen in each eye.

Follow, poet, follow right
To the bottom of the night,
With your unconstraining voice
Still persuade us to rejoice;

With the farming of a verse
Make a vineyard of the curse,
Sing of human unsuccess
In a rapture of distress;

In the deserts of the heart
Let the healing fountain start,
In the prison of his days
Teach the free man how to praise.

February 1939

XL

Where do They come from? Those whom we so much dread
As on our dearest location falls the chill
            Of the crooked wing and endangers
            The melting friend, the aqueduct, the flower.

Terrible Presences that the ponds reflect
Back at the famous, and when the blond boy
            Bites eagerly into the shining
            Apple, emerge in their shocking fury.

And we realise the woods are deaf and the sky
Nurses no one, and we are awake and these
            Like farmers have purpose and knowledge,
            And towards us their hate is directed.

We are the barren pastures to which they bring
The resentment of outcasts; on us they work
            Out their despair; they wear our weeping
            As the disgraceful badge of their exile.

O we conjured them here like a lying map;
Desiring the extravagant joy of life
        We lured with a mirage of orchards
        Fat in the lazy climate of refuge.

Our money sang like streams on the aloof peaks
Of our thinking that beckoned them on like girls;
        Our culture like a West of wonder
        Shone a solemn promise in their faces.

We expected the beautiful or the wise
Ready to see a charm in our childish fib,
        Pleased to find nothing but stones and
        Able at once to create a garden.

But those who come are not even children with
The big indiscriminate eyes we had lost,
        Occupying our narrow spaces
        With their anarchist vivid abandon.

They arrive, already adroit, having learned
Restraint at the table of a father's rage;
        In a mother's distorting mirror
        They discovered the Meaning of Knowing.

These pioneers have long adapted themselves
To the night and the nightmare; they come equipped
        To reply to terror with terror,
        With lies to unmask the least deception.

For a future of marriage nevertheless
The bed is prepared; though all our whiteness shrinks
        From the hairy and clumsy bridegroom,
        We conceive in the shuddering instant.

For the barren must wish to bear though the Spring
Punish; and the crooked that dreads to be straight
        Cannot alter its prayer but summons
        Out of the dark a horrible rector.

O the striped and vigorous tiger can move
With style through the borough of murder; the ape
        Is really at home in the parish
        Of grimacing and licking: but we have

Failed as their pupils. Our tears well from a love
We have never outgrown; our cities predict
        More than we hope; even our armies
        Have to express our need of forgiveness.

April 1939

XLI · September 1, 1939

I sit in one of the dives
On Fifty-Second Street
Uncertain and afraid
As the clever hopes expire
Of a low dishonest decade:
Waves of anger and fear
Circulate over the bright
And darkened lands of the earth,
Obsessing our private lives;
The unmentionable odour of death
Offends the September night.

Accurate scholarship can
Unearth the whole offence
From Luther until now
That has driven a culture mad,
Find what occurred at Linz,
What huge imago made
A psychopathic god:
I and the public know
What all schoolchildren learn,
Those to whom evil is done
Do evil in return.

Exiled Thucydides knew
All that a speech can say
About Democracy,
And what dictators do,
The elderly rubbish they talk
To an apathetic grave;
Analysed all in his book,
The enlightenment driven away,
The habit-forming pain,
Mismanagement and grief:
We must suffer them all again.

Into this neutral air
Where blind skyscrapers use
Their full height to proclaim
The strength of Collective Man,
Each language pours its vain
Competitive excuse:
But who can live for long
In an euphoric dream;
Out of the mirror they stare,
Imperialism's face
And the international wrong.

Faces along the bar
Cling to their average day:
The lights must never go out,
The music must always play,
All the conventions conspire
To make this fort assume
The furniture of home;
Lest we should see where we are,
Lost in a haunted wood,
Children afraid of the night
Who have never been happy or good.

The windiest militant trash
Important Persons shout
Is not so crude as our wish:
What mad Nijinsky wrote
About Diaghilev
Is true of the normal heart;
For the error bred in the bone
Of each woman and each man
Craves what it cannot have,
Not universal love
But to be loved alone.

From the conservative dark
Into the ethical life
The dense commuters come,
Repeating their morning vow,
'I *will* be true to the wife,
I'll concentrate more on my work',
And helpless governors wake
To resume their compulsory game:
Who can release them now,
Who can reach the deaf,
Who can speak for the dumb?

All I have is a voice
To undo the folded lie,
The romantic lie in the brain
Of the sensual man-in-the-street
And the lie of Authority
Whose buildings grope the sky:
There is no such thing as the State
And no one exists alone;
Hunger allows no choice
To the citizen or the police;
We must love one another or die.

Defenceless under the night
Our world in stupor lies;
Yet, dotted everywhere,
Ironic points of light
Flash out wherever the Just
Exchange their messages:
May I, composed like them
Of Eros and of dust,
Beleaguered by the same
Negation and despair,
Show an affirming flame.

September 1939

Part VII

In Time of War

A SONNET SEQUENCE WITH A VERSE COMMENTARY

(TO E. M. FORSTER)

Here, though the bombs are real and dangerous,
And Italy and King's are far away,
And we're afraid that you will speak to us,
You promise still the inner life shall pay.

As we run down the slope of Hate with gladness
You trip us up like an unnoticed stone,
And just as we are closeted with Madness
You interrupt us like the telephone.

For we are Lucy, Turton, Philip, we
Wish international evil, are excited
To join the jolly ranks of the benighted

Where Reason is denied and Love ignored:
But, as we swear our lie, Miss Avery
Comes out into the garden with the sword.

I

So from the years the gifts were showered; each
Ran off with his at once into his life:
Bee took the politics that make a hive,
Fish swam as fish, peach settled into peach.

And were successful at the first endeavour;
The hour of birth their only time at college,
They were content with their precocious knowledge,
And knew their station and were good for ever.

Till finally there came a childish creature
On whom the years could model any feature,
And fake with ease a leopard or a dove;

Who by the lightest wind was changed and shaken,
And looked for truth and was continually mistaken,
And envied his few friends and chose his love.

II

They wondered why the fruit had been forbidden;
It taught them nothing new. They hid their pride,
But did not listen much when they were chidden;
They knew exactly what to do outside.

They left: immediately the memory faded
Of all they'd learnt; they could not understand
The dogs now who, before, had always aided;
The stream was dumb with whom they'd always planned.

They wept and quarrelled: freedom was so wild.
In front, maturity, as he ascended,
Retired like a horizon from the child;

The dangers and the punishments grew greater;
And the way back by angels was defended
Against the poet and the legislator.

III

Only a smell had feelings to make known,
Only an eye could point in a direction;
The fountain's utterance was itself alone;
The bird meant nothing: that was his projection

Who named it as he hunted it for food.
He felt the interest in his throat, and found
That he could send his servant to the wood,
Or kiss his bride to rapture with a sound.

They bred like locusts till they hid the green
And edges of the world: and he was abject,
And to his own creation became subject;

And shook with hate for things he'd never seen,
And knew of love without lover's proper object,
And was oppressed as he had never been.

IV

He stayed: and was imprisoned in possession.
The seasons stood like guards about his ways,
The mountains chose the mother of his children,
And like a conscience the sun ruled his days.

Beyond him his young cousins in the city
Pursued their rapid and unnatural course,
Believed in nothing but were easy-going,
And treated strangers like a favourite horse.

And he changed little,
But took his colour from the earth,
And grew in likeness to his sheep and cattle.

The townsman thought him miserly and simple,
The poet wept and saw in him the truth,
And the oppressor held him up as an example.

V

His generous bearing was a new invention:
For life was slow; earth needed to be careless:
With horse and sword he drew the girls' attention;
He was the Rich, the Bountiful, the Fearless.

And to the young he came as a salvation;
They needed him to free them from their mothers,
And grew sharp-witted in the long migration,
And round his camp fires learnt all men are brothers.

But suddenly the earth was full: he was not wanted.
And he became the shabby and demented,
And took to drink to screw his nerves to murder;

Or sat in offices and stole,
And spoke approvingly of Law and Order,
And hated life with all his soul.

VI

He watched the stars and noted birds in flight;
The rivers flooded or the Empire fell:
He made predictions and was sometimes right;
His lucky guesses were rewarded well.

And fell in love with Truth before he knew her,
And rode into imaginary lands,
With solitude and fasting hoped to woo her,
And mocked at those who served her with their hands.

But her he never wanted to despise,
But listened always for her voice; and when
She beckoned to him, he obeyed in meekness,

And followed her and looked into her eyes;
Saw there reflected every human weakness,
And saw himself as one of many men.

VII

He was their servant—some say he was blind—
And moved among their faces and their things;
Their feeling gathered in him like a wind
And sang: they cried—'It is a God that sings'—

And worshipped him and set him up apart,
And made him vain, till he mistook for song
The little tremors of his mind and heart
At each domestic wrong.

Songs came no more: he had to make them.
With what precision was each strophe planned.
He hugged his sorrow like a plot of land,

And walked like an assassin through the town,
And looked at men and did not like them,
But trembled if one passed him with a frown.

VIII

He turned his field into a meeting-place,
And grew the tolerant ironic eye,
And formed the mobile money-changer's face,
And found the notion of equality.

And strangers were as brothers to his clocks,
And with his spires he made a human sky;
Museums stored his learning like a box,
And paper watched his money like a spy.

It grew so fast his life was overgrown,
And he forgot what once it had been made for,
And gathered into crowds and was alone,

And lived expensively and did without,
And could not find the earth which he had paid for,
Nor feel the love that he knew all about.

IX

They died and entered the closed life like nuns:
Even the very poor lost something; oppression
Was no more a fact; and the self-centred ones
Took up an even more extreme position.

And the kingly and the saintly also were
Distributed among the woods and oceans,
And touch our open sorrow everywhere,
Airs, waters, places, round our sex and reasons;

Are what we feed on as we make our choice.
We bring them back with promises to free them,
But as ourselves continually betray them:

They hear their deaths lamented in our voice,
But in our knowledge know we could restore them;
They could return to freedom; they would rejoice.

X

As a young child the wisest could adore him;
He felt familiar to them like their wives:
The very poor saved up their pennies for him,
And martyrs brought him presents of their lives.

But who could sit and play with him all day?
Their other needs were pressing, work, and bed:
The beautiful stone courts were built where they
Could leave him to be worshipped and well fed.

But he escaped. They were too blind to tell
That it was he who came with them to labour,
And talked and grew up with them like a neighbour:

To fear and greed those courts became a centre;
The poor saw there the tyrant's citadel,
And martyrs the lost face of the tormentor.

XI

He looked in all His wisdom from the throne
Down on the humble boy who kept the sheep,
And sent a dove; the dove returned alone:
Youth liked the music, but soon fell asleep.

But He had planned such future for the youth:
Surely His duty now was to compel;
For later he would come to love the truth,
And own his gratitude. The eagle fell.

It did not work: His conversation bored
The boy who yawned and whistled and made faces,
And wriggled free from fatherly embraces;

But with the eagle he was always willing
To go where it suggested, and adored
And learnt from it the many ways of killing.

XII

And the age ended, and the last deliverer died
In bed, grown idle and unhappy; they were safe:
The sudden shadow of the giant's enormous calf
Would fall no more at dusk across the lawn outside.

They slept in peace: in marshes here and there no doubt
A sterile dragon lingered to a natural death,
But in a year the spoor had vanished from the heath;
The kobold's knocking in the mountain petered out.

Only the sculptors and the poets were half sad,
And the pert retinue from the magician's house
Grumbled and went elsewhere. The vanquished powers
were glad

To be invisible and free: without remorse
Struck down the sons who strayed into their course,
And ravished the daughters, and drove the fathers mad.

1936

XIII

Certainly praise: let the song mount again and again
For life as it blossoms out in a jar or a face,
For the vegetable patience, the animal grace;
Some people have been happy; there have been great men.

But hear the morning's injured weeping, and know why:
Cities and men have fallen; the will of the Unjust
Has never lost its power; still, all princes must
Employ the Fairly-Noble unifying Lie.

History opposes its grief to our buoyant song:
The Good Place has not been; our star has warmed to birth
A race of promise that has never proved its worth;

The quick new West is false; and prodigious, but wrong
This passive flower-like people who for so long
In the Eighteen Provinces have constructed the earth.

XIV

Yes, we are going to suffer, now; the sky
Throbs like a feverish forehead; pain is real;
The groping searchlights suddenly reveal
The little natures that will make us cry,

Who never quite believed they could exist,
Not where we were. They take us by surprise
Like ugly long-forgotten memories,
And like a conscience all the guns resist.

Behind each sociable home-loving eye
The private massacres are taking place;
All Women, Jews, the Rich, the Human Race.

The mountains cannot judge us when we lie:
We dwell upon the earth; the earth obeys
The intelligent and evil till they die.

XV

Engines bear them through the sky: they're free
And isolated like the very rich;
Remote like savants, they can only see
The breathing city as a target which

Requires their skill; will never see how flying
Is the creation of ideas they hate,
Nor how their own machines are always trying
To push through into life. They chose a fate

The islands where they live did not compel.
Though earth may teach our proper discipline,
At any time it will be possible

To turn away from freedom and become
Bound like the heiress in her mother's womb,
And helpless as the poor have always been.

XVI

Here war is simple like a monument:
A telephone is speaking to a man;
Flags on a map assert that troops were sent;
A boy brings milk in bowls. There is a plan

For living men in terror of their lives,
Who thirst at nine who were to thirst at noon,
And can be lost and are, and miss their wives,
And, unlike an idea, can die too soon.

But ideas can be true although men die,
And we can watch a thousand faces
Made active by one lie:

And maps can really point to places
Where life is evil now:
Nanking; Dachau.

XVII

They are and suffer; that is all they do:
A bandage hides the place where each is living,
His knowledge of the world restricted to
The treatment that the instruments are giving.

And lie apart like epochs from each other
—Truth in their sense is how much they can bear;
It is not talk like ours, but groans they smother—
And are remote as plants; we stand elsewhere.

For who when healthy can become a foot?
Even a scratch we can't recall when cured,
But are boisterous in a moment and believe

In the common world of the uninjured, and cannot
Imagine isolation. Only happiness is shared,
And anger, and the idea of love.

XVIII

Far from the heart of culture he was used:
Abandoned by his general and his lice,
Under a padded quilt he closed his eyes
And vanished. He will not be introduced

When this campaign is tidied into books:
No vital knowledge perished in his skull;
His jokes were stale; like wartime, he was dull;
His name is lost for ever like his looks.

He neither knew nor chose the Good, but taught us,
And added meaning like a comma, when
He turned to dust in China that our daughters

Be fit to love the earth, and not again
Disgraced before the dogs; that, where are waters,
Mountains and houses, may be also men.

April 1938

XIX

But in the evening the oppression lifted;
The peaks came into focus; it had rained:
Across the lawns and cultured flowers drifted
The conversation of the highly trained.

The gardeners watched them pass and priced their shoes;
A chauffeur waited, reading in the drive,
For them to finish their exchange of views;
It seemed a picture of the private life.

Far off, no matter what good they intended,
The armies waited for a verbal error
With all the instruments for causing pain:

And on the issue of their charm depended
A land laid waste, with all its young men slain,
The women weeping, and the towns in terror.

XX

They carry terror with them like a purse,
And flinch from the horizon like a gun;
And all the rivers and the railways run
Away from Neighbourhood as from a curse.

They cling and huddle in the new disaster
Like children sent to school, and cry in turn;
For Space has rules they cannot hope to learn,
Time speaks a language they will never master.

We live here. We lie in the Present's unopened
Sorrow; its limits are what we are.
The prisoner ought never to pardon his cell.

Can future ages ever escape so far,
Yet feel derived from everything that happened,
Even from us, that even this was well?

XXI

The life of man is never quite completed;
The daring and the chatter will go on:
But, as an artist feels his power gone,
These walk the earth and know themselves defeated.

Some could not bear nor break the young and mourn for
The wounded myths that once made nations good,
Some lost a world they never understood,
Some saw too clearly all that man was born for.

Loss is their shadow-wife, Anxiety
Receives them like a grand hotel; but where
They may regret they must; their life, to hear

The call of the forbidden cities, see
The stranger watch them with a happy stare,
And Freedom hostile in each home and tree.

XXII

Simple like all dream wishes, they employ
The elementary language of the heart,
And speak to muscles of the need for joy:
The dying and the lovers soon to part

Hear them and have to whistle. Always new,
They mirror every change in our position;
They are our evidence of what we do;
They speak directly to our lost condition.

Think in this year what pleased the dancers best:
When Austria died and China was forsaken,
Shanghai in flames and Teruel re-taken,

France put her case before the world: 'Partout
Il y a de la joie.' America addressed
The earth: 'Do you love me as I love you?'

XXIII

When all the apparatus of report
Confirms the triumph of our enemies;
Our bastion pierced, our army in retreat,
Violence successful like a new disease,

And Wrong a charmer everywhere invited;
When we regret that we were ever born:
Let us remember all who seemed deserted.
To-night in China let me think of one,

Who through ten years of silence worked and waited,
Until in Muzot all his powers spoke,
And everything was given once for all:

And with the gratitude of the Completed
He went out in the winter night to stroke
That little tower like a great animal.

XXIV

No, not their names. It was the others who built
Each great coercive avenue and square,
Where men can only recollect and stare,
The really lonely with the sense of guilt

Who wanted to persist like that for ever;
The unloved had to leave material traces:
But these need nothing but our better faces,
And dwell in them, and know that we shall never

Remember who we are nor why we're needed.
Earth grew them as a bay grows fishermen
Or hills a shepherd; they grew ripe and seeded;

And the seeds clung to us; even our blood
Was able to revive them; and they grew again;
Happy their wish and mild to flower and flood.

XXV

Nothing is given: we must find our law.
Great buildings jostle in the sun for domination;
Behind them stretch like sorry vegetation
The low recessive houses of the poor.

We have no destiny assigned us:
Nothing is certain but the body; we plan
To better ourselves; the hospitals alone remind us
Of the equality of man.

Children are really loved here, even by police:
They speak of years before the big were lonely,
And will be lost.

                    And only
The brass bands throbbing in the parks foretell
Some future reign of happiness and peace.

We learn to pity and rebel.

XXVI

Always far from the centre of our names,
The little workshop of love: yes, but how wrong

We were about the old manors and the long
Abandoned Folly and the children's games.

Only the acquisitive expects a quaint
Unsaleable product, something to please
An artistic girl; it's the selfish who sees
In every impractical beggar a saint.

We can't believe that we ourselves designed it,
A minor item of our daring plan
That caused no trouble; we took no notice of it.

Disaster comes, and we're amazed to find it
The single project that since work began
Through all the cycle showed a steady profit.

XXVII

Wandering lost upon the mountains of our choice,
Again and again we sigh for an ancient South,
For the warm nude ages of instinctive poise,
For the taste of joy in the innocent mouth.

Asleep in our huts, how we dream of a part
In the glorious balls of the future; each intricate maze
Has a plan, and the disciplined movements of the heart
Can follow for ever and ever its harmless ways.

We envy streams and houses that are sure:
But we are articled to error; we
Were never nude and calm like a great door,

And never will be perfect like the fountains;
We live in freedom by necessity,
A mountain people dwelling among mountains.

1938 (see App. II)

Commentary

Season inherits legally from dying season;
Protected by the wide peace of the sun, the planets
Continue their circulations; and the galaxy

Is free for ever to revolve like an enormous biscuit:
With all his engines round him and the summer flowers,
Little upon his little earth, man contemplates

The universe of which he is both judge and victim;
A rarity in an uncommon corner, gazes
On the great trackways where his tribe and truth are nothing.

Certainly the growth of the fore-brain has been a success:
He has not got lost in a backwater like the lampshell
Or the limpet; he has not died out like the super-lizards.

His boneless worm-like ancestors would be amazed
At the upright position, the breast, the four-chambered heart,
The clandestine evolution in the mother's shadow.

'Sweet is it', say the doomed, 'to be alive though wretched',
And the young emerging from the closed parental circle,
To whose uncertainty the certain years present

Their syllabus of limitless anxiety and labour,
At first feel nothing but the gladness of their freedom,
Are happy in the new embraces and the open talk.

But liberty to be and weep has never been sufficient;
The winds surround our griefs, the unfenced sky
To all our failures is a taciturn unsmiling witness.

And not least here, among this humorous and hairless people
Who like a cereal have inherited these valleys:
Tarim nursed them; Thibet was the tall rock of their protection,

And where the Yellow River shifts its course, they learnt
How to live well, though ruin threatened often.
For centuries they looked in fear towards the northern defiles,

But now must turn and gather like a fist to strike
Wrong coming from the sea, from those whose paper houses
Tell of their origin among the coral islands;

Who even to themselves deny a human freedom,
And dwell in the estranging tyrant's vision of the earth
In a calm stupor under their blood-spotted flag.

Here danger works a civil reconciliation,
Interior hatreds are resolved upon this foreign foe,
And will-power to resist is growing like a prosperous city.

For the invader now is deadly and impartial as a judge:
Down country footpaths, from each civic sky,
His anger blows alike upon the rich, and all

Who dwell within the crevices of destitution,
On those with a laborious lifetime to recall, and those,
The innocent and short whose dreams contain no children.

While in an international and undamaged quarter,
Casting our European shadows on Shanghai,
Walking unhurt among the banks, apparently immune

Below the monuments of an acquisitive society,
With friends and books and money and the traveller's freedom,
We are compelled to realise that our refuge is a sham.

For this material contest that has made Hongkew
A terror and a silence, and Chapei a howling desert,
Is but the local variant of a struggle in which all,

The elderly, the amorous, the young, the handy and the thoughtful,
Those to whom feeling is a science, those to whom study
Of all that can be added and compared is a consuming love,

With those whose brains are empty as a school in August,
And those in whom the urge to action is so strong
They cannot read a letter without whispering, all

In cities, deserts, ships, in lodgings near the port,
Discovering the past of strangers in a library,
Creating their own future on a bed, each with his treasure,

Self-confident among the laughter and the *petits verres*,
Or motionless and lonely like a moping cormorant,
In all their living are profoundly implicated.

This is one sector and one movement of the general war
Between the dead and the unborn, the Real and the Pretended,
Which for the creature who creates, communicates, and chooses,

The only animal aware of lack of finish,
In essence is eternal. When we emerged from holes
And blinked in the warm sunshine of the Laufen Ice Retreat,

Thinking of Nature as a close and loyal kinsman,
On every acre the opponents faced each other,
And we were far within the zone where casualties begin.

Now in a world that has no localised events,
Where not a tribe exists without its dossier,
And the machine has taught us how, to the Non-Human,

That unprogressive blind society that knows
No argument except the absolute and violent veto,
Our colours, creeds and sexes are identical,

The issue is the same. Some uniforms are new,
Some have changed sides; but the campaign continues:
Still unachieved is *Jen*, the Truly Human.

This is the epoch of the Third Great Disappointment:
The First was the collapse of that slave-owning empire
Whose yawning magistrate asked, 'What is truth?'

Upon its ruins rose the Universal Churches:
Men camped like tourists under their tremendous shadows,
United by a common sense of human failure,

Their certain knowledge only of the timeless fields
Where the Unchanging Happiness received the faithful,
And the Eternal Nightmare waited to devour the wicked.

In which a host of workers, famous and obscure,
Meaning to do no more than use their eyes,
Not knowing what they did, then sapped belief;

Put in its place a neutral dying star,
Where Justice could not visit. Self was the one city,
The cell where each must find his comfort and his pain,

The body nothing but a useful favourite machine
To go upon errands of love and to run the house,
While the mind in its study spoke with its private God.

But now that wave which already was washing the heart,
When the cruel Turk stormed the gates of Constantine's city,
When *Galileo* muttered to himself, '*sed movet*',

And *Descartes* thought, 'I am because I think',
To-day, all spent, is silently withdrawing itself:
Unhappy he or she who after it is sucked.

Never before was the Intelligence so fertile,
The Heart more stunted. The human field became
Hostile to brotherhood and feeling like a forest.

Machines devised by harmless clergymen and boys
Attracted men like magnets from the marl and clay
Into towns on the coal-measures, to a kind of freedom,

Where the abstinent with the landless drove a bitter bargain,
But sowed in that act the seeds of an experienced hatred,
Which, germinating long in tenement and gas-lit cellar,

Is choking now the aqueducts of our affection.
Knowledge of their colonial suffering has cut off
The Hundred Families like an attack of shyness;

The apprehensive rich pace up and down
Their narrow compound of success; in every body
The ways of living are disturbed; intrusive as a sill,

Fear builds enormous ranges casting shadows,
Heavy, bird-silencing, upon the outer world,
Hills that our grief sighs over like a Shelley, parting

All that we feel from all that we perceive,
Desire from Data; and the Thirteen gay Companions
Grow sullen now and quarrelsome as mountain tribes.

We wander on the earth, or err from bed to bed
In search of home, and fail, and weep for the lost ages
Before Because became As If, or rigid Certainty

The Chances Are. The base hear us, and the violent
Who long to calm our guilt with murder, and already
Have not been slow to turn our wish to their advantage.

On every side they make their brazen offer:
Now in that Catholic country with the shape of Cornwall,
Where Europe first became a term of pride,

North of the Alps where dark hair turns to blonde,
In Germany now loudest, land without a centre
Where the sad plains are like a sounding rostrum,

And on these tidy and volcanic summits near us now,
From which the Black Stream hides the Tuscarora Deep,
The voice is quieter but the more inhuman and triumphant.

By wire and wireless, in a score of bad translations,
They give their simple message to the world of man:
'*Man can have Unity if Man will give up Freedom.*

The State is real, the Individual is wicked;
Violence shall synchronise your movements like a tune,
And Terror like a frost shall halt the flood of thinking.

Barrack and bivouac shall be your friendly refuge,
And racial pride shall tower like a public column
And confiscate for safety every private sorrow.

Leave Truth to the police and us; we know the Good;
We build the Perfect City time shall never alter;
Our Law shall guard you always like a cirque of mountains,

Your Ignorance keep off evil like a dangerous sea;
You shall be consummated in the General Will,
Your children innocent and charming as the beasts.'

All the great conquerors sit upon their platform,
Lending their sombre weight of practical experience:
Ch'in Shih Huang Ti who burnt the scholars' books,

Chaka the mad who segregated the two sexes,
And *Genghis Khan* who thought mankind should be destroyed,
And *Diocletian* the administrator make impassioned speeches.

Napoleon claps who found religion useful,
And all who passed deception on the People, or who said
Like Little *Frederick*, 'I shall see that it is done.'

While many famous clerks support their programme:
Plato the good, despairing of the average man,
With sad misgivings signs their manifesto;

Shang-tzu approves their principle of Nothing Private;
The author of *The Prince* will heckle; *Hobbes* will canvass,
With generalising *Hegel* and quiet *Bosanquet*.

And every family and every heart is tempted:
The earth debates; the Fertile Crescent argues;
Even the little towns upon the way to somewhere,

Those desert flowers the aeroplane now fertilises,
Quarrel on this; in England far away,
Behind the high tides and the navigable estuaries;

In the Far West, in absolutely free America,
In melancholy Hungary, and clever France
Where ridicule has acted a historic role,

And here where the rice-grain nourishes these patient households
The ethic of the feudal citadel has impregnated,
Thousands believe, and millions are half-way to a conviction.

While others have accepted *Pascal's* wager and resolve
To take whatever happens as the will of God,
Or with *Spinoza* vote that evil be unreal.

Nor do our leaders help: we know them now
For humbugs full of vain dexterity, invoking
A gallery of ancestors, pursuing still the mirage

Of long dead grandeurs whence the interest has absconded,
As Fahrenheit in an odd corner of great Celsius' kingdom
Might mumble of the summers measured once by him.

Yet all the same we have our faithful sworn supporters
Who never lost their faith in knowledge or in man,
But worked so eagerly that they forgot their food

And never noticed death or old age coming on,
Prepared for freedom as *Kuo Hsi* for inspiration,
Waiting it calmly like the coming of an honoured guest.

Some looked at falsehood with the candid eyes of children,
Some had a woman's ear to catch injustice,
Some took Necessity, and knew her, and she brought forth Freedom.

Some of our dead are famous, but they would not care:
Evil is always personal and spectacular,
But goodness needs the evidence of all our lives,

And, even to exist, it must be shared as truth,
As freedom or as happiness. (For what is happiness
If not to witness joy upon the features of another?)

They did not live to be remembered specially as noble,
Like those who cultivated only cucumbers and melons
To prove that they were rich; and when we praise their names,

They shake their heads in warning, chiding us to give
Our gratitude to the Invisible College of the Humble,
Who through the ages have accomplished everything essential,

And stretch around our struggle as the normal landscape,
And mingle, fluent with our living, like the winds and waters,
The dust of all the dead that reddens every sunset;

Giving us courage to confront our enemies,
Not only on the Grand Canal, or in Madrid,
Across the campus of a university city,

But aid us everywhere, that in the lovers' bedroom,
The white laboratory, the school, the public meeting,
The enemies of life may be more passionately attacked.

And, if we care to listen, we can always hear them:
'Men are not innocent as beasts and never can be,
Man can improve himself but never will be perfect.

Only the free have disposition to be truthful,
Only the truthful have the interest to be just,
Only the just possess the will-power to be free.

For common justice can determine private freedom,
As a clear sky can tempt men to astronomy,
Or a peninsula persuade them to be sailors.

You talked of Liberty, but were not just; and now
Your enemies have called your bluff; for in your city,
Only the man behind the rifle had free-will.

One wish is common to you both, the wish to build
A world united as that Europe was in which
The flint-faced exile wrote his three-act comedy.

Lament not its decay; that shell was too constricting:
The years of private isolation had their lesson,
And in the interest of intelligence were necessary.

Now in the clutch of crisis and the bloody hour
You must defeat your enemies or perish, but remember,
Only by those who reverence it can life be mastered;

Only a whole and happy conscience can stand up
And answer their bleak lie; among the just, .
And only there, is Unity compatible with Freedom.'

Night falls on China; the great arc of travelling shadow
Moves over land and ocean, altering life:
Thibet already silent, the packed Indias cooling,

Inert in the paralysis of caste. And though in Africa
The vegetation still grows fiercely like the young,
And in the cities that receive the slanting radiations

The lucky are at work, and most still know they suffer,
The dark will touch them soon: night's tiny noises
Will echo vivid in the owl's developed ear,

Vague in the anxious sentry's; and the moon look down
On battlefields and dead men lying, heaped like treasure,
On lovers ruined in a brief embrace, on ships

Where exiles watch the sea: and in the silence
The cry that streams out into the indifferent spaces,
And never stops or slackens, may be heard more clearly,

Above the everlasting murmur of the woods and rivers,
And more insistent than the lulling answer of the waltzes,
Or hum of printing-presses turning forests into lies;

As now I hear it, rising round me from Shanghai,
And mingling with the distant mutter of guerrilla fighting,
The voice of Man: '*O teach me to outgrow my madness.*

It's better to be sane than mad, or liked than dreaded;
It's better to sit down to nice meals than to nasty;
It's better to sleep two than single; it's better to be happy.

Ruffle the perfect manners of the frozen heart,
And once again compel it to be awkward and alive,
To all it suffered once a weeping witness.

Clear from the head the masses of impressive rubbish;
Rally the lost and trembling forces of the will,
Gather them up and let them loose upon the earth,

Till they construct at last a human justice,
The contribution of our star, within the shadow
Of which uplifting, loving, and constraining power
All other reasons may rejoice and operate.'

Autumn 1938

Part VIII

Theatre, Film, Radio

I

Drama began as the act of a whole community. Ideally there would be no spectators. In practice every member of the audience should feel like an understudy.

Drama is essentially an art of the body. The basis of acting is acrobatics, dancing, and all forms of physical skill. The music hall, the Christmas pantomime, and the country house charade are the most living drama of to-day.

The development of the film has deprived drama of any excuse for being documentary. It is not in its nature to provide an ignorant and passive spectator with exciting news.

The subject of drama, on the other hand, is the commonly known, the universally familiar stories of the society or generation in which it is written. The audience, like the child listening to the fairy tale, ought to know what is going to happen next.

Similarly the drama is not suited to the analysis of character, which is the province of the novel. Dramatic characters are simplified, easily recognisable and over life-size.

Dramatic speech should have the same confessed, significant, and undocumentary character, as dramatic movement.

Drama in fact deals with the general and universal, not with the particular and local, but it is probable that drama can only deal, at any rate directly, with the relations of human beings with each other, not with the relation of man to the rest of nature.

September 1935

II · Choruses and Songs

I

You who have come to watch us play and go
Openly to face the outer sky, you may
As guest or as possessor enter in
To the mysterious joy of a lighted house.
But never think our thoughts are strange to yours;
We, too, have watched life's circular career
How seed woken by touches in the dark
Out of this inarticulate recognition

And changing every moment come at last
By fortunate prejudice to delighting form
And the indifference of profuse production.
We saw all this, but what have we to do
With the felicities of natural growth?
What reference theirs to ours, where shame
Invasive daily into deeper tissues
Has all convicted? Remain we here
Sitting too late among the lights and music
Without hope waiting for a soothing hush;
Never to day-break can we say 'at last'
And eyes from vistas have brought nothing back;
The pane of glass is always there, looked through,
Bewilders with left-handed images.
If when the curtain falls, if you should speak,
Turning together, as of neighbours lately gone,
Although our anguish seem but summer lightning,
Sudden, soon over, in another place,
Although immune then, do not say of us
'It was nothing, their loss.' It was all.

April 1929

2

You who return to-night to a narrow bed
With one name running sorrowfully through your sorrowful head,
You who have never been touched, and you, pale lover,
Who left the house this morning kissed all over,
You little boys also of quite fourteen
Beginning to realise just what we mean,
Fill up glasses with champagne and drink again.

It's not a new school or factory to which we summon,
We're here today because of a man and a woman.
O Chef, employ your continental arts
To celebrate the union of two loving hearts!
Waiters, be deft, and slip, you pages, by
To honour the god to name whom is to lie:
Fill up glasses with champagne and drink again.

Already he has brought the swallows past the Scillies
To chase each other skimming under English bridges,
Has loosed the urgent pollen on the glittering country
To find the pistil, force its burglar's entry,
He moves us also and up the marble stair
He leads the figures matched in beauty and desire:
Fill up glasses with champagne and drink again.

It's not only this we praise, it's the general love:
Let cat's mew rise to a scream on the tool-shed roof,
Let son come home to-night to his anxious mother,
Let the vicar lead the choirboy into a dark corner.
The orchid shall flower to-night that flowers every hundred years,
The boots and the slavey be found dutch-kissing on the stairs:
Fill up glasses with champagne and drink again.

Let this be kept as a generous hour by all,
This once let the uncle settle his nephew's bill,
Let the nervous lady's table gaucheness be forgiven,
Let the thief's explanation of the theft be taken,
The boy caught smoking shall escape the usual whipping,
To-night the expensive whore shall give herself for nothing:
Fill up glasses with champagne and drink again.

The landlocked state shall get its port to-day,
The midnight worker in the laboratory by the sea
Shall discover under the cross-wires that which he looks for,
To-night the asthmatic clerk shall dream he's a boxer,
Let the cold heart's wish be granted, the desire for a desire,
O give to the coward now his hour of power:
Fill up glasses with champagne and drink again.

? Summer 1930

3

Alice is gone and I'm alone,
    Nobody understands
How lovely were her Fire Alarms,
    How fair her German Bands.

O how I cried when Alice died
    The day we were to have wed.
We never had our Roasted Duck
    And now she's a Loaf of Bread.

At nights I weep, I cannot sleep:
    Moonlight to me recalls
I never saw her Waterfront
    Nor she my Waterfalls.

? 1931

4

You were a great Cunarder, I
Was only a fishing smack.
Once you passed across my bows
And of course you did not look back.

275

It was only a single moment yet
I watch the sea and sigh,
Because my heart can never forget
The day you passed me by.

? 1932

5

Chorus.   Hail the strange electric writing
             Alma Mater on the door
             Like a secret sign inviting
             All the rich to meet the poor:
             Alma Mater, ave, salve,
             Floreas in secula.

Girls.   You sent us men with lots of money,
             You sent us men you knew were clean,
             You sent us men as sweet as honey,
             Men to make us really keen.
             Always, even though we marry,
             Though we wear ancestral pearls,
             One memory we'll always carry,
             We were Alma Mater girls.

Chorus.   Alma Mater, ave, salve, etc.

Thieves.   Let Americans with purses
             Go for short strolls after dark,
             Let the absent-minded nurses
             Leave an heiress in the park,
             Though the bullers soon or later
             Clap us handcuffed into jail,
             We'll remember Alma Mater,
             We'll remember without fail.

Chorus.   Alma Mater, ave, salve, etc.

Boys.   The French are mean and Germans lazy,
             Dutchmen leave you in the end.
             Only the English, though they're crazy,
             They will keep you for a friend.
             Always, though a king in cotton
             Waft us hence to foreign parts,
             Alma Mater shall not be forgotten,
             She is written on our hearts.

Chorus.   Alma Mater, ave, salve, etc.

Blackmailers. We must thank our mugs' relations,
               For our income and man's laws.

But the first congratulations,
Alma Mater, they are yours.

Coiners.   When the fool believes our story,
When he thinks our coins are true,
To Alma Mater be the glory
For she taught us what to do.

Chorus.   Alma Mater, ave, salve, etc.

Old Hacks
and Trots.   We cannot dance upon the table
Now we're old as souvenirs
Yet as long as we are able
We'll remember bygone years.
Still, as when we were the attraction,
Come the people from abroad,
Spending, though we're out of action,
More than they can well afford.

Chorus.   Alma Mater, ave, salve, etc.

Grand Chorus.   Navies rust and nations perish,
Currency is never sure,
But Alma Mater she shall flourish
While the sexes shall endure:
Alma Mater, ave, salve,
Floreas in secula.

? 1932

6

Seen when night was silent,
The bean-shaped island

And our ugly comic servant
Who is observant

O the verandah and the fruit
   The tiny steamer in the bay
Startling summer with its hoot.
   You have gone away.

? 1933

7

Love, loath to enter
The suffering winter
Still willing to rejoice
With the unbroken voice

At the precocious charm
Blithe in the dream
Afraid to wake, afraid
To doubt one term
Of summer's perfect fraud,
Enter and suffer
Within the quarrel
Be most at home,
Among the sterile prove
Your vigours, love.

? 1933

8

A beastly devil came last night,
He said he was going to kill you quite.
I was going to faint;
The virgin came down and made me a saint.
Olive, I am renowned,
For the devil I have drowned.
A saint am I and a saint are you,
It's perfectly, perfectly, perfectly true.

Olive will you be my wife?
I have saved your life.
Just say you'll be mine,
You shall have kisses like wine,
When the wine gets into your head
I will see that you're not misled.
A saint am I and a saint are you,
It's perfectly, perfectly, perfectly true.

Olive, when we are wed,
We shall have a lovely clean bed.
You know how little babies are made,
Now don't be afraid,
You understand
They are made with God's hand.
A saint am I and a saint are you,
It's perfectly, perfectly, perfectly true.

Olive, O I love your hair,
I love your clothes, I love you bare.
A cathedral we will build
When the devil I have killed.
We'll go up to the skies
And eat sweet mince pies.
A saint am I and a saint are you,
It's perfectly, perfectly, perfectly true.

? 1934

You with shooting-sticks and cases for field-glasses, your limousines
    parked in a circle: who visit the public games, observing in
    burberries the feats of the body:
You who stand before the west fronts of cathedrals: appraising the
    curious carving:
The virgin creeping like a cat to the desert, the trumpeting angels, the
    usurers boiling:
And you also who look for truth: alone in tower:
Follow our hero and his escort on his latest journey: From the square
    surrounded by Georgian houses, taking the lurching tram
    eastward
South of the ship-cranes, of the Slythe canal: Stopping at Fruby and
    Drulger Street,
Past boys ball-using: shrill in alleys.
Passing the cinemas blazing with bulbs: bowers of bliss
Where thousands are holding hands: they gape at the tropical
    vegetation, at the Ionic pillars and the organ solo.
Look left: The moon shows locked sheds, wharves by water,
On your right is the Power House: its chimneys fume gently above us
    like rifles recently fired.
Look through the grating at the vast machinery: at the dynamos and
    turbines
Grave, giving no sign of the hurricane of steam within their huge steel
    bottles,
At the Diesel engines like howdahed elephants: at the dials with their
    flickering pointers:
Power to the city: where loyalties are not those of the family.

And now, enter:
O human pity, gripped by the crying of a captured bird, wincing at
    sight of surgeon's lance,
Shudder indeed: that life on its narrow littoral so lucky
Can match against eternity a time so cruel!
The street we enter with setts is paved: cracked and uneven as an
    Alpine glacier,
Garbage chucked in the gutters has collected in the hollows in
    loathsome pools,
Back to back houses on both sides stretch: a dead-straight line of dung-
    colored brick
Wretched and dirty as a run for chickens.
Full as a theatre is the foul thoroughfare: some sitting like sacks, some
    slackly standing.
Their faces grey in the glimmering gaslight: their eyeballs drugged
    like a dead rabbit's.
From a window a child is looking, by want so fretted his face has
    assumed the features of a tortoise:
A human forest: all by one infection cancelled.
Despair so far invading every tissue has destroyed in these the hidden
    seat of the desire and the intelligence.

A little further, and now: Enter the street of some of your dreams:
Here come the untidy jokers and the spruce who love military secrets
And those whose houses are dustless and full of Ming vases:
Those rebels who have freed nothing in the whole universe from the
     tyranny of the mothers, except a tiny sensitive area:
Those who are ashamed of their baldness or the size of their members,
Those suffering from self-deceptions necessary to life
And all who have compounded envy and hopelessness into desire
Perform here nightly their magical acts of identification
Among the Chinese lanterns and the champagne served in shoes.
You may kiss what you like; it has often been kissed before.
Use what words you wish; they will often be heard again.

                                                              ? 1934

10

So, under the local images your blood has conjured,
We show you man caught in the trap of his terror, destroying himself.
From his favourite pool between the yew-hedge and the roses, it is no
     fairy-tale his line catches
But grey-white and horrid, the monster of his childhood raises its huge
     domed forehead
And death moves in to take his inner luck,
Lands on the beaches of his love, like Coghlan's coffin.

Do not speak of a change of heart, meaning five hundred a year and a
     room of one's own,
As if that were all that is necessary. In these islands alone there are
     some forty-seven million hearts, each of four chambers:
You cannot avoid the issue by becoming simply a community digger,
O you who prattle about the wonderful Middle Ages: You who expect
     the millennium after a few trifling adjustments.

Visit from house to house, from country to country: consider the
     populations
Beneath the communions and the coiffures: discover your image.
Man divided always and restless always: afraid and unable to forgive:
Unable to forgive his parents, or his first voluptuous rectal sins,
Afraid of the clock, afraid of catching his neighbour's cold, afraid of his
     own body,
Desperately anxious about his health and his position: calling upon the
     Universe to justify his existence,
Slovenly in posture and thinking: the greater part of the will devoted
To warding off pain from the water-logged areas,
An isolated bundle of nerve and desire, suffering alone,
Seeing others only in reference to himself: as a long-lost mother or as
     his ideal self at sixteen.

Watch him asleep and waking:
Dreaming of continuous sexual enjoyment or perpetual applause;
Reading of accidents over the breakfast-table, thinking: 'This could
  never happen to me.'
Reading the reports of trials, flushed at the downfall of a fellow
  creature.
Examine his satisfactions:
Some turn to the time-honoured solutions of sickness and crime: some
  to the latest model of aeroplane or the sport of the moment.
Some to good works, to a mechanical ritual of giving.
Some have adopted an irrefragable system of beliefs or a political
  programme, others have escaped to the ascetic mountains
Or taken refuge in the family circle, among the boys on the bar-stools,
  on the small uncritical islands.
Men will profess devotion to almost anything; to God, to Humanity,
  to Truth, to Beauty: but their first thought on meeting is:
  'Beware!'
They put their trust in Reason or the Feelings of the Blood, but they
  will not trust a stranger with half-a-crown.
Beware of those with no obvious vices; of the chaste, the non-smoker
  and drinker, the vegetarian:
Beware of those who show no inclination towards making money:
  there are even less innocent forms of power.
Beware of yourself:
Have you not heard your own heart whisper: 'I am the nicest person in
  this room'?
Asking to be introduced to someone 'real': someone unlike all those
  people over there?

You have wonderful hospitals and a few good schools:
Repent.
The precision of your instruments and the skill of your designers is
  unparalleled:
Unite.
Your knowledge and your power are capable of infinite extension:
Act.

                                                        ? *1934*

                              II

    The Summer holds: upon its glittering lake
    Lie Europe and the islands; many rivers
    Wrinkling its surface like a ploughman's palm.
    Under the bellies of the grazing horses
    On the far side of posts and bridges
    The vigorous shadows dwindle; nothing wavers.
    Calm at this moment the Dutch sea so shallow
    That sunk St. Paul's would ever show its golden cross
    And still the deep water that divides us still from Norway.

We would show you at first an English village: You shall choose its
   location
Wherever your heart directs you most longingly to look; you are loving
   towards it:
Whether north to Scots Gap and Bellingham where the black rams
   defy the panting engine:
Or west to the Welsh Marches; to the lilting speech and the magicians'
   faces:
Wherever you were a child or had your first affair
There it stands amidst your darling scenery:
A parish bounded by the wreckers' cliff; or meadows where browse the
   Shorthorn and maplike Friesian
As at Trent Junction where the Soar comes gliding; out of green
   Leicestershire to swell the ampler current.

Hiker with sunburn blisters on your office pallor,
Cross-country champion with corks in your hands,
When you have eaten your sandwich, your salt and your apple,
When you have begged your glass of milk from the ill-kept farm,
What is it you see?

I see barns falling, fences broken,
Pasture not ploughland, weeds not wheat.
The great houses remain but only half are inhabited,
Dusty the gunrooms and the stable clocks stationary.
Some have been turned into prep-schools where the diet is in the hands
   of an experienced matron,
Others into club-houses for the golf-bore and the top-hole.
Those who sang in the inns at evening have departed; they saw their
   hope in another country,
Their children have entered the service of the suburban areas; they
   have become typists, mannequins and factory operatives; they
   desired a different rhythm of life.
But their places are taken by another population, with views about
   nature,
Brought in charabanc and saloon along arterial roads;
Tourists to whom the Tudor cafés
Offer Bovril and buns upon Breton ware
With leather-work as a sideline: Filling stations
Supplying petrol from rustic pumps.
Those who fancy themselves as foxes or desire a special setting for
   spooning
Erect their villas at the right places,
Airtight, lighted, elaborately warmed;
And nervous people who will never marry
Live upon dividends in the old-world cottages
With an animal for friend or a volume of memoirs.

Man is changed by his living; but not fast enough.
His concern to-day is for that which yesterday did not occur.
In the hour of the Blue Bird and the Bristol Bomber, his thoughts are

appropriate to the years of the Penny Farthing:
He tosses at night who at noonday found no truth.

Stand aside now: The play is beginning
In the village of which we have spoken; called Pressan Ambo:
Here too corruption spreads its peculiar and emphatic odours
And Life lurks, evil, out of its epoch.

? December 1934

12

Happy the hare at morning, for she cannot read
The Hunter's waking thoughts. Lucky the leaf
Unable to predict the fall. Lucky indeed
The rampant suffering suffocating jelly
Burgeoning in pools, lapping the grits of the desert:
The elementary sensual cures,
The hibernations and the growth of hair assuage:
Or best of all the mineral stars disintegrating quietly into light.
But what shall men do, who can whistle tunes by heart,
Know to the bar when death shall cut him short, like the cry of the
  shearwater?
We will show you what he has done.
How comely are his places of refuge and the tabernacles of his peace,
The new books upon the morning table, the lawns and the afternoon
  terraces!
Here are the playing-fields where he may forget his ignorance
To operate within a gentleman's agreement: twenty-two sins have
  here a certain licence.
Here are the thickets where accosted lovers combatant
May warm each other with their wicked hands,
Here are the avenues for incantation and workshops for the cunning
  engravers.
The galleries are full of music, the pianist is storming the keys, the
  great cellist is crucified over his instrument,
That none may hear the ejaculations of the sentinels
Nor the sigh of the most numerous and the most poor; the thud of their
  falling bodies
Who with their lives have banished hence the serpent and the faceless
  insect.

? December 1934

13

Now through night's caressing grip
Earth and all her oceans slip,
Capes of China slide away
From her fingers into day
And the Americas incline

283

Coasts towards her shadow line.
Now the ragged vagrants creep
Into crooked holes to sleep:
Just and unjust, worst and best,
Change their places as they rest:
Awkward lovers lie in fields
Where disdainful beauty yields:
While the splendid and the proud
Naked stand before the crowd
And the losing gambler gains
And the beggar entertains:
May sleep's healing power extend
Through these hours to our friend.
Unpursued by hostile force,
Traction engine, bull or horse
Or revolting succubus;
Calmly till the morning break
Let him lie, then gently wake.

? 1935

14

The General Public has no notion
    Of what's behind the scenes.
They vote at times with some emotion
    But don't know what it means.
Doctored information
    Is all they have to judge things by;
The hidden situation
    Develops secretly.

If the Queen of Poland swears,
    If the Pope kicks his cardinals down the stairs,
If the Brazilian Consul
    Misses his train at Crewe,
If Irish Clergy
Lose their en*e*rgy
    And dons have too much to do:
The reason is just simply this:
    They're in the racket, too.

To grasp the morning dailies you must
    Read between the lines.
The evening specials make just nonsense
    Unless you've shares in mines.
National estrangements
    Are not what they seem to be;
Underground arrangements
    Are the master-key.

If Chanel gowns have a train this year,
    If Morris cars fit a self-changing gear,
If Lord Peter Wimsey
    Misses an obvious clue,
If Wallace Beery
Should act a fairy
    And Chaplin the Wandering Jew;
The reason is just simply this:
    They're in the racket, too!

There's lots of little things that happen
    Almost every day
That show the way the wind is blowing
    So keep awake, we say.
We have got the lowdown
    On all European affairs;
To History we'll go down
    As the men with the longest ears.

If the postman is three minutes late,
    If the grocer's boy scratches your gate,
If you get the wrong number,
    If Cook has burnt the stew,
If all your rock-plants
Come up as dock-plants
    And your tennis-court turns blue;
The reason is just simply this:
    You're in the racket, too!

? 1935

15

Evening. A slick and unctuous Time
Has sold us yet another shop-soiled day,
Patently rusty, not even in a gaudy box.
I have dusted the six small rooms:
The parlour, once the magnificent image of my freedom,
And the bedroom, which once held for me
The mysterious languors of Egypt and the terrifying Indias.
The delivery-vans have paid their brief impersonal visits.
I have eaten a scrappy lunch from a plate on my knee.
I have spoken with acquaintances in the Stores;
Under our treble gossip heard the menacing throb of our hearts
As I hear them now, as all of us hear them,
Standing at our stoves in these villas, expecting our husbands:
The drums of an enormous and routed army,
Throbbing raggedly, fitfully, scatteredly, madly.
We are lost. We are lost.

March 1936

The chimney sweepers
  Wash their faces and forget to wash the neck;
The lighthouse keepers
  Let the lamps go out and leave the ships to wreck;
The prosperous baker
  Leaves the rolls in hundreds in the oven to burn;
The undertaker
  Puts a small note on the coffin saying 'Wait till I return,
I've got a date with Love!'

And deep-sea divers
  Cut their boots off and come bubbling to the top;
And engine-drivers
  Bring expresses in the tunnel to a stop;
The village rector
  Dashes down the side-aisle half-way through a psalm;
The sanitary inspector
  Runs off with the cover of the cesspool on his arm—
To keep his date with Love!

? March 1936

Death like his is right and splendid;
That is how life should be ended!
He cannot calculate nor dread
The mortifying in the bed,
Powers wasting day by day
While the courage ebbs away.
Ever-charming, he will miss
The insulting paralysis,
Ruined intellect's confusion,
Ulcer's patient persecution,
Sciatica's intolerance
And the cancer's sly advance;
Never hear, among the dead,
The rival's brilliant paper read,
Colleague's deprecating cough
And the praises falling off;
Never know how in the best
Passion loses interest;
Beauty sliding from the bone
Leaves the rigid skeleton.

? April 1936

Let the eye of the traveller consider this country and weep,
For toads croak in the cisterns; the aqueducts choke with leaves:
The highways are out of repair and infested with thieves:
The ragged population are crazy for lack of sleep:
Our chimneys are smokeless; the implements rust in the field
And our tall constructions are felled.

Over our empty playgrounds the wet winds sough;
The crab and the sandhopper possess our abandoned beaches;
Upon our gardens the dock and the darnel encroaches;
The crumbling lighthouse is circled with moss like a muff;
The weasel inhabits the courts and the sacred places;
Despair is in our faces.

For the Dragon has wasted the forest and set fire to the farm;
He has mutilated our sons in his terrible rages
And our daughters he has stolen to be victims of his dissolute
                                                          orgies;
He has cracked the skulls of our children in the crook of his arm;
With the blast of his nostrils he scatters death through the land;
We are babes in his hairy hand.

O, when shall the deliverer come to destroy this dragon?
For it is stated in the prophecies that such a one shall appear,
Shall ride on a white horse and pierce his heart with a spear;
Our elders shall welcome him home with trumpet and organ,
Load him with treasure, yes, and our most beautiful maidenhead
He shall have for his bed.

                                                    ? April 1936

At last the secret is out, as it always must come in the end,
The delicious story is ripe to tell to the intimate friend;
Over the tea-cups and in the square the tongue has its desire;
Still waters run deep, my dear, there's never smoke without fire.

Behind the corpse in the reservoir, behind the ghost on the links,
Behind the lady who dances and the man who madly drinks,
Under the look of fatigue, the attack of migraine and the sigh
There is always another story, there is more than meets the eye.

For the clear voice suddenly singing, high up in the convent wall,
The scent of the elder bushes, the sporting prints in the hall,
The croquet matches in summer, the handshake, the cough, the kiss,
There is always a wicked secret, a private reason for this.

                                                    ? April 1936

O quick and furtive is the lovers' night.
Pausing to marvel at their poisoned grace,
The moon's accusing lantern brings to light
The sleepers ruined in a brief embrace.
O quick and furtive is the lovers' night.

O silly and unlucky are the brave,
Who tilt against the world's enormous wrong.
Their serious little efforts will not save
Themselves or us. The enemy is strong.
O silly and unlucky are the brave.

O happy the free cities of the dead
Which ask no questions of what life was for,
Where nothing matters that was ever said,
And no one need take trouble any more.
O happy the free cities of the dead.

August 1937

21

Ben was a four foot seven Wop,
He worked all night in a bucket-shop
On cocoa, and sandwiches,
And bathed on Sunday evenings.

In winter when the woods were bare
He walked to work in his underwear
With his hat in his hand,
But his watch was broken.

He met his Chief in the Underground,
He bit him hard till he turned round
In the neck, and the ear,
And left-hand bottom corner.

He loved his wife though she was cruel,
He gave her an imitation jewel
In a box, a black eye,
And a very small packet of Woodbines.

August 1937

22

The biscuits are hard and the beef is high,
The weather is wet and the drinks are dry,
We sit in the mud and wonder why.

With faces washed until they shine
The G.H.Q. sit down to dine
A hundred miles behind the line.

The Colonel said he was having a doze;
I looked through the window; a rambler rose
Climbed up his knee in her underclothes.

The chaplain paid us a visit one day,
A shell came to call from over the way,
You should have heard the bastard pray!

The subaltern's heart was full of fire,
Now he hangs on the old barbed wire
All blown up like a motor-tyre.

The sergeant-major gave us hell.
A bullet struck him and he fell.
Where did it come from? Who can tell?

Kurt went sick with a pain in his head.
Malingering, the Doctor said.
Gave him a pill. Next day he was dead.

Fritz was careless, I'm afraid.
He lost his heart to a parlour-maid.
Now he's lost his head to a hand-grenade.

Karl married a girl with big blue eyes.
He went back on leave; to his surprise
The hat in the hall was not his size.

O, No Man's Land is a pleasant place,
You can lie there as long as you lie on your face
Till your uniform is an utter disgrace.

I'd rather eat turkey than humble pie,
I'd rather see mother than lose an eye,
I'd rather kiss a girl than die.

We're sick of the rain and the lice and the smell,
We're sick of the noise of shot and shell,
And the whole bloody war can go to hell!

August 1937

23 · ROMAN WALL BLUES

Over the heather the wet wind blows,
I've lice in my tunic and a cold in my nose.

The rain comes pattering out of the sky,
I'm a Wall soldier, I don't know why.

The mist creeps over the hard grey stone,
My girl's in Tungria; I sleep alone.

Aulus goes hanging around her place,
I don't like his manners, I don't like his face.

Piso's a Christian, he worships a fish;
There'd be no kissing if he had his wish.

She gave me a ring but I diced it away;
I want my girl and I want my pay.

When I'm a veteran with only one eye
I shall do nothing but look at the sky.

October 1937

III · Three Fragments for Films

1 · COAL FACE

O lurcher-loving collier, black as night,
Follow your love across the smokeless hill;
Your lamp is out and all the cages still;
Course for her heart and do not miss,
For Sunday soon is past and, Kate, fly not so fast,
For Monday comes when none may kiss:
Be marble to his soot, and to his black be white.

June 1935

2 · NIGHT MAIL

North, north, north,
To the country of the Clyde and the Firth of Forth.

This is the night mail crossing the border,
Bringing the cheque and the postal order,
Letters for the rich, letters for the poor,
The shop at the corner and the girl next door.

Through sparse counties she rampages,
Her driver's eye upon her gages.
Panting up past lonely farms,
Fed by the fireman's restless arms.
Uplands heaped like slaughtered horses,
Rushing stony water courses,
Lurching through the cutting, and beneath the bridge,

Into the gap in the distant ridge.
Winding up the valley and the water-shed
Through the heather and the weather and the dawn overhead.
Pulling up Beattock, a steady climb—
The gradient's against her, but she's on time.

Past cotton grass and moorland boulder,
Shovelling white steam over her shoulder,
Snorting noisily as she passes
Silent miles of wind-bent grasses;
Birds turn their heads as she approaches,
Stare from the bushes at her blank-faced coaches;
Sheepdogs cannot turn her course,
They slumber on with paws across,
In the farm she passes no one wakes,
But a jug in a bedroom gently shakes.

Dawn freshens, the climb is done.
The train tilts forward for the downhill run.
Down towards Glasgow she descends
Towards the steam tugs, yelping down the glade of cranes.
Towards the fields of apparatus, the furnaces
Set on the dark plain like gigantic chessmen.
All Scotland waits for her.
Yes, this country, whose scribbled coastline traps the wild Atlantic
                                        in a maze of stone,
And faces Norway with its doubled notches.
In the dark glens, beside the pale-green sea-lochs,
Men long for news.

Letters of thanks, letters from banks,
Letters of joy from the girl and boy,
Receipted bills and invitations
To inspect new stock or visit relations,
And applications for situations,
And timid lovers' declarations,
And gossip, gossip from all the nations;
News circumstantial, news financial,
Letters with holiday snaps to enlarge in,
Letters with faces scrawled in the margin,
Letters from uncles, cousins and aunts,
Letters to Scotland from the South of France,
Letters of condolence to Highlands and Lowlands,
Notes from overseas to the Hebrides;
Written on paper of every hue,
The pink, the violet, the white and the blue.
The chatty, the catty, the boring, adoring,
The cold and official and the heart's outpouring,
Clever, stupid, short and long,
The typed and the printed and the spelt all wrong.

Thousands are still asleep
Dreaming of terrifying monsters
Or a friendly tea beside the band at Cranston's or Crawford's;
Asleep in working Glasgow, asleep in well-set Edinburgh,
Asleep in granite Aberdeen.
In grimed Dundee that weaves a white linen from the Indian fibre,
In Stornaway smoking its heavy wools,
And where the rivers feel the long salmon threshing in their netted
                                                                    mouths,
They continue their dreams,
But shall wake soon and long for letters.
And none will hear the postman's knock
Without a quickening of the heart,
For who can bear to feel himself forgotten?

July 1935

3 · NEGROES

Still at their accustomed hour, the cities and oceans swing westward into the segment of eternal shadow, their revolutions unaltered since first to this chain of islands, motionless in the Caribbean Sea like a resting scorpion, the Captains came, eager from Europe, white to the West.

And still they come, new from those nations to which the study of that which can be weighed and measured is a consuming love.

We show these pictures as evidence of their knowledge; its nature and its power.

Power to employ the waters and the winds for their human and peculiar purposes; power to convert the lives of others to their kind of willing.

Such as these, in the circuit of whose bodies turns the blood of Africa.

Consider their works, their weeks, their contact with those who can design instruments of precision; and what compels both races into one enterprise—the wish for life: their concern in these places for the production of foods and beverages.

Acts of injustice done
Between the setting and the rising sun
In history lie like bones, each one.

Memory sees them down there,
Paces alive beside his fear,
That's slow to die and still here.

The future hard to mark
Of a world turning in the dark
Where ghosts are walking and dogs bark.

But between the day and night
The choice is free to all; and light
Falls equally on black and white.

1935

Part IX

Essays and Reviews

I

Free will degenerates through habit to physical laws. The laws of matter, statements of averages, are inveterate habits. Matter has morality instead of religion.

The inorganic world is like the elementary pieces with which a pianist begins his study. As his taste and technique improve, more of these are left in the drawer. Thus actions such as breathing, unconscious, become reflexes, mechanical save in regressive disaster.

Where there is conflict, free will is a necessity. Conflict occurs whenever two different stimuli are presented simultaneously. This is possible where there is (1) a co-ordinated nervous system, and (2) memory.

Under pressure of stimuli an organ is developed to cope with them (e.g., the concentration of sensory organs in the head with the assumption of bilateral symmetry). Such an organ becomes at once selective. Specialisation of organ involves specialisation of environment, and tends to exclude free will.

Man is relatively unspecialised at the periphery and highly organised at the centre, allowing a much greater freedom of environment than is possible to animals such as insects whose appendages are specialised.

Having unspecialised limbs man was driven to make specialised detachable ones, or tools. When limbs are not detachable the stimulus can be supplied to the limb itself and motor-memory is enough. As soon as limbs are detachable, an intellectual memory is necessary.

When man became self-conscious, he created his most important detachable organ, the intellect, and since it was itself living, the most dangerous. Intellect alone can co-ordinate desires. It alone can set them at each other's throats.

*   *   *

Body and Soul (Not-Me and Me) can have no independent existence, yet they are distinct, and an attempt to make one into the other destroys. The Pagans tried to convert mind into body, and went mad or just apathetic. We attempt to turn body into mind and become diseased. The heresy in both cases is Unitarianism.

Our second error is that we have tried to develop both in the wrong direction. We have tried to make the body more and more individualistic (hygiene) and the mind more and more communistic (newspapers). The result being that on the one hand we lose the capacity to love and on the other we lose the capacity to think. The love of one's neighbour is a bodily, a blood relationship; the development of the mind is one more and more of differentiation, individualistic, away from nature.

It is the body's job to make, the mind's to destroy.

*   *   *

The sex act is a mixture of mind destroying itself and body making itself. To body, the child is more body like itself, the assurance of body's immortality; to mind, the child is new mind, hostile to itself, the assurance of the destruction of its ideas.

*   *   *

The progress of man seems to be in a direction away from nature. The development of consciousness may be compared with the breaking away of the child from the Oedipus relation. Just as one must be weaned from one's mother, one must be weaned from the Earth Mother (Unconscious?). Along with the growing self-consciousness of man during the last 150 years, as illustrated for example by Dostoevsky, has developed Wordsworthian nature-worship, the nostalgia for the womb of Nature which cannot be re-entered by a consciousness increasingly independent but afraid. Rousseau is a nice example of the two tendencies. The motor-car and other improvements in quick transport are altering this and I am glad. The first sign of change is an impoverishment in feeling, noticed and criticised by many. This is necessary accompaniment to weaning; every adolescent feels it.

*   *   *

Man is a product of the refined distintegration of nature by time.

*   *   *

Mind has been evolved from body, i.e. from the Not-self, whose thinking is community-thinking, and therefore symbolic. While Yeats is right that great poetry in the past has been symbolic, I think we are reaching the point in the development of the mind where symbols are becoming obsolete in poetry, as the mind, or non-communistic self, does not think in this way. This does not invalidate its use in past poetry, but it does invalidate it in modern poetry, just as an attempt to write in Chaucerian English would be academic.

*   *   *

Only body can be communicated.

*   *   *

Infectious diseases: a sign of the unconscious sense of unity between men.

*   *   *

Psychology.

How silly to talk of ideas as being far-fetched. The attitude of psychology should always be 'Have you heard this one?'

*   *   *

Transference: the re-creation of the original attitude of dependence towards the parents. It does not involve, as Freud says, the acquired attitudes of resentment. All that means is that Freud is behaving as foolishly as the parents did.

*   *   *

Pleasure.

The error of Freud and most psychologists is making pleasure a negative thing, progress towards a state of rest. This is only one half of pleasure and the least important half. Creative pleasure is, like pain, an increase in tension. What does the psychologist make of contemplation and joy?

The essence of creation is doing things for no reason; it is pointless. Possessive pleasure is always rational. Freud really believes that pleasure is immoral, i.e., happiness is displeasing to God.

If you believe this, of course, the death-wish becomes the most important emotion, and the 'reinstatement of the earlier condition'. Entropy is another name for despair.

*   *   *

The real 'life-wish' is the desire for separation, from family, from one's literary predecessors.

*   *   *

The Tyranny of the Dead. One cannot react against them.

*   *   *

The middle class: an orphan class, with no fixed residence, capable of snobbery in both directions. From class insecurity it has developed the family unit as a defence. Like the private bands in the tribal migrations. It is afraid of its fortunate position.

*   *   *

Humanism.

Will never do since it believes that the duality of Higher and Lower will is inevitable and desirable. This dualism is the result of the Fall, i.e. the dissociated consciousness of man. We can only live properly when this fissure is repaired. 'Which of you by taking thought can add one cubit unto his stature?' This is the final answer to believers in the efficacy of the will. Resist not evil; or as Lane puts it, 'It is no good fighting evil as it only fights back and there is no energy left for creating knowledge.'

*   *   *

'Be good and you will be happy' is a dangerous inversion. 'Be happy and you will be good' is the truth.

The only good reason for doing anything is for fun.

*   *   *

A colonel captures a position, after receiving severe wounds himself and the loss of three-quarters of his regiment, to find that the enemy are his own side. Repression is equally heroic and equally foolish.

*   *   *

Realism in Art—the Zola sort—is a form of anxiety neurosis, one of the many varieties of the jackdaw mind, one of the collectors. Against the reckoning day. Narcissism enters in dealing with one's own experience, and inferiority feeling in dealing with other people's.

*   *   *

Three kinds of verbal dexterity.

A. α. The picked word.	*Antres vast and deserts idle.*
β. Rhyme discoveries.	*Your head would have achèd*
	To see her naked.
B. The manipulation of common	*Where you would not, lie you must.*
abstract words.	*Lie you must, but not with me.*

B is the rarest and means the most to me, I think. There is always something exhibitionistic, and Society for Pure English, about Aα. But what a temptation, and how satisfied one is with oneself when one does it.

*   *   *

300

Do I want poetry in a play, or is Cocteau right: 'There is a poetry of the theatre, but not in it'? I shall use poetry in *The Reformatory*[1] as interlude. Poetry after all should be recited, not read. I don't want any characters, any ideas in my play, but stage-life, something which is no imitation but a new thing.

*   *   *

A play is poetry of action. The dialogue should be correspondingly a simplification. (E.g. Hrotswitha.) The Prep School atmosphere: that is what I want.

Journal entries, 1929

II

Instinct and Intuition: A Study in Mental Duality. By George Binney Dibblee.

Duality is one of the oldest of our concepts; it appears and reappears in every religion, metaphysic, and code of ethics; it is reflected in (or perhaps reflects) the earliest social system of which we have knowledge—the Dual Organisation in Ancient Egypt; one of its most important projections is war.

In Chapters XI to XVII of *Instinct and Intuition*, Mr. Dibblee discusses various dualities, such as pleasure–pain, feeling–thought, conscious–unconscious, and decides, with good reason, that they are not fundamental. In their place he offers a thesis which may be summarised thus:—from introspection and from physiological evidence such as the Rivers-Head experiments on protopathic and epicritic sensibility—and the work on visual perception of Sir John Parsons, we may conclude that the mind is divided into two parts, an instinctive intelligent faculty on the one hand, acting both consciously and extra-consciously, the seat of which is the optic thalamus, and the intellect proper on the other, resident in the cortex and cerebral hemispheres, termed reason when acting consciously, when extra-consciously intuition.

The argument is worked out with a caution, a wealth of detail, and a beauty of style that makes it difficult to criticise, nor is there space in a review to exhaust the many interesting questions it raises. We must confine ourselves to two—What is human 'instinctive behaviour'? and Is there in any sense a thalamo-cortical rivalry?

Mr. Dibblee points out the impossibility of arguing from the instinctive behaviour of animals and insects to that of man, but his conception of instinct seems more suitable to the former.

> It is the coincidence of three kinds of fitness which establishes instinct: the external network of circumstances in which alone the species can flourish and in which therefore it is fixed: the mediating

[1][Evidently the working title for the play that became *The Enemies of a Bishop*, Auden's first unpublished collaboration with Isherwood.]

corporal mechanism whereby the necessary routine is made so easy as to be the readiest solution of a particular difficulty; and the deep traces of some neural path conducting unconscious intelligence, which has often presented before in the history of the fixed species the same obvious and appropriate solution to the same regularly recurring problem ... It is the joint product of living afferent, central and efferent mechanisms with an accent on the central link.

Such a definition will do in the case of animals, where, to our knowledge at least, all behaviour is instinctive, but in speaking of man it includes too much. Human instinct, if the term is to have meaning, must be limited to the subjective demands, proceeding from within outwards, existing independently of their objects (e.g. the instincts of creation and security). In so far as instinct may be gratified by the same behaviour towards the same objects, a habit is set up both of thought and action. (Is this Mr. Dibblee's Advanced Instinct?) In so far as the behaviour or the object fail to satisfy, non-habitual reactions will tend to take place (emergency behaviour). Directed thinking is no less action than motor-activity, and is alike provoked by instinct. The sudden indiscretion of a middle-aged man is neither more nor less instinctive than his previous respectability, neither more nor less rational.

Mr. Dibblee is hard to follow in his assumption of an 'instinctive intelligence' of a different order from the rational and intuitional intelligence. The thalamus is phylogenetically older than the cortex, and there may well be division of labour, e.g. the thalamus may be the organ differentiating protopathic and epicritic sensations; though here and elsewhere Mr. Dibblee seems to rely too much on the Rivers-Head experiments which were too few not to admit of other interpretations. But that they are different in nature, or that one can act without the other, there is no evidence. The motor-control is cortical and the memory reserves of the hemispheres are dependent upon the sensory-receptor mechanism of the thalamus for their supply. The author is careful not to stress a rivalry between the two systems, but he does sometimes suggest it.

The reason is an instrument, and cannot of itself control or inhibit anything; what it can do is to cause one desire to modify another. Reason alone can co-ordinate desires; reason alone can set them at each other's throats. Dual conceptions, of a higher and lower self, of instinct and reason, are only too apt to lead to the inhibition rather than the development of desires, to their underground survival in immature forms, the cause of disease, crime, and permanent fatigue. The only duality is that between the whole self at different stages of development—e.g. a man before and after a religious conversion. The old life must die in giving birth to the new. That which desires life to itself, be it individual, habit, or reason, casts itself, like Lucifer, out of heaven.

The Criterion, April 1930

III · Writing

If an Australian aborigine sits down on a pin he says 'Ow'. Dogs with bones growl at the approach of other dogs. English, Russian, Brazilian, all mothers, 'coo' to their babies. Sailors at any port, pulling together on a hawser: watch them and listen—heaving, they grunt together 'Ee-Ah'.

This is the first language.

We generally think of language being words used to point to things, to say that something is *this* or *that*, but the earliest use of language was not this; it was used to express the feelings of the speaker; feelings about something happening to him (the prick of the pin), or attitudes towards other things in the world (the other hungry dog; the darling baby), or, again, as a help to doing something with others of his own kind (pulling the boat in). The first two uses are common to many animals, but the last is peculiar to the most highly organised, and contains more possibilities of development.

Life is one whole thing made up of smaller whole things, which again are made up of smaller whole things, and so on. The largest thing we can talk about is the universe, the smallest the negative electrons of the atom which run round its central positive nucleus, already a group. So too for us, nucleus and cell, cell and organ, organ and the human individual, individual and family, nation and world, always groups linked up with larger groups, each group unique, different from every other, but without meaning except in its connection with others. The whole cannot exist without the part, nor the part without the whole; and each whole is more than just the sum of its parts; it is a new thing.

But suppose the part begins to work, not only as if it were a whole (which it is), but as if there were no larger whole, then there is a breakdown (e.g. a cancer growth in the body). And this is what has happened to us. At some time or other in human history, when and how we don't know, man became self-conscious; he began to feel, I am I, and you are not I; we are shut inside ourselves and apart from each other. There is no whole but the self.

The more this feeling grew, the more man felt the need to bridge over the gulf, to recover the sense of being as much part of life as the cells in his body are part of him. Before he had lost it, when he was still doing things together in a group, such as hunting, when feeling was strongest, as when, say, the quarry was first sighted, the group had made noises, grunts, howls, grimaces. Noise and this feeling he had now lost had gone together; then, if he made the noise, could he not recover the feeling? In some way like this language began, but its development must have been very slow. Among savage tribes, for example, news travels much quicker than a messenger could carry it, by a sympathy which we, ignorant of its nature and incapable of practising it, call telepathy. Dr. Rivers tells a story of some natives in Melanesia getting into a rowing-boat. There was no discussion as to who should stroke or steer. All found their places, as we should say, by instinct.

Even among ourselves, two friends have to say very much less to understand each other's meaning than two strangers. Their conversation is often unintelligible to a third person. Even when we are listening to anyone, it is not only the words themselves which tell us what he means, but his gestures (try listening with your eyes shut), and also the extent to which he is talking to us personally. (It is always difficult to understand what people are saying at another table in a restaurant. We are outside the group.)

Words are a bridge between a speaker and a listener. What the bridge carries, i.e. what the speaker gives and the listener receives, we call the *meaning* of the words.

MEANING

In anything we say there are four different kinds of meaning; any one of them may be more important than the other three, but there is generally something of all four.

(1) *Sense* (typical case, fat stock prices on the wireless). We say *something*, or expect *something* to be said to us about something. 'Snig is a man.' We now know that there is a thing called Snig, and that thing is a man and not a dog or anything else.

(2) *Feeling* (typical case, the conversation of lovers). We generally have feelings about the things of which we are talking. 'There's that horrible man Snig.' We now know that the speaker does not like Snig.

(3) *Tone* (typical case, an after-dinner speech). We generally have an attitude to the person we are talking to. We say the same thing in a different way to different people. 'There's that swine Snig.' 'There's Mr. Snig; of course, I expect he's charming, really, but I don't like him very much, I'm afraid.'

(4) *Intention* (typical case, a speech at a General Election). Apart from what we say or feel we often want to make our listeners act or think in a particular way. 'There's that man Snig. I shouldn't have much to do with him if I were you.' The speaker is trying to stop us seeing Mr. Snig.

LANGUAGE AND WORDS

Language, as we know it, consists of words—that is, a comparatively small number of different sounds (between forty and fifty in English) arranged in different orders or groups, each sound, or group of sounds, standing for something; an object, an action, a colour, an idea, etc.

To go back to our sketch of the origin of language. Before language we have the people who feel something (the hunting group), the feeling (feeling of unity in the face of hunger or danger, etc.), the object which excites the feeling (the hunted bison), and the noise which expressed the feeling. If the noise was later used to recover the feeling, it would also present to the memory the idea or the image of the animal, or whatever it was excited the feeling. Thus sounds would begin to have sense meaning, to stand for things, as well as having meaning as an expression of feeling.

It is unlikely, therefore, even at the first that language was entirely onomatopœic—that is, that words were sounds imitating the sounds of things spoken about. Many words, no doubt, did, just as they still do (e.g. hissing, growling, splashing). It is only possible to imitate in this way actions or objects which make a noise. You could never, for example, imitate the sound of a mountain. In fact, most of the power of words comes from their *not* being like what they stand for. If the word 'ruin', for instance, was only like a particular ruin, it would only serve to describe the one solitary building; as it is, the word conjures up all the kinds of ruins which we know, and our various feelings about them—ruined churches, ruined houses, ruined gasworks, loss of money, etc.

INFLECTION

All languages are originally inflected; that is to say, the sounds standing for a particular object or action change slightly according to how we are looking at it. E.g. the Roman said:

Homo canem amat (The man loves the dog).
Canis hominem amat (The dog loves the man).

He felt that the man is a different man and the dog is a different dog if he is loving or being loved. But, as people get more self-conscious, more aware of what they are feeling and thinking, they separate their feelings and thoughts from the things they are feeling and thinking about. They show the difference in attitude either by changing the word order or by using special words like prepositions. Thus in English, the least inflected language:

The man loves the dog.
The dog loves the man.
The man gives a bone *to* the dog.

All languages show some inflection. (*I* love *him*. *He* loves *me*.)

WRITING

Writing and speech are like two tributary streams, rising at different sources, flowing apart for a time until they unite to form a large river. Just as it is possible for sounds conveying their meaning by the ear to stand for things, pictures conveying their meaning through the eye can do the same.

The earliest kinds of writing, such as Egyptian hieroglyphs, or Mexican writings, are a series of pictures telling a story, as a sentence tells a story. The urge to write, like the urge to speak, came from man's growing sense of personal loneliness, of the need for group communication. But, while speech begins with the feeling of separateness in space, of I-here-in-this-chair and you-there-in-that-chair, writing begins from the sense of separateness in time, of 'I'm here to-day, but I shall be dead to-morrow, and you will be active in my place, and how can I speak to you?'

Primitive people, living in small groups, have very little idea of death, only a very strong sense of the life of the tribe, which, of course, never dies. The moment man loses this sense of the continuously present group life, he becomes increasingly aware of the shortness and uncertainty of the life of the individual. He looks round desperately for some means of prolonging it, of living into the future, of uniting the past with the present. The earliest writings of which we know tell the exploits of dead kings. The writer is like a schoolboy who carves his initials on a desk; he wishes to live for ever.

How early speech joined up with writing it is impossible to say, but writing must soon have stopped being purely pictorial—drawings of each separate object. A language of this kind would have had to contain thousands of letters, and would have been very difficult to know, and slow and clumsy to write. Chinese is still a language of this kind. Further, abstract ideas would be impossible to represent by pictures (how, for example, could you draw a picture of 'habit'?). Luckily, the fact that the number of different sounds which it is possible to make are comparatively few presented a solution to the difficulty. In inventing an alphabet, or code, where one kind of mark stands for one kind of sound, any word could be written by arranging the marks or letters in the order in which the sounds were made. (Our own alphabet comes originally from Egypt, through Phœnicia, Colchis, and Italy.)

SPOKEN AND WRITTEN LANGUAGE

As long as people are living in small societies, and living generation after generation in one place, they have little need of writing. Poems, stories, moral advice, are learnt by heart and handed down by word of mouth from father to son. Oral tradition has certain advantages and certain disadvantages over writing. Generally speaking, the *feelings* meaning is transmitted with extraordinary accuracy, as the gestures and the tone of voice that go with the words are remembered also. (With a statement in writing it is often impossible, after a time, to decide exactly what the author meant. Think how easy it is to misunderstand a letter.) On the other hand, in speaking, the *sense* meaning is apt to get strangely distorted. It is easy not to catch or to forget the exact words told to one, and to guess them wrongly; again, we may be asked to explain something and add our own explanation, which is passed on with the story; e.g. this message was passed back from the front lines from mouth to mouth to the officer commanding the reserve: 'Send reinforcements; the regiment is going to advance.' What actually reached him was: 'Send three and fourpence; the regiment is going to a dance.'

But as the communities became larger and government became more centralised, writing became more and more important. Still, as long as copying of original manuscripts had to be done by hand, books were rare and too costly for any but the few. The invention of printing in the fifteenth century greatly increased the power of the written word, but the cost of books still limited their circulation. Popular printed literature during the sixteenth and seventeenth centuries, apart from some religious books, was confined to broadsheets and pamphlets peddled in the streets. The eighteenth century saw the rise of the magazine and the newspaper; and the introduction of steam power at the beginning of the nineteenth century, by cheapening the cost of production, put printed matter within the reach of anyone who could read or write. (Think also of the introduction of the penny post, and the effect of universal education. The last five years, with the wireless and the talkies, have produced a revival of the spoken word.)

The effect of this has been a mixed one. It has made the language able to deal with a great many more subjects, particularly those which are abstract, like some of the sciences; it can be more accurate, draw finer distinctions of meaning. Words written down in one language can be translated into another. Thus the world's knowledge can be pooled, and words borrowed from another language for which the borrower has no word in his own, with the exact shade of meaning which he wants (clock—chronometer: stranger—alien, etc.). But increase in vocabulary makes a language more difficult to learn—not only just to learn the words, but to learn to use them. Education in the use of the language becomes more and more necessary. At present nobody gets such an education. The speech of a peasant is generally better, i.e. more vivid, better able to say what he wants to say, than the speech of the average University graduate. It's like juggling with balls. You may be able to juggle fairly well with three, but, if you try six, without careful practice you will probably drop them all. It is not the language that is to blame, but our skill in using it.

VERSE FORMS

Speech originated in noises made during group excitement. Excitement seems naturally to excite movement. When we are excited, we want to dance about. Noise was thus in the beginning associated with movements of a group—perhaps dancing round food or advancing together to attack. The greater the excitement, the more in sympathy with each other each member of the group is, the more regular the movements; they keep time with each other; every foot comes down together.

Again, imagine a circle of people dancing; the circle revolves and comes back to its starting-place; at each revolution the set of movements is repeated.

When the words move in this kind of repeated pattern, we call the effect of the movement in our minds the metre. Words arranged in metre are verse. Just as in a crowd we are much more easily carried away by feeling than when alone, so metre excites us, prepares us to listen readily to what is being said. We expect something to happen, and therefore it does. When a poet is writing verse, the feeling, as it were, excites the words and makes them fall into a definite group, going through definite dancing movements, just as feeling excites the different members of a crowd and makes them act together. Metre is group excitement among words, a series of repeated movements. The weaker the excitement, the less the words act together and upon each other. (Rhythm is what is expected by one word of another.) In scientific prose, for example, what words do is only controlled by the sense of what is being said. They are like people in a street on an ordinary day. They can be or do anything they like as long as they keep to the left of the pavement and don't annoy each other. But even here this much is expected. There is always some degree of rhythm in all language. The degree depends on the power of feeling.

Accents, long and short syllables, feet and all that, are really quite simple. You will always read a line of poetry rightly if you know its meaning (all four kinds). There are certain traditional rules in writing poetry, just as there are traditional steps in a dance, but every good poet, like every good dancer, uses them in his own way, which is generally quite distinct from that of any other poet. If you were describing a certain dance, you could do it in various ways—as consisting of ten steps, or of four long steps and six little steps, or of three heavy steps and six light ones; in the same way the motion or metre of a line of poetry can be described in different ways according as to how you choose to look at it. In English poetry, for example, we generally describe it by accents—light and heavy steps—because that is the most obvious feature about the movements of English speech. But remember always that such a description of movement is only a description; it isn't the movement itself.

Lastly, language may be ornamented in various ways. The two most familiar ornaments are alliteration (e.g. In a *s*ummer *s*eason when *s*oft was the *s*un), and rhyme (Old King *Cole* was a merry old *soul*). Alliteration is found in the early verse of the Teutonic people, and rhyme, beginning perhaps in the marching-songs of the Roman soldiers, was adopted by the early Christian hymn-writers and so came into modern verse. Alliteration is the effect produced by an arrangement of words beginning with a similar sound; rhyme that produced by an arrangement of words ending in a similar sound. The sounds are similar, but belong to different words, and, therefore, have different meanings in each place. Through the likeness, thoughts and feelings hitherto distinct in the mind are joined together. They are, in fact, sound metaphors.

DIFFERENT KINDS OF WRITING

The difference between different kinds of writing lies not so much in the writing itself, but in the way we look at it (and, of course, in the way the author wished us to look at it; but we often know very little about that). Literary forms do not exist outside our own minds. When we read anything, no matter what—a description of a scientific experiment, a history book, a ballad, or a novel—in so far as we pay attention only to what things are happening one after another to something or somebody, it is a story; in so far as we read it only to learn the way in which something or someone behaves in certain circumstances, it is science; in so far as we read it only to find out what has actually happened in the past, it is history.

People often ask what is the difference between poetry and prose. The only difference is in the way the writer looks at things. (There is another difference between prose and *verse*; see above.) For instance, the novelist starts with a general idea in his mind; say, that people are always trying to escape from their responsibilities, and that escape only leaves them in a worse mess. Then he writes a story about what happened to Mr. and Mrs. Smith. He may never say, in so many words, that they tried to escape, never mention his idea, but this idea is the force that drives the story along. The poet, on the other hand, hears people talking in his club about the sad story of Mr. and Mrs. Smith. He thinks, 'There now, that's very interesting. They are just like everybody else; trying to get round life. It's like those sailors who tried to get to India by the North-West Passage. On they go, getting farther and farther into the ice, miles from home. Why, that's a good idea for a poem.' He writes a poem about explorers; he may never mention Mr. and Mrs. Smith at all. The novelist then goes from the general to the particular, the poet from the particular to the general, and you can see this also in the way they use words. The novelist uses words with their general meaning, and uses a whole lot of them to build up a particular effect: his character. The poet uses words with their particular meanings and puts them together to give a general effect: his ideas. Actually, of course, nearly all novels and all poems except very short ones have both ways of looking at things in them (e.g. Chaucer's *Canterbury Tales* is more like a novel in verse; Melville's *Moby Dick* is more like a poem in prose). All you can say is that one way is typical of the novelist and the other of the poet.

WHY PEOPLE WRITE BOOKS

People write in order to be read. They would like to be read by everybody and for ever. They feel alone, cut off from each other in an indifferent world where they do not live for very long. How can they get in touch again? How can they prolong their lives? Children by their bodies live on in a life they will not live to see, meet friends they will never know, and will in their turn have children, some tiny part of them living on all the time. These by their bodies; books by their minds.

But the satisfaction of any want is pleasant: we not only enjoy feeling full, we enjoy eating; so people write books because they enjoy it, as a carpenter enjoys making a cupboard. Books are written for money, to convert the world, to pass the time; but these reasons are always trivial, beside the first two—company and creation.

HOW PEOPLE WRITE BOOKS

We know as much, and no more, about how books are made as we know about the making of babies or plants. Suddenly an idea, a feeling, germinates in the mind of the author and begins to grow. He has to look after it, and water the soil with his own experience—all that he knows and has felt, all that has happened to him in his life; straightening a shoot here, pruning a bit there, never quite certain what it is going to do next, whether it will just wither and die, come up in a single night like a mushroom, or strengthen quietly into a great oak-tree. The author is both soil and gardener; the soil part of him does not know what is going on, the gardener part of him has learnt the routine. He may be a careful gardener but poor soil; his books are then beautifully written, but they seem to have nothing in them. We say he lacks inspiration. Or he may be excellent soil but a careless gardener. His books are exciting, but badly arranged, out of proportion, harsh to the ear. We say he lacks technique. Good soil is more important than good gardening, but the finest plants are the product of both.

WHY PEOPLE READ BOOKS

When we read a book, it is as if we were with a person. A book is not only the meaning of the words inside it; it is the person who means them. In real life we treat people in all sorts of ways. Suppose we ask a policeman the way. As long as he is polite we do not bother whether he beats his wife or not; in fact, if he started to tell us about his wife we should get impatient; all we expect of him is that he shall know the way and be able clearly to explain it. But other people we treat differently; we want more from them than information; we want to live *with* them, to feel and think *with* them. When we say a book is good or bad, we mean that we feel towards it as we feel towards what we call a good or bad person. (Remember, though, that a book about bad characters is not therefore bad, any more than a person is bad because he talks about bad people.) Actually we know that we cannot divide people into good and bad like that; everyone is a mixture; we like some people in some moods and some in others, and as we grow older our taste in people changes. The same is true of books. People who say they only read good books are prigs. We all like some good books and some bad. The only silly thing to do is to pretend that bad books are good. The awful nonsense that most people utter when they are discussing or criticising a book would be avoided if they would remember that they would never think of criticising a person in the same way.

For instance, people will often say that they don't like the book because they don't agree with it. We think it rather silly when people can only be friends with those who hold the same views in everything.

Reading is valuable just because books are like people, and make the same demands on us to understand and like them. Our actual circle of friends is generally limited; we feel that our relations with them are not as good as they might be, more muddled, difficult, unsatisfying than necessary. Just as a boxer exercises for a real fight with a punchball or a sparring-partner, so you can train yourself for relations with real people with a book. It's not easy, and you can't begin until you have had some experience of real people first (any more than a boxer can practise with a punch-ball until he has learnt a little about boxing), but books can't die or quarrel or go away as people can. Reading and living are not two watertight compartments. You must use your knowledge of people to guide you when reading books, and your knowledge of books to guide you when living with people. The more you read the more you will realise what difficult and delicate things relations with people are, but how worth while they can be when they really come off; and the more you know of other people, the more you will be able to get out of each kind of book, and the more you will realise what a true good a really great book can be, but that great books are as rare as great men.

Reading is valuable when it improves our technique of living, helps us to live fuller and more satisfactory lives. It fails when we can't understand or feel with what we read, either because of ignorance of our own or obscurity in the writing.

It is a danger when we only read what encourages us in lax and crude ways of feeling and thinking: like cheap company (too many people only read what flatters them; they like to be told they are fine fellows, and all is for the best in the best of all possible worlds; or they only want to be excited or to forget to-morrow's bills). It is also dangerous when it becomes a substitute for living, when we get frightened of real people and find books safer company; they are a rehearsal for living, not living itself. Swots and 'bookish' people have stage fright.

BOOKS AND LIFE

A book is the product of somebody living in a particular place at a particular time. People have a nature they are born with, and they have a life which they lead and live through, which alters that original nature. They may be born with great talents but live in a society where they can't develop or use them; or they may be only averagely gifted but get the opportunity to make the most of them. Great men are a combination of talent and opportunity. Great books are as rare as great men, and, like them, they often come in batches. It is improbable that the men living in England in the sixteenth century were more naturally talented than those living in the eleventh, but they had a better chance, a more stimulating world. Take the greatest names in literature—Homer, Dante, Shakespeare. Homer is typical of a kind of writing called epic—long stories in verse about the exploits of a small group of young warriors under a leader, the pioneer or pirate band society, held together by their devotion to their leader, and by common interests in fighting and farming and wife-getting. Dante was a citizen of Florence, a small and ambitious city State (he was also a citizen of the universal religious State, the Catholic Church). Shakespeare was born in a small, young country, fighting for its existence as an independent nation. There is something common to all three: the small size of the society and the unity of interests. Whenever a society is united (and the larger the society the harder it is to unite and the cruder and more violent the only feelings which come) it has a great outburst of good writing; we don't only find one or two first-class writers, we find a whole mass of good small writers (think of Athens in the fifth century and the Elizabethan song-writers). Being made one, like the sailors pulling on the rope, it has all power.

But whenever society breaks up into classes, sects, townspeople and peasants, rich and poor, literature suffers. There is writing for the gentle and writing for the simple, for the highbrow and the lowbrow; the latter gets cruder and coarser, the former more and more refined. And so, to-day, writing gets shut up in a circle of clever people writing about themselves for themselves, or ekes out an underworld existence, cheap and nasty. Talent does not die out, but it can't make itself understood. Since the underlying reason for writing is to bridge the gulf between one person and another, as the sense of loneliness increases, more and more books are written by more and more people, most of them with little or no talent. Forests are cut down, rivers of ink absorbed, but the lust to write is still unsatisfied. What is going to happen? If it were only a question of writing it wouldn't matter; but it is an index of our health. It's not only books, but our lives, that are going to pot.

An Outline for Boys and Girls and Their Parents,
ed. by Naomi Mitchison, 1932

IV · Private Pleasure

The Year Book of Education 1932. Edited by Lord Eustace Percy.
The Triumph of the Dalton Plan. By C. W. Kimmins and Belle Rennie.
Reminiscences of a Public Schoolboy. By W. Nichols Marcy.

Here are three books—a bird's-eye view of the world of school—a puff of a teaching method—a defence of a way of living. Here you may learn that Monmouth demands a quarter of an hour longer for scripture than Cornwall, that Ernie Todd aged twelve prefers the Dalton plan because you can spend more time on the subjects in which you are weak, that louts who accuse prefects of immoral relations with fags are, unless they quickly apologise, justly and soundly thrashed. Data to support almost any contention. Ratepayer, well-fed, daring his wife to contradict, may thump the breakfast table, shout 'Disgraceful. They're playing ducks and drakes with our money. The nation can't afford it.' Folk-dancer, remembering a once-sore behind, thinks 'Ah, had the masters loved me, I should have expanded like a flower.' Old boy in club, having another, solemn as a clergyman, declares 'You can't get away from it. A good school stamps a man.'

It is going on. It is going to be like this to-morrow. Attendance-officer will flit from slum to slum, educational agencies will be besieged by promising young men who have no inclination to business, examiners chuckle over a novel setting of the problem of Achilles and the Tortoise, fathers sell grand pianos or give up tobacco, that little Adrian or Derek may go to Marlborough or Stowe.

Like everything else in our civilisation, the system we have made has become too much for us; we can't stop the boat and we can't get out into the cold sea. The snail is obeying its shell. All we can do is to become specialists. Just as the soldier devises new methods of gas attack, or the poet a new technique of verbal association, the teacher vigorously pursues the logic of his tiny department. 'How many pupils can I get?' 'What is the optimum method for getting the greatest number of them through school certificate?' No one can afford to stop and ask what is the bearing of his work on the rest of the world, its ultimate value. It's his job, his bread and butter. Should he stop for one moment, there's his ego dinning like a frightened woman 'But what's going to happen to me? You'll be sacked without a testimonial.'

Education, all smoothly say, is the production of useful citizens. But, good God, what on earth is a useful citizen just now? If you are a policeman or a cabinet minister, it's a person who won't give you any trouble. Education is a dope to allay irritation. If he is poor, now that you no longer want him very much on the land but in mass-production plants, better give him something to think about lest he sense the absurd inadequacy of the operations he is made to do, and start to smash. Better teach him enough to read the *News of the World*. Every worker shall attend an elementary school. If he's rich, your sort, then segregate him with the other young of your sort, let him year by year through his school-days feel all the excitement of a social climber, and make him so afraid of the opinions of your sort, that you may be sure he'll never do anything silly, like forgetting his class. Public school men will always lend each other money.

But there are some, who, though comfortably off, with no right to fear, have nightmares. 'Of course, the world is really alright', they say, 'it's only the way I look at it. If I'd been differently brought up, if men had understood me, life would be the jolly thing it ought to be. Besides, even if there is anything wrong with the world, if I do try to do anything about it, I shouldn't make any difference: I should only lose my money. It's all so very diffy. Let's go and ask the children. Perhaps they will know. Now remember; no slapping. The most wonderful thing in the world is love.'

And off they go to live with the children, and splendid they are at it too. The children brighten up no end—in their heads. Stupidity which is a natural defence against living beyond one's means collapses under the intense fire of their kindness. Girls of eleven paint like Picasso, boys of sixteen write pastiches of Joyce. Every child responds to the love smarm—for a bit. But emotionally it withers. Before a man wants to understand, he wants to command or obey instinctively, to live with others in a relation of power; but all power is anathema to the liberal. He hasn't any. He can only bully the spirit.

And so unconsciously the liberal becomes the secret service of the ruling class, its most powerful weapon against social revolution.

For the freedom they boast of is bogus, management by flattery, persuading people that your suggestions are really their own. Its power lies in the inexhaustible vanity of the human heart. Don't think that you can behave as you like in a liberal school—a little recalcitrance, yes that is amusing. But a will of your own! Make no mistake about that.

The public schools are at least better than that. They offer an intense social field, the satisfactory nature of which can be seen in the fact that, their members, like bees taken from a colony, when they leave it, spiritually die. They fail because they are only for the splendid people:

they are economically parasitic. Those who leave them will not attempt to create a similar kind of society in the world because that would mean admitting the others, those who have frizzed hair, or eat peas with a knife.

But what can one do? Dearie, you can't do anything for the children till you've done something for the grown-ups. You've really got nothing to teach and you know it. When you have repapered the walls perhaps you will be allowed to tell your son how to hold the brush. In the meantime some of us will go on teaching what we can for a sum which even in its modesty we do not really deserve. Teaching will continue to be, not a public duty, but a private indulgence.

Scrutiny, September 1932

V · Problems of Education

Education and the Social Order. By Bertrand Russell.

This book is excellent propaganda. Like most propagandists, Mr. Russell is subtle to detect the psychological weakness of his opponents, but sometimes blind to his own. His book is full of valuable things.

> Conservatives and Imperialists lay stress on heredity, because they belong to the white race but are rather uneducated. Radicals lay stress on education, because it is potentially democratic . . .
>
> The town-dweller has, instead [of patriotism], a sentiment largely artificial, largely the product of his education and his newspapers.
>
> Progressive educators . . . have been inclined to generate self-importance in the child, and to let him feel himself a little aristocrat whom adults must serve.

And the whole of the chapter on class feeling in education shows Mr. Russell as a brilliant critic, from an intellectual standpoint. For he is a propagandist for disinterested curiosity, the promotion of rational enquiry. One is tempted to feel that that is all he really does care about, that his only reason for disliking injustice is that it makes research difficult. 'If a conquering dogmatic Marxism were to replace Christianity, it might be as great an obstacle to scientific progress as Christianity has been.'

There is to be a ruling class, but it is to be a class of the clever boys who will be educated apart. As the cognitive part of man is the basis of his excellence, the only mortal sin is to be closed to argument, or to teach doctrines which cannot be intellectually proved.

It is curious that Mr. Russell should be drawn to Communism, because he does not give the impression of liking community life very much. The physical presence of other people hinders thinking, and he would hate that. He says rightly that 'science has so altered our technique as to make the world one economic unit' but omits to say that this has no connection with the psychological unit, to point out that Nationalism fails not because the nation is too small a group but because it is too large. It would be presumptuous of me to pretend to know what the proletariat think of Communism; but its increasing attraction for the bourgeois lies in its demand for self-surrender for those individuals who, isolated, feel themselves emotionally at sea. Does Mr. Russell never contemplate the possibility that intellectual curiosity is neurotic, a compensation for those isolated from a social group, sexually starved, or physically weak?

In his treatment of sex and of religion he hates, not only the wrong kind of mystery, but any mystery, all that cannot be reduced to rational proportions or test tube knowledge. Knowledge will save the lover and the worshipper. All that is not understandable is 'childish emotion'. The trouble is that Mr. Russell refuses to admit that man's nature is dual, and that each part of him has its own conception of justice and morality. In his passionate nature man wants lordship, to live in a relation of power with others, to obey and to command, to strut and to swagger. He desires mystery and glory. In his cerebral nature he cares for none of these things. He wants to know and be gentle; he feels his other passionate nature is frightening and cruel.

The liberal methods of education are far better for the latter; whether they are as satisfying to the former as the old methods, with all their grave faults, is more doubtful. Liberals like Mr. Russell hate aristocracy and would substitute bureaucracy, since they hate personal power because of its frequent cruelty. The danger is, though, that, destroying it, man will grow dingy, society a collection of rentiers governed by an intellectual watch committee; instead of the terror, the spiritual bully.

Education, whatever it pretend, can do nothing for the individual; it is always social. The growth of an individual cannot be planned; it is the outcome of passionate relationships (hence the importance of the family. All the criticisms levelled at it are just and yet, as Mr. Russell bravely admits, we cannot picture the world without it), and these exist under any society or system of education. Kropotkin owed as much to the *Corps des pages* as to anything else.

The failure of modern education lies not in its attention to individual needs, nor to methods, nor even to the moral ideas it preaches, but in the fact that nobody genuinely believes in our society, for which the children are being trained. All books—and this is one of them—which help to make people conscious of this lack of belief are valuable and should be read.

The New Statesman, 15 October 1932

VI · How to Be Masters of the Machine

The machine is a mechanised tool; a tool in that it is a device for the economical use of power; mechanised in that the manipulation of the tool is transferred from a human being to a mechanism.

To the consumer then the machine is a means of obtaining an abundance of goods; to the producer a means of lightening his labour and increasing his leisure.

It sounds ideal: a four-hour working day; steam yachts and cigarette lighters all round. There aren't yet. Is it the fault of the capitalists? Not at all.

On the contrary, it is just what they might soon provide—except, of course, to the unemployed.

Imagine yourself in the near future a worker in some gigantic factory. For four hours every day you screw one nut on to each of a succession of chassis moving along a belt. By doing this you earn £6 a week.

You live in a villa, have your own car, a wireless in the sitting-room, an electrical refrigerator in the kitchen, everything that the advertisements tell you you need, much that in the nineteenth century could not be had for love or money.

You have the goods, and you have the leisure; goods, the material with which to satisfy your wants, and leisure, the time in which to satisfy them. Are you happy? If not, why not?

The question is, what do you really want? You want, I think, two things. First security, not to be afraid that you may lose your job. To be certain that other people like you and respect you, not only your friends, but the people you see in trams, or the policeman at the corner.

Secondly, you want to do something, to make things, to discover new facts, prove to yourself and others by your skill or brains that you are worth something, in fact, to give your existence a material meaning.

How does machinery help you? At present, not much. Security?—if you are a wage-earner, machinery means more unemployment; one person can look after many machines, and the work requires little skill but great intensity of labour, so that only the young are required.

The worker is too old at thirty. If you are a shareholder, the fierceness of competition and the constant trade booms and depressions keep you in a perpetual state of anxiety about your investments.

When people are anxious, leisure becomes a vacuum to be forcibly filled—never be alone, never stop to think. Half the machinery of the world is running to-day not to satisfy any real want, but to stop us remembering that we are afraid.

Does the machine help us to do or make things which make us proud of ourselves? Take the ordinary machine-minder. Most of the operations in a mass production plant are of such slight importance in themselves that no one could possibly feel that doing them made him a man.

They are only labour for wages, not work. The case of the machine-carter is different. Engine or crane drivers, for example, who have a powerful machine completely dependent on their judgment, or skilled electricians installing a lighting system, have a real job, needing all their faculties of body and mind.

But there are a limited number of such; there will always be required a mass of unskilled workers for whom their real life must lie outside their employment.

What of the machine, then, during leisure? Lack of security is attributable to a machined economic and social system, and the deluge of fancy luxury articles is largely an effect of capitalism, but in any kind of modern State the abundance of goods which machinery makes possible will still raise the questions: Do I want all these things? What do I want them for?

If you are a mechanic, interested in the construction and technical working of machinery, the questions answer themselves.

If you are not, remember that while one machine can only do one thing, and do it all the time, human desire is intermittent, variable, and many-sided.

The machine therefore tends to dictate that the particular desire it satisfies is like it, unique and ever active, and to suppress those for which it is not constructed, unless you, its owner, are quite certain exactly what you want it for, e.g., I want this wireless set to listen to the concert next Wednesday, to hear the news at 9.20. I do not want it to be turned on all day while I read.

Do not let the possession of a motorcycle oblige you to use it at times when you really want to go for a walk. Find out what you want first of all, and then if a machine will help you, use it.

In theory machines have made it possible for everyone to reach a standard of living formerly unattainable even by the very rich. In practice they have so far made a majority of mankind wretched and a minority unhappy, spoiled children.

If you are to make the theory fact, you must first establish a Socialist State in which everyone can feel secure, and, secondly, have enough self-knowledge and common sense to ensure that machines are employed by your needs, and not your needs by the machinery.

Daily Herald, 28 April 1933

VII

Culture and Environment. By F. R. Leavis and Denys Thompson.
How to Teach Reading. By F. R. Leavis.
How Many Children Had Lady Macbeth? By L. C. Knights.

What is a highbrow? Someone who is not passive to his experience but who tries to organise, explain and alter it, someone in fact, who tries to influence his history: a man struggling for life in the water is for the time being a highbrow. The decisive factor is a conflict between the person and his environment; most of the people who are usually called highbrows had either an unhappy childhood and adolescence or suffer from physical defects. Mr. Leavis, Mr. Thompson, Mr. Knights, Mr. Pound, the author and the reader of this review, are highbrows, and these books are a plea for the creation of more.

I think rightly. We live in an age in which the collapse of all previous standards coincides with the perfection in technique for the centralised distribution of ideas; some kind of revolution is inevitable, and will as inevitably be imposed from above by a minority; in consequence, if the result is not to depend on the loudest voice, if the majority is to have the slightest say in its future, it must be more critical than it is necessary for it to be in an epoch of straightforward development.

All these three books are concerned with school education. *How Many Children Had Lady Macbeth?* is an attack on the bunk in most teaching of Shakespeare, with its concentration on the characters and plot, and its omission of the poetry. *How to Teach Reading* is a demand for training in the technique of critical reading. *Culture and Environment* is a practical text book for assisting children to defeat propaganda of all kinds by making them aware of which buttons are being pressed.

All three books are good and will, I hope, be read seriously by all school teachers. *Culture and Environment* is particularly excellent because it sets the examination papers; teachers are usually hard-worked, and, while agreeing with the importance of this kind of instruction, are either too busy or too tired to prepare it themselves.

Also I am inclined to think that advertising is a better field than literature for such work, the aim of which, like that of psycho-analysis, is primarily destructive, to dissipate a reaction by becoming conscious of it. Advertising and machines are part of the environment of which literature is a reaction; those who are critically aware of their environment and of themselves will be critical of what they read, and not otherwise. I think it extremely doubtful whether any direct training of literary sensibility is possible.

Our education is far too bookish. To give children masterpieces to read, the reaction of exceptional adult minds to vast experiences, is fantastic. A boy in school remains divorced from the means of production, from livelihood; it is impossible to do much, but I believe that for the time being the most satisfactory method of teaching English to children is through their environment and their actions in it; e.g., if they are going to read or write about sawing wood, they should saw some themselves first: they should have plenty of acting, if possible, and under their English teacher movement classes as well, and very, very little talk.

These books all imply the more general question 'What is to be done?' though, perhaps intentionally, they all avoid specifically stating or answering it. Mass production, advertising, the divorce between mental and manual labour, magazine stories, the abuse of leisure, all these are symptoms of an invalid society, and can only be finally cured by attending to the cause. You can suppress one symptom but only to create another, just as you can turn a burglar into an epileptic. Opinions differ both on cause and cure, but it is the duty of an investigator to state his own, and if possible the more important conflicting ones. Consciousness always appears to be uncontaminated by its object, and the danger of the methods advocated in these books is of making the invalid fascinated by his disease, of enabling the responsible minority to derive such intellectual satisfaction from contemplating the process of decay, from which by the nature of consciousness itself they feel insulated, that they lose the will and power to arrest it.

The Twentieth Century, May 1933

VIII

The Book of Talbot. By Violet Clifton.

Perhaps it is not the reviewer's business to criticise the dust-cover of a book, but I feel bound to say that in this case the remarks quoted very nearly made one reader throw the book straight in the fire. *The Book of Talbot* is too excellent to need a puff redolent of the worst features of Sunday journalism.

It is difficult to say more about it than to recommend everyone to read it and judge for themselves. It is the life of a husband written by a wife who loved him; of a man of old family whom fortune enables to realize every phantasy in action, by a woman who, I should imagine, read little but Homer, Dante, and Shakespeare. Both of them were devout Roman Catholics.

Henry James once said, reviewing a batch of novels: 'Yes, the circumstances of the interest are there, but where is the interest itself?' How easily might that have been true of a book like this. The lives of explorers are not necessarily interesting: records of physical sensations can be as dull as any analysis of mental states. *The Book of Talbot* is a great book, not because he went to Verkhoyansk, the coldest place in the world, but because Lady Clifton would have been just as interested in his adventures if he had gone to Wigan.

It shows more clearly than anything I have read for a long time that the first criterion of success in any human activity, the necessary preliminary, whether to scientific discovery or to artistic vision, is intensity of attention or, less pompously, love.

Love has allowed Lady Clifton to constellate round Talbot the whole of her experience and to make it significant. One cannot conceive of her needing to write another line; one feels that she has put down everything. One is quite incurious to know whether Talbot was in actual life as magnificent a figure as he is in his book. Whatever his origins he is completely convincing. There is no trace of day-dreaming.

Almost any passage will illustrate the writer's fixity of purpose.

A walk by the sea might bring an unforgettable experience, as on that summer day when Violet had thought: 'I must walk alone near the sea'. She followed the causeway; she was exhilarated by her feeling of unity with nature, of unity with God. Like a breeze, blowing among the marsh flowers, so God was the breath of common life—'we living creatures are all akin.' She rounded a crag; a heron saw her, sent out a harsh warning and flapped away. A chough echoed the cry, gulls and curlews took up the chorus of fear; the sanderlings and the godwits sped off in silvery sweep. A red-deer leapt up from the bracken, a fallow bounded away. She had given out love, but fear had come back to her, and that so sharply that she was stunned. She saw herself cut off from the common breath, like a dead part in a living whole.

Talbot came upon her, past the flooded causeway, but he never quite understood why, at the moment, she seemed a being at ebb;

nor why she caught hold of his hand and held it for the brief time he
left it to her. He but half heard her say—something about his being
her only friend.

It is this single-minded devotion that gives her her remarkable
technical skill at combining the words of Talbot's diary and her own
comments into a consistent texture of narrative. It also makes it
possible for her to say things which in isolation look silly. For example,
I doubt if many can read the following passage out of its context
without embarrassment, yet few, I am certain, coming upon it in its
proper place will feel it unjustified.

> Foreseeing the desolate time when he would no longer speak her
> name she treasured his every call upon her. For the night, to prove
> love, she made a game. Every time that he woke or turned she would
> give a little cooing sound to show her wakefulness, but if he had to
> say her name—then he had won. In those weeks he twice won the
> game. But every night she struck many matches, for he woke often.

One may be repelled by Roman Catholicism; one may regard the
system of society which made Talbot's life and character possible as
grossly unjust, but I cannot imagine that anyone who is fortunate
enough to read this book, will not experience that sense of glory which
it is the privilege of great art to give.

The Criterion, October 1933

IX

T. E. Lawrence. By B. H. Liddell Hart.

If this article is very little about Captain Liddell Hart's book, it is
because he has presented his matter so clearly and convincingly that
the reader forgets all about him. Excepting the almost mythical *Seven
Pillars* there is no better account of the Arabian campaign than this,
and no more living portrait of Lawrence: nor is there likely to be.

Thinking of Lawrence, I am reminded of two stories; the first
Turgenev's *A Desperate Character*, particularly the incident of the
hero found sitting in an inn with the notice in front of him 'Anyone
who wishes to flip a nobleman on the nose may do so for two roubles',
and how he nearly killed one who tried to take two flips for his money.
The second, which I read I believe in McDougall's *Abnormal
Psychology* was the statement made by a man after he had cut the
throats of his wife and family. 'No, I am not the truly strong man. The
truly strong man lounges about in bars and does nothing at all.'

To me Lawrence's life is an allegory of the transformation of the
Truly Weak Man into the Truly Strong Man, an answer to the
question 'How shall the self-conscious man be saved?' and the moral
seems to be this; 'self-consciousness is an asset, in fact the only friend
of our progress. We can't go back on it. But its demands on our little
person and his appetites are so great that most of us, terrified, try to
escape or make terms with it, which is fatal. As a pursuer it is deadly.'

Only the continuous annihilation of the self by the Identity, to use Blake's terminology, will bring us to the freedom we wish for, or in Lawrence's own phrase 'Happiness comes in absorption'.

But a misinterpretation of absorption is one of the great heresies of our generation. To interpret it as blind action without consideration of meaning or ends, as an escape from reason and consciousness; that is indeed to become the Truly Weak Man, to enlist in the great Fascist retreat which will land us finally in the ditch of despair, to cry like Elijah: 'Lord take away my life for I am not better than my fathers.'

From Lawrence's own account of himself, no one has found his temptation harder, nor conquered it more resolutely, better demonstrated the truth that action and reason are inseparable; it is only in action that reason can realise itself, and only through reason that action can become free. Consciousness necessitates more action not less, and *vice versa*.

To the problem of human relations he has an equally important contribution to make. Different as they appear on the surface, both he and his namesake, D. H. Lawrence, imply the same, that the Western-romantic conception of personal love is a neurotic symptom only inflaming our loneliness, a bad answer to our real wish to be united to and rooted in life. They both say *'noli me tangere'*. It is at least doubtful, if in our convalescence sexual relations can do anything but postpone our cure. It is quite possible that the way back to real intimacy is through a kind of asceticism. The self must first learn to be indifferent; as Lenin said, 'To go hungry, work illegally and be anonymous.' Lawrence's enlistment in the Air Force and Rimbaud's adoption of a trading career are essentially similar. 'One must be absolutely modern.'

I mentioned Lenin. He and Lawrence seem to me the two whose lives exemplify most completely what is best and significant in our time, our nearest approach to a synthesis of feeling and reason, act and thought, the most potent agents of freedom and to us, egotistical underlings, the most relevant accusation and hope.

Now and Then, Spring 1934

X · The Liberal Fascist

[HONOUR]

No account of school life ever appears disinterested to those who disagree with it: it will always appear the work of either a nest-fouler or a nest-whitewasher. I can only say that if, in my account of Gresham's School, Holt, I am sometimes critical, it is not, I hope, from personal motives. Of its fairness and accuracy I must leave those directly acquainted with the school in the first half of the last decade to judge.

As what one sees depends on what one is, I must begin with a description of myself at that time. The son of book-loving, Anglo-Catholic parents of the professional class, the youngest of three brothers, I was—and in most respects still am—mentally precocious, physically backward, short-sighted, a rabbit at all games, very untidy and grubby, a nail-biter, a physical coward, dishonest, sentimental, with no community sense whatever, in fact a typical little highbrow and difficult child. It says much—or perhaps little—for Holt that I was never bullied or molested, I was allowed to make my friends where I chose, and was, taking everything into consideration, very happy throughout my time there.

The first condition for a successful school is a beautiful situation and in that respect we were at Holt very fortunate. The school authorities, with extraordinary good sense, set virtually no bounds, a liberty rarely I believe abused. Watching a snow storm come up from the sea over the marshes at Salthouse, and walking in a June dawn (not so legally) by Hempstead Mill are only the two most vivid of a hundred such experiences.

If the buildings were not lovely—their date precluded that—they were better than many, and comfortable. Class-rooms were warm and well-lit. In my own house we had dormitories with cubicles (smaller dormitories of 4 or 6 beds without cubicles would be better I think) and studies, shared with two or three others for the first two years, and single afterwards: so we cannot be said to have been unduly herded together. Fagging, during one's first year or so, was extremely light, hot water was plentiful, and the cooking, if undistinguished—no one seems ever to have solved the problem of school maids who are almost invariably slatternly and inefficient—was quite adequate.

So much for the surroundings which were all that a parent could desire. What about the education?

On the academic side I can't say much because I remember so little, but I imagine it was pretty good. Holt is a modern school, i.e. it does not teach Greek and concentrates on science, history, etc. We had a magnificent library, perhaps the only requisite because real people, who can learn, given that chance, will teach themselves; the labs were excellently equipped, all the staff were conscientious and some efficient, and our scholarship list was quite satisfactory.

As regards out-of-school activities the school was extremely sensible. Athletics were treated as they ought to be treated, as something to be enjoyed and not made a fetish of, every kind of hobby was encouraged (I remember with special pleasure the expeditions of the sociological society which did no more sociology than my foot, but had a grand time visiting factories in a charabanc). There was plenty of acting, house plays in the winter and a Shakespeare play in an open-air theatre in the summer. And if I think that all out-of-door plays are detestable, that is a personal prejudice.

I can't say that we were given any real sense of the problems of the world, or of how to attack them, other than in vague ideals of service, but then I have never heard of any school that did, and my own convictions are perhaps too extreme for me to expect to see them acted upon. Indeed it is impossible to see how any school, which is not directly attached in some way to an industrial or agricultural unit, and where boys and staff are both drawn from the monied classes, can hope to see the world picture of that class objectively. The mass production

322

of gentlemen is their *raison-d'être,* and one can hardly suggest that they should adopt principles which would destroy them. The fact remains that the public school boy's attitude to the working-class and to the not-quite-quite has altered very little since the war. He is taught to be fairly kind and polite, provided of course they return the compliment, but their lives and needs remain as remote to him as those of another species. And I doubt very much if the same isn't true of the staff as well. I do remember hearing however that a master was sacked for taking part in left-wing politics outside the school, which if true, and I cannot vouch for the accuracy of the story, seems to me a shameful thing.

The only concrete suggestion I have to make here is that the staff might give up wearing those ridiculous black clothes (if they still do) which made them look like unsuccessful insurance agents, and certainly did not increase our respect for them; if we were allowed— and rightly—to wear blazers and flannel trousers, the staff as well might surely be allowed a sensible costume.

I suppose no one ever remembers actually being taught anything, though one remembers clearly enough when one failed to learn. My efforts at engineering, which must have been as distressing to the very nice military man who taught that subject as they were boring to me— the sum total of my achievement was two battered ash-trays and any number of ruined tools—are still vivid.

Where one was more successful, one remembers only the idiosyncrasies of the masters, that X shouted in class—a horrible habit—that Y would come up behind one on a bicycle ride and pinch one's seat, that Z wore his cap like a racing-tout, and so on. For, as people, those who at one time or another have taught me stand out in memory very clearly, far more clearly in fact than my friends, and this seems a common experience.

It is perhaps as well that teachers can never realise how intensely aware of their personalities their charges are, because if they could they would be too terrified to move or to open their mouths. A single act or remark is quite sufficient to queer the pitch. For example a certain master once caught me writing poetry in prep, writing a poem which I knew to be a bad one. He said 'You shouldn't waste your sweetness on the desert air like this, Auden'; to-day I cannot think of him without wishing him evil.

It is pleasant to turn from such thoughts to remember two men to whom I owe an immense debt, the master who taught Classics and English, and the Music master. The former, who was never tired of showing us the shallowness of those who despised the classics, had the most magnificent bass reading voice I have ever heard, and from listening to him read the Bible or Shakespeare I learnt more about poetry and the humanities than from any course of University lectures.

To the latter I owe not only such knowledge of music as I possess, but my first friendship with a grown up person, with all that that means. As a musician he was in the first rank. I do not think it was only partiality that made me feel, when later I heard Schweitzer play Bach on the organ, that he played no better.

As a person he was what the ideal schoolmaster should be, ready to be a friend and not a beak, to give the adolescent all the comfort and stimulus of a personal relation, without at the same time making any demands for himself in return, a temptation which must assail all those who are capable of attracting and influencing their juniors. He was in the best sense of the word indifferent, and if the whole of the rest of my schooldays had been hateful, which they weren't, his existence alone would make me recall them with pleasure.

Finally, no acknowledgments of mine would be complete without a reference to one—call him Wreath—who though not a member of the staff, yet as captain of my house when I was still a junior, stood to me in much the same relation. A really good prefect is as rare as a comet— authority makes most boys of eighteen or any other age into stuck-up little idiots, but he was a born leader and the only person, boy or master, who ever made the conventional house and school loyalties have any meaning for me.

I have no wish to belittle a profession to which I have the honour to belong. Its members are practically all extremely conscientious, hard working, keen on their job, and sometimes very intelligent. At the same time if one were invited to dine with a company representing all trades and professions, the schoolmaster is the last person one would want to sit next to. Being a schoolmaster is not like being a Bank Clerk—it is not enough just to be efficient at teaching; one must be a remarkable person. Some schoolmasters are, but far, far too many are silted-up old maids, earnest young scoutmasters, or just generally dim.

Some of the reasons for this are clear; in the first place the profession has generally to be entered young, and those of university age who are attracted to it are rarely the most vital and adventurous spirits. On the contrary they are only too often those who are afraid of the mature world, either the athletic whose schooldays were the peak of their triumph from which they dread to recede, or else the timid academic whose qualifications or personal charm are insufficient to secure them a fellowship; in either case the would-be children. It is not improbable that those who enter teaching as a *pis-aller*, as they might become stevedores or bootleggers, are often the best; which may be the reason why the staffs of preparatory schools seem so superior to those of public schools.

In the second place, partly because they have never had the chance, and sometimes I am ashamed to say as the result of a definite policy of the school authorities, they have no outside interests. This seems to me disastrous, leading inevitably to them becoming either lifeless prunes or else spiritual vampires, sucking their vitality from the children. Indeed if I were a headmaster—which heaven forbid—I would have no unmarried man on my staff who was not definitely engaged on some work outside the school. Better still, the number of professional teachers would be very small, the product of a very vigorous selection. The rest would be conscripted, every citizen after some years in the world would be called up to serve his two or three years teaching for the state, after which he would return to his job again. However that is only a daydream and I must return to Holt and its education of our morals.

That side was run on what was called the honour system, and for the benefit of those who do not know the school, some explanation of this is necessary.

About a week after arrival every new boy was interviewed separately by his housemaster and the headmaster—half watt hypnotism we used to call it—and was asked—I need hardly say how difficult it would have been to refuse—to promise on his honour three things:

(1) Not to swear.

(2) Not to smoke.

(3) Not to say or do anything indecent.

Having done so, two consequences followed:

(1) If you broke any of these promises you should report the breakage to your housemaster.

(2) If you saw anyone else break them, you should endeavour to persuade him to report and if he refused you should report him yourself.

Before I say anything in criticism, I must add that the system worked, in public at any rate. One almost never saw anyone smoking, heard anyone swear, or came across any smut. From the point of view of master and parent it would seem ideal. Here at last was the clean and healthy school they had been looking for.

From the boy's point of view on the other hand, I feel compelled to say that I believe no more potent engine for turning them into neurotic innocents, for perpetuating those very faults of character which it was intended to cure, was ever devised.

Everyone knows that the only emotion that is fully developed in a boy of fourteen is the emotion of loyalty and honour. For that very reason it is so dangerous. By appealing to it, you can do almost anything you choose, you can suppress the expression of all those emotions, particularly the sexual, which are still undeveloped; like a modern dictator you can defeat almost any opposition from other parts of the psyche, but if you do, if you deny these other emotions their expression and development, however silly or shocking they may seem to you, they will not only never grow up, but they will go backward, for human nature cannot stay still; they will, like all things that are shut up, go bad on you.

Of the two consequences of our promises, the second, the obligation to interfere with one's neighbour, is of course much the more serious. It meant that the whole of our moral life was based on fear, on fear of the community, not to mention the temptation it offered to the natural informer, and fear is not a healthy basis. It makes one furtive and dishonest and unadventurous. The best reason I have for opposing Fascism is that at school I lived in a Fascist state. Of the effect of the system on the boys after they left school I have little direct experience outside my own and those whom I knew personally, but all those with whom I have spoken, whether old boys or others who have come into contact with old boys, have borne out my conclusion that the effect is a serious one in many cases. I am fully aware that the first five years of life are more important than any others and that those cases I am thinking of would have had a difficult time anyway, but I am convinced that their difficulties were enormously and unnecessarily increased by the honour system. Though the system was a peculiarity of Holt, it is only an extreme example of a tendency which can be seen in the running of every school: the tendency to identify the welfare of the school with the welfare of the boys in it, to judge school life not by its own peculiar standards as a stage in the development towards maturity, but as an end in itself by adult standards. Every headmaster is inclined to think that so long as all's fair in his own little garden he has succeeded. When later he sees what some of his old boys have turned into he seldom realises that the very apparent perfection he was so proud of is partly responsible.

You can, I repeat, do almost anything by utilising the sense of community so long as the community is there, but as soon as the pressure is removed your unfortunate pupils are left defenceless. Either the print has taken so deeply that they remain frozen and undeveloped, or else, their infantilised instinct suddenly released, they plunge into foolish and damaging dissipation.

The first truth a schoolmaster has to learn is that if the fool would persist in his folly he would become wise; in other words, to leave well alone and not to give advice until it is asked for, remembering that nearly all his education is done by the boy himself with the help of other boys of his own age. There is far too much talk about ideals at all schools. Ideals are the conclusions drawn from a man's experience, not the data: they are essentially for the mature.

Whether for good or ill dogmatic religion, that is to say a Christian world-picture, has broken down among schoolmasters, and religion without dogma soon becomes, as it was at Holt, nothing but vague uplift, as flat as an old bottle of soda water. For the young without experience ideals are as grave a danger in the moral sphere as book learning is in the intellectual, the danger of becoming a purely mental concept, mechanising the soul.

In the absence of an orthodoxy, and we shall have to reconcile ourselves to that for some time, education has to rely almost entirely upon the quality of the teacher. For a teacher to be of real value to his pupils, he must be a mature and above all a happy person, giving the young the feeling that adult life is infinitely more exciting and interesting than their own; he must be prepared to give them all his powers of affection and imaginative understanding when they want them, yet to forget them completely the moment they are gone, to be indifferent to them personally; and lastly he must have no moral bees-in-his-bonnet, no preconceptions of what the good child should be; he must be shocked or alarmed at nothing, only patient to understand the significance of any piece of behaviour from the child's point of view, not his own; to see in the perfect little ape his most promising charge, and watchful to remove as tactfully and unobtrusively as possible such obstacles to progress as he can. He must, to use a phrase of Mr. Gerald Heard's, and I know no better, 'be an anthropologist'.

More nonsense is talked about education than about anything else, and I cannot hope to do better than my fellow amateurs. I have written about Holt because I was there and therefore have known it from the inside, but any other school would have done as well. If I have criticised certain things, it is not because I think Holt is worse than other schools—in many respects it is probably considerably in advance of them—but because at a time like the present when the world into which our young emerge is bound to be a very difficult one, it is particularly important that they should get the best start we can give them, and too many suggestions are better than none. I offer mine for what they are worth.

The Old School, ed. by Graham Greene, 1934

XI · Introduction to 'The Poet's Tongue'

Of the many definitions of poetry, the simplest is still the best: 'memorable speech'. That is to say, it must move our emotions, or excite our intellect, for only that which is moving or exciting is memorable, and the stimulus is the audible spoken word and cadence, to which in all its power of suggestion and incantation we must surrender, as we do when talking to an intimate friend. We must, in fact, make exactly the opposite kind of mental effort to that we make in grasping other verbal uses, for in the case of the latter the aura of suggestion round every word through which, like the atom radiating lines of force through the whole of space and time, it becomes ultimately a sign for the sum of all possible meanings, must be rigorously suppressed and its meaning confined to a single dictionary one. For this reason the exposition of a scientific theory is easier to read than to hear. No poetry, on the other hand, which when mastered is not better heard than read is good poetry.

All speech has rhythm, which is the result of the combination of the alternating periods of effort and rest necessary to all living things, and the laying of emphasis on what we consider important; and in all poetry there is a tension between the rhythms due to the poet's personal values, and those due to the experiences of generations crystallised into habits of language such as the English tendency to alternate weak and accented syllables, and conventional verse forms like the hexameter, the heroic pentameter, or the French Alexandrine. Similes, metaphors of image or idea, and auditory metaphors such as rhyme, assonance, and alliteration help further to clarify and strengthen the pattern and internal relations of the experience described.

Poetry, in fact, bears the same kind of relation to Prose, using prose simply in the sense of all those uses of words that are not poetry, that algebra bears to arithmetic. The poet writes of personal or fictitious experiences, but these are not important in themselves until the reader has realised them in his own consciousness.

> Soldier from the war returning,
> Spoiler of the taken town.

It is quite unimportant, though it is the kind of question not infrequently asked, who the soldier is, what regiment he belongs to, what war he had been fighting in, etc. The soldier is you or me, or the man next door. Only when it throws light on our own experience, when these lines occur to us as we see, say, the unhappy face of a stockbroker in the suburban train, does poetry convince us of its significance. The test of a poet is the frequency and diversity of the occasions on which we remember his poetry.

Memorable speech then. About what? Birth, death, the Beatific Vision, the abysses of hatred and fear, the awards and miseries of desire, the unjust walking the earth and the just scratching miserably for food like hens, triumphs, earthquakes, deserts of boredom and featureless anxiety, the Golden Age promised or irrevocably past, the gratifications and terrors of childhood, the impact of nature on the adolescent, the despairs and wisdoms of the mature, the sacrificial victim, the descent into Hell, the devouring and the benign mother? Yes, all of these, but not these only. Everything that we remember no matter how trivial: the mark on the wall, the joke at luncheon, word games, these, like the dance of a stoat or the raven's gamble, are equally the subject of poetry.

We shall do poetry a great disservice if we confine it only to the major experiences of life:

> The soldier's pole is fallen,
> Boys and girls are level now with men,
> And there is nothing left remarkable
> Beneath the visiting moon.

> They had a royal wedding.
> All his courtiers wished him well.
> The horses pranced and the dancers danced.
> O Mister it was swell.

> And masculine is found to be
> Hadria the Adriatic Sea.

have all their rightful place, and full appreciation of one depends on full appreciation of the others.

A great many people dislike the idea of poetry as they dislike over-earnest people, because they imagine it is always worrying about the eternal verities.

Those, in Mr. Spender's words, who try to put poetry on a pedestal only succeed in putting it on the shelf. Poetry is no better and no worse than human nature; it is profound and shallow, sophisticated and naïve, dull and witty, bawdy and chaste in turn.

In spite of the spread of education and the accessibility of printed matter, there is a gap between what is commonly called 'highbrow' and 'lowbrow' taste, wider perhaps than it has ever been.

The industrial revolution broke up the agricultural communities, with their local conservative cultures, and divided the growing population into two classes: those whether employers or employees who worked and had little leisure, and a small class of shareholders who did no work, had leisure but no responsibilities or roots, and were therefore preoccupied with themselves. Literature has tended therefore to divide into two streams, one providing the first with a compensation and escape, the other the second with a religion and a drug. The Art for Art's sake of the London drawing-rooms of the '90's, and towns like Burnley and Rochdale, are complementary.

Nor has the situation been much improved by the increased leisure and educational opportunities which the population to-day as a whole possess. Were leisure all, the unemployed would have created a second Athens.

Artistic creations may be produced by individuals, and because their work is only appreciated by a few it does not necessarily follow that it is not good; but a universal art can only be the product of a community united in sympathy, sense of worth, and aspiration; and it is improbable that the artist can do his best except in such a society.

Something of this lies behind the suspicion of and attack upon the intellectual which is becoming more and more vocal. It is hardly possible to open a number of *Punch* without seeing him spectacled, round-shouldered, rabbit-toothed, a foil to a landscape of beautifully unconscious cows, or a whipping-boy for a drawing-room of dashing young sahibs and elegant daughters of the chase. Cross the channel and this dislike, in more countries than one, has taken a practical form, to which the occasional ducking of an Oxford æsthete seems a nursery tiff.

If we are still of the opinion that poetry is worth writing and reading, we must be able to answer such objections satisfactorily at least to ourselves.

The 'average' man says: 'When I get home I want to spend my time with my wife or in the nursery; I want to get out on to the links or go for a spin in the car, not to read poetry. Why should I? I'm quite happy without it.' We must be able to point out to him that whenever, for example, he makes a good joke he is creating poetry, that one of the motives behind poetry is curiosity, the wish to know what we feel and think, and how, as E. M. Forster says, can I know what I think till I see what I say, and that curiosity is the only human passion that can be indulged in for twenty-four hours a day without satiety.

The psychologist maintains that poetry is a neurotic symptom, an attempt to compensate by phantasy for a failure to meet reality. We must tell him that phantasy is only the beginning of writing; that, on the contrary, like psychology, poetry is a struggle to reconcile the unwilling subject and object; in fact, that since psychological truth depends so largely on context, poetry, the parabolic approach, is the only adequate medium for psychology.

The propagandist, whether moral or political, complains that the writer should use his powers over words to persuade people to a particular course of action, instead of fiddling while Rome burns. But Poetry is not concerned with telling people what to do, but with extending our knowledge of good and evil, perhaps making the necessity for action more urgent and its nature more clear, but only leading us to the point where it is possible for us to make a rational and moral choice.

In compiling an anthology such considerations must be borne in mind. First, one must overcome the prejudice that poetry is uplift and show that poetry can appeal to every level of consciousness. We do not want to read 'great' poetry all the time, and a good anthology should contain poems for every mood. Secondly, one must disabuse people of the idea that poetry is primarily an escape from reality. We all need escape at times, just as we need food and sleep, and some escape poetry there must always be. One must not let people think either that poetry never enjoys itself, or that it ignores the grimmer aspects of existence. Lastly, one must show those who come to poetry for a message, for calendar thoughts, that they have come to the wrong door, that poetry may illuminate but it will not dictate.

As regards arrangement we have, after some thought, adopted an alphabetical, anonymous order. It seems best to us, if the idea of poetry as something dead and suitable for a tourist-ridden museum—a cultural tradition to be preserved and imitated rather than a spontaneous living product—is to be avoided, that the first approach should be with an open mind, free from the bias of great names and literary influences, the first impression that of a human activity, independent of period and unconfined in subject.

The Poet's Tongue, ed. by W. H. Auden
and John Garrett, 1935

XII · The Bond and the Free

Growing Opinions. Edited by Alan Campbell Johnson.
I Was a Prisoner. By William Holt.
Means Test Man. By W. Brierley.
Caliban Shrieks. By Jack Hilton.

If the business of a reviewer is to describe the contents of the books he reviews and to appraise their value, this is not going to be a review.

Growing Opinions is a collection of articles by members of the rising generation who, like the readers of this magazine, have had luck. They can and do read difficult books, they have no reason to con the road in order to avoid meeting a policeman. If their ideas are not startling, they are cogently reasoned and well expressed. Mr. Stovin and Mr. Lovelock's articles on Education and Sport respectively seem to me particularly good.

Anyone who does not know what the intelligent young man or woman with a university education is thinking about Life may learn it here. As a whole they seem well-informed and well-intentioned, sensible and serious, unrhetorical and a trifle dull. Perhaps, though here I may be doing them an injustice, they are a little self-satisfied, a little too conscious of their good sense, and their status as the Free.

The writers of the other three books, on the other hand, are all below the salt. Two of them have done time. The third is technically at liberty to walk out of his front door but as he cannot afford to go anywhere else, he may also be included among the Bond.

Those who cannot imagine for themselves what a modern prison is like, a fairly easy task, may learn to do so from Mr. Holt. Those who cannot imagine for themselves what the Means Test is like, a very difficult task, may learn to do so from Mr. Brierley. Those who for whatever reason feel a bitterness and hatred against life will find such a feeling expressed in magnificent Moby Dick rhetoric by Mr. Hilton, the finest writer of them all.

And then.
What is to be done?

'What we need is a new faith' say the growing opinions, but wait for a leader to provide one.

'Make up your minds. Act', shouts the politician to the eight-year-old, knowing that the latter will be only too delighted to hear that he hasn't got to learn any more.

'The whole bloody chute is going to bust soon, and a damn good job too', shrieks Caliban, but shrinks from wielding the crowbar because he doesn't like the sight of a bloody crown.

Every sensitive and intelligent person knows that the Means Test and the Prison are as these books describe them, and that a social system under which they are possible is grotesque. Then why does it endure a second longer?

It does so in the first place because of the quiet unostentatious courage, honesty, intelligence, kindliness and good-will of millions of individuals in their own small circle. Those therefore like the Communist, who see most clearly the defects of the system, are inclined to distrust and even dislike the considerate employer or the unembittered wage-earner. If things have got to grow worse before they can improve, then the bigger the bully chosen as Means Test inspector, the greater martinet the Prison governor, the better.

And in the second place, to those who feel that perhaps the Communist does not hold all the cards, the most disquieting fact is that the armament firms, the yellow and gutter press, the advertising agencies are staffed, not by monsters, but by extremely intelligent young men of liberal opinions.

Is the economic argument then unanswerable, or have we got to be even more pessimistic about the future of the human race?

For there are two things that every educated middle-class man (or woman) really knows to be true:

(1) That violence is always and unequivocally bad. No personal experience, no scientific knowledge, gives any other verdict than that what you can self-forgetfully love, you can cure.

> As I fall sometime in the dark,
> Do not shout as dogs do bark.
> Give me sympathy and example
> So that in your steps I will surely trample.
> Spare the rod and save the child,
> Imprisonment is bleak and punishment wild.

We know this perfectly well, but we are only prepared to act on it as long as it's no trouble and there's no difficult problem. When there is we send for the hangman and the bombing plane and shut our eyes and ears.

Bernard Shaw remarks somewhere that in a really civilised community flogging would be impossible because no man could be persuaded to flog another. But as it is, any decent warder will do it for half-a-crown, not probably because he likes it or even thinks it desirable on penal grounds, but because it is expected of him. 'There! you see', says the economist, 'the economic reason again.'

(2) That he is spending more on himself than he need, and is doing less for others than he could. But he doesn't want to seem a prig. We

ought to move in such and such a direction, towards, say, a moral life or universal disarmament but let's move all together.

In other words, 'I don't want the responsibility, let a revolution do it for me.'

The difficulty is that we all know, the Communist himself is a splendid example, that if we choose, we can reject self-interest, and that only when we do so, do we achieve anything worth while.

'But I can't do that, without a faith.' But in these words we reject one. And hope that an easier one will be forced on us.

Bernard Shaw's speech in *Too True to be Good*, quoted in *Growing Opinions*, is a warning:

> I must have affirmations to preach [We have but we don't]. Without them the young will not listen to me; for even the young grow tired of denials. The negative-monger falls before the soldiers, the men of action, the fighters, strong in the old uncompromising affirmations which give them status, duties, certainty of consequences; so that the pugnacious spirit of man in them can reach out and strike deathblows with steadfastly closed minds. Their way is straight and sure; but it is the way of death.

Scrutiny, September 1935

XIII · Psychology and Art To-day

> Neither in my youth nor later was I able to detect in myself any particular fondness for the position or work of a doctor. I was, rather, spurred on by a sort of itch for knowledge which concerned human relationships far more than the data of natural science.—*Freud*.

> Mutual forgiveness of each vice
> Such are the gates of paradise.—*Blake*.

To trace, in the manner of the textual critic, the influence of Freud upon modern art, as one might trace the influence of Plutarch upon Shakespeare, would not only demand an erudition which few, if any, possess, but would be of very doubtful utility. Certain writers, notably Thomas Mann and D. H. Lawrence, have actually written about Freud, certain critics, Robert Graves in *Poetic Unreason* and Herbert Read in *Form in Modern Poetry*, for example, have made use of Freudian terminology, surrealism has adopted a technique resembling the procedure in the analyst's consulting-room;[1] but the importance of Freud to art is greater than his language, technique or the truth of theoretical details. He is the most typical but not the only representative of a certain attitude to life and living relationships, and to define that attitude and its importance to creative art must be the purpose of this essay.

[1] But not the first. The Elizabethans used madness, not as a subject for clinical description but as opportunity for a particular kind of associational writing (e.g., *Lear* or *The Duchess of Malfi*). Something of the kind occurs even earlier in the nonsense passages in the mummer's play.

332

Of the earliest artists, the palæolithic rock-drawers, we can of course know nothing for certain, but it is generally agreed that their aim was a practical one, to gain power over objects by representing them; and it has been suggested that they were probably bachelors, i.e., those who, isolated from the social group, had leisure to objectify the phantasies of their group, and were tolerated for their power to do so. Be that as it may, the popular idea of the artist as socially ill adapted has been a constant one, and not unjustified. Homer may have been blind, Milton certainly was, Beethoven deaf, Villon a crook, Dante very difficult, Pope deformed, Swift impotent, Proust asthmatic, Van Gogh mental, and so on. Yet parallel with this has gone a belief in their social value. From the chiefs who kept a bard, down to the Shell-Mex exhibition, patronage, however undiscriminating, has never been wanting as a sign that art provides society with something for which it is worth paying. On both these beliefs, in the artist as neurotic, and in the social value of art, psychology has thrown a good deal of light.

THE ARTIST AS NEUROTIC

There is a famous passage in Freud's introductory lectures which has infuriated artists, not altogether unjustly:

Before you leave to-day I should like to direct your attention for a moment to a side of phantasy-life of very general interest. There is, in fact, a path from phantasy back again to reality, and that is—art. The artist has also an introverted disposition and has not far to go to become neurotic. He is one who is urged on by instinctive needs which are too clamorous; he longs to attain to honour, power, riches, fame, and the love of women; but he lacks the means of achieving these gratifications. So, like any other with an unsatisfied longing, he turns away from reality and transfers all his interest, and all his Libido, too, on to the creation of his wishes in life. There must be many factors in combination to prevent this becoming the whole outcome of his development; it is well known how often artists in particular suffer from partial inhibition of their capacities through neurosis. Probably their constitution is endowed with a powerful capacity for sublimation and with a certain flexibility in the repressions determining the conflict. But the way back to reality is found by the artist thus: He is not the only one who has a life of phantasy; the intermediate world of phantasy is sanctioned by general human consent, and every hungry soul looks to it for comfort and consolation. But to those who are not artists the gratification that can be drawn from the springs of phantasy is very limited; their inexorable repressions prevent the enjoyment of all but the meagre daydreams which can become conscious. A true artist has more at his disposal. First of all he understands how to elaborate his day-dreams, so that they lose that personal note which grates upon strange ears and become enjoyable to others; he knows too how to modify them sufficiently so that their origin in prohibited sources is not easily detected. Further, he possesses the mysterious ability to mould his particular material until it expresses the idea of his phantasy faithfully; and then he knows how to attach to this reflection of his phantasy-life so strong a stream of pleasure that, for a time at least, the repressions are out-balanced and dispelled by it. When he can do all this, he opens out to others the way back to the comfort and consolation of their own unconscious sources of pleasure, and so reaps their gratitude and admiration; then he has won—through his phantasy—what before he could only win in phantasy: honour, power, and the love of women.

Misleading though this may be, it draws attention to two facts, firstly that no artist, however 'pure', is disinterested: he expects certain rewards from his activity, however much his opinion of their nature may change as he develops; and he starts from the same point as the neurotic and the day-dreamer, from emotional frustration in early childhood.

The artist like every other kind of 'highbrow' is self-conscious, i.e., he is all of the time what everyone is some of the time, a man who is active rather than passive to his experience. A man struggling for life in the water, a schoolboy evading an imposition, or a cook getting her mistress out of the house is in the widest sense a highbrow. We only think when we are prevented from feeling or acting as we should like. Perfect satisfaction would be complete unconsciousness. Most people, however, fit into society too neatly for the stimulus to arise except in a crisis such as falling in love or losing their money.[2] The possible family situations which may produce the artist or intellectual are of course innumerable, but those in which one of the parents, usually the mother, seeks a conscious spiritual, in a sense, adult relationship with the child, are probably the commonest. E.g.,

(1) When the parents are not physically in love with each other. There are several varieties of this: the complete fiasco; the brother-sister relationship on a basis of common mental interests; the invalid-nurse relationship when one parent is a child to be maternally cared for; and the unpassionate relation of old parents.

(2) The only child. This alone is most likely to produce early life confidence which on meeting disappointment, turns like the unwanted child, to illness and anti-social behaviour to secure attention.

(3) The youngest child. Not only are the parents old but the whole family field is one of mental stimulation.[3]

Early mental stimulation can interfere with physical development and intensify the conflict. It is a true intuition that makes the caricaturist provide the highbrow with a pair of spectacles. Myopia,

[2] E.g., the sale of popular text-books on economics since 1929.

[3] The success of the youngest son in folk tales is instructive. He is generally his mother's favourite as physically weaker and less assertive than his brothers. If he is often called stupid, his stupidity is physical. He is clumsy and lazy rather than dull. (Clumsiness being due to the interference of fancies with sense data.) He succeeds partly out of good nature and partly because confronted with a problem he overcomes it by understanding rather than with force.

deafness, delayed puberty, asthma—breathing is the first independent act of the child—are some of the attempts of the mentally awakened child to resist the demands of life.

To a situation of danger and difficulty there are five solutions:

(1) To sham dead: The idiot.
(2) To retire into a life of phantasy: The schizophrene.
(3) To panic, i.e., to wreak one's grudge upon society: The criminal.
(4) To excite pity, to become ill: The invalid.
(5) To understand the mechanism of the trap: The scientist and the artist.

ART AND PHANTASY

In the passage of Freud quoted above, no distinction was drawn between art and phantasy, between—as Mr. Roger Fry once pointed out—*Madame Bovary* and a *Daily Mirror* serial about earls and housemaids. The distinction is one which may perhaps be best illustrated by the difference between two kinds of dream. 'A child has in the afternoon passed the window of a sweetshop, and would have liked to buy some chocolate it saw there, but its parents have refused the gift—so the child dreams of chocolate'—here is a simple wish fulfilment dream of the *Daily Mirror* kind, and all art, as the juvenile work of artists, starts from this level. But it does not remain there. For the following dream and its analysis I am indebted to Dr. Maurice Nicoll's *Dream Psychology*:

A young man who had begun to take morphia, but was not an addict, had the following dream:

'I was hanging by a rope a short way down a precipice. Above me on the top of the cliff was a small boy who held the rope. I was not alarmed because I knew I had only to tell the boy to pull and I would get to the top safely.' The patient could give no associations.

The dream shows that the morphinist has gone a certain way from the top of the cliff—the position of normal safety—down the side of the precipice, but he is still in contact with that which remains on the top. That which remains on the top is now relatively small, but is not inanimate like a fort, but alive: it is a force operating from the level of normal safety. This force is holding the dreamer back from the gulf, but that is all. It is for the dreamer himself to say the word if he wants to be pulled up (i.e., the morphinist is *deliberately* a morphinist).

When the common phrase is used that a man's will is weakening as he goes along some path of self-indulgence, it implies that something is strengthening. What is strengthening is the attractive power of vice. But in the dream, the attractive power of morphia is represented by the force of gravitation, and the force of gravitation is constant.

But there are certain variable elements in the dream. The position of the figure over the cliff can vary and with it the length of the rope. The size of the figure at the top of the cliff might also vary without in any way violating the spirit of the dream. If then, we examine the length of the rope and the size of the figure on the cliff top in the light of relatively variable factors, the explanation of the *smallness* of the figure on the cliff top may be found to lie in the length of the rope, as if the rope drew itself out of the figure, and so caused it to shrink.

Now the figure at the top of the cliff is on firm ground and may there symbolise the forces of some habit and custom that exist in the morphinist and from which he has departed over the edge of the cliff, but which still hold him back from disaster although they are now shrunken. The attractive power of the morphia is not increasing, but *the interest the morphinist takes in morphia* is increasing.

A picture of the balance of interest in the morphinist is thus given, and the dream shows that the part of interest situated in the cliff top is now being drawn increasingly over the precipice.

In this dream, we have something which resembles art much more closely. Not only has the censor transformed the latent content of the dream into symbols but the dream itself is no longer a simple wish fulfilment, it has become constructive, and, if you like, moral. 'A picture of the balance of interest'—that is a good description of a work of art. To use a phrase of Blake's, 'It's like a lawyer serving a writ.'

CRAFTSMANSHIP

There have always been two views of the poetic process, as an inspiration and as a craft, of the poet as the Possessed and as the Maker, e.g.,

> All good poets, epic as well as lyric, compose their beautiful poems not by art, but because they are inspired and possessed.—*Socrates.*

> That talk of inspiration is sheer nonsense: there is no such thing; it is a matter of craftsmanship.—*William Morris.*

And corresponding to this, two theories of imagination:

> Natural objects always weaken, deaden, and obliterate imagination in me.—*Blake.*

> Time and education beget experience: experience begets memory; memory begets judgment and fancy. . . . Imagination is nothing else but sense decaying or weakened by the absence of the object.—*Hobbes.*

The public, fond of marvels and envious of success without trouble, has favoured the first (see any film of artists at work); but the poets themselves, painfully aware of the labour involved, on the whole have inclined towards the second. Psycho-analysis, naturally enough, first turned its attention to those works where the workings of the unconscious were easiest to follow—Romantic literature like *Peer Gynt*, 'queer' plays like *Hamlet*, or fairy tales like *Alice in Wonderland*. I should doubt if Pope's name occurs in any text-book. The poet is inclined to retort that a great deal of literature is not of this kind, that even in a short lyric, let alone a sustained work, the material immediately 'given' to consciousness, the automatic element, is very small, that, in his own experience, what he is most aware of are technical problems, the management of consonants and vowels, the counterpointing of scenes, or how to get the husband off the stage before the lover's arrival, and that psychology concentrating on the symbols, ignores words; in his treatment of symbols and facts he fails to explain why of two works dealing with the same unconscious material, one is æsthetically good and the other bad; indeed that few psycho-analysts in their published work show any signs of knowing that æsthetic standards exist.

Psycho-analysis, he would agree, has increased the artist's interest in dreams, mnemonic fragments, child art and graffiti, etc., but that the interest is a *conscious* one. Even the most surrealistic writing or Mr. James Joyce's latest prose shows every sign of being non-automatic and extremely carefully worked over.

THE CONSCIOUS ELEMENT

Creation, like psycho-analysis, is a process of re-living in a new situation. There are three chief elements:

(1) The artist himself, a certain person at a certain time with his own limited conflicts, phantasies and interests.

(2) The data from the outer world which his senses bring him, and which, under the influence of his instincts, he selects, stores, enlarges upon, and by which he sets value and significance.

(3) The artistic medium, the new situation, which because it is not a personal, but a racial property (and psychological research into the universality of certain symbols confirms this), makes communication possible, and art more than an autobiographical record. Just as modern physics teaches that every physical object is the centre of a field of force which radiating outwards occupies all space and time, so psychology states that every word through fainter and fainter associations is ultimately a sign for the universe. The associations are always greater than those of an individual. A medium complicates and distorts the creative impulse behind it. It is, in fact, largely the medium, and thorough familiarity with the medium, with its unexpected results, that enables the artist to develop from elementary uncontrolled phantasy, to deliberate phantasy directed towards understanding.

WHAT WOULD BE A FREUDIAN LITERATURE

Freudianism cannot be considered apart from other features of the contemporary environment, apart from modern physics with its conception of transformable energy, modern technics, and modern politics. The chart here given makes no attempt to be complete, or accurate; it ignores the perpetual overlap of one historical period with another, and highly important transition periods, like the Renaissance. It is only meant to be suggestive, dividing the Christian era into three periods, the first ending with the fifteenth century, the second with the nineteenth, and the third just beginning; including what would seem the typical characteristics of such periods.

337

	1st Period.	2nd Period.	3rd Period
First Cause:	God immanent and transcendent.	Official: God transcendent. The universal mechanic. Opposition: God immanent. Pantheism. Romantic.	Energy appearing in many measurable forms, fundamental nature unknown.
World View:	The visible world as symbol of the eternal.	Official: The material world as a mechanism. Opposition: The spiritual world as a private concern.	The interdependence of observed and observer.
The End of Life:	The City of God.	Official: Power over material. Opposition: Personal salvation.	The good life on earth.
Means of Realisation:	Faith and work. The rule of the Church.	Official: Works without moral values. Opposition: Faith.	Self-understanding.
Personal Driving Forces:	Love of God. Submission of private will to will of God.	Official: Conscious will. Rationalised. Mechanised. Opposition: Emotion. Irrational.	The unconscious directed by reason.
The Sign of Success:	The mystical union	Wealth and power.	Joy.
The Worst Sinner:	The heretic.	The idle poor (Opposition view— the respectable bourgeois).	The deliberate irrationalist.
Scientific Method:	Reasoning without experiment.	Experiment and reason: the experimenter considered impartial. Pure truth. Specialisation.	Experiment directed by conscious human needs.
Sources of Power:	Animal. Wind. Water.	Water. Steam.	Electricity.
Technical Materials:	Wood. Stone.	Iron. Steel.	Light alloys.
Way of Living:	Agricultural and trading. Small towns. Balance of town and country.	Valley towns. Industrialism. Balance of town and country upset.	Dispersed units connected by electrical wires. Restored balance of town and country.
Economic System:	Regional units. Production for use. Usury discouraged.	Laissez-faire Capitalism. Scramble for markets.	Planned socialism.
Political System:	Feudal hierarchy.	National democracy. Power in hands of capitalists.	International Democracy. Government by an Order.

338

Freud belongs to the third of these phases, which in the sphere of psychology may be said to have begun with Nietzsche (though the whole of Freud's teaching may be found in *The Marriage of Heaven and Hell*). Such psychology is historically derived from the Romantic reaction, in particular from Rousseau, and this connection has obscured in the minds of the general public, and others, its essential nature. To the man in the street, 'Freudian' literature would embody the following beliefs:

(1) Sexual pleasure is the only real satisfaction. All other activities are an inadequate and remote substitute.
(2) All reasoning is rationalisation.
(3) All men are equal before instincts. It is my parents' fault in the way they brought me up if I am not a Napoleon or a Shakespeare.
(4) The good life is to do as you like.
(5) The cure for all ills is (*a*) indiscriminate sexual intercourse; (*b*) autobiography.

THE IMPLICATIONS OF FREUD

I do not intend to take writers one by one and examine the influence of Freud upon them. I wish merely to show what the essence of Freud's teaching is, that the reader may judge for himself. I shall enumerate the chief points as briefly as possible:

(1) The driving force in all forms of life is instinctive; a libido which of itself is undifferentiated and unmoral, the 'seed of every virtue and of every act which deserves punishment'.
(2) Its first forms of creative activity are in the ordinary sense of the word physical. It binds cells together and separates them. The first bond observable between individuals is a sexual bond.
(3) With the growth in importance of the central nervous system with central rather than peripheral control, the number of modes of satisfaction to which the libido can adapt itself become universally increased.
(4) Man differs from the rest of the organic world in that his development is unfinished.
(5) The introduction of self-consciousness was a complete break in development, and all that we recognise as evil or sin is its consequence. Freud differs both from Rousseau who denied the Fall, attributing evil to purely local conditions ('Rousseau thought all men good by nature. He found them evil and made no friend'), and also from the theological doctrine which makes the Fall the result of a deliberate choice, man being therefore morally responsible.
(6) The result of this Fall was a divided consciousness in place of the single animal consciousness, consisting of at least three parts: a conscious mind governed by ideas and ideals; the impersonal

unconscious from which all its power of the living creature is derived but to which it was largely denied access; and a personal unconscious, all that morality or society demanded should be forgotten and unexpressed.[4]

(7) The nineteenth century doctrine of evolutionary progress, of man working out the beast and letting the ape and tiger die, is largely false. Man's phylogenetic ancestors were meek and sociable, and cruelty, violence, war, all the so-called primitive instincts, do not appear until civilisation has reached a high level. A golden age, comparatively speaking (and anthropological research tends to confirm this), is an historical fact.

(8) What we call evil was once good, but has been outgrown, and refused development by the conscious mind with its moral ideas. This is the point in Freud which D. H. Lawrence seized and to which he devoted his life:

> Man is immoral because he has got a mind
> And can't get used to the fact.

The danger of Lawrence's writing is the ease with which his teaching about the unconscious, by which he means the impersonal unconscious, may be read as meaning, 'let your personal unconscious have its fling', i.e., the *acte gratuit* of André Gide. In personal relations this itself may have a liberating effect for the individual. 'If the fool would persist in his folly he would become wise.' But folly is folly all the same and a piece of advice like 'Anger is just. Justice is never just', which in private life is a plea for emotional honesty, is rotten political advice, where it means 'beat up those who disagree with you'. Also Lawrence's concentration on the fact that if you want to know what a man is, you must look at his sexual life, is apt to lead many to believe that pursuit of a sexual goal is the only necessary activity.

(9) Not only what we recognise as sin or crime, but all illness, is purposive. It is an attempt at cure.

(10) All change, either progressive or regressive, is caused by frustration or tension. Had sexual satisfaction been completely adequate human development could never have occurred. Illness and intellectual activity are both reactions to the same thing, but not of equal value.

(11) The nature of our moral ideas depends on the nature of our relations with our parents.

(12) At the root of all disease and sin is a sense of guilt.

(13) Cure consists in taking away the guilt feeling, in the forgiveness of sins, by confession, the re-living of the experience, and by absolution, understanding its significance.

(14) The task of psychology, or art for that matter, is not to tell people how to behave, but by drawing their attention to what the impersonal unconscious is trying to tell them, and by increasing

---

[4] The difference between the two unconscious minds is expressed symbolically in dreams, e.g., motor-cars and manufactured things express the personal unconscious, horses, etc., the impersonal.

their knowledge of good and evil, to render them better able to choose, to become increasingly morally responsible for their destiny.

(15) For this reason psychology is opposed to all generalisations; force people to hold a generalisation and there will come a time when a situation will arise to which it does not apply. Either they will force the generalisation, the situation, the repression, when it will haunt them, or they will embrace its opposite. The value of advice depends entirely upon the context. You cannot tell people what to do, you can only tell them parables; and that is what art really is, particular stories of particular people and experiences, from which each according to his immediate and peculiar needs may draw his own conclusions.

(16) Both Marx and Freud start from the failures of civilisation, one from the poor, one from the ill. Both see human behaviour determined, not consciously, but by instinctive needs, hunger and love. Both desire a world where rational choice and self-determination are possible. The difference between them is the inevitable difference between the man who studies crowds in the street, and the man who sees the patient, or at most the family, in the consulting-room. Marx sees the direction of the relations between outer and inner world from without inwards, Freud vice versa. Both are therefore suspicious of each other. The socialist accuses the psychologist of caving in to the status quo, trying to adapt the neurotic to the system, thus depriving him of a potential revolutionary: the psychologist retorts that the socialist is trying to lift himself by his own boot tags, that he fails to understand himself, or the fact that lust for money is only one form of the lust for power; and so that after he has won his power by revolution he will recreate the same conditions. Both are right. As long as civilisation remains as it is, the number of patients the psychologist can cure are very few, and as soon as socialism attains power, it must learn to direct its own interior energy and will need the psychologist.

CONCLUSION

Freud has had certain obvious technical influences on literature, particularly in its treatment of space and time, and the use of words in associational rather than logical sequence. He has directed the attention of the writer to material such as dreams and nervous tics hitherto disregarded; to relations as hitherto unconsidered as the relations between people playing tennis; he has revised hero-worship.

He has been misappropriated by irrationalists eager to escape their conscience. But with these we have not, in this essay, been concerned. We have tried to show what light Freud has thrown on the genesis of the artist and his place and function in society, and what demands he would make upon the serious writer. There must always be two kinds of art, escape-art, for man needs escape as he needs food and deep sleep, and parable-art, that art which shall teach man to unlearn hatred

341

and learn love, which can enable Freud to say with greater conviction:

> We may insist as often as we please that the human intellect is
> powerless when compared with the impulses of man, and we may be
> right in what we say. All the same there is something peculiar about
> this weakness. The voice of the intellect is soft and low, but it is
> persistent and continues until it has secured a hearing. After what
> may be countless repetitions, it does get a hearing. This is one of the
> few facts which may help to make us rather more hopeful about the
> future of mankind.

The Arts To-day, ed. by Geoffrey Grigson, 1935

XIV · The Good Life

Man is an organism with certain desires existing in an environment
which fails to satisfy them fully. His theories about the universe are
attempts, whether religious, scientific, philosophical, or political, to
explain or overcome this tension. If we regard the environment as
static, then the problem is one of modifying our desires; if we take the
organism as static, one of modifying the environment. Religion and
psychology begin with the first; science and politics with the second.

If we choose the first, we have to answer three questions:

(1) What are our desires? Why do we do what we do do?
(2) If our desires are mutually incompatible, which are we to choose?
i.e. what ought we to desire and do, and what ought we not to
desire and do?
(3) How are we to desire what we ought to desire?

If we choose the second, the questions are:

(1) In what respects does our environment fail to satisfy us?
(2) How can we change it?

Further, whichever side we approach the problem from, there are
three possible kinds of resolution:

(1) Those which assert that what is, must be, and that progress of any
kind is a vain delusion. This defeatist view appears in Stoicism and
in Fascist ideology, and is in general associated with a ruling class
which is losing ground. Oppressed classes, without hope, desire
vengeance, and may easily adopt a blind eschatology.
(2) The contradiction between what is, and what ought to be, is an
illusion arising from the finite nature of human knowledge. In
reality there is no Good and Bad.
(3) What is, is a necessary stage in the realisation of what ought to be.
This realisation may be:
(*a*) Sudden and catastrophic.
(*b*) A slow evolution.
(*x*) Voluntary—depending on the determination of the majority
of individuals, i.e. it is possible for the consummation to be
rejected.

(*y*) Determined—though the individual can accept or reject it; if he rejects it he joins the losing side.

Christianity is undecided about (*a*) and (*b*), but holds (*y*) not (*x*).
Social Democracy holds (*b*), and is undecided about (*x*) and (*y*).
Psychology, on the whole, holds (*b*) and (*x*).
Communism holds (*a*) and (*y*).

I · THE POLITICS OF THE GOSPELS

(1) *God or Cæsar?* To extract a political theory from the teaching of Jesus requires the ingenuity of a Seventh-Day Adventist. The suggestion that the cleansing of the Temple is a watered-down version of a revolutionary act—that the disciples were to form the corps of a militant International, that Jesus was really a Communist, can only be maintained by entirely unjustifiable manipulation of the evidence, which on the contrary, as in the account of the Temptation, Cæsar's coin, or the Trial, states that He decisively rejected the political solution. The whole of His direct teaching is concerned with the relation of the individual to God and to his neighbour, irrespective of the political system under which he may happen to live—though, as in the parables of the Pharisee and the publican, and the Good Samaritan, or the story of the healing of the centurion's daughter, He demonstrates the evil and absurdity of class and racial prejudice; but the emphasis is laid, not on the necessity for consciously setting out to abolish these, but on behaving as if class and race did not exist, on the supposition that if we so live, they will automatically disappear.

In this sense the teaching of Jesus is fundamentally non-political in that it regards all institutions as a product of the heart, the form of which can be changed, and only changed by a change in the latter. The parable of the house swept and garnished emphasises this.

(2) *Economic inequality.* The cause of inequality is Greed. The cure is the abandonment of money-getting as a motive.

(3) *Eschatology.* It is possible for the historian to say that, even supposing Jesus to have believed the ideal society to be a Communist one, the circumstances and date of His birth would have made revolutionary advice to His disciples both foolish and immoral. A militant Communist movement at such a period of technological advance would have been destroyed as quickly and brutally as the Anabaptists were later, but the eschatological teaching of Jesus makes such reflections irrelevant; e.g. Mark ix, 1, viii. 26, xiv. 62, despite the efforts of Jerome, Origen, and others to explain them away, making a distinction, for example, between 'tasting' and 'seeing' death, cannot mean anything except that Jesus Himself believed: (i) That the Parousia was imminent, an event to take place within the disciples' lifetime. (ii) That even before the final consummation the Kingdom of God is present on earth in the remnant of which He Himself is the head, the *saving* remnant of Deutero-Isaiah, that is, rather than the saved remnant of earlier prophecies. (iii) That it is not a compensation for the sufferings of the remnant, but the result of them. (iv) That it

343

will come suddenly and not by a slow evolution. (Parable of the robbed householder in Luke xii.) (v) It will be a judgment at which the principal criterion will be the attitude taken up by men to Jesus Himself, or, in a general sense, each individual is judged on his merits as determined by the disposition of his will towards the Kingdom of God, as manifest in his day and generation. (vi) It will be a moral, not a political, victory. The world powers are not to be overthrown by earthly or supernatural weapons. (vii) It marks the division between the past age and the age to come. It ushers in a universe purged of evil.

To such beliefs politics can have no meaning. All through history men have attempted to prove that Christianity stood for Feudalism, Absolute Monarchy, Democracy, and what not, and the political activities of the Church remain obscure until we see them as those of an organised and therefore political society professing an a-political faith.

Christianity, then, like most religions, is one which accepts the environment as given and concerns itself with controlling man's behaviour towards it.

What our desires are. Since the cause and sustainer of the universe is God, who is good, our real desire is to be at one with Him. When human the relationship between ourselves and Him is one of father to son. Ultimately that is the purpose of our actions.

What we ought to desire. In practice we desire all sorts of other things. Some of these may be explained as being modes of desiring God—immature stages in development, good in so far as they lead us to God. Others are evil—evil being anything that is self-centred. To them must be attributed the overt symptoms of suffering that we experience. Their existence in us is to be explained by the Fall—an inherited defect in our nature, which, since God is good, must be attributed to a volitional act of rebellion at some period of human development. Further, there is in the universe an evil principle— Satan—hostile to good—but finally inevitably to be vanquished.

II · THE MEANS OF REALISATION

The teaching of Jesus is unique in that it is absolutely non-moralistic. It contains little dogmatic teaching about the nature of evil, but, as regards the methods of overcoming it, He is very definite. His repeated attacks on the scribes and Pharisees, not as individuals, but as a class (except your righteousness exceed the righteousness of the scribes and Pharisees, ye shall in no wise enter the Kingdom of Heaven), His verdict on John the Baptist (nevertheless I say unto you, the least in the Kingdom of God is greater than he), and the sayings about resisting evil, and those who take the sword, condemn as useless—and, more than that, as provoking those very evils it is designed to cure—the whole intellectual system of moral imperatives which had governed human life up to this time and has continued to govern it. The two commandments of loving God and thy neighbour imply that the good life is a product, and only a product, of an attitude of complete love and faith towards both. On repeated occasions He indicated that the term neighbour admits of no distinction or qualification whatever. Every individual is of equal value.

'If a man love not his brothers whom he hath seen, how shall he love God whom he hath not seen?'

'Not everyone that saith unto Me, "Lord, Lord", shall enter into the Kingdom of Heaven; but he that doeth the will of My Father which is in Heaven.'

'Inasmuch as ye did it unto the least of these My brethren, ye did it unto Me.'

'Every good tree bringeth forth good fruit, but a corrupt tree bringeth forth a corrupt fruit.'

Christianity is not a quietist religion—it does not in fact really take the environment as given and static, but states that a change of heart can, and must, bring about a change in the environment. The test of the former, indeed, is the latter. Behaviour—and behaviour is always material action—is the only criterion. Whatever creed or social code men profess, if the results are evil, either the creed or code, or men's interpretation of it, is condemned. Faith and works—which last cannot possibly be construed to mean 'works' in the district-visitor sense—are not independent. A faith stands or falls by its results.

'Except ye be born again, ye cannot enter into the Kingdom of Heaven.'

'Be ye perfect—even as your Father in Heaven is perfect.'

Christianity is a twice-born catastrophic religion. Jesus teaches that a real conversion is required, not a slow amelioration. Further, that the good life is possible here and now. The call to enter the Kingdom is an immediate one, not a reference to something which may take place after death. A theology which stresses an absolute gulf between God and man, and the *inevitable* corruption of the world, is not really consonant with his teaching.

Psychology

Psychology is principally an investigation into the nature of evil. Its essential problem is to discern what it is that prevents people having the good will. It holds:

(1) The driving force in living things is a *libido* which is unconscious and creative—Dante's 'Amor Naturalis' which is always without error. Beyond that psychology does not go—that is to say, it is a naturalistic theory which refuses to raise the question of the Unmoved Mover, which it would say is not a real question at all. 'No intelligent question can be framed concerning causality unless there exist two co-isolates of a larger neutral isolate. The question, 'What is the cause of the changing universe? accepts the existence of a co-isolate of the universe' (Professor Levy). When we ask the question, 'Who made the world?' we are really asking, 'Why isn't it made as we should like it?'

It does not conceive of this *libido* apart from matter or having a personality other than that it acquires in individual consciousness. The psychologist's unconscious could only be equated with a God

345

of Blake's kind 'which only acts and is in existing beings and men'.

(2) The development of self-consciousness in man marked a break with the rest of the organic world. Henceforward the conscious image or idea could interfere and govern[1] the unconscious impulse which had hitherto governed it. What we call evil is a consequence of this. Man developed a personal unconscious. As D. H. Lawrence wrote, in *Psychoanalysis and the Unconscious*, Adam and Eve fell, not because they had sex or even because they committed the sexual act, but because they became aware of their sex and of the possibility of the act. When sex became to them a mental object—that is, when they discovered that they could deliberately enter upon and enjoy and even provoke sexual activity in themselves—then they were cursed and cast out of Eden. Then man became self-responsible; he entered on his own career. When the analyst discovers the incest motive in the unconscious, surely he is only discovering a term of humanity's repressed *idea* of sex. It is not even suppressed sex-consciousness, but *repressed*—that is, it is nothing pristine and anterior to mentality. It is in itself the mind's ulterior motive—that is, the incest motive is propagated in the pristine unconscious by the mind itself, and in its origin is not a pristine impulse but a logical extension of the existent idea of sex and love. Or more succinctly: 'Man is immoral because he has got a mind and can't get used to the fact.' Such a theory differs sharply from the nineteenth-century evolutionary doctrine of man moving

> upward, working out the beast,
> And let the ape and tiger die.

On the contrary it suggests that most of what we call evil is not primitive at all. The 'cave man'—and recent anthropology confirms this—is a product of a relatively high civilisation. The Garden of Eden has more historical justification than is usually believed.

Again, it is opposed to Rousseau in that it regards evil as being due to more than immediate environmental conditions, and differs from the theological doctrine, at least in its Augustinian form, in that it does not make the Fall the result of a conscious moral choice, but regards it as inevitable. It denies original guilt.

(3) What we call evil is something that was once good but has been outgrown. Ignorance begets the moralistic censor as the only means of control. Impulses which are denied expression remain undeveloped in the personal unconscious. From this it follows that the impulse behind all acts which we term evil is good. Psychology will have nothing to do with dualistic theories of Satan or the higher and lower self.

(4) What can be loved can be cured. The two chief barriers are ignorance and fear. Ignorance must be overcome by confession— i.e. drawing attention to unnoticed parts of the field of experience; fear by the exercise of *caritas* or *eros paidogogos*.

Psychology, like Christianity, is pacifist, with a pacifism that

---

[1] See *The Science of Character*, by Klages.

enjoins abstention not only from physical violence, but also from all kinds of dogmatic generalisation and propaganda—from spiritual coercion. The only method of teaching it recognises is parabolic. You cannot convince anyone of anything until they have reached the stage in development when they can relate it to their personal experience—i.e. until they can convince themselves. You must never tell people what to do—only tell them particular stories of particular people with whom they may voluntarily identify themselves, and from which they voluntarily draw conclusions. A dogmatic intellectual expression of a truth can be accepted consciously by those who have not related it to their experience, but this always results either in their holding it in a simplified view, which, when it is met by facts they had not envisaged, is rejected (the parable of the man who built on sand), or its meaning is twisted to suit the personal unconscious (Satan in the Temptation). People are not cured by reading psychological textbooks. The mistake of liberalism was imagining that free discussion was all that was needed to let truth triumph, whereas, unless people have substantially the same experience, logical controversy is nothing more than systemised misunderstanding.[2] The task of revealing the hidden field of experience, of understanding and curing by love, is a very slow, but ultimately the only satisfactory, one. 'The chief sin', wrote Kafka, in one of his aphorisms, 'is impatience. Through impatience man lost Eden, and it is impatience that prevents him from regaining it.' People take to violence because they haven't the strength and nerve to be absorbent.

(5) Psychology is fundamentally a rationalist movement. It does not say, as some, like Lawrence, have been inclined to say, 'Trust your instincts blindly'. Just because it believes that the exercise of the reason is the only way through, its first task is to show how little the reason is able to effect directly. Nor does it deny the possibility of free will, except in a sense which is also true of Christian theology. Just as the theologian says that every man is fallen and in bondage to Satan, so the psychologist says that everyone is neurotic, at the mercy therefore of his repressed impulses, and unable to escape from his image. At the same time his aim is to release his patient through increased self-knowledge, so that he may really exercise his reason and make a genuine choice. The ideally 'cured' patient would be one in whom the unconscious and the conscious were at one, and who would obey his impulses—which is only deterministic in the sense of 'in his will is our peace'. No more than Communism rejects Capitalism does psychology reject selfconsciousness and reason. Both theories believe in the law of the negation of the negation, and that attempts to put the clock back, either in economic or psychical life, are reactionary and disastrous.

(6) Lastly, psychology does not wish, as both it and Communism have been accused of wishing, to make everyone the same. It has no conception of normality. Like both Communism and Christianity, it believes in the equal value of every individual—i.e. potential

[2] See *Mencius on the Mind*, by I. A. Richards.

value. It does not claim to turn all the geese into swans. It aims at making each discover for himself his unique treasure. What you lose on the swings you gain on the roundabouts, and, further, you can *only* gain on the roundabouts if you lose on the swings.

The Church

As long as Christianity remained the religion of small 'converted' groups, expecting an imminent second coming, in an empire to which it was conscientiously bound to refuse allegiance, it could preserve its enthusiastic, non-economic, anarchic character. But as it grew in numbers and importance, as it became the recognised State religion, as whole countries became converted *en bloc*—sometimes, as in Norway, extremely forcibly—this became impossible. Augustine's *communio sanctorum*, whose minds and lives were directed towards God instead of self, could no longer be identified with the baptised, or even with the Church. Dante was not unorthodox in placing a pope in Hell. It became organised, wealthy, and powerful, and no society which is these, however unworldly its final ends, can be anything but worldly in its immediate ends (which, as the hope of an immediate Parousia faded, became more important); it will favour those forces and persons who favour its organisation, wealth, and power, and oppose those which oppose it, without considering too closely their individual moral value. However much it seeks to define in theory what belongs to God and what to Cæsar, in practice it is obliged not only to make generous terms with Cæsar,[3] but itself to make Cæsar's claims. Offering a socially honourable career, it offers worldly inducement. And, as the standard religion, it ceases to demand conversion as a condition of membership. Men are Christian, not necessarily because of a revelation, but because their parents were. As Professor Powicke says,

What we call abuses or superstition in the medieval Church were part of the price paid for, not obstacles to, its universality. They were due to the attempt of pagans to appropriate a mystery. If the people paid, so did the Church. We distort the facts if we try to separate clergy and laity too sharply, for paganism was common to both. . . . By paganism I mean a state of acquiescence, or merely professional activity, unaccompanied by sustained religious experience and inward discipline. It is not a state of vacancy and scepticism. It is confined to no class of persons, and is not hostile to, though it is easily wearied by, religious observance. It accepts what is offered without any sense of responsibility, has no sense of sin, and easily recovers from twinges of conscience. At the same time it is full of curiosity and is easily moved by what is now called the group-mind. It is sensitive to the activities of the crowd, is often emotional, and can be raised to those moods of passion, superstition, and love of persecution into which religion, on its side, can degenerate. A medieval, like a modern, man remained a Christian because he was born a Christian and most medieval Christians were probably men of this kind. . . . In the eleventh century Cardinal Peter Damiani

[3] E.g. the modification of the strict theological condemnation of usury.

348

pointed out in his lurid way that it was of no use to try to keep the clergy apart from the laity unless strict evangelical poverty were insisted upon for all clergy alike. But Damiani and all the preachers of Apostolic poverty who came after him were entangled on the horns of a dilemma. If it is the function of the Church to drive out sin, it must separate itself from sin; if the Church separates itself from sin it becomes a clique. (*Legacy of the Middle Ages*, ed. Crump & Jacob.)

The task of the Church became to act for the mass of more or less pagan and ignorant people as a spiritual pacifier; to protect them from their terrors, and to provide the opportunities for those who wished to live a genuinely Christian life, to do so.

Hence the problem of dogma and the liberty of the private conscience. Divergent theoretical views, whether religious or political, result in divergent actions. What at first seems to be a merely academic difference of opinion may finally land the disputants on opposite sides of the barricade. 'The records of the Holy Inquisition are full of histories which we dare not give to the world, because they are beyond the belief of honest men and innocent women; yet they all began with saintly simpletons. Mark what I say: the woman who quarrels with her clothes, and puts on the dress of a man, is like the man who throws off his fur gown and dresses like John the Baptist: they are followed, as surely as the night follows the day, by bands of wild women and men, who refuse to wear any clothes at all.' (*St. Joan.*)

So the Catholic. The Protestant can retort, and with equal truth, that orthodoxy does not necessarily result in goodness, that many of the orthodox are more wicked than those whom they persecute. In fact, such an orthodoxy is extremely rare; the intellectual acceptance of an idea, without its experience, is no guarantee of its effectiveness. There is little doubt, for example, that, whatever the correct theological attitude, a great many people regard Heaven as a good time, and a reward for not having a good time in this world (i.e. you mustn't enjoy yourself in this world; i.e. the working classes should congratulate themselves); and infer from the doctrine of the Virgin Birth that sexual intercourse is wicked.

III · THE POLITICAL MIND

No politician can really be a liberal in practice, for no society can be liberal unless membership is voluntary; we become members of a State by birth, and we do not choose to be born. Similarly the governor cannot choose the governed; he must accept them all—the just and the unjust, the rich and the poor, the selfless and the self-seeking—and the bias of his own mind, for he himself is within the State.

Many political theories are vitiated, either:

(1) By confusing what the State is with what it ought to be. Few people, for example, consciously desire Dante's *vita felice*, the actualising of the potential intellect, or, with Aristotle, to live virtuously. The majority want security, to be free from material

349

and psychological anxiety, to be liked, and to feel of some importance.

(2) By assuming that there is in fact a community of will. The social contract is a grotesque simplification. In animal herds, or Dr. Rivers' boat crew, the unconscious formation of a group pattern, a united will, may be an adequate description of what happens, but in any more conscious and specialised community the social order is accepted;

(a) Because it is customary;

(b) Because one is fortunately placed;

(c) Because, though unfortunately placed, one lacks the knowledge and power to change it.

There is no such thing as a community of will, nor has the will of the majority any effectiveness apart from the material power it is able to wield. A successful change depends on the support of the armed forces.

(3) By using false analogies, e.g. the biological theory of the State (the story of the belly and the members), a theory which could only be invented by a cell in the central nervous system. Every unit in the State is a conscious one and capable of different functions. Since the governor has always immediate ends to consider, and since the unity of will is a fiction, he cannot afford to wait until this unity is voluntarily reached—i.e. he must coerce either physically, or by the propagandist organisation of public opinion. He may believe, and most of the experimental evidence in the treatment of individuals, either in education, medicine,[4] or the training of animals, will confirm this belief, that violence is inefficient; but he will point to history to refute the view that violence has never accomplished anything, and he knows that he is compelled to use it, to bring about that organisation of society which can make a real unity of will possible.

Ruling a mass, and knowing that you cannot convert a mass as a mass, because they are individually at different stages and in different positions, he must accept the actual rather than the potential character of the governed, and attempt to modify them by modifying those things which are alone in his power to modify—material conditions and social structure. His view of morality must be one of social utility. For him, that is immoral, and that only, which causes a conflict of will—e.g. theft or ownership relations are rightly a matter of legal regulation, but sexual behaviour, which is by mutual consent, is not. The authoritative exercise of what we usually call moral judgment is only justifiable in a society where membership is entirely voluntary.

IV · PSYCHOLOGY AND RELIGION

Psychology does not deny the fact of religious experience, the usefulness of religious theory, in the past, to assist men to live well. In

[4] See a very interesting essay on constipation, in Dr. Groddeck's *Exploring the Unconscious*, on the evils of forcible purgative treatment.

offering an explanation of the idea of God as a projection of parental images, or as what is left over of the sense of group identity after the individual has taken his lion's share, or of the mystical experience as an eruption from the subconscious, and in condemning the religious explanation as one which the world has outgrown, it asks to be tested by results. It believes that it has a more scientific theory—i.e. one which will work better—and claims that, given a free hand, and time, more people will lead better lives than they would with the help of religion. The Christian will retort that the findings of psychology do not necessarily invalidate a belief in God—that, for example, there is no reason why the parental relation should not be a symbol of the divine relation, instead of vice versa, and can point to a weak spot in psychology, the problem of transference. In order to free the patient from himself, the psychologist must make his claims in the name of something greater. What is it to be?

Every confession, within whatever framework it may be made, passes through two phases of a curative effect. First: that one opens oneself to another person, breaks through those walls of loneliness, wherein all guilt, whether in the sense of sacrilege or of sin, whether it was due to rebellion, oversight, error, weakness, the lust of destruction or whatever other incitement, at first imprisons every upright man. Confession, simply as openly answering for oneself and one's conduct, puts an end to the danger of self-deception, by taking this first step towards a fellow-man, and sets foot on the slender bridge of trust in humanity, by choosing another as humanity's representative. This step of voluntary surrender, this renunciation of cowardly cunning, and of lying on behalf of one's imposing public façade, as does the man of the world, is like a deep expiration in the open air. Secondly: into the lungs thus freed, there follows with the second step a deep inspiration: the father-confessor gives what he has to give. If the answer of the private person with difficulty conceals his lower thoughts of tricks and power-policy even to active intrigue, so that a sensitive person is stricken with horror like the bird before the snake—then surely we must introduce poison-gas into the parable. If the private person answers with the fascination of his own ripe and broad humanity, so that the lonely one, suddenly freed, feels—whether he represses it or shows it: 'Thou, my redeemer!'—then we must speak of intoxicating gas. But when one who knows answers so that he, with all his private humanity, is as a speaking-tube for something which is not his, but in whose service he is and in whose name he acts—only then can we say that he pours forth the free strong breath of life, which so fills the lungs of the other that at one stroke the poison-air is overcome. (Prinzhorn—*Psychotherapy*.)

V · COMMUNISM AND PSYCHOLOGY

Psychology and Communism have certain points in common:

(1) They are both concerned with unmasking hidden conflicts.

351

(2) Both regard these conflicts as inevitable stages which must be made to negate themselves.

(3) Both regard thought and knowledge not as something spontaneous and self-sufficient, but as purposive and determined by the conflict between instinctive needs and a limited environment. Communism stresses hunger and the larger social mass affected by it; psychology, love and the small family unit. (Biologically nutrition is anterior to reproduction, so that the Communist approach would seem from this angle the more basic one.) E.g. the psychologist explains the clinging child by the doting mother. Communism explains the doting mother by the social conditions which drive her to be doting.

A discovery, like that of Malinowski, that the typical Œdipus dream of murdering the father and committing incest with the mother, occurs only in patriarchal communities, while in matriarchal communities it is one of murdering the mother's brother and committing incest with the sister, shows the importance of social structure in influencing character formation.

(4) Both desire and believe in the possibility of freedom of action and choice, which can only be obtained by unmasking and making conscious the hidden conflict.

The hostility of Communism to psychology is that it accuses the latter of failing to draw correct conclusions from its data. Finding the neurotic a product of society, it attempts to adjust him to that society, i.e. it ignores the fact that the neurotic has a real grievance. It should say to him, 'Your phantasies are just, but powerless, and a distorted version of something which, if you choose to act, you can alter.' The failure to say this has reduced psychology to a quack religion for the idle rich.

VI · COMMUNISM AND RELIGION

The hostility of Communism to religion has two sides:

(1) The religious approach, it says, is the method of those who see no hope of understanding and altering the environment. As long as in one human lifetime no material progress is visible, man is bound to rely upon individual moral progress. The more power he obtains over material objects, the more he finds he is able to make changes which seemed previously to depend solely on moral attitudes— e.g. the influence of the ductless glands on character.

(2) When a religious body becomes an organised Church it becomes a political movement, and the historical evidence can point to no occasion on which the Church has been able to avert either war or economic changes, however contrary to their theories. On the contrary, it has always made the maintenance of its official position its criterion of conduct, accepted the political status quo, shut its eyes to the violence and mad character of its supporters, persistently lent its strength to crush proletarian movements, and whilst preaching the necessity for settlement by agreement,

whenever the violent crisis has occurred, has stood by the forces of reaction. A tree must be judged by its fruits.

The contrary objections of the Church to Communism are:

(1) That, without the Christian transcendental beliefs, the Communist will fail to secure the results, in so far as they are good, which he intends. Further, that there is a wretchedness in man's condition without God, that is independent of material conditions.
(2) The Communist use of violence is indefensible.
(3) He wishes to destroy the individual and make a slave State.
(4) That private property is necessary to develop human personality and responsibility.
(5) That he wishes to destroy the family.

The use of violence (2). Unless the Christian denies the value of any Government whatsoever, he must admit, as Schweitzer did when destroying trypanosomes, the necessity for violence, and judge the means by its end. He cannot deny, if he is honest, the reality of the class conflict, and unless he can offer a better method of surpassing it (supposing that he is not stupid enough to be taken in by the fiction of the corporative State, which is the word and not the thing) than the Communists, he must accept it.

The individual (3). A theory which culminates in the words, 'To each according to his needs, from each according to his powers', cannot be accused of denying the individual in intention. In fact Communism is the only political theory that really holds the Christian position of the absolute equality in value of every individual, and the evil of all State restraint. It is hardly necessary to add that this doctrine of equality does not assert that everyone has the same talents—i.e. that the individual has no uniqueness and is interchangeable with another—nor does it necessarily imply absolute equality of social reward. Communism looks on coercion, the dictatorship of the proletariat, neither as the redemption which it is to the Fascist, nor as an inevitable and perpetual punishment of original sin, but solely as a transitory means to an end.

Property (4) has been the subject of subtle and obscure study, particularly by French Catholic writers. Their arguments would be more convincing if they condemned monastic orders, in which the individual's sense of responsibility is developed by the administration of community property. Further, Communism has never suggested that no one should have private belongings; it only condemns that possession which gives its owner power over the personality of others.

The family (5). Communism has been subjected to the most fantastic attacks, by ignorant and interested persons, on this score. It has no quarrel whatever with the family, as such—only with the narrowing of loyalties to a single one. In depriving the family of economic power, it leaves it free to be what it should be—an emotional bond—instead of what, as psychologists or common-sense observation can testify, it, at present, so often is—a strangling prison, whose walls are not love, but money.

In that the Christian is a member of society he must have an attitude towards political movements, and increasingly so as he discovers that many things which he recognised as evil, but believed were unchangeable, the consequences of sin, to be endured, can be changed. The behaviour and utterances of indiscreet Fascists should be enough to disillusion him of that solution, which would otherwise, by its bogus idealist appeal, and its attempt to return to pre-industrial conditions, be a temptation to a religion founded on a pre-industrial event. Social Democracy claims to achieve the same end as the Communist, by non-violent means and with religious tolerance; it is questionable, however, whether its behaviour in Europe, its pretence that it uses no violence, or its assumption that the possessing classes, however ready to make concessions, will ever voluntarily abdicate, can much longer convince.

At the same time it would be foolish to gloss over the antagonism of Communism to religion, or to suppose that, if Communism were to triumph in England, the Church would not be persecuted. The question for the Christian, however, is not whether Communism is hostile to Christianity, but whether Christianity is less hostile to Communism than to any other political movement—for no political movement is Christian. If it is, then this very persecution is his chance of proving, if he can, that religion is not the opium of the people, not something that has long been outgrown, but a vital truth. Deprived of all economic and social support, with no axe to grind, he can make no illegitimate appeal. The Christian will have to see if what occurred in the first century can occur again in the twentieth. A truth is not tested until, oppressed and illegal, it still shows irresistible signs of growth.

Christianity and the Social Revolution,
ed. by John Lewis et al., 1935

XV

Documentary Film. By Paul Rotha.

Mr. Rotha has written a very interesting book, and an opportune one too. It is particularly encouraging that the author, who is himself one of our best known documentary directors, should criticise so acutely his own movement. 'One of the most serious shortcomings of the documentary film has been its continued evasion of the human being.' The so-called documentary film began in reaction to the commercial cinema, and has suffered, like all reaction movements, from its negative qualities. Disgusted, and rightly, with the standardisation of theme and the star system of personality exploitation, it began by saying: 'The private life is unimportant. We must abandon the story and report facts, i.e., we must show you people at their daily work, show you how modern industry is organised, show you what people do for their living, not what they feel'. But the private life and the emotions are facts like any others, and one cannot understand the public life of action without them. This puritanical attitude of 'reality' and entertainment to what even Mr. Rotha can call '*mere* fiction' resulted in films which had many excellent qualities, but to the ordinary film-goer were finally and fatally dull. It was valuable, however, in two ways. Firstly a film is expensive to make, and it was this attitude of the British documentary directors in the early days to work and industry that brought them the support of public bodies like the E.M.B. and the G.P.O., without which they could have made no films at all, nor learnt from their mistakes. Secondly, the intractability of the subject matter incited the directors to experiments in technical problems, which would not otherwise have been undertaken and which have proved of permanent importance.

The only genuine meaning of the word 'documentary' is true-to-life. Any gesture, any expression, any dialogue or sound effect, any scenery that strikes the audience as true-to-life is documentary, whether obtained in the studio or on location. Because of the irreversibility and continuous unvaried movement of the film, it is not the best medium for factual information. It is impossible to remember the plot of the simplest commercial film, let alone the intricacies of, say, the sugar beet industry. The effect of a film is to create a powerful emotional attitude towards the material presented.

Because of the mass of realistic detail which the camera records, no medium has ever been invented which is so well suited to portray individual character, and so badly suited to the portrayal of types. On the screen you never see *a* man digging in *a* field, but always Mr. Macgregor digging in a ten acre meadow. It goes far beyond the novel in this.

Every good story is what Mr. Flaherty calls 'the theme of the location'. A story is the device by which the public and private life are related to each other for the purposes of presentation, and no film which ignores either completely can be good. The first, second and third thing in cinema, as in any art, is subject. Technique follows from and is governed by subject.

Mr. Rotha is alive to all this, but does not point out quite clearly enough the exact nature of the obstacles. The first and most important of these is the time factor. No reputable novelist would dare write his novel before he has spent years acquiring and digesting his material, and no first-class documentary will be made until the director does not begin shooting before he has the same degree of familiarity with his. Inanimate objects, like machines, or facts of organisation, can be understood in a few weeks, but not human beings, and if documentary films have hitherto concentrated on the former, it is not entirely the fault of the directors, but is also due to the compulsion on them to turn out a film in a ridiculously short period. It is a misfortune that the art which is the slowest to create, should at the same time be the most expensive. The second obstacle is class. It is doubtful whether an artist can ever deal more than superficially (and cinema is not a superficial art) with characters outside his own class, and most British documentary directors are upper middle.

Lastly, there is the question of financial support. A documentary film is a film that tells the truth, and truth rarely has advertisement value. One remains extremely sceptical about the disinterestedness of large-scale industry and government departments, or about the possibility that they will ever willingly pay for an exact picture of the human life within their enormous buildings.

The Listener, 19 February 1936

XVI · Psychology and Criticism

In Defence of Shelley. By Herbert Read.

It is probable that the only method of attacking or defending a poet is to quote him. Other kinds of criticism whether strictly literary, or psychological or social, serve only to sharpen our appreciation or our abhorrence by making us intellectually conscious of what was previously but vaguely felt; it cannot change one into the other.

In his title essay Mr. Read takes his stand upon what he calls ontogenetic criticism.

> Mr. Eliot's objection to Shelley's poetry is irrelevant prejudice . . .; and such, I would suggest, is the kind of poetic approach of all who believe, with Mr. Eliot, that 'literary criticism should be completed by criticism from a definite ethical and theological standpoint'. I do not deny that such criticism may have its interest; but the only kind of criticism which is basic, and therefore complementary not only to literary but also to ethical, theological and every other kind of ideological criticism, is ontogenetic criticism, by which I mean criticism which traces the origins of the work of art in the psychology of the individual and in the economic structure of society.

He dissects lucidly though perhaps not fully enough—in a psychological analysis one expects to hear something about the parents—certain traits in Shelley's character, his liability to hallucinations, his interest in incest, and his lack of objectivity in his modes of self-expression, and demonstrates their emergence in his poetry. This is interesting but does not explain why Mr. Read admires Shelley, and Mr. Eliot does not.

He continues, with the help of Dr. Burrow's *Social Basis of Consciousness*, by showing that Shelley, like every neurotic, had a just grievance, and that his very neurosis was the source of his insight.

> 'It is the distinction of the neurotic personality that he is at least consciously and confessedly *nervous*', so the special value of Shelley is that he was conscious of his direction; he had, in the modern sense, but without expressing himself in modern terminology, analysed his own neurosis. He did not *define* his autosexuality; but he allowed the reaction full scope. That is to say, he allowed his feelings and ideas to develop integrally with his neurotic personality; and the élan of that evolution inevitably led to the formulation of 'a clearer, more conscious social order'.

This is extremely interesting but still I am no clearer why I cannot read Shelley with pleasure.

Is it then a difference of moral opinion? I would disagree with Mr. Read when he implies that ontogenetic criticism makes no moral judgements. Every psychology, certainly Dr. Burrow's, every economic analysis contains therapeutic intentions, i.e. they presuppose an idea of what the individual or society could and should become, and Mr. Read himself comes down heavily in favour of 'sympathy and infinitude'; but still we are no nearer the nature of our difference. I find, and I imagine Mr. Read does too, the Weltanschauung of Prometheus more to my taste than that of Coriolanus, but I would rather read the latter. It is not a question of expressed belief.

No, the crucial difference between us is reached, I think, in Section VII.

> There are always these two types of originality: originality that responds like the Æolian harp to every gust of contemporary feeling, pleasing by its anticipation of what is half-formed in the public consciousness; and *originality that is not influenced by anything outside the poet's own consciousness, but is the direct product of his individual mind and independent feeling.*

What does Mr. Read mean by not influenced by *anything*? Consciousness is filled by outside impressions and could not exist without them. If he means other men's intellectual ideas, it certainly does not apply to Shelley. Rilke in a fine passage which Mr. Read has himself quoted in *Form in Modern Poetry* enumerates the human mass of sensory experiences that should go to the making of a single poem. That is precisely my objection to Shelley. Reading him, I feel that he never looked at or listened to anything, except ideas. There are some poets, Housman for example, whose poetic world contains very few properties, but the few are objectively presented; others again, like Edward Lear, construe them according to laws other than those of socialised life, but the owl and the pussy cat are real.

I cannot believe—and this incidentally is why I cannot sympathise with Mr. Read in his admiration for abstract art (symbolic art is another matter)—that any artist can be good who is not more than a bit of a reporting journalist.

To the journalist the first thing of importance is subject and, just as I would look at a painting of the Crucifixion before a painting of a still life, and cannot admit that 'the pattern may have some more or less remote relation to objects, but such a relation is not necessary', so in literature I expect plenty of news.

Admittedly the journalistic side of the artist can easily and frequently does kill his sensibility; there must always be a tension between them (allied perhaps to the tension Mr. Read describes in the essay on Hopkins, the conflict between 'sensibility and belief') but a lack of interest in objects in the outside world, the complete triumph of the wish to be 'a man without passions—party passions, national passions, religious passions' is equally destructive.

Abstractions which are not the latest flowers of a richly experienced and mature mind are empty and their expression devoid of poetic value. The very nature of Shelley's intellectual interests demanded a far wider range of experiences than most poets require (the more 'autosexual' a poet, the more necessary it is for him to be engaged in material action), and his inability to have or to record them makes, for me, the bulk of his work, with the exception of a few short pieces, empty and unsympathetic.

New Verse, April–May 1936

XVII · Poetry, Poets, and Taste

One hundred per cent he-men, very grown-up doctors, and a certain kind of social reformer have no use for poetry. The first thinks it a cissy occupation, the second an infantile and neurotic method of escape, and the third fiddling while Rome burns. As a poet I am naturally interested in persuading people to buy poetry, so I shall try to answer these objections.

The first gentleman is easy. I shall only ask him if he knows the one about the Lady of Gloucester. His objection is largely the result of bad education. School teachers, and, I'm afraid, a lot of other people who ought to know better, think of Poetry with a P, as something which concerns itself only with the Higher Life, or what some snob with a genius for nauseating titles has called 'Higher-grade living'. This is, of course, quite untrue. Poetry has as varied a subject matter and treatment as human character. It deals with the mysteries of the universe certainly—well even the most hard-headed business man sometimes thinks if only when convalescent after influenza, 'Why am I here?'—but it deals just as much with the joke at lunch or the face of the lady opposite.

'Cover her face; mine eyes dazzle: she died young', is poetry. So is—

> Early in the morning at half-past three
> They were all lit up like a Christmas tree.
> Lil got up and started for bed,
> Took another sniff and then she fell down dead.

And so is—

> And masculine is found to be
> Hadria, the Adriatic sea.

There is solemn poetry and light poetry, comic poetry and serious poetry, pure poetry and obscene poetry, and to say that you only like one kind, is like saying 'I only like Archdeacons' or 'The only people I have any use for are barmaids'. Really to appreciate archdeacons, you must know some barmaids and vice versa. The same applies to poetry.

The doctor and the social reformer are tougher opponents. I lump them together because both their criticisms raise the question of the nature of artistic activity. The doctor's argument is something like this: 'I've had plenty of these artists in my consulting-room and I know what I'm talking about. Their health's generally rotten, they're mentally completely unstable, their private lives are a disgrace and they never pay my bills. Look at Homer, blind as a bat. Look at Villon, a common or garden crook. Look at Proust, asthmatic, a typical case of mother fixation, etc., etc.'

And he's quite right. As a matter of fact, I think we shall find that all intelligent people, even the great doctor himself, are the product of psychological conflict in childhood, and generally share some neurotic traits. I rather suspect that if the world consisted solely of the psychologically perfect, we should still be eating roots in the jungle. But I'll leave that and concentrate on the artist. When we are confronted with an emotional difficulty or danger, there are three things we can do. We can pretend that *we* are not there, i.e. we can become feeble-minded or ill; we can pretend that *it* isn't there, i.e. we can daydream; or we can look at it carefully and try to understand it, understand the mechanism of the trap. Art is a combination of these last two; there is an element of escape in it, and an element of science, which only differs from what we generally call by that name, in that its subject is a different order of data.

The first half of art, then, is perceiving. The artist is the person who stands outside and looks, stands even outside himself and looks at his daydreams.

The second half of art is telling. If you asked any artist why he works, I think he would say, 'To make money and to amuse my friends'.

He is a mixture of spy and gossip, a cross between the slavey, with her eye glued to the keyhole of the hotel bedroom, and the wife of a minor canon; he is the little boy who comes into the drawing-room and says, 'I saw St. Peter in the hall' or 'I saw Aunt Emma in the bath without her wig'.

So the doctor is wrong. If the artists sometimes give us escape, let us be grateful, for we all need a certain amount of escape, just as we need sleep; but he also tells us the truths which we are too busy or too ashamed to see.

And the social reformer is wrong, too. When an artist writes about the slums or disease or Hell, it is quite true that he wants them to be there because they are his material, just as dentists want people to have decaying teeth. You can rarely expect him to be a good politician, but you can use what he gives you, the truths he tells, to strengthen your will, and amuse you in your hours of relaxation. Aunt Emma may buy some hair restorer after all.

There are two more points I should like to touch on, one trivial, the other more important. Firstly, what is poetry as distinct from the other arts, and secondly, how do you distinguish good poetry from bad. I think there is no absolute division between poetry and prose. 'Pure' poetry would, I think, be words used with only emotional significance and without any logical significance, and prose be the reverse. In practice pure poetry and prose do not exist, any more than pure substances do in nature, and if they did would be unreadable, just as pure chemicals do not react. All you can say is that

> Sing a song of sixpence,
> A pocket full of rye,

is near the pure poetry end of the scale, and

is near the pure prose end, and there is every possible shade between them.

As for taste, it ultimately rests with the individual reader. Every reader and every age think naturally enough that they have the key to absolute taste, but history should make us humble. There is only one general rule and that is sincerity, which is easy to say, but impossible to obey perfectly. Admit to yourself that you like quite different kinds of poetry in different moods, and if you find you really prefer Ella Wheeler Wilcox to Shakespeare, for heaven's sake admit it. Some people can never be poets because they don't happen to have any genuine interest in words, in the telling side of the art; i.e. they are not really interested in poetry. Others fail because they are not interested in their subject, in the perceiving side. But the commonest cause of badness in any of the arts is being really interested in one subject while pretending to be interested in another. The secret of good art is the same as the secret of a good life; to find out what you are interested in, however strange, or trivial, or ambitious, or shocking, or uplifting, and deal with that, for that is all you can deal with well.

'To each according to his means; from each according to his powers', in fact. Personally the kind of poetry I should like to write but can't is 'the thoughts of a wise man in the speech of the common people'.

The Highway (Workers' Educational Association),
December 1936

XVIII · Impressions of Valencia

The pigeons fly about the square in brilliant sunshine, warm as a fine English May. In the centre of the square, surrounded all day long by crowds and surmounted by a rifle and fixed bayonet, 15ft. high, is an enormous map of the Civil War, rather prettily illustrated after the manner of railway posters urging one to visit Lovely Lakeland or Sunny Devon. Badajoz is depicted by a firing-party; a hanged man represents Huelva; a doll's train and lorry are heading for Madrid; at Seville Quiepo el Llano is frozen in an eternal broadcast. The General seems to be the Little Willie of the war; in a neighbouring shop window a strip of comic woodcuts shows his rake's progress from a perverse childhood to a miserable and well-merited end.

Altogether it is a great time for the poster artist and there are some very good ones. Cramped in a little grey boat the Burgos Junta, dapper Franco and his bald German adviser, a cardinal and two ferocious Moors are busy hanging Spain; a green Fascist centipede is caught in the fanged trap of Madrid; in photomontage a bombed baby lies couchant upon a field of aeroplanes.

To-day a paragraph in the daily papers announces that since there have been incidents at the entrances to cabarets, these will in future be closed at nine p.m. Long streamers on the public buildings appeal for unity, determination and discipline. Three children, with large brown eyes like some kind of very rich sweet, are playing trains round the fountain. On one of the Ministries a huge black arrow draws attention to the fact that the front at Teruel is only 150 km. away. This is the Spain for which charming young English aviators have assured us that the best would be a military dictatorship backed by a foreign Power.

Since the Government moved here the hotels are crammed to bursting with officials, soldiers and journalists. There are porters at the station and a few horse-cabs, but no taxis, in order to save petrol. Food is plentiful, indeed an hotel lunch is heavier than one could wish. There is a bull-fight in aid of the hospitals; there is a variety show where an emaciated-looking tap-dancer does an extremely sinister dance of the machine-guns. The foreign correspondents come in for their dinner, conspicuous as actresses.

And everywhere there are the people. They are here in corduroy breeches with pistols on their hip, in uniform, in civilian suits and berets. They are here, sleeping in the hotels, eating in the restaurants, in the cafés drinking and having their shoes cleaned. They are here, driving fast cars on business, running the trains and the trams, keeping the streets clean, doing all those things that the gentry cannot believe will be properly done unless they are there to keep an eye on them. This is the bloodthirsty and unshaven Anarchy of the bourgeois cartoon, the end of civilisation from which Hitler has sworn to deliver Europe.

For a revolution is really taking place, not an odd shuffle or two in cabinet appointments. In the last six months these people have been learning what it is to inherit their own country, and once a man has tasted freedom he will not lightly give it up; freedom to choose for himself and to organise his life, freedom not to depend for good fortune on a clever and outrageous piece of overcharging or a windfall of drunken charity. That is why, only eight hours away at the gates of Madrid where this wish to live has no possible alternative expression than the power to kill, General Franco has already lost two professional armies and is in the process of losing a third.

The New Statesman, 30 January 1937

XIX · Jehovah Housman and Satan Housman

A.E.H.: A Memoir. By Laurence Housman.

Heaven and Hell. Reason and Instinct. Conscious Mind and Unconscious. Is their hostility a temporary and curable neurosis, due to our particular pattern of culture, or intrinsic in the nature of these faculties? Can man only think when he is frustrated from acting and feeling? Is the intelligent person always the product of some childhood neurosis? Does Life only offer two alternatives: 'You shall be happy, healthy, attractive, a good mixer, a good lover and parent, but on condition that you are not overcurious about life. On the other hand you shall be attentive and sensitive, conscious of what is happening round you, but in that case you must not expect to be happy, or successful in love, or at home in any company. There are two worlds and you cannot belong to them both. If you belong to the second of these worlds you will be unhappy because you will always be in love with the first, while at the same time you will despise it. The first world on the other hand will not return your love because it is in its nature to love only itself. Socrates will always fall in love with Alcibiades; Alcibiades will only be a little flattered and rather puzzled'?

To those who are interested in this problem, A. E. Housman is one of the classic case histories. Few men have kept Heaven and Hell so rigidly apart. Jehovah Housman devoted himself to the emendation of texts of no æsthetic value and collected thunderbolts of poisoned invective in notebooks to use when opportunity arose against the slightest intellectual lapses; Satan Housman believed that the essence of poetry was lack of intellectual content. Jehovah Housman lived the virginal life of a don; Satan Housman thought a good deal about stolen waters and the bed. Jehovah Housman believed that slavery was necessary to support the civilised life; Satan Housman did not accept injustice so lightly.

> But they've pulled the beggar's hat off for the world to see and stare,
> And they're haling him to justice for the colour of his hair.

But they had one common ground upon which they could meet: the grave. Dead texts; dead soldiers; Death the Reconciler, beyond sex and beyond thought. There, and there only, could the two worlds meet.

Mr. Laurence Housman's memoir of his brother records a great many interesting facts from which the reader must construct his own theory of what happened to Housman to cause this division, of why, for instance, he did not work for Greats, and why he did not allow his family to come to see him in those critical years from 1882 to 1892. But however fascinating such speculations may be, they are of minor importance. What happened to Housman happens in one way or another to most intellectuals, though few exhibit the symptoms in so pure a form.

> The stars have not dealt me the worst they could do:
> My pleasures are plenty, my troubles are two.
> But oh, my two troubles they reave me of rest,
> The brains in my head and the heart in my breast.
>
> Oh, grant me the ease that is granted so free,
> The birthright of multitudes, give it to me,
> That relish their victuals and rest on their bed
> With flint in the bosom and guts in the head.

Yes, the two worlds. Perhaps the Socialist State will marry them; perhaps it won't. Perhaps it will always be true that

> Wer das Tiefste gedacht, liebt das Lebendigste,
> Hohe Jugend versteht, wer in die Welt geblickt
> Und es neigen die Weisen
> Oft am Ende zu Schönem sich.

Perhaps again the only thing which can bring them together is the exercise of what Christians call Charity, a quality for which, it will be remembered, neither Jehovah nor Satan Housman had much use, but of which perhaps they were both not a little frightened.

New Verse, January 1938

XX · Light Verse

I

Behind the work of any creative artist there are three principal wishes: the wish to make something; the wish to perceive something, either in the external world of sense or the internal world of feeling; and the wish to communicate these perceptions to others. Those who have no interest in or talent for making something, i.e. no skill in a particular artistic medium, do not become artists; they dine out, they gossip at street corners, they hold forth in cafés. Those who have no interest in communication do not become artists either; they become mystics or madmen.

There is no biological or mathematical law which would lead us to suppose that the quantity of innate artistic talent varies very greatly from generation to generation. The major genius may be a rare phenomenon, but no art is the creation solely of geniuses, rising in sudden isolation like craters from a level plain; least of all literature, whose medium is language—the medium of ordinary social intercourse.

If, then, we are to understand the changes that do in fact take place, why in the history of poetry there should be periods of great fertility, and others comparatively barren, why both the subject-matter and the manner should vary so widely, why poetry should sometimes be easy to understand, and sometimes very obscure, we must look elsewhere than to the idiosyncrasies of the individual poets themselves.

The wish to make something, always perhaps the greatest conscious preoccupation of the artist himself, is a constant, independent of time. The things that do change are his medium, his attitude to the spoken and written word, the kind of things he is interested in or capable of perceiving, and the kind of audience with whom he wants to communicate. He wants to tell the truth, and he wants to amuse his friends, and what kind of truth he tells and what kind of friends he has depend partly on the state of society as a whole and partly on the kind of life which he, as an artist, leads.

When the things in which the poet is interested, the things which he sees about him, are much the same as those of his audience, and that audience is a fairly general one, he will not be conscious of himself as an unusual person, and his language will be straightforward and close to ordinary speech. When, on the other hand, his interests and perceptions are not readily acceptable to society, or his audience is a highly specialised one, perhaps of fellow poets, he will be acutely aware of himself as the poet, and his method of expression may depart very widely from the normal social language.

In the first case his poetry will be 'light' in the sense in which it is used in this anthology. Three kinds of poetry have been included:

(1) Poetry written for performance, to be spoken or sung before an audience [e.g. Folk-songs, the poems of Tom Moore].

(2) Poetry intended to be read, but having for its subject-matter the everyday social life of its period or the experiences of the poet as an ordinary human being [e.g. the poems of Chaucer, Pope, Byron].

(3) Such nonsense poetry as, through its properties and technique, has a general appeal [Nursery rhymes, the poems of Edward Lear].[1]

Light verse can be serious. It has only come to mean *vers de société*, triolets, smoke-room limericks, because, under the social conditions which produced the Romantic Revival, and which have persisted, more or less, ever since, it has been only in trivial matters that poets have felt in sufficient intimacy with their audience to be able to forget themselves and their singing-robes.

II

But this has not always been so. Till the Elizabethans, all poetry was light in this sense. It might be very dull at times, but it was light.

As long as society was united in its religious faith and its view of the universe, as long as the way in which people lived changed slowly, audience and artists alike tended to have much the same interests and to see much the same things.

It is not until the great social and ideological upheavals of the sixteenth and seventeenth centuries that difficult poetry appears, some of Shakespeare, Donne, Milton, and others. The example of these poets should warn us against condemning poetry because it is difficult. Lightness is a great virtue, but light verse tends to be conventional, to accept the attitudes of the society in which it is written. The more homogeneous a society, the closer the artist is to the everyday life of his time, the easier it is for him to communicate what he perceives, but the harder for him to see honestly and truthfully, unbiased by the conventional responses of his time. The more unstable a society, and the more detached from it the artist, the clearer he can see, but the harder it is for him to convey it to others. In the greatest periods of English Literature, as in the Elizabethan period, the tension was at its strongest. The artist was still sufficiently rooted in the life of his age to feel in common with his audience, and at the same time society was in a sufficient state of flux for the age-long beliefs and attitudes to be no longer compulsive on the artist's vision.

In the seventeenth century poetry, like religion, had its eccentric sports. Milton, with the possible exception of Spenser, is the first eccentric English poet, the first to make a myth out of his personal experience, and to invent a language of his own remote from the spoken word. Poets like Herbert and Crashaw and prose-writers like Sir Thomas Browne are minor examples of the same tendency.

[1] A few pieces, e.g. Blake's *Auguries of Innocence* and Melville's *Billy in the Darbies*, do not really fall into any of these categories, but their technique is derived so directly from the popular style that it seemed proper to include them. When Blake, for instance, deserts the proverbial manner of the *Auguries* for the eccentric manner of the Prophetic Books, he ceases to write 'light verse'.

Marvell and Herrick are 'traditional' in a way that these others are not, even though the former often uses the same kind of tricks.

The Restoration marks a return both to a more settled society and to a more secure position for the artist under aristocratic patronage. His social status rose. When Dryden in his 'Essay on the Dramatic Poetry of the Last Age' ascribes the superiority in correctness of language of the new dramatists to their greater opportunities of contact with genteel society, he is stating something which had great consequences for English poetry. With a settled and valued place in society, not only minor poets, but the greatest, like Dryden and Pope, were able to express themselves in an easy manner, to use the speaking-voice, and to use as their properties the images of their everyday, i.e. social, life.

Their poetry has its limits, because the society of which they were a part was a limited part of the community, the leisured class, but within these limits, certain that the aim of poetry was to please, and certain of whom they had to please, they moved with freedom and intelligence.

This ease continued until the Romantic Revival which coincided with the beginning of the Industrial Revolution. From a predominantly agricultural country, where the towns were small and more important as places for social intercourse than as wealth-producing centres, England became a country of large manufacturing towns, too big for the individual to know anybody else except those employed in the same occupation. The divisions between classes became sharper and more numerous. At the same time there was a great increase in national wealth, and an increase in the reading public. With the increase in wealth appeared a new class who had independent incomes from dividends, and whose lives felt neither the economic pressure of the wage-earner nor the burden of responsibility of the landlord. The patronage system broke down, and the artist had either to write for the general public, whose condition was well described by Wordsworth in his preface to the *Lyrical Ballads*,

> A multitude of causes, unknown to former times, are now acting with a combined force to blunt the discriminating powers of the mind, and, unfitting it for all voluntary exertion, to reduce it to a state of almost savage torpor. The most effective of these causes are the great national events which are daily taking place, and the increasing accumulation of men in cities, where the uniformity of their occupations produces a craving for extraordinary incident, which the rapid communication of intelligence hourly gratifies;

or if he had an artistic conscience he could starve, unless he was lucky enough to have independent means.

As the old social community broke up, artists were driven to the examination of their own feelings and to the company of other artists. They became introspective, obscure, and highbrow.

The case of Wordsworth, the greatest of the Romantic poets, is instructive. While stating that he intended to write in the language really used by men, in particular by Westmorland farmers, whenever he tries to do so he is not completely successful, while in his best work, the *Odes* and *The Prelude*, his diction is poetic, and far removed from the spoken word. The sub-title of *The Prelude*, *The Growth of a Poet's*

Mind, is illuminating. Wordsworth was a person who early in life had an intense experience or series of experiences about inanimate nature, which he spent the rest of his poetical life trying to describe. He was not really interested in farm-labourers or any one else for themselves, but only in so far as they helped to explain this vision, and his own relation to it. When he objects to eighteenth-century diction as 'artificial', what he really means is artificial for his particular purpose. The diction of the Immortality Ode would be as artificial for Pope's purposes as Pope's was for Wordsworth's.

Wordsworth's case is paralleled by the history of most of the Romantic poets, both of his day and of the century following. Isolated in an amorphous society with no real communal ties, bewildered by its complexity, horrified by its ugliness and power, and uncertain of an audience, they turned away from the life of their time to the contemplation of their own emotions and the creation of imaginary worlds, Wordsworth to Nature, Keats and Mallarmé to a world of pure poetry, Shelley to a future Golden Age, Baudelaire and Hölderlin to a past,

> . . . ces époques nues
> Dont Phoebus se plaisait à dorer les statues.[2]

Instead of the poet regarding himself as an entertainer, he becomes the prophet, 'the unacknowledged legislator of the world', or the Dandy who sits in the café, 'proud that he is less base than the passers-by, saying to himself as he contemplates the smoke of his cigar: "What does it matter to me what becomes of my perceptions?"'

This is not, of course, to condemn the Romantic poets, but to explain why they wrote the kind of poetry they did, why their best work is personal, intense, often difficult, and generally rather gloomy.

The release from social pressure was, at first, extremely stimulating. The private world was a relatively unexplored field, and the technical discoveries made were as great as those being made in industry. But the feeling of excitement was followed by a feeling of loss. For if it is true that the closer bound the artist is to his community the harder it is for him to see with a detached vision, it is also true that when he is too isolated, though he may see clearly enough what he does see, that dwindles in quantity and importance. He 'knows more and more about less and less'. It is significant that so many of these poets either died young like Keats, or went mad like Hölderlin, or ceased producing good work like Wordsworth, or gave up writing altogether like Rimbaud—'I must ask forgiveness for having fed myself on lies, and let us go. . . . One must be absolutely modern.' For the private world is fascinating, but it is exhaustible. Without a secure place in society,

---

[2] Mr. Stephen Spender, in his essay on Keats in *From Anne to Victoria*, has analysed the gulf between the world of the poems and the world of the letters. Keats's abandonment of 'Hyperion' with the remark that there were too many Miltonic inversions in it, is a sign that he was becoming aware of this gulf. When the subject-matter of poetry ceases to be the social life of man, it tends to dispense with the social uses of language, grammar, and word-order, a tendency which Mallarmé carried to its logical conclusion.

Browning is an interesting case of a poet who was intensely interested in the world about him and in a less socially specialised period might well have been the 'easiest' poet of his generation, instead of the most 'difficult'.

without an intimate relation between himself and his audience, without, in fact, those conditions which make for Light Verse, the poet finds it difficult to grow beyond a certain point.

III

But Light Verse has never entirely disappeared. At the beginning of the Romantic age stand two writers of Light Verse who were also major poets, Burns and Byron, one a peasant, the other an aristocrat. The former came from a Scottish parish which, whatever its faults of hypocrisy and petty religious tyranny, was a genuine community where the popular tradition in poetry had never been lost. In consequence Burns was able to write directly and easily about all aspects of life, the most serious as well as the most trivial. He is the last poet of whom this can be said. Byron, on the other hand, is the first writer of Light Verse in the modern sense. His success lasts as long as he takes nothing very seriously; the moment he tried to be profound and 'poetic' he fails. However much they tried to reject each other, he was a member of 'Society', and his poetry is the result of his membership. If he cannot be poetic, it is because smart society is not poetic. And the same is true, in a minor way, of Praed, whose serious poems are as trivial as his *vers de société* are profound.

IV

The nineteenth century saw the development of a new kind of light poetry, poetry for children and nonsense poetry. The breakdown of the old village or small-town community left the family as the only real social unit, and the parent–child relationship as the only real social bond. The writing of nonsense poetry which appeals to the Unconscious, and of poetry for children who live in a world before self-consciousness, was an attempt to find a world where the divisions of class, sex, occupation did not operate, and the great Victorian masters of this kind of poetry, Lewis Carroll and Edward Lear, were as successful in their day as Mr. Walt Disney has been in ours. The conditions under which folk-poetry is made ensure that it shall keep its lightness or disappear, but the changing social conditions are reflected in its history by a degeneration both in technique and in treatment. The Border ballad could be tragic; the music-hall song cannot.[3] Directness and ease of expression has been kept, but at the cost of excluding both emotional subtlety and beauty of diction. Only in America, under the conditions of frontier expansion and prospecting and railway development, have the last hundred years been able to produce a folk-poetry which can equal similar productions of pre-industrial Europe, and in America, too, this period is ending.

The problem for the modern poet, as for every one else to-day, is how to find or form a genuine community, in which each has his valued

[3] Kipling, who identified himself with British middle-class imperialism, as Pope identified himself with the 18th-century landed gentry, wrote serious light verse; and it is, perhaps, no accident that the two best light-verse writers of our time, Belloc and Chesterton, are both Catholics.

place and can feel at home. The old pre-industrial community and culture are gone and cannot be brought back. Nor is it desirable that they should be. They were too unjust, too squalid, and too custom-bound. Virtues which were once nursed unconsciously by the forces of nature must now be recovered and fostered by a deliberate effort of the will and the intelligence. In the future, societies will not grow of themselves. They will either be made consciously or decay. A democracy in which each citizen is as fully conscious and capable of making a rational choice, as in the past has been possible only for the wealthier few, is the only kind of society which in the future is likely to survive for long.

In such a society, and in such alone, will it be possible for the poet, without sacrificing any of his subtleties of sensibility or his integrity, to write poetry which is simple, clear, and gay.

For poetry which is at the same time light and adult can only be written in a society which is both integrated and free.

The Oxford Book of Light Verse, ed. by Auden, 1938

XXI · The Sportsmen: A Parable

Long ago, on a certain tract of country, some men were out shooting. The country was pretty open, so that who secured the biggest bag depended mainly upon who was the best shot. Perhaps the standard of marksmanship was not very high:—the sportsmen were only the best shots from the village, who had come out for a bit of shooting in the slack season between harvest and ploughing. They were out to shoot duck, for they knew that no one in their senses would want to eat anything else; and their sporting instincts were not very English: it is hard enough to hit a duck at all, they would have argued, and if one is lucky enough to spot one sitting, so much the better.

A few hundred years passed, and men were still shooting over the same country. This had now become much overgrown, which was more favourable for some kinds of birds than the open country and less so for others: some new species had appeared, and some old ones died out. Another result of the growth of vegetation was that now some of the butts were much more advantageously placed than others, so that even a good shot, if he got a bad butt, might be unlucky. The sportsmen had changed too. Though most of them still shot duck to sell in the open market, the best shots had been hired by the village squire who preferred partridge, a taste with which they were inclined to agree; in fact, it was they who had first persuaded him to try one for a change. They still hadn't dared try and sell him a grouse which, in their opinion tasted even better, and which they always took home with them when they were lucky enough to hit one. The standard of marksmanship was high, as it well might be, seeing that most of them did nothing else, and wouldn't have known what to do with a sickle if they saw one.

They were proud of their job, and determined to keep up a high standard of skill and sportsmanship, so that those who took shots at sitting birds were fined and regarded as outsiders.

Another few hundred years passed. The country had now become so densely wooded that from most of the butts it was only possible to see a tiny circle of sky immediately overhead, and the bags so small that both the village and the squire had almost forgotten what birds tasted like, had stopped sending out any more sportsmen, and were living on tinned food sent down in vans from the city. Such sportsmen as there were, were now, most of them, boys from rich homes who had run away because they did not get on with their parents and were attracted by the idea of a wild life in the woods, with an occasional eccentric who, even when he was in the nursery, had a passion for playing with toy firearms. It was now so difficult to hit anything, that those who went on shooting at all became very fine shots indeed. And, as no one wanted any birds any more anyway, the sportsmen had begun to feel that the only excitement in shooting lay in the skill required. It had become a point of honour not to fire at a common bird or an easy target, even if they should see one. Each had his own set of rules: one would only fire at birds a thousand feet up; another neglected all but woodpeckers with white tails; a third always took aim standing on his head. And how they quarrelled over the relative merits of their different methods in the *Sporting Quarterly*.

Now about the time I am describing, a curious thing happened. Rumours began to reach the village of a far country where the inhabitants had cleared the land of timber, so that duck had once more become plentiful and shooting parties were again in fashion. Stirred by the news, some of the villagers formed a party and went out into the woods to fell the trees, despite the threat of the squire to prosecute them if they did. There they met the few remaining sportsmen and began to tell them what they had heard; how, in that far country, he who brought home the biggest bag of duck was fêted by the village and handsomely rewarded. When they heard this, the sportsmen were divided in their opinions. Some said: 'I would rather die than shoot such an ugly bird as a duck.' Others said: 'The squire is my first cousin, and I am expecting a legacy when he dies; I mustn't do anything that would offend him.' And all these retired in dudgeon to their butts. One, an older man and, perhaps, the finest marksman of them all, stood for a long time in silence and then said: 'I think you are right in what you say, and I wish you every success in your efforts to clear the country and encourage the duck to breed as they used to, but I must ask you to forgive me if I do not help you. For many years now I have been spending all my waking hours in the study of eagles. I do not know if there are any others who share my passion; I do not suppose that there will ever be many who feel as I do about these rare and beautiful birds; but for me, it is my vocation and my life. So I must ask you to excuse me.' And having said this, he went his way.

Those who remained behind asked the villagers what they should do, as they rarely saw any duck nowadays. The villagers replied that the first thing necessary was to fell the trees and clear away the undergrowth and they suggested that the sportsmen should lend a hand with this. A few thought this a reasonable suggestion, but the greater part were alarmed and offended, saying: 'Me, turn woodcutter? I am a sportsman.' And indeed, when one looked at them, one was inclined to feel that they were right. Most of them would have been very unskilful woodcutters. So they, too, retired to their butts. There, in the days that followed, they had plenty of time to reflect upon what had been said on all sides, and one or two began to keep an eye open for duck, thinking: 'How surprised and impressed the village would be, if I were to stroll in one evening with a couple of fine duck over my shoulder.' But watch as they might, they seldom saw a sign of one, and, even when they did, they were so accustomed to trick targets that they missed. This was very humiliating to crack shots such as they were. 'Bah!' they said, 'those villagers are a stupid lot: if they want duck, they shall have them'; and, putting their guns aside, they sat down to model duck out of clay and old newspapers, using to guide them some coloured plates which they had torn out of ornithological textbooks in their fathers' libraries.

When the models were finished and dry, they returned with them to the village, and said: 'Look what we have shot.' Some of the younger villagers who had never seen a duck except in a museum were impressed, and praised the sportsmen highly for their skill; but the older and wiser among them fingered the models, and smelt them, and said: 'These are not duck; they are only clay and old newspapers.'

New Verse, Autumn 1938

XXII · Introduction to 'Poems of Freedom'

Great claims have been made for poets as a social force: they have been called the critics of life, the trumpets that sing men to battle, the unacknowledged legislators of the world. On the other hand they have been accused of being introverted neurotics who find in infantile word-play an escape from the serious duties of adult life, the irresponsible fiddlers deserting a Rome in flames. Both opinions are bosh, but the second is the inevitable reaction from the first. Those who go to poetry expecting to find a complete guide to religion, or morals, or political action, will very soon be disillusioned and condemn poets, though what they are really condemning is their own attitude towards poetry.

Because the medium of poetry is language, the medium in which all social activities are conducted, demands are made on it which it would never occur to people to make on the other arts like painting or music (although, in fact, music is probably a far more effective stimulus to action).

Poets are rarely and only incidentally priests or philosophers or party agitators. They are people with a particular interest and skill in handling words in a particular kind of way which is extremely difficult to describe and extremely easy to recognise. Apart from that, they are fairly ordinary men and women, neither better nor worse, with the same limitations of nationality and class, with the same feelings and thoughts and prejudices. Some have been rich, some have been poor, some intelligent, others stupid.[1]

[1] It is true, however, that during the last hundred years, artists have tended to become a social class of their own, in parallel with the general trend to specialisation, or class

Because language is communicable, what they do for society is much the same as what they do for themselves. They do not invent new thoughts or feelings, but out of their skill with words they crystallise and define with greater precision thoughts and feelings which are generally present in their class and their age. To adapt the saying of the old lady: 'We know what we think when we see what they say.'

Take for example Timon's speech:

> Why this
> Will lug your priests and servants from your sides,
> Pluck stout men's pillows from below their heads:
> This yellow slave
> Will knit and break religions; bless the accurs'd;
> Make the hoar leprosy ador'd; place thieves,
> And give them title, knee and approbation
> With senators on the bench;—this is it
> That makes the wappen'd widow wed again.

Nothing is said here that either we or Shakespeare's contemporaries did not already know, but our awareness of the power of money is extended and intensified.

Reading this anthology will teach no one how to run a state or raise a revolution; it will not even, I think, tell them what freedom is. But it is a record of what people in many different social positions, from a peer like Lord Byron to a poor priest like Langland, and in many different Englands, from Wat Tyler's to Stephen Spender's, have noticed and felt about oppression, and so also it is a record of what we still feel. The details of our circumstances of injustice change, so does our knowledge of what is unjust and how best to remedy it, but our feelings change little which is why it is possible still to read poems written by those who are now dead.

> Avenge, O Lord, thy slaughtered saints, whose bones
> Lie scattered on the Alpine mountains cold

was what Milton felt about the Albigensians, but it is equally well what we feel about the Basques, and

> I can't take up my musket and fight them now, no mo!
> But I'm not going to love 'em and that is certain sho!
> And I don't want no pardon for what I was or am,
> I won't be reconstructed and I don't give a damn

will remain a perfect expression of dislike of pompous authority, long after the American Civil War has been forgotten.

The primary function of poetry, as of all the arts, is to make us more aware of ourselves and the world around us. I do not know if such increased awareness makes us more moral or more efficient: I hope not.

I think it makes us more human, and I am quite certain it makes us more difficult to deceive, which is why, perhaps, all totalitarian theories of the State, from Plato's downwards, have deeply mistrusted

division, in social organisation, a tendency which has had serious consequences for both the artist and the public, but that is not a question which I wish to raise over this anthology.

the arts. They notice and say too much, and the neighbours start talking:

There's many a beast, then, in a populous city
And many a civil monster.

Poems of Freedom, ed. by John Mulgan, 1938

XXIII

Everything that lives is Holy.—*Blake*.

I

(1) Goodness is easier to recognise than to define; only the greatest novelists can portray good people. For me, the least unsatisfactory description is to say that any thing or creature is good which is discharging its proper function, using its powers to the fullest extent permitted by its environment and its own nature—though we must remember that 'nature' and 'environment' are intellectual abstractions from a single, constantly changing reality. Thus, people are happy and good who have found their vocation: what vocations there are will depend upon the society within which they are practised.

There are two kinds of goodness, 'natural' and 'moral'. An organism is naturally good when it has reached a state of equilibrium with its environment. All healthy animals and plants are naturally good in this sense. But any change toward a greater freedom of action is a morally good change. I think it permissible, for example, to speak of a favourable mutation as a morally good act. But moral good passes into natural good. A change is made and a new equilibrium stabilised. Below man, this happens once for each species; the change toward freedom is not repeated. In man, the evolution can be continued, each stage of moral freedom being superseded by a new one. For example, we frequently admire the 'goodness' of illiterate peasants as compared with the 'badness' of many townees. But this is a romantic confusion. The goodness we admire in the former is a natural, not a moral, goodness. Once, the life of the peasant represented the highest use of the powers of man, the farthest limit of his freedom of action. This is no longer true. The townee has a wider range of choice and fuller opportunities of using his power. He frequently chooses wrongly, and so becomes morally bad. We are right to condemn him for this, but to suggest that we should all return to the life of the peasant is to deny the possibility of moral progress. Worship of youth is another romantic pessimism of this kind.

(2) Similarly, there is natural and moral evil. Determined and unavoidable limits to freedom of choice and action, such as the necessity for destroying life in order to eat and live, climate, accidents, are natural evils. If, on the other hand, I, say, as the keeper of a boarding-house, knowing that vitamins are necessary to health, continue, for reasons of gain or laziness, to feed my guests on an insufficient diet, I commit moral evil. Just as moral good tends to pass into natural good, so, conversely, what was natural evil tends, with

every advance in knowledge, to become moral evil.

(3) The history of life on this planet is the history of the ways in which life has gained control over and freedom within its environment. Organisms may either adapt themselves to a particular environment— e.g., the fleshy leaves of the cactus permit it to live in a desert—or develop the means to change their environment—e.g., organs of locomotion.

Below the human level, this progress has taken place through structural biological changes, depending on the luck of mutations or the chances of natural selection. Only man, with his conscious intelligence, has been able to continue his evolution after his biological development has finished. By studying the laws of physical nature, he has gained a large measure of control over them and insofar as he is able to understand the laws of his own nature and of the societies in which he lives, he approaches that state where what he wills may be done. 'Freedom', as a famous definition has it, 'is consciousness of necessity.'

(4) The distinguishing mark of man as an animal is his plastic, unspecialised 'foetalised' nature. All other animals develop more quickly and petrify sooner. In other words, the dictatorship of heredity is weakest in man. He has the widest choice of environment, and, in return, changes in environment, either changes in nature or his social life, have the greatest effect on him.

(5) In contrast to his greatest rivals for biological supremacy, the insects, man has a specialised and concentrated central nervous system, and unspecialised peripheral organs, i.e., the stimuli he receives are collected and pooled in one organ. Intelligence and choice can only arise when more than one stimulus is presented at the same time in the same place.

(6) Man has always been a social animal living in communities. This falsifies any theories of Social Contract. The individual *in vacuo* is an intellectual abstraction. The individual is the product of social life; without it, he could be no more than a bundle of unconditioned reflexes. Men are born neither free nor good.

(7) Societies and cultures vary enormously. On the whole, Marx seems to me correct in his view that physical conditions and the forms of economic production have dictated the forms of communities: e.g., the geographical peculiarities of the Aegean peninsula produced small democratic city-states, while the civilisations based on river irrigation like Egypt and Mesopotamia were centralised autocratic empires.

(8) *But* we are each conscious of ourselves as a thinking, feeling, and willing whole, and this is the only whole of which we have direct knowledge. This experience conditions our thinking. I cannot see how other wholes, family, class, nation, etc., can be wholes to us except in a purely descriptive sense. We do not see a state, we see a number of individuals. Anthropological studies of different communities, such as Dr. Benedict's work on primitive American cultures, or that of the Lynds on contemporary Middletown, have shown the enormous power of a given cultural form to determine the nature of the individuals who live under it. A given cultural pattern develops those traits of character and modes of behaviour which it values, and suppresses those which it does not. But this does not warrant ascribing

to a culture a superpersonality, conscious of its parts as I can be conscious of my hand or liver. A society consists of a certain number of individuals living in a particular way, in a particular place, at a particular time; nothing else.

(9) The distinction drawn by Locke between society and government is very important. Again, Marx seems to me correct in saying that sovereignty or government is not the result of a contract made by society as a whole, but has always been assumed by those people in society who owned the instruments of production.

Theories of Rights arise as a means to attack or justify a given social form, and are a sign of social strain. Burke, and later thinkers, who developed the idealist theory of the state, were correct in criticising the *a priori* assumptions of Social Contract and in pointing out that society is a growing organism. But, by identifying society and government, they ignored the power of the latter to interfere with the natural growth of the former, and so were led to denying the right of societies to revolt against their governments, and to the hypostatisation of the *status quo*.

(10) A favourite analogy for the state among idealist political thinkers is with the human body. This analogy is false. The constitution of the cells in the body is determined and fixed; nerve cells can only give rise to more nerve cells, muscle cells to muscle cells, etc. But, in the transition from parent to child, the whole pack of inherited genetic characters is shuffled. The King's son may be a moron, the coal heaver's a mathematical genius. The entire pattern of talents and abilities is altered at every generation.

(11) Another false analogy is with the animal kingdom. Observed from the outside (how it appears to them no one knows), the individual animal seems to be sacrificed to the continuance of the species. This observation is used to deny the individual any rights against the state. But there is a fundamental difference between man and all other animals in that an animal which has reached maturity does not continue to evolve, but a man does. As far as we can judge, the only standard in the animal world is physical fitness, but in man a great many other factors are involved. What has survival value can never be determined; man has survived as a species through the efforts of individuals who at the time must often have seemed to possess very little biological survival value.

(12) Man's advance in control over his environment is making it more and more difficult for him, at least in the industrialised countries with a high standard of living, like America or England, to lead a naturally good life, and easier and easier to lead a morally bad one.

Let us suppose, for example, that it is sometimes good for mind and body to take a walk. Before there were means of mechanical transport, men walked because they could not do anything else; i.e., they committed naturally good acts. To-day, a man has to choose whether to use his car or walk. It is possible for him, by using the car on an occasion when he ought to walk, to commit a morally wrong act, and it is quite probable that he will. It is despair at finding a solution to this problem which is responsible for much of the success of Fascist blood-and-soil ideology.

(1) A society, then, is good insofar as

a) it allows the widest possible range of choices to its members to follow those vocations to which they are suited;

b) it is constantly developing, and providing new vocations which make a fuller demand upon their increasing powers.

The Greeks assumed that the life of intellectual contemplation was the only really 'good' vocation. It has become very much clearer now that this is only true for certain people, and that there are a great many other vocations of equal value: human nature is richer and more varied than the Greeks thought.

(2) No society can be absolutely good. Utopias, whether like Aldous Huxley's Brave New World or Dante's Paradiso, because they are static, only portray states of natural evil or good. (Someone, I think it was Landor, said of the characters in the *Inferno*: 'But they don't want to get out.') People committing acts in obedience to law or habit are not being moral. As voluntary action always turns, with repetition, into habit, morality is only possible in a world which is constantly changing and presenting a fresh series of choices. No society is absolutely good; but some are better than others.

(3) If we look at a community at any given moment, we see that it consists of good men and bad men, clever men and stupid men, sensitive and insensitive, law-abiding and lawless, rich and poor. Our politics, our view of what form our society and our government should take here and now, will depend on

a) how far we think the bad is due to preventable causes;

b) what, if we think the causes preventable, we find them to be. If we take the extremely pessimistic view that evil is in no way preventable, our only course is the hermit's, to retire altogether from this wicked world. If we take a fairly pessimistic view, that badness is inherited (i.e., that goodness and badness are not determined by social relations), we shall try to establish an authoritarian regime of the good. If, on the other hand, we are fairly optimistic, believing that bad environment is the chief cause of badness in individuals, and that the environment can be changed, we shall tend toward a belief in some sort of democracy. Personally I am fairly optimistic, partly for reasons which I have tried to outline above, and partly because the practical results of those who have taken the more pessimistic view do not encourage me to believe that they are right.

(4) *Fairly* optimistic. In the history of man, there have been a few civilised individuals but no civilised community, not one, ever. Those who talk glibly of Our Great Civilisation, whether European, American, Chinese, or Russian, are doing their countries the greatest disservice. We are still barbarians. All advances in knowledge, from Galileo down to Freud or Marx, are, in the first impact, humiliating; they begin by showing us that we are not as free or as grand or as good as we thought; and it is only when we realise this that we can begin to study how to overcome our own weakness.

(5) What then are the factors which limit and hinder men from developing their powers and pursuing suitable vocations?

375

a) Lack of material goods. Man is an animal and until his immediate material and economic needs are satisfied, he cannot develop further. In the past this has been a natural evil: methods of production and distribution were too primitive to guarantee a proper standard of life for everybody. It is doubtful whether this is any longer true; in which case, it is a moral and remediable evil. Under this head I include all questions of wages, food, housing, health, insurance, etc.

b) Lack of education. Unless an individual is free to obtain the fullest education with which his society can provide him, he is being injured by society. This does not mean that everybody should have the *same* kind of education, though it does mean, I think, education of some kind or other, up to university age. Education in a democracy must have two aims. It must give vocational guidance and training, assist each individual to find out where his talents lie, and then help him to develop these to the full—this for some people might be completed by sixteen; and it must also provide a general education, develop the reason and the consciousness of every individual, whatever his job, to a point where he can for himself distinguish good from bad, and truth from falsehood—this requires a much longer educational period.

At present education is in a very primitive stage; we probably teach the wrong things to the wrong people at the wrong time. It is dominated, at least in England, by an academic tradition which, except for the specially gifted, only fits its pupils to be schoolteachers. It is possible that the time for specialisation (i.e., vocational training) should be in early adolescence, the twelve-to-sixteen group, and again in the latter half of the university period; but that the sixteen-to-twenty age group should have a general education.

c) Lack of occupations which really demand the full exercise of the individual's powers. This seems to me a very difficult problem indeed. The vast majority of jobs in a modern community do people harm. Children admire gangsters more than they admire factory operatives because they sense that being a gangster makes more demands on the personality than being a factory operative and is therefore, for the individual, morally better. It isn't that the morally better jobs are necessarily better rewarded economically: for instance, my acquaintance with carpenters leads me to think carpentry a very good profession, and my acquaintance with stockbrokers to think stockbroking a very bad one. The only jobs known to me which seem worthy of respect, both from the point of view of the individual and society, are being a creative artist, some kind of highly skilled craftsman, a research scientist, a doctor, a teacher, or a farmer. This difficulty runs far deeper than our present knowledge or any immediate political change we can imagine, and is therefore still, to a certain extent, a natural rather than a moral evil, though it is obviously much aggravated by gross inequalities in economic reward, which could be remedied. I don't myself much like priggish phrases such as 'the right use of leisure'; I agree with Eric Gill that work is what one does to please oneself, leisure the time one has to serve the community. The most one can say is that we must never forget that most people are being degraded by the work they do, and that the possibilities of sharing the duller jobs through the whole community will have to be explored much more fully. Incidentally, there is reason for thinking that the routine manual and machine-minding jobs are better tolerated by those whose talents are for book-learning than by those whose talents run in the direction of manual skill.

d) Lack of suitable psychological conditions. People cannot grow unless they are happy and, even when their material needs have been satisfied, they still need many other things. They want to be liked and to like other people; to feel valuable, both in their own eyes and in the eyes of others; to feel free and to feel responsible; above all, not to feel lonely and isolated. The first great obstacle is the size of modern communities. By nature, man seems adapted to live in communities of a very moderate size; his economic life has compelled him to live in ever-enlarging ones. Many of the damaging effects of family life described by modern psychologists may be the result of our attempt to make the family group satisfy psychological needs which can only be satisfied by the community group. The family is based on inequality, the parent-child relationship; the community is, or should be, based on equality, the relationship of free citizens. We need both. Fortunately, recent technical advances, such as cheap electrical power, are making smaller social units more of a practical possibility than they seemed fifty years ago, and people with as divergent political views as the anarchists and Mr. Ford are now agreed about the benefits of industrial decentralisation.

The second obstacle is social injustice and inequality. A man cannot be a happy member of a community if he feels that the community is treating him unjustly; the more complicated and impersonal economic life becomes, the truer this is. In a small factory where employer and employees know each other personally, i.e., where the conditions approximate to those of family life, the employees will accept without resentment a great deal more inequality than their fellows in a modern large-scale production plant.

III

(1) Society consists of a number of individual wills living in association. There is no such thing as a general will of society, except insofar as all these individual wills agree in desiring certain material things, e.g., food and clothes. It is also true, perhaps, that all desire happiness and goodness, but their conceptions of these may and do conflict with each other. Ideally, government is the means by which all the individual wills are assured complete freedom of moral choice and at the same time prevented from ever clashing. Such an ideal government, of course, does not and could not ever exist. It presupposes that every individual in society possesses equal power, and also that every individual takes part in the government.

(2) In practice, the majority is always ruled by a minority, a certain number of individuals who decide what a law shall be, and who command enough force to see that the majority obeys them. To do this, they must also command a varying degree of consent by the majority, though this consent need not be and never is complete. They must, for

example, have the consent of the armed forces and the police, and they must either control the financial resources of society, or have the support of those who do.

(3) Democracy assumes, I think correctly, the right of every individual to revolt against his government by voting against it. It has not been as successful as its advocates hoped, firstly, because it failed to realise the pressure that the more powerful and better educated classes could bring to bear upon the less powerful and less educated in their decisions—it ignored the fact that in an economically unequal society votes may be equal but voters are not—and secondly, because it assumed, I think quite wrongly, that voters living in the same geographical area would have the same interests, again ignoring economic differences and the change from an agricultural to an industrial economy. I believe that representation should be by trade or profession. No one person has exactly the same interests as another, but I, say, as a writer in Birmingham, have more interests in common with other writers in Leeds or London than I have with my next-door neighbour who manufactures cheap jewelry. This failure of the geographical unit to correspond to a genuine political unit is one of the factors responsible for the rise of the party machine. We rarely elect a local man whom we know personally; we have to choose one out of two or three persons offered from above. This seems to me thoroughly unsatisfactory. I think one of our mistakes is that we do not have enough stages in election; a hundred thousand voters are reduced by a single act to one man who goes to Parliament. This must inevitably mean a large degree of dictatorship from above. A sane democracy would, I feel, choose its representatives by a series of electoral stages, each lower stage electing the one above it.

(4) Legislation is a form of coercion, of limiting freedom. Coercion is necessary because societies are not free communities; we do not choose the society into which we are born; we can attempt to change it, but we cannot leave it. Ideally, people should be free to know evil and to choose the good, but the consequences of choosing evil are often to compel others to evil. The guiding principle of legislation in a democracy should be, not to make people good, but to prevent them making each other bad against their will. Thus we all agree that there should be laws against theft or murder, because no one chooses to be stolen from or murdered. But it is not always so simple. It is argued by laissez-faire economists that legislation concerning hours of work, wages, etc., violates the right of individual wills to bargain freely. But this presupposes that the bargaining powers of different wills are equal, and that each bargain is an individual act. Neither of these assumptions is true, and economic legislation is justified because they are not.

But there are other forms of legislation which are less justified. It is true that the individual will operating in a series of isolated acts is an abstraction—our present acts are the product of past acts and in their turn determine future ones—but I think the law has to behave as if this abstraction were a fact, otherwise there is no end to legislative interference. Take the case, for instance, of drink. If I become a drunkard, I may not only impair my own health, but also that of my children; and it can be argued, and often is, that the law should see that

I do not become one by preventing me from purchasing alcohol. I think, however, that this is an unjustifiable extension of the law's function. Everything I do, the hour I go to bed, the literature I read, the temperature at which I take my bath, affects my character for good or bad and so, ultimately, the characters of those with whom I come in contact. If the legislator is once allowed to consider the distant effects of my acts, there is no reason why he should not decide everything for me. The law has to limit itself to considering the act in isolation: if the act directly violates the will of another, the law is justified in interfering; if only indirectly, it is not. Nearly all legislation on 'moral' matters, such as drink, gambling, sexual behaviour between adults, etc., seems to me bad.

(5) In theory, every individual has a right to his own conception of what form society ought to take and what form of government there should be and to exercise his will to realise it; on the other hand, everyone else has a right to reject his conception. In practice, this boils down to the right of different political parties to exist, parties representing the main divisions of interest in society. As the different sectional interests cannot form societies on their own—e.g., the employees cannot set up one state by themselves and the employers another—there is always coercion of the weaker by the stronger by propaganda, legislation, and sometimes physical violence; and the more evenly balanced the opposing forces are, the more violent that coercion is likely to become.

I do not see how in politics one can decide *a priori* what conduct is moral, or what degree of tolerance there should be. One can only decide which party in one's private judgment has the best view of what society ought to be, and to support it; and remember that, since all coercion is a moral evil, we should view with extreme suspicion those who welcome it. Thus I cannot see how a Socialist country could tolerate the existence of a Fascist party any more than a Fascist country could tolerate the existence of a Socialist party. I judge them differently because I think that the Socialists are right and the Fascists are wrong in their view of society. (It is always wrong in an absolute sense to kill, but all killing is not equally bad; it does matter who is killed.)

Intolerance is an evil and has evil consequences we can never accurately foresee and for which we shall always have to suffer; but there are occasions on which we must be prepared to accept the responsibility of our convictions. We must be as tolerant as we dare— only the future can judge whether we were tyrants or foolishly weak— and if we cannot dare very far, it is a serious criticism of ourselves and our age.

(6) But we do have to choose, every one of us. We have the misfortune or the good luck to be living in one of the great critical historical periods, when the whole structure of our society and its cultural and metaphysical values are undergoing a radical change. It has happened before, when the Roman Empire collapsed, and at the Reformation, and it may happen again in the future.

In periods of steady evolution, it is possible for the common man to pursue his private life without bothering his head very much over the

379

principles and assumptions by which he lives, and to leave politics in the hands of professionals. But ours is not such an age. It is idle to lament that the world is becoming divided into hostile ideological camps; the division is a fact. No policy of isolation is possible. Democracy, liberty, justice, and reason are being seriously threatened and, in many parts of the world, destroyed. It is the duty of every one of us, not only to ourselves but to future generations of men, to have a clear understanding of what we mean when we use these words, to remember that while an idea can be absolutely bad, a person can never be, and to defend what we believe to be right, perhaps even at the cost of our lives and those of others.

I Believe, ed. by Clifton Fadiman, 1939

XXIV · Educational Theory

All education is a preparation for life. It must teach people how to do the things which will keep them alive, agriculture, hunting, fighting and what not, and it must teach them how to live together, the laws, customs and beliefs of the community.

In a primitive community with an undifferentiated economy, there is no quarrel between the vocational and the social aspect, for, apart from the division of labour between the sexes, all have to do the same things and lead the same kind of life. Religious instruction is practical, and practical instruction religious.

Educational theory begins when society has become differentiated, when different classes are living so differently, and doing such different things that the question arises: 'What shall we teach and to whom?'

THE MIDDLE AGES

Our present education has developed out of the theory and practice of the Middle Ages. Mediæval social theory divided society into three classes:

1. Those who pray.
2. Those who guard.
3. Those who work.

Those Who Pray.

Their social function was to mediate between God and man; their practical occupation a life of contemplation. That is to say, their life was a mental one, a training of the mind rather than the body, the more so because the flesh was held to be evil. Originally they were vowed to poverty, and in many monastic communities manual labour was an important part of their life, but their intellectual training was an abstract and philosophical one. Believing that the material world was as straw beside the heavenly mysteries, and that the truth had been revealed once and for all, and that their task was one of interpretation only, they did not pursue a scientific method of inquiry.

In addition, their professional language was Latin. As they were the only literate part of society, they became responsible for educational, legal and administrative duties. It is from them that the academic tradition with its bias towards abstract knowledge divorced from action, its preference for interpretation rather than creation, its formalism, and its emphasis on Latin, is derived.

Those Who Guard.

Their function was to guard property; their occupation the life of the courtier and the soldier; and their training, a training of the body and the social manners of a governing class. To them the military virtues of physical strength, courage, loyalty and social discipline were important, and neither intelligence nor technical skill of much value. It is on them that the public school social code is based.

Those Who Work.

Their function was to provide society with goods, their occupation manual labour, and their training purely vocational. The peasant child began to work in the fields as soon as he could, and as economic life became increasingly complicated, an organised apprentice system grew up in the skilled trades. For them education was empirical and specialised.

This view of society involves three assumptions:

1. That the structure of society is static.
2. That it is just.
3. That the special aptitudes suited to each class are inherited. (Except of course in the Church, where the laying on of hands took the place of birth-right.)

Christianity was committed to the belief that all human souls were of equal value. To square this with the manifest inequality of social reward, the theologians were forced to explain it by the Fall of Man. Society, then, was corrupt, but it was just. Further, if children are born evil, then they will always tend not to want the things they ought to want, such as learning or courage or manual skill, and must be forced to want them. The traditional disciplinary technique was due partly to ignorance, but was aggravated by an *a priori* doctrine of what the child must be like.

THE RENAISSANCE AND THE REFORMATION

Both had important influences upon education. The study of Greek brought knowledge of an intellectually educated ruling class and a secular culture. It was not incompatible with being a gentleman to be also a scholar. This encouraged speculation at the expense of authority, but it only intensified the gulf between thought and action, by making learning an aristocratic privilege. The pursuit of disinterested knowledge like pure mathematics and the practice of disinterested action like sport was socially respectable. Applied science or manual labour were not.

The Reformation coincides with the rise to political and economic power of the middle classes, and as a new class they had a new conception of society. Puritanism accepted the first two tenets of mediæval social theory but denied the third, i.e. it held that:

1. The structure of society is static.
2. It is just.
3. Special aptitudes are not inherited.

It accepted the class stratification, but asserted that the class in which the individual found himself depended upon his own efforts. The Middle Ages had believed, in theory at least, that the beggar was as good as the rich man. The Puritans denied this. The beggar was a beggar because he was wicked. All classes must pray and all classes must work. It is from them, both for themselves, and as employers, that the demand for a more vocational and scientific education and the attack on the Humanities has come.

ROUSSEAU AND ROMANTIC ANARCHISM

The increasing complexity of social and economic life and their growing moral and physical ugliness stimulated a reaction which began with Rousseau and is ending with Freud. The fundamental beliefs on which it is based are:

1. The structure of society is static.
2. It is unjust.
3. The individual is born good and is made evil by society. 'Man is born free and is everywhere in chains.'

The effects of these beliefs on the theory and practice of education have been immense. If the individual is born good, then the child is better than the adult, and it is the adult who must learn from the child.

However questionable in some respects their theories may have been, they had the practical effect of making people study children to see what they were really like, and it is to the followers of Rousseau that we owe most of the advance that has been made in teaching and disciplinary technique.

Comments

1. The single point upon which all these theories agree, and upon which they are all wrong, is that the structure of society is static and unchangeable.

2. The Middle Ages were right in supposing that the poor are not necessarily poor because they are wicked, nor the rich necessarily rich because they are virtuous. The Puritans were wrong.

3. The Puritans were right in supposing that ability or the lack of it are not necessarily inherited. The Middle Ages were wrong.

4. Rousseau was right in supposing that society is not necessarily just. The Middle Ages and the Puritans were wrong.

382

5. The Middle Ages and the Puritans were right in supposing that Society is a necessary fact. Rousseau was wrong.

With the middle classes established in the saddle after the industrial revolution, came the consolidation of their private educational system, the reform of the old public schools, the creation of a great many new ones, and a systematisation of the principles on which they were to be run. The public schools before Arnold began to reform them had been tough, barbarian places which produced the kind of brave and unscrupulous adventurers who get an Empire. Arnold's job was to turn them into incubators for the type of narrow-minded, active, unquestioning administrators who would develop and keep it, and the same type was needed for the reformed army and the new Civil Services, all the key positions of a new dominant class.

The contribution of Arnold and his followers was the invention of the prefect system, the emphasis on 'character' rather than intelligence, and the discovery of organised games as the best means of developing it. By the prefect system boys were given a training in the theory and practice of authoritarian discipline; while their character-training taught them to regard themselves as natural leaders, owing a rigid loyalty to their group; and as they lived in boarding schools where only their own class was admitted from the ages of 8 to 18, it was hardly surprising that they identified their group completely with the nation. These features remain to-day the foundations of the public school system.

A national public education begins at the end of the nineteenth century, when industrial processes demand technically educated masses and recruits for the lower grade executive posts. If the evangelicals of the nineteenth century wanted the poor to be taught to read so that they could read the Bible, the more far-sighted of the bourgeoisie wanted it so that they should understand blue-prints and modern book-keeping. That, instead of either, they should come to understand Karl Marx, was no part of anyone's design, though it was a danger which the diehards foresaw.

TRANSITION TO DEMOCRACY

The establishment of universal compulsory education created a new problem which the liberal conscience attempted to solve by the 'ladder' theory. Government should be by the best men irrespective of class, and the problem was to make access to the highest positions as easy and generous as possible. This theory is a barely concealed 'leadership theory', the logical end of which is seen in the modern Nazi training colleges. But it has never been brought to anything like its logical conclusions in England.

The exclusiveness of the public schools was largely retained, and justified on the grounds that their products were the leaders who *served* the nation; while at the other end an attempt was made to limit their exclusiveness by opening them to a small creamed selection of working-class boys. This movement has never touched the more important schools, and the less important, whose finances have forced them to enter it, have never had to admit more than 10 per cent. of their total numbers.

This half-heartedness is defended by the assertion that the public schools have something very precious (their tradition) which might be swamped by too great an influx of the lower classes. This gives the game away. The middle classes *are* the best, but, under this liberal theory, they may recruit into their ranks a small selection from the lower classes who are then submitted to a thorough de-classing process. The class structure remains unaltered, but a certain number of the lower classes are taken out of their class and trained as leaders. But it still remains that to be leader you must be middle class.

Liberal education also implies the academic bias; liberal, in this sense, meaning fit for an Athenian free man as opposed to a slave. And the Athenian tradition that a real free man despises trade as well as manual labour still lingers, rather mustily, in our educational approach.

The practical success of Rousseau's methods in education only shows that if you treat children with a modicum of kindliness and common sense, in other words, if you make the society in which they live a reasonably decent one, they will thrive on it. A good society makes people good, as bad society makes them bad. Therefore if you can discover the factors which make a society what it is, you can educate people to virtue. The failure of education to have any appreciable effect upon the behaviour of adults or nations shows that most people adapt themselves very quickly to whatever society or section of society they happen to fall into. The charming young public school athlete becomes the Great Portland Street tyke.

This is not to say that school society ought to be no better than society outside, but to say that it cannot be; different schools imitate different sections. The State school imitates the mass-production factory, the public school the army and the Colonial Civil Services, while the progressive school community resembles that of the *rentier* who is free to devote himself to higher things, and is under no obligation to develop his courage or his cunning.

Education can never be more effective than the structure of society as a whole will let it, and the teacher who imagines that you can effectively change education without first changing society will end either by throwing the whole contraption overboard in despair like D. H. Lawrence, or by deceiving himself with a lot of gas about Service like Dr. Norwood.

D. H. LAWRENCE, ANTI-IDEALISM, AND FASCISM

All English education pays lip-service to the Liberal ideal, though the public schools have pursued it rather half-heartedly. The most serious attack on Liberal education has been made by D. H. Lawrence, and the fact that the Fascist countries appear on the surface to be putting his theories into practice makes their study extremely important to socialists. Very briefly summarised they amount to this:

1. Man fell when he became self-conscious.
2. Mental life and physical life are at odds; each secretly despises the other.
3. Idealism, the running of the instinctive life by the self-conscious mind, corrupts life.
4. Europeans have lived so long under the rule of idealism that they have become deranged, and think they want what they ought to want. They are, most of them, self-conscious neurasthenic ninnies, afraid of life.
5. Every individual is unique, with his unique needs. You cannot live by a set of Sunday-school rules.
6. Very few people either really want or are suited to a life of thought. Most can only learn a few tricks.
7. The aim of education should be to help people to realise their deepest instinctive needs.

Education should therefore:

1. Turn its back on the whole academic tradition. The majority of pupils will need no more than the three Rs. The basis of training should be the primary manual trades, farming, building, tinkering, cooking, etc., not book-learning nor ornamental arts and crafts.
2. Train the body and spirit by the tougher sports like boxing and swimming which develop courage and personal pride. Gymnastics begin at the wrong end by setting out to train the body through the mind.
3. Select its candidates for mind-training very carefully.

Many of Lawrence's observations are true, and perhaps several of his practical suggestions are sound, but his refusal to admit that on the whole people are like what they are because society is like what it is instead of the reverse makes his conclusions dangerous. As a matter of observation it is true that book-learning has a bad effect on many people, and that manual work is viewed with horror. But it is not true to say:

1. That you know that mental activity *must always* be only suited to a few.
2. That you know who they are.

It is a very attractive doctrine for an authoritarian state, because once you begin by saying that some people are born to think and therefore to rule, while the mass are born not to think but to carry out the way of life which the thinkers decide is best for them, it is a short step to saying that those who are actually ruling are born to think and those who oppose them must not be allowed to think. It is Plato's old problem of how to secure rule by the Good Men. No one can decide who they are, and no one has ever succeeded in convincing those who are in power that they are bad or that they are incompetent to judge who is.

Headmasters of old schools and new schools alike are always

proclaiming that their aim is to produce leaders. This only shows that they are conceited. Every teacher knows in his heart of hearts that he has not the slightest idea of what effect he is having, that he is working largely in the dark, that on most of his pupils he has no effect at all, and probably a bad effect on half the rest.

It also shows that they are reactionary. The leaders of the second generation are the rebels of the first. A leader is the very last person they would recognise or like to see in their schools; what they want is a pleasant-mannered yes-man with executive ability.

We come back again to the old fallacy that there can be a state of society which is final and absolutely just. The moment we forget that

1. All forms of society are imperfect,
2. Some are better than others,

that is to say, if we become romantically utopian or other-worldly, if we deny the movement of history, we surrender to the first tyrant who can seize power.

Loyalty and intelligence are mutually hostile. The intelligence is always disloyal. There must always be a conflict between the loyalty necessary for society to be, and the intelligence necessary for society to become. The question of whether there are some people who are followers by nature, and others who are leaders, can only be discussed when education up to the age of maturity is open to all.

Meanwhile the important part of Lawrence's attack is his attack on the school curriculum. Every educationalist agrees that education should be general and not vocational, yet, in fact, everyone receives a vocational education in academic teaching. It is not a question of whether some people do not need an academic training but of whether all people do not need a practical manual one in some real trade, and need to realise that the mind is only a part of the whole man.

Education To-day—and To-morrow,
by Auden and T. C. Worsley, 1939

XXV · A Great Democrat

The Spirit of Voltaire. By Norman L. Torrey.
Voltaire. By Alfred Noyes.

Voltaire was not only one of the greatest Europeans of all time but, though he might be surprised to hear it, one of the greatest fighters for democracy, and one who should be as much a hero to us as Socrates or Jefferson. As Professor Torrey says: 'Voltaire has an important message for the present age. His readers in the period preceding the World War were mildly amused or mildly shocked but not deeply moved. . . . To-day our hopes are not so sanguine. . . . It is in such periods of increasing fanaticism that generations will turn again to the spirit of Voltaire.' Professor Torrey has certainly done his best to insure that they shall. Voltaire has suffered the greatest misfortune that can befall a writer: he has become a legend, which insures that he will not be read until someone destroys the legend. This Professor Torrey has done with scholarship and perfect taste. If these admirable books of Professor Torrey and Mr. Noyes are as widely read as they ought to be, it will be an encouraging sign. For democracy is not a political system or party but an attitude of mind. There is no such thing as the perfect democratic state, good for all time. What political form is most democratic at any given period depends on geography, economic development, educational level, and the like. But in any particular issue it is always possible to say where a democrat should stand, and to recognise one, whatever party label he may bear.

It is a pity that the most widely known of Voltaire's works should be *Candide*, for the facile optimism of Leibniz, which it attacks, the view that 'everything that is, is right', is a side issue. Such a view bears only a superficial resemblance to the profound intuitions of Spinoza or to Rilke's '*dennoch preisen*', which are the basis for all reverence for life and belief in the future. It is too patently contradicted by daily experience to be held for long, even by the rich.

Democracy has three great enemies: the mystic pessimism of the unhappy, who believe that man has no free will, the mystic optimism of the romantic, who believes that the individual has absolute free will, and the mystic certainty of the perfectionist, who believes that an individual or a group can know the final truth and the absolutely good. For Voltaire these beliefs were embodied, the first in Pascal, the second in Rousseau, and the last in the Catholic church.

Pascal's extreme view about original sin, by denying to fallen man any free will, makes the intellect useless, all human relations a hindrance, and all social forms meaningless. We feel, he says, that we must have absolute certainty; therefore absolute certainty must exist. Only the Catholic religion professes to offer certainty. Therefore we should accept it. Rousseau, starting from the other extreme of asserting the absolute free will of the natural individual, came to similar conclusions. Man is good and corrupted by society; therefore all social forms are bad. If every individual will were allowed to operate freely, there would emerge a general social will. Like Pascal he felt that certainty should exist, and since the intellect could not give it, one should trust to feeling. In the end, since it was impossible for him to become a savage, and no absolute political creed had been invented, he accepted Pascal's wager and died a Catholic.

Voltaire's reply to them both was, in essence, very simple. Examine all the evidence and don't try to go beyond it.

Pascal says that all men are wicked and unhappy. They are, but not all the time. People are often happy and do good acts. Pascal says that the human passions are the cause of all evil. They are, but also they are the cause of all good. They are an integral part of the creation.

> The miseries of life no more prove the fall of man than the miseries of a hackney coach-horse prove that once upon a time all horses were fat and sleek, and were never beaten; and that, since one of them ate forbidden hay, all its descendants have been condemned to draw hackney-coaches.

Rousseau says that civilisation is horrible. Much of it is, but not all.

We neither can nor want to become savages or babies again.

Never has anyone employed so much wit in trying to make us witless; the reading of your book makes us want to creep on all fours. However, as it is now more than sixty years since I lost that habit, I feel unfortunately that it is impossible for me to take it up again, and I leave that natural attitude to those who are more worthy of it than you or I. Neither can I embark to go and live with the savages of Canada. ... The ailments with which I am afflicted retain me by the side of the greatest doctor of Europe and I could not find the same attentions among the Missouri Indians.

Voltaire saw that those who say that they cannot live without absolute certainty end by accepting some person or institution that offers it. In his day there was only one such offer, that of the Catholic church.

Mr. Noyes disposes once for all of the popular conception of Voltaire as a shallow cynic who felt and believed in nothing. The man was not lacking in reverence who wrote:

I was meditating last night, I was absorbed in the contemplation of nature, I admired the immensity, of course, the harmony of those infinite globes. ... One must be blind not to be dazzled by the spectacle, one must be stupid not to recognise the author of it, one must be mad not to worship him.

When he wrote, '*Ecrasez l'infâme*', he had in mind the assumption, under whatever disguise, religious, philosophical, political, that the final absolute truth has been revealed.

Allow that assumption, and tyranny and cruelty are not only inevitable but just and necessary. For if I know the good, then it is my moral duty to persecute all who disagree with me. That is why the Catholic church can never compromise with liberalism or democracy, and why it must prefer even fascism to socialism. Fascism may persecute Catholicism, but as a competitor; it is based on the same premise of being in possession of the final truth, and if it persecutes, in the end it can only strengthen its persecuted rivals. The first principle of democracy, on the other hand, is that no one knows the final truth about anything, and that the most one can say is: 'At this particular moment, and in this particular instance, the nearest approximation we can get to the truth seems to be this. We do not know what absolute goodness is, but this man seems to be better than that man.' In such an atmosphere Catholicism withers. There are many liberal Catholics, like Noyes and Maritain, some of them the salt of the earth, but they will always see their hopes defeated. They will deplore the politics of their church without realising their necessity, for a revealed religion must be centralised and authoritarian, and must oppose any political system which encourages the freedom of the individual conscience.

At the time when Voltaire wrote, social change seemed impossible, and supernatural security was the only refuge for the unhappy; Catholicism, as in any backward country to-day, had no rival. But as soon as misery is seen to have natural causes which might be removed by political action, absolutist political creeds appear.

388

Pascal and Rousseau illustrate like parables how people come to prefer certainty to freedom. Both were sick men, and sickness is one cause of unhappiness. Poverty and feelings of social inferiority or insecurity are others. Like Rousseau, liberal capitalism began in the belief that all individuals are equally free to will, and just as Rousseau died a Catholic, so the masses, disillusioned, are beginning to welcome the barrack life of fascism, which at least offers security and certainty. Voltaire was no social revolutionary, but within the economic and social conditions of his time he attempted on his estate at Ferney to create a community of which the members would feel happy enough to allow the spirit of democracy to flower. For one of the symptoms of happiness is a lively curiosity that finds others as interesting and worth knowing as oneself, and it is only by removing the obvious causes of misery, poverty, and social injustice that a democracy like the United States can protect itself against the specious appeals of the enemies of freedom.

The Nation, 25 March 1939

XXVI · The Public v. the Late Mr. William Butler Yeats

THE PUBLIC PROSECUTOR:

Gentlemen of the Jury. Let us be quite clear in our minds as to the nature of this case. We are here to judge, not a man, but his work. Upon the character of the deceased, therefore, his affectations of dress and manner, his inordinate personal vanity, traits which caused a fellow countryman and former friend to refer to him as 'the greatest literary fop in history', I do not intend to dwell. I must only remind you that there is usually a close connection between the personal character of a poet and his work, and that the deceased was no exception.

Again I must draw your attention to the exact nature of the charge. That the deceased had talent is not for a moment in dispute; so much is freely admitted by the prosecution. What the defence are asking you to believe, however, is that he was a *great* poet, the greatest of this century writing in English. That is their case, and it is that which the prosecution feels bound most emphatically to deny.

A great poet. To deserve such an epithet, a poet is commonly required to convince us of these things: firstly a gift of a very high order for memorable language, secondly a profound understanding of the age in which he lived, and thirdly a working knowledge of and sympathetic attitude towards the most progressive thought of his time.

Did the deceased possess these? I am afraid, gentlemen, that the answer is, no.

On the first point I shall be brief. My learned friend, the counsel for the defence, will, I have no doubt, do his best to convince you that I am wrong. And he has a case, gentlemen. O yes, a very fine case. I shall only ask you to apply to the work of the deceased a very simple test. How many of his lines can you remember?

Further, it is not unreasonable to suppose that a poet who has a gift for language will recognise that gift in others. I have here a copy of an anthology edited by the deceased entitled *The Oxford Book of Modern Verse*. I challenge anyone in this court to deny that it is the most deplorable volume ever issued under the imprint of that highly respected firm which has done so much for the cause of poetry in this country, the Clarendon Press.

But in any case you and I are educated modern men. Our fathers imagined that poetry existed in some private garden of its own, totally unrelated to the workaday world, and to be judged by pure aesthetic standards alone. We know that now to be an illusion. Let me pass, then, to my second point. Did the deceased understand his age?

What did he admire? What did he condemn? Well, he extolled the virtues of the peasant. Excellent. But should that peasant learn to read and write, should he save enough money to buy a shop, attempt by honest trading to raise himself above the level of the beasts, and O, what a sorry change is there. Now he is the enemy, the hateful huxter whose blood, according to the unseemly boast of the deceased, never flowed through *his* loins. Had the poet chosen to live in a mud cabin in Galway among swine and superstition, we might think him mistaken, but we should admire his integrity. But did he do this? O dear no. For there was another world which seemed to him not only equally admirable, but a deal more agreeable to live in, the world of noble houses, of large drawing rooms inhabited by the rich and the decorative, most of them of the female sex. We do not have to think very hard or very long, before we shall see a connection between these facts. The deceased had the feudal mentality. He was prepared to admire the poor just as long as they remained poor and deferential, accepting without protest the burden of maintaining a little Athenian band of literary landowners, who without their toil could not have existed for five minutes.

For the great struggle of our time to create a juster social order, he felt nothing but the hatred which is born of fear. It is true that he played a certain part in the movement for Irish Independence, but I hardly think my learned friend will draw your attention to that. Of all the modes of self-evasion open to the well-to-do, Nationalism is the easiest and most dishonest. It allows to the unjust all the luxury of righteous indignation against injustice. Still, it has often inspired men and women to acts of heroism and self-sacrifice. For the sake of a free Ireland the poet Pearse and the countess Markiewicz gave their all. But if the deceased did give himself to this movement, he did so with singular moderation. After the rebellion of Easter Sunday 1916, he wrote a poem on the subject which has been called a masterpiece. It is. To succeed at such a time in writing a poem which could offend neither the Irish Republican nor the British Army was indeed a masterly achievement.

And so we come to our third and last point. The most superficial glance at the last fifty years is enough to tell us that the social struggle towards greater equality has been accompanied by a growing intellectual acceptance of the scientific method and the steady conquest of irrational superstition. What was the attitude of the deceased towards this? Gentlemen, words fail me. What are we to say of a man whose earliest writings attempted to revive a belief in fairies and whose favourite themes were legends of barbaric heroes with unpronounceable names, work which has been aptly and wittily described as Chaff about Bran?

But you may say, he was young; youth is always romantic; its silliness is part of its charm. Perhaps it is. Let us forgive the youth, then, and consider the mature man, from whom we have a right to expect wisdom and common sense. Gentlemen, it is hard to be charitable when we find that the deceased, far from outgrowing his folly, has plunged even deeper. In 1900 he believed in fairies; that was bad enough; but in 1930 we are confronted with the pitiful, the deplorable spectacle of a grown man occupied with the mumbo-jumbo of magic and the nonsense of India. Whether he seriously believed such stuff to be true, or merely thought it pretty, or imagined it would impress the public, is immaterial. The plain fact remains that he made it the centre of his work. Gentlemen, I need say no more. In the last poem he wrote, the deceased rejected social justice and reason, and prayed for war. Am I mistaken in imagining that somewhat similar sentiments are expressed by a certain foreign political movement which every lover of literature and liberty acknowledges to be the enemy of mankind?

THE COUNSEL FOR THE DEFENCE:

Gentlemen of the Jury. I am sure you have listened with as much enjoyment as I to the eloquent address of my learned friend. I say enjoyment because the spectacle of anything well-done, whether it be a feat of engineering, a poem, or even an outburst of impassioned oratory, must always give pleasure.

We have been treated to an analysis of the character of the deceased which, for all I know, may be as true as it is destructive. Whether it proves anything about the value of his poetry is another matter. If I may be allowed to quote my learned friend: 'We are here to judge, not a man, but his work.' We have been told that the deceased was conceited, that he was a snob, that he was a physical coward, that his taste in contemporary poetry was uncertain, that he could not understand physics and chemistry. If this is not an invitation to judge the man I do not know what is. Does it not bear an extraordinary resemblance to the belief of an earlier age that a great artist must be chaste? Take away the frills, and the argument of the prosecution is reduced to this: 'A great poet must give the right answers to the problems which perplex his generation. The deceased gave the wrong answers. Therefore the deceased was not a great poet.' Poetry in such a view is the filling up of a social quiz; to pass with honours the poet must score not less than 75%. With all due respect to my learned friend, this is nonsense. We are tempted so to judge contemporary poets because we really do have problems which we really do want solved, so that we are inclined to expect everyone, politicians, scientists, poets, clergymen, to give us the answer, and to blame them indiscriminately when they do not. But who reads the poetry of the past in this way? In an age of rising nationalism, Dante looked back with envy to the Roman Empire. Was this socially progressive? Will only a Catholic admit that Dryden's 'The Hind and the Panther' is a good poem? Do we condemn Blake because he rejected Newton's theory of light, or rank Wordsworth lower than Baker, because the latter had a deeper appreciation of the steam engine?

Can such a view explain why

> Mock Emmet, Mock Parnell
> All the renown that fell

is good; and bad, such a line as

> Somehow I think that you are rather like a tree.

In pointing out that this is absurd, I am not trying to suggest that art exists independently of society. The relation between the two is just as intimate and important as the prosecution asserts.

Every individual is from time to time excited emotionally and intellectually by his social and material environment. In certain individuals this excitement produces verbal structures which we call poems; if such a verbal structure creates an excitement in the reader, we call it a good poem. Poetic talent, in fact, is the power to make personal excitement socially available. Poets, i.e. persons with poetic talent, stop writing good poetry when they stop reacting to the world they live in. The nature of that reaction, whether it be positive or negative, morally admirable or morally disgraceful, matters very little; what is essential is that the reaction should genuinely exist. The later Wordsworth is not inferior to the earlier because the poet had altered his political opinions, but because he had ceased to feel and think so strongly, a change which happens, alas, to most of us as we grow older. Now, when we turn to the deceased, we are confronted by the amazing spectacle of a man of great poetic talent, whose capacity for excitement not only remained with him to the end, but actually increased. In two hundred years when our children have made a different and, I hope, better social order, and when our science has developed out of all recognition, who but a historian will care a button whether the deceased was right about the Irish Question or wrong about the transmigration of souls? But because the excitement out of which his poems arose was genuine, they will still, unless I am very much mistaken, be capable of exciting others, different though their circumstances and beliefs may be from his.

However since we are not living two hundred years hence, let us play the schoolteacher a moment, and examine the poetry of the deceased with reference to the history of our time.

The most obvious social fact of the last forty years is the failure of liberal capitalist democracy, based on the premises that every individual is born free and equal, each an absolute entity independent of all others; and that a formal political equality, the right to vote, the right to a fair trial, the right of free speech, is enough to guarantee his freedom of action in his relations with his fellow men. The results are only too familiar to us all. By denying the social nature of personality, and by ignoring the social power of money, it has created the most impersonal, the most mechanical and the most unequal civilisation the world has ever seen, a civilisation in which the only emotion common to all classes is a feeling of individual isolation from everyone else, a civilisation torn apart by the opposing emotions born of economic injustice, the just envy of the poor and the selfish terror of the rich.

If these latter emotions meant little to the deceased, it was partly because Ireland compared with the rest of western Europe was economically backward, and the class struggle was less conscious there. My learned friend has sneered at Irish Nationalism, but he knows as well as I that Nationalism is a necessary stage towards Socialism. He has sneered at the deceased for not taking arms, as if shooting were the only honourable and useful form of social action. Has the Abbey Theatre done nothing for Ireland?

But to return to the poems. From first to last they express a sustained protest against the social atomisation caused by industrialism, and both in their ideas and their language a constant struggle to overcome it. The fairies and heroes of the early work were an attempt to find through folk tradition a binding force for society; and the doctrine of Anima Mundi found in the later poems is the same thing in a more developed form, which has left purely local peculiarities behind, in favour of something that the deceased hoped was universal; in other words, he was looking for a world religion. A purely religious solution may be unworkable, but the search for it is, at least, the result of a true perception of a social evil. Again, the virtues that the deceased praised in the peasantry and aristocracy, and the vices he blamed in the commercial classes, were real virtues and vices. To create a united and just society where the former are fostered and the latter cured is the task of the politician, not the poet.

For art is a product of history, not a cause. Unlike some other products, technical inventions for example, it does not re-enter history as an effective agent, so that the question whether art should or should not be propaganda is unreal. The case for the prosecution rests on the fallacious belief that art ever makes anything happen, whereas the honest truth, gentlemen, is that, if not a poem had been written, not a picture painted, not a bar of music composed, the history of man would be materially unchanged.

But there is one field in which the poet is a man of action, the field of language, and it is precisely in this that the greatness of the deceased is most obviously shown. However false or undemocratic his ideas, his diction shows a continuous evolution towards what one might call the true democratic style. The social virtues of a real democracy are brotherhood and intelligence, and the parallel linguistic virtues are strength and clarity, virtues which appear ever more clearly through successive volumes by the deceased.

The diction of *The Winding Stair* is the diction of a just man, and it is for this reason that just men will always recognise the author as a master.

Partisan Review, Spring 1939

XXVII · The Prolific and the Devourer

PART I

> To the Devourer it seems as if the producer was in his
> chains: but it is not so, he only takes portions of
> existence and fancies that the whole.
>   But the Prolific would cease to be Prolific unless the
> Devourer, as a sea, received the excess of his delights.
>   These two classes of men are always upon earth, and
> they should be enemies: whoever tries to reconcile them
> seeks to destroy existence.
>   —*William Blake*, THE MARRIAGE OF HEAVEN AND HELL

Not only does Man create the world in his own image, but the different
types of man create different kinds of world. Cf. Blake: 'A fool sees not
the same tree that a wise man sees.'

All the striving of life is a striving to transcend duality, and establish
unity or freedom. The Will, the Unconscious, is this desire to be free.
Our wants are our conception of what dualities exist, i.e., of what the
obstacles are to our will. We are not free to will not to be free.

Freud has led us astray in opposing the Pleasure Principle to the
Reality Principle. This is concealed Puritanism. 'What I want, the
world outside myself cannot give. Therefore what I want is wrong.
The Death Wish: Never to have been born is beyond all comparison
the best.' On the contrary, my wants are just as much a part of reality as
anything else.

It is untrue to say that we really desire to return to the womb. We
picture freedom thus, because it was our earliest experience of Unity,
and we can only picture the unknown future in terms of the known
past.

At first the baby sees his limbs as belonging to the outside world. When
he has learnt to control them, he accepts them as parts of himself. What
we call the 'I', in fact, is the area over which our will is immediately
operative. Thus, if we have a toothache, we seem to be two people, the
suffering 'I' and the hostile outer world of the tooth. His penis never
fully belongs to a man.

The Dictator who says 'My People': the Writer who says 'My Public'.

People seem 'real' to us, i.e., part of our life, in proportion as we are
conscious that our respective wills affect each other.

Part of our knowledge of reality comes to us automatically through
unavoidable personal contacts. The rest through the use of the
intellect.

The intellect, by revealing to us unsuspected relations between facts of which we have no personal and therefore emotional experience and facts of which we have, enables us to feel about and therefore to be affected in our actions by the former. It widens the horizon of the heart.

The religious definitions of salvation (i.e., Unity or Freedom), 'The Kingdom of Heaven', 'In His Will is our Peace', are the best because the most general. To be saved is to want only what one has.

To be wicked or neurotic in the moral or popular sense is to want what the majority do not want. To be wicked or neurotic in the religious or real sense is to want what one cannot have. These often coincide, but not always.

Even the ascetic who condemns all who consciously seek honour, power, and the love of women is less evil than the psychologist who condemns as neurotic all who don't. Judge not.

The neurotic is someone who draws a false general conclusion from a particular instance. X was once slapped unjustly by his papa and goes through life thinking that the world must always treat him unjustly. Sometimes the identification is only partial: symbolic fears—lobsters and castration.

There is only one salvation but there are as many roads thither as there are kinds of people.
  Three kinds of people: three roads to salvation.
  Those who seek it
    1) through the manipulation of non-human things: the farmer, the engineer, the scientist
    2) through the manipulation of other human beings: the politician, the teacher, the doctor
    3) through the manipulation of their own phantasies: the artist, the saint.

Everyone combines these three lives in varying proportions, e.g., when we are eating we are scientists, when we are in company we are politicians, when we are alone we are artists. Nevertheless, the proportions vary enough to make individuals inhabit such different worlds that they have great difficulty in understanding each other.

In its essence, Science is the exercise of the faculties to secure our physical existence in the material world. The baby seeking the breast is a scientist.
  Art is the spiritual life, made possible by science.
  Material happiness is created by science.
  Spiritual happiness is created by art.
  Politics creates nothing, but is a technique for their distribution.

The average man, the man-in-the-street, is the person who is passive towards experience: his knowledge is limited to what comes to him automatically through immediate personal experience. The scientist, artist, and politician proper are intellectuals, i.e., they seek to extend their experience beyond the immediately given.

We are all of us average men outside our particular fields. If we are not politicians we fail to understand politics that lie outside personal relations, if we are not artists we fail to understand art that does not reflect our own private phantasies, if we are not scientists we are bewildered by science that is not obviously based on common-sense experience.

'Work' is action forced on us by the will of another. 'Unless you do this, I won't give you anything to eat. Unless you learn this irregular verb, I shall beat you.' When I was at school, lessons were play to me. Work meant playing football.

The goal of everyone is to live without working. To do this one must either have inherited or stolen money, or one must persuade society to pay one for doing what one likes, i.e., for playing.

The true aim of the politician (whether a politician proper, teacher, doctor, etc.) should be the creation of a society where no one has to work, where everyone is conscious, that is, of what they like doing, and nothing else has to be done. The politician who begins at the other end and tries to persuade men that it is their social duty to like doing what has to be done (or more usually what he thinks has to be done) is a tyrant.

How often one hears a young man with no talent say when asked what he intends to do, 'I want to write'. What he really means is, 'I don't want to work'. Politics and science can be play too, but art is the least dependent on the good-will of others and looks the easiest.

The Ivory Tower. Like the Point, this is really only a useful mathematical concept without actual existence, meaning complete isolation from all experience. The closest approximation in real life is schizophrenia.

The commonest ivory tower is that of the average man, the state of passivity towards experience.

We can justly accuse the poets of the nineties of ivory-towerism, not because they said they were non-political, but because the portion of life which they saw as poets was such a tiny fragment. Politics and science, indeed, they saw as average men of their social position, education, and income.

'To know a lot about something and a little about everything' is a rotten maxim. Rather, first discover what manner of person you are, and then learn to see everything through the lens of your gift. One destroys one's ivory tower only when one has learnt to see the whole universe as an artist, or as a scientist, or as a politician.

'The Child is Father to the Man.' We do not become a different person as we grow up, but remain the same from infancy to old age. Maturity, however, knows who he is, and childhood does not. To mature means to become conscious of necessity, to know what one wants and to be prepared to pay the price for it. Failures either do not know what they want, or jib at the price.

The Parable of the Labourers in the Vineyard. Nature has her favourites whom she lets have everything at sale-price. There are others who get nothing except at famine prices. But they must pay them all the same.

The youngest of three brothers, I grew up in a middle-class professional family. My father was a doctor, my mother had a university degree. The study was full of books on medicine, archaeology, the classics. There was a rain-gauge on the lawn and a family dog. There were family prayers before breakfast, bicycle-rides to collect fossils or rub church-brasses, reading aloud in the evenings. We kept pretty much to ourselves. Mother was often ill.

In one way we were eccentric: we were Anglo-Catholics. On Sundays there were services with music, candles, and incense, and at Christmas, a crèche was rigged up in the dining-room, lit by an electric-torch battery, round which we sang hymns.

There I learnt certain attitudes, call them prejudices if you like, which I shall never lose: that knowledge is something to seek for its own sake; an interest in medicine and disease, and theology; a conviction (though I am unaware of ever having held any supernatural beliefs) that life is ruled by mysterious forces; a dislike of strangers and cheery gangs; and a contempt for businessmen and all who work for profits rather than a salary (my father was in municipal medicine, not private practice).

My father's library not only taught me to read, but dictated my choice of reading. It was not the library of a literary man nor of a narrow specialist, but a heterogeneous collection of books on many subjects, and including very few novels. In consequence my reading has always been wide and casual rather than scholarly, and in the main non-literary.

As a child I had no interest in poetry, but a passion for words, the longer the better, and appalled my aunts by talking like a professor of geology. To-day words so affect me that a pornographic story, for example, excites me sexually more than a living person can do.

Besides words, I was interested almost exclusively in mines and their machinery. An interest in people did not begin till adolescence.

My interest and knowledge were such that I deceived not only myself but my parents into thinking that it was a genuine scientific interest and that I was gifted to become, what I said I was going to become, a mining engineer. A psychologist, noticing that I had no practical mechanical gift whatsoever, would have realised that the interest was a symbolic one. From the age of four to thirteen I had a series of passionate love-affairs with pictures of, to me, particularly attractive water-turbines, winding-engines, roller-crushers, etc., and I was never so emotionally happy as when I was underground.

The same psychologist would have also detected easily enough the complexes which were the cause of these affairs, but what was important for the future was not the neurotic cause but the fact that I should have chosen to express my conflicts in symbolic phantasy rather than in action or any other way. I cannot now look at anything without looking for its symbolic relation to something else.

I doubt if a person with both these passions, for the word and for the symbol, could become anything but a poet. At any rate, when at the age of sixteen a schoolfriend casually asked me one day if I wrote poetry, I, who had never written a line or even read one with pleasure, decided at that moment that poetry was my vocation, and though, when I look at my work, I am often filled with shame and disgust, I know that, however badly I may write, I should do anything else even worse, and that the only way in which I shall ever see anything clearly is through the word and the symbol.

My political education began at the age of seven when I was sent to a boarding school. Every English boy of the middle class spends five years as a member of a primitive tribe ruled by benevolent or malignant demons, and then another five years as a citizen of a totalitarian state.

For the first time I came into contact with adults outside the family circle and found them to be hairy monsters with terrifying voices and eccentric habits, completely irrational in their bouts of rage and good-humour, and, it seemed, with absolute power of life and death. Those who deep in the country at a safe distance from parents spend their lives teaching little boys, behave in a way which would get them locked up in ordinary society. When I read in a history book of King John gnawing the rush-mat in his rage, it did not surprise me in the least: that was just how the masters behaved.

So, despite all I have learnt since, my deepest feeling about politicians is that they are dangerous lunatics to be avoided when possible, and carefully humoured: people, above all, to whom one must never tell the truth.

In an English Public School there are no economic classes, but instead rigid class divisions based on seniority. The new boy starts as a member of the proletariat, menial and exploited, climbs by his third year into the respectable bourgeoisie, and by his fifth if he is politically reliable has become a responsible policeman or civil servant, honoured by the confidence of the Cabinet which may even sometimes ask his advice.

An admirable laboratory for the study of class-feeling and political ambition.

Such a State seems to be of the kind in which each individual has an equal chance to rise, and social reward depends solely upon merit. No doubt this is preferable to one in which social position is fixed, but it is certainly no Utopia.

I soon learnt to distinguish three kinds of citizens: the political, the apolitical, and the anti-political.

The political is one whose values coincide with the State values. In a school, he is athletic, a good mixer, ambitious but not too ambitious, moral but not too moral. He climbs the social ladder rapidly, becomes a competent, unimaginative administrator of laws the rightness of which he does not question, is approved of and happy.

The apolitical is one whose interests are not those of the State but do not clash with them, which usually means that they have nothing to do with people. Perhaps he is a photographer or a bird-watcher or a radio mechanic. As he is only anxious to be left alone, he performs his social duties well enough to keep out of trouble, and climbs slowly to a position of obscure security. He is the natural and sensible anarchist.

The anti-political is one whose interests and values clash with those of the State. He is not interested in athletics and shows it, his moral behaviour is incorrect, he deliberately sabotages. There are however two sub-species of the anti-political: the one who, were the values of society more to his taste, would become apolitical, and the one who in that case would become political. The latter is the true revolutionary: his anarchism is only a means to a political end. Whether he is a potential reformer or a potential tyrant depends on whether or no his personal ambition is combined with intellectual ability.

I also learnt by bitter experience to recognise yet another type, the ambitious anti-political who, ashamed of not being a social success, tries to disguise himself as a political. It is the type that becomes the police informer or the sadistic bureaucrat.

School life taught me that I was an anti-political. I wanted to be left alone, to write poetry, to choose my own friends and lead my own sex-life. The Enemy was and still is the politician, i.e., the person who wants to organise the lives of others and make them toe the line. I can recognise him instantly in any disguise, whether as a civil servant, a bishop, a schoolmaster, or a member of a political party, and I cannot meet him however casually without a feeling of fear and hatred and a longing to see him (or her, for the worst ones are women) publicly humiliated.

At first I thought I was a simple apolitical anarchist forced into being an anti-political saboteur by a peculiar environment, but when I became a schoolteacher I discovered that I had more political ambition, that I enjoyed influencing others, more than I had imagined.

When I left school, I became for a few years a rentier, which meant that through the power of an allowance from my parents, the State for me ceased to exist.

It is easy to criticise the rentier for being a parasite upon the labours of others, but no one who is honest would not change places with him if he could. A private income enables its fortunate possessor to be affectionate, tolerant, gay, to visit foreign countries and mix with all kinds of people, and such civilisation as we have is largely the creation of the rentier class. Many of its members are selfish and unpleasant, but if they do harm, it is usually only to themselves, and I think it probable that the percentage of unpleasant people is lower than in any other class.

The so-called ivory-tower artist is supposed to be typically a rentier. In actual fact the intelligent and sensitive rentier writer, owing to his greater freedom of movement and lack of economic pressure to produce hurried work, has a deeper and wider experience of life than his poorer colleague who is condemned to a fixed job.

I notice with alarm that those political systems which to a greater or lesser degree attempt to remove economic pressures and incentives, seem compelled to substitute for them social and governmental ones, to resemble in fact, and far too closely for my liking, an English public school. The politician will have succeeded only when and if he can create a society that preserves the freedom from social pressure of the rentier class while removing the economic injustice on which it rests.

I do not know if this is possible, but even if it is, I am doubtful if the politician can ever make it his aim, for to achieve it would be to destroy his profession, since social pressure is as much his medium as language is that of the poet.

At twenty-two, my allowance stopped, I ceased to be a rentier and became a master in a preparatory boarding school for the sons of the well-to-do. The primitive tribe ruled by demons which had terrified and fascinated the small boy, now appeared to the employee in a more prosaic light as a private business enterprise operating under a laissez-faire capitalism, a shop in which, as in all other kinds of shop, success depended upon our ability to be more attractive to customers than our competitors. For the first time in my life I became aware of the power of money, the technique of advertisement, and the gullibility of the public.

Politically a private school is an absolute dictatorship where the assistant staff play, as it were, Goering Roehm Goebbels Himmler to a headmaster Hitler. There are the same intrigues for favour, the same gossip campaigns, and from time to time the same purges. No one who is dependent upon the good-will of others (and even headmasters are dependent upon the good-will of the parents, just as a dictator has to cajole the masses) can avoid becoming a politician, and that involves not only many disingenuous compliances but a good deal of downright lying.

To be forced to be political is to be forced to lead a dual life. Perhaps this would not matter if one could consciously keep them apart and know which was the real one. But to succeed at anything, one must believe in it, at least for the time being, and only too often the false public life absorbs and destroys the genuine private life. Nearly all public men become booming old bores.

It is folly to imagine that one can live two lives, a public and a private one. No man can serve two masters.

In the struggle between the public life and the private life, the former will always win because it is the former that brings home the bacon.

To survive spiritually as a member of an organisation, one must possess some special talent which makes one so indispensable that almost any outrageous behaviour is pardoned. Prostitutes and opera singers survive revolutions.

There is one other way. The anarchist hidden in the heart of everyone, even the administrator, has made every society tolerate and even demand the existence of the Fool, the licensed buffoon critic. Witness the popularity of Charlie Chaplin and the Marx Brothers. But it only tolerates a very few, and furthermore, this enviable position is precarious. At any moment the Fool may go too far and be whipped.

Teaching is a political activity, a playing at God the political father, an attempt to create others in one's own likeness. Since every individual is unique, this self-reproduction is luckily impossible. Bad teachers do not know this, or fondly imagine that they are not trying to interfere.

A teacher soon discovers that there are only a few pupils whom he can help, many for whom he can do nothing except teach a few examination tricks, and a few to whom he can do nothing but harm. The children who interested me were either the backward, i.e., those who had not yet discovered their real nature, the bright with similar interests to my own, or those who, like myself at their age, were school-hating anarchists. To these last I tried, while encouraging their rebellion, to teach a technique of camouflage, of how to avoid martyrdom. For the political I could do nothing except try to undermine their faith.

A teacher who keeps in touch with his pupils after they have left school and gone into the world, is in a peculiarly advantageous position to study the effect on a person of his job.

Occupational diseases. A political problem of the first order. A large percentage of the occupations open to people to-day do them harm.

The Victorian father who said he would rather see his daughter dead than on the stage was less foolish than the modern parent who cheerfully allows his children to go into advertising or journalism.

His occupation dictates to a man what he does and selects his company. His actions and his company make the man. There is no such thing as an idealistic stockbroker.

One cannot walk through a mass-production factory and not feel that one is in Hell. And no amount of Workers' Control will alter that feeling.

There is a merciful mechanism in the human mind that prevents one from knowing how unhappy one is. One only realises it if the unhappiness passes, and then one wonders how on earth one was ever able to stand it. If the factory workers once got out of factory life for six months, there would be a revolution such as the world have never seen.

The Farmer—the Skilled Worker—the Scientist—the Cook—the Innkeeper—the Doctor—the Teacher—the Athlete—the Artist. Are there really any other occupations fit for human beings?

Judges, Policemen, Critics. These are the real Lower Orders, the low, sly lives, whom no decent person should receive in his house.

Lucky indeed the young man who is conscious of a vocation such as scientific research which is recognised and rewarded by society, and smooth his path to the Good Life.

Many careers are closed to me because I lack the necessary qualifications. I have no mathematical understanding; I can never become an engineer. But of those that remain open to me there are some which will employ my talents to make me more and more human, and others which, employing exactly the same talents, will make me more and more brutish. The Doctor and the Public Hangman require the same qualifications.

But, you will say, this is unrealistic bourgeois idealism. We must have policemen: only mass-production can bring motor-cars, refrigerators, electric razors within the pocket range of the workers. Perhaps you are right. Perhaps it is necessary that thousands should be martyred for the sake of that General Good which Blake called the plea of the hypocrite and the scoundrel. But neither I nor anyone I care for shall be among the martyrs if I can help it, and I find your complaisance disgusting.

Because the rich hypocritically denied the importance of material things, is no reason why Socialists should adopt the values of an American vacuum-cleaner salesman.

Distrust the man who says, 'First things first! First let us raise the material standard of living among the Masses, and then we will see what we can do about the spiritual problems.'
    In accomplishing the first without considering the second, he will have created an enormous industrial machine that cannot be altered without economic dislocation and ruin.

Crisis. Civilisation is in danger. Artists of the world unite. Ivory Tower. Escapist. Ostrich.
    Yes, the Crisis is serious enough, but we shall never master it, if we

rush blindly hither and thither in blind obedience to the frantic cries of panic.

Few of the artists who round about 1931 began to take up politics as an exciting new subject to write about, had the faintest idea what they were letting themselves in for. They have been carried along on a wave which is travelling too fast to let them think what they are doing or where they are going. But if they are neither to ruin themselves nor harm the political causes in which they believe, they must stop and consider their position again. Their follies of the last eight years will provide them with plenty of food for thought.

If one reviews the political activity of the world's intellectuals during the past eight years, if one counts up all the letters to the papers which they have signed, all the platforms on which they have spoken, all the congresses which they have attended, one is compelled to admit that their combined effect, apart from the money they have helped to raise for humanitarian purposes (and one must not belittle the value of that) has been nil. As far as the course of political events is concerned they might just as well have done nothing. As regards their own work, a few have profited, but how few.

That movement will fail: the intellectuals are supporting it.

The World does not pardon political failure. No one can succeed at anything unless he is not only passionately interested in it, but absolutely confident of success. Are you so interested, are you so confident? If not, then you must be deaf to the voices of duty and your friend, the cries of the fatherless and widows, for you cannot help them.

He who undertakes anything, thinking he is doing it out of a sense of duty, is deceiving himself and will ruin everything he touches.

You cannot give unless you also receive. What is it that you hope to receive from politics? excitement? experience? Be honest.

The artist qua artist is no reformer. Slums, war, disease are part of his material, and as such he loves them. The writers who, like Hemingway and Malraux, really profited as writers from the Spanish Civil War, and were perhaps really some practical use as well, had the time of their lives there.

The voice of the Tempter: 'Unless you take part in the class struggle, you cannot become a major writer.'

The value of a framework of general ideas, e.g., Catholicism or Marxism, in organising the writer's experience, varies from writer to writer. One can point to Dante as a proof of their value, and to Shakespeare as a proof of their unimportance. But the value of such a framework lies, not in its scientific truth, but in its immediate convenience. A scientific hypothesis is a provisional framework for organising future experience: an artistic Weltanschauung is a fixed framework chosen by the artist as the most suitable for the organisation of past experience.

To be useful to an artist a general idea must be capable of including the most contradictory experiences, and of the most subtle variations and ironic interpretations. The politician also finds a general idea useful, but for this purpose, which is to secure unanimity in action, subtlety and irony are drawbacks. The political virtues of an idea are simplicity and infallibility.

'How can one think to fill people with blind faith in the correctness of a doctrine if by continued changes in its outward construction one spreads uncertainty and doubt?' (Hitler)

The artist's maxim: 'Whoso generalises, is lost.'
The politician's maxim: 'Hard cases make bad law.'

We do not criticise the artists of the past for holding religious or political or scientific beliefs which differ from our own. We do so criticise contemporary artists, because we are perplexed by our age and, looking round desperately for the answers to our problems, blame all indiscriminately who fail to give them, forgetting that the artist is not pretending to give an answer to anything.

Artists, even when they appear to hold religious or political dogmas, do not mean the same thing by them as the organisers of their church or party. There is more in common between my view of life and that of Claudel than there is between Claudel's and that of the Bishop of Boston.

The Prolific and the Devourer: the Artist and the Politician. Let them realise that they are enemies, i.e., that each has a vision of the world which must remain incomprehensible to the other. But let them also realise that they are both necessary and complementary, and further, that there are good and bad politicians, good and bad artists, and that the good must learn to recognise and to respect the good.

On meeting a stranger, the artist asks himself: 'Do I like or dislike him?'
The politician asks: 'Is he a Democrat or a Republican?'
Writers who try, like D. H. Lawrence in *The Plumed Serpent*, to construct political systems of their own, invariably make fools of themselves because they construct them in terms of their own experience, and treat the modern State as if it were a tiny parish and politics as if it were an affair of personal relations, whereas modern politics is almost exclusively concerned with relations that are impersonal.
Thus Lawrence's dictum 'Anger is sometimes just, justice is never just', which is admirable advice to lovers, applied politically can only mean: 'Beat up those who disagree with you'.

One of the strongest appeals of Fascism lies in its pretence that the State is one Big Family: its insistence on Blood and Race is an attempt to hoodwink the man-in-the-street into thinking that political relations are personal. The man-in-the-street whose political education is confined to personal relations, and who is bewildered by and resentful of the impersonal complexity of modern industrial life, finds it hard to resist a movement which talks to him so comfortingly in personal terms. One of the best reasons I have for knowing that Fascism is bogus is that it is much too like the kinds of Utopias artists plan over café tables very late at night.

Works of art are created by individuals working alone. The relation between artist and public is one to which, in spite of every publisher's trick, laissez-faire economics really applies, for there is neither compulsion nor competition. In consequence artists, like peasant proprietors, are anarchists who hate the Government for whose interference they have no personal cause to see the necessity.

I have never yet met a Left-Wing intellectual for whom the real appeal of Communism did not lie in its romantic promise that with the triumph of Communism the State shall wither away.

Similarly, if one reads, say, the poems of Roy Campbell, it is not hard to see that to him Fascism means a heroic life of bull-fighting, motor-racing, mounting beautiful women, and striding bare-headed and square-shouldered magnificently towards the dawn.

The fate of Gide and Unamuno testify to what happens when the artistic dream is confronted with the political reality.

A desire for fresh experiences, humanitarian indignation at injustice and cruelty, are, even if short-sighted, at least honourable motives for taking to politics. But there are others, and few of us are quite innocent of them, which are less pretty.

In our political activities there is a larger element of old-fashioned social climbing than we care to admit. To receive social approval, to have one's work praised, even for the wrong reasons, is always gratifying, but it does not make for either artistic or political success. I have spoken too often myself about the need for popular art to feel comfortable when I hear this subject mentioned.

'Among the hardest workers in political parties will be found, like Rimbaud at Harar, those whom the God has deserted.' (Connolly)

Too often, alas, instead of cheerfully admitting the desertion, and betaking themselves to activities to which they are better fitted, they cannot leave the arts alone, but set up as critics. The bitterness of failure distorts everything they write.

There are many people, and they number some artists among them, who today seek in politics an escape from the unhappiness of their private lives, as once people sought refuge in the monastery and convent. Driven by envy and hatred they spread discomfort wherever they go and ruin everything they touch. A wise political party will have nothing to do with them.

But if artists are silly about politics, so are politicians about art. In the past it was sometimes possible for an individual of a secure ruling class to have the leisure to become a connoisseur as well as a politician. But not to-day.

Modern State patronage of the Arts. How awful it is. Think of the buildings in Washington. Think of those gigantic statues set up all over the world representing the Worker, the Triumph of Fascism, the Freedom of the Press. Think of the National Anthems.

Artists and politicians would get along better in a time of crisis like the present, if the latter would only realise that the political history of the world would have been the same if not a poem had been written, not a picture painted nor a bar of music composed.

If the criterion of art were its power to incite to action, Goebbels would be one of the greatest artists of all time.

Tolstoi, who, knowing that art makes nothing happen, scrapped it, is more to be respected than the Marxist critic who finds ingenious reasons for admitting the great artists of the past to the State Pantheon.
from an unpublished book, 1939

Appendices and Index

Appendix I

An Early Version of 'Paid on Both Sides'

This previously unpublished version of the charade was complete by
July (or possibly early August) 1928, and is printed from a typescript
which Auden gave Isherwood. It adapts some poems written earlier
(listed in their order of appearance in the text):

> The four sat on in the bare room . . . *December 1927*
> Some say that handsome raider, still at large . . . *Spring 1928*
> The summer quickens all . . . *April 1928*
> To-night the many come to mind . . . *January 1928*
> The Spring will come . . . *Spring 1928*
> Light strives with darkness, right with wrong . . . *January 1928*

The rest of the text probably dates from June and July 1928.

The final version, printed as Part I of the present edition, was ready
by the end of December 1928, when Auden sent it to Eliot as a
submission to *The Criterion*. (It was published there, after a year's
delay, in January 1930.) The final text takes over some of the early one,
and adds some poems written before December 1928:

> Not from this life, not from this life is any . . . *September 1928*
> Can speak of trouble, pressure on men . . . *October 1928*
> Always the following wind of history . . . *November 1928*
> The Spring unsettles sleeping partnerships . . . *August 1928*
> Because I'm come it does not mean to hold . . . *November 1928*
> Sometime sharers of the same house . . . *November 1928*
> There is the city . . . *November 1928*
> To throw away the key and walk away . . . *August 1928*

Other verse in the final text dates from December 1928.

PAID ON BOTH SIDES

A CHARADE

CHARACTERS

Lintzgarth
John Nower
William Nower
F′ Gunmen
F″

Nattrass
Aaron Shaw
Anne Shaw
FF′ Gunmen
FF″
Seth
Seth's Mother

The Midwife
The Announcer
The Guest
The Butler
People

The Chorus

DRESSES

John Nower.	Tails.
Anne Shaw.	Evening frock.
Aaron Shaw.	Plus-fours and a cap, preferably tweeds.
William and Gunmen.	Dinner jackets for the last scene. For the first they wear trench coats. William and FF′ wear homburgs, the others bowlers. F″ and FF′ have field glasses. All carry sportsman's guns.
Seth.	A straw panama with an elastic under the chin. Clothes tight and too small. A large revolver.
Seth's Mother.	An iron on one leg as for rickets. A stick.
Midwife.	Untidy. A blue apron. Soiled lavatory towels on arm.
Announcer.	The uniform of a cinema commissionaire. A megaphone.
Guest.	Dress suit with a yellow waistcoat. A paper cap out of a cracker.
Chorus.	Rugger things. The leader wears a scrum cap.

The Lintzgarth party will wear its handkerchiefs round their left arms.

Both sides are to be seated on chairs on the R and L of the stage until their disappearance in the last scene. *Exeunt* means going back to their chairs.

The stage is a plain one with a raised recess which has drawing curtains in front and back-cloth behind.

Chorus.   Often the man, alone shut, shall consider
            The killings in old winters, death of friends;
            Sitting with stranger shall expect no good.

            There was no food in the assaulted city;
            Men spoke at corners asking for news, saw
            Outside the watchfires of a stronger army.

            Spring came urging to ships, a casting off,
            But one would stay, vengeance not done: it seemed
            Doubtful to them that they should meet again.

            Fording in the cool of the day they rode
            To meet at crossroads when the year was over:
            Dead is Brody; such a man was Morl.

            I will say this not falsely; I have seen
            The just and the unjust die in the day,
            All, willing or not; and some were willing.

[*Enter midwife.*]

Midwife.   Sometimes we read a sign; cloud in the sky,
            The wet tracks of a hare, quicken the step,
            Promise the best day. But here no remedy
            Is to be thought of; no news but the new death,
            A Nower dragged out in the night, a Shaw
            Ambushed behind the wall. Blood on the ground
            Would welcome fighters: last night at Hammergill
            A boy was born fanged like a weasel. I am old,
            Will die this winter, but more than once shall hear
            The cry for help, the shooting round the house.

[*Exit C midwife. During her speech F″ enters R and squats in the centre of
the stage looking L through field glasses. Enter William and F′ R.*]

William.   Are you hurt?
F′.   Nothing much, sir; only a slight flesh wound. Did you get
            him, sir?
William.   On ledge above the gully, aimed at, seen moving, fell;
            looked down on, sprawls in the stream.
F′.   Good. He sniped poor Dick last Easter, riding to Flash.
William.   I have some lint and bandages in my haversack, and
            there's a spring here. I'll dress your arm.

[*Enter L FF′ and FF″.*]

FF′.   Did you find Tom's body?
FF″.   Yes, sir. It's lying in the Hangs.
FF′.   Which way did they go?
FF″.   Down there, sir.

[*F″ observes them and runs R.*]

411

F''.   There are twenty men from Nattrass, sir, over the gap,
              coming at once.
William.   Have they seen us?
F''.   Not yet.
William.   We must get out. You go round by the copse and make for
              the Barbon road. We'll follow the old tramway. Keep low
              and run like hell.

[*Exeunt R. FF' watches through field glasses.*]

FF'.   Yes. No. No. Yes. I can see them. They are making for the
              Barbon road. Go down and cut them off. There is good
              cover by the bridge. We've got them now.

[*A whistle. The back curtain draws showing John, Anne, Aaron and the
Announcer grouped. Both sides enter L and R.*]

Aaron.   There is a time for peace; too often we
              Have gone on cold marches, have taken life,
              Till wrongs are bred like flies; the dreamer wakes
              Beating a smooth door, footsteps behind, on the left
              The pointed finger, the unendurable drum,
              To hear of horses stolen or a house burned.
              Now this shall end with marriage as it ought:
              Love turns the wind, brings up the salt smell,
              Shadow of gulls on the road to the sea.
Announcer.   The engagement is announced of John Nower, eldest son
              of the late Mr. and Mrs. George Nower of Lintzgarth,
              Rookhope, and Anne Shaw, only daughter of the late Mr.
              and Mrs. Joseph Shaw of Nattrass, Garrigill.
All.   Hurrah.

[*Someone does a cartwheel across the stage. Exeunt L and R. Back
curtains close.*]

Chorus.   The four sat on in the bare room
              Together and the fire unlighted:
              One said, 'We played duets, she turned the page,
              More quavers on the other side.'

              'We parted in the waiting-room
              Scraping back chairs for the wrong train,'
              Said Two; and Three, 'All kinds of love
              Are obsolete or extremely rare.'

              'Yesterday', Four said, 'falling on me
              Through the glass pavement overhead
              The shadow of returning girls
              Proclaimed an insolent new Spring.'

              They said, the four distinguished men
              Who sat waiting the enemy,
              Saw closing upon the bare room

The weight of a whole winter night,
Beyond the reef high-breaking surf.

[*Back curtains draw. John and Anne alone. John blows on a grass held between the thumbs and listens.*]

John.   On Cautley where a peregrine has nested, iced heather
          hurt the knuckles. Fell on the ball near time, the rushing
          of forwards stopped. Good-bye now, he said, would open
          the swing doors. These I remember but not love till now.
          We cannot tell where we shall find it though we all look for
          it till we do, and what others tell us is no use to us.
          Some say that handsome raider, still at large,
          A terror to the Marches, in truth is love;
          And we must listen for such messengers
          To tell us daily, 'To-day a saint came blessing
          The huts', 'Seen lately in the provinces
          Reading behind a tree and people passing.'
          But love returns:
          At once all heads are turned this way, and love
          Calls order—silenced the angry sons—
          Steps forward, greets, repeats what he has heard
          And seen, feature for feature, word for word.

Anne.   Yes, love does not begin with meeting, nor end in parting.
          We are always in love though we know love only by
          moments, and perhaps it is only ourselves that we love.
          Mouth to mouth is no nearer. Now I see you, but if I shut
          my eyes I forget. Words fail us and truth eludes us and we
          cannot be satisfied. But I am glad this evening that we are
          together.
          Look. The flushed waterfall
          Sprouts from the hanging valley; but for us
          The silence is unused, and life and death
          Seem no more than the echo of an axe.

[*One of the chorus sings :*]

          The summer quickens all,
          Scatters its promises
          To you and me no less,
          Though neither can compel.

          The wish to last the year,
          The longest look to live,
          The urgent word survive
          The movement of the air.

          But loving now let none
          Think of divided days
          When we shall choose from ways,
          All of them evil, one:

413

Look on with stricter brows
The sacked and burning town,
The ice-sheet moving down,
The fall of an old house.

Anne.   John, I have a car waiting. Let's get away from here. We
           sleep in beds where men have died howling.
John.   You may be right, but we shall stay. No one can avoid to-
           morrow.
Anne.   To-morrow may change us.
John.   We only love what changes.
Anne.   To-night the many come to mind
           Sent forward in the thaw with anxious marrow,
           For such might now return with a bleak face,
           An image pause half-lighted in the door,
           A greater but not fortunate in all;
           Come home deprived of an astonishing end—
           Morgan's who took a clean death in the north
           Shouting against the wind, or Cousin Dodds'
           Passed out asleep in her chair, the snow falling.
           The too-loved clays, borne over by diverse drifts,
           Fallen upon the far side of all enjoyment,
           Unable to move closer, shall not speak
           Out of that grave stern on no capital fault:
           Enough to have lightly touched the unworthy thing.
John.   We live still.
Anne.   But what has become of the dead? They forget.
John.   These. Smilers, all who stand on promontories, slinkers,
           whisperers; deliberate approaches, echoes, time, prom-
           ises of mercy, what dreams or goes masked, embraces
           that fail, insufficient evidence, touches of the old wound.
           . . . But let us not think of things which we hope will be
           long in coming.

Chorus.   The Spring will come,
           Not hesitate for one employer who
           Though a fine day and every pulley running
           Would quick lie down; nor save the wanted one
           That wounded in escaping swam the lake
           Safe to the reeds, collapsed in shallow water.

           You have tasted good and what is it? For you
           Sick in the green plain, healed in the tundra, shall
           Turn westward back from your alone success
           Under a dwindling Alp to see your friends
           Cut down the wheat.
John.   It's getting cold, dear. Let's go in.

[*Exeunt C. Back curtains close.*]

Chorus.   For where are Basley who won the Ten,
           Dickon so tarted by the House,

Thomas who kept a sparrow-hawk?
The clock strikes, it is time to go,
The tongue ashamed, deceived by a shake of the hand.

[*Enter bridal party L, guests R. The chief guest comes forward and presents a bouquet to the bride.*]

Guest.   With gift in hand we come
From every neighbour farm
To celebrate in wine
The certain union of
A woman and a man;
And may their double love
Be shown to the stranger's eye
In a son's symmetry.
Now hate is swallowed down,
All anger put away;
The spirit comes to its own,
The beast to its play.

[*All clap. The guest addresses the audience.*]

Guest.   Will any lady be so kind as to oblige us with a dance? Thank you very much. This way, miss. What tune would you like?

[*Gramophone. Dance. Enter butler.*]

Butler.   Dinner is served

[*Aaron goes to the dancer.*]

Aaron.   You'll dine with us, of course.
People.   It will be a good year for them I think.
You don't mean that he—well you know what.
Rather off his form lately.
The vein is showing well in the Quarry Hazel.
One of Edward's friends.
Well it does seem to show.
Etc.

[*Exeunt except Seth and his Mother. This time they go right off.*]

Mother.   Seth.
Seth.   Yes, mother.
Mother.   William Nower is here.
Seth.   I know that. What do you want me to do?
Mother.   Kill him.
Seth.   I can't do that. There is peace now, besides he is our guest.
Mother.   Have you forgotten your brother's death at the Hangs? It is a nice thing for me to hear people saying that I have a coward for a son. I am thankful your father is not alive to see it.
Seth.   I am not afraid of anybody or anything; but I don't want to.

Mother.   I shall have to take steps.

Seth.   It shall be as you like. But I think that much will come of
            this, chiefly harm.

Mother.   I have thought of that.

[*Exeunt. A shot. More shots. Shouting.*]

People outside.   A trap. I might have known.
                     Take that damn you.
                     Open the window.
                     You swine.
                     Jimmy. O my God.
                     Etc.

[*Two of the Shaw party enter L and R.*]

FF'.   The Master's killed. Some of them got away: fetching
            help, will attack in an hour.

FF''.   See that all the doors are bolted.

[*Exeunt R and L. Back curtains draw. Anne with the dead.*]

Anne.   Now we have seen the story to its end.
            The hands that were to help will not be lifted,
            And bad followed by worse leaves us to tears,
            An empty bed, hope from less noble men.
            I had seen joy
            Received and given upon both sides for years,
            Now not.

Chorus.   Light strives with darkness, right with wrong:
            Man thinks to be called the fortunate,
            To bring home a wife, to live long.

            But he is defeated; let the son
            Sell the farm lest the mountain fall:
            His mother and her mother won.

            His fields are used up where the moles visit,
            The contours worn flat; if there show
            Passage for water he will miss it;

            Give up his breath, his woman, his team;
            No life to touch, though later there be
            Big fruit, eagles above the stream.

CURTAIN

416

Appendix II

Textual Notes

These notes, which are selective not comprehensive, call attention to some special problems in the text and to some of the more interesting revisions Auden made during the 1930's. They do not pretend to provide a full account of Auden's textual history.

The dates of composition appended to the poems in the main text, and in some instances discussed here, derive from a mixed bag of sources. During his early years Auden kept a series of notebooks in which he wrote out fair copies of his poems with the date and place of composition. Four of these notebooks survive: one from May 1927 to March 1929 (with many excisions); one from April 1929 to March 1930; then, following a lacuna extending to some point in August 1930, one from August 1930 to August 1932; and a final notebook beginning September 1932 and apparently complete until May 1933, with only intermittently dated poems after that date, extending through 1934. It is probably not accidental that Auden's careful preservation of the history of his work ended at the time of his 'Vision of Agape' in June 1933. Further dates come from copies of Auden's books that he annotated for friends. I have found two dated copies of *Poems* (one marked in the early 1940's, the other around 1965) and three such copies of *Another Time* (all from the early 1940's; I have made most use of the earliest). Although I have not been able to find a dated copy of *Look, Stranger!* or its American edition *On This Island* it seems likely that one exists.

Minor variations between the text of this edition and the original editions usually represent restorations of manuscript readings, or corrections Auden made in friends' copies. I have noted the more important editorial emendations below.

PART I: PAID ON BOTH SIDES

For the dates of composition of the separate poems in the charade, see the headnote to Appendix I.

PART II: POEMS 1927–1931

This section corresponds to the two published editions of *Poems*, and retains the book's dedicatory poem to Isherwood. Two poems are added as noted below. The poems here numbered I, II, IV, V, VI, XXV, and XXVII were omitted from the 1933 second edition of *Poems*; all other substantive variants between the two editions are noted below.

V : The crowing of the cock To a reviewer of the first edition who complained of the obscurity of this poem Auden defended himself, in a letter, with an explanation of part of the final stanza. Lines 1 and 2 of the stanza, he wrote, were 'a symptomatic movement towards emotional satisfaction'; and lines 3 and 4, 'The result of repression, the divided self, Puritan right and wrong'. The poem disappeared from the second edition.

XI : Again in conversations In the 1930 edition line 7 reads 'Than peace-time occupations.'

XVI : Watch any day The comma in line 7 is restored from a manuscript.

XXIV : It was Easter Auden compiled this poem, probably late in 1929 or early 1930, from four separate poems; the first of these was originally part of a verse-letter to Isherwood. In part 2, a manuscript has inverted commas around the last word of the first line of the sixth verse-paragraph, thus:

> Yet sometimes man look and say 'good'

In the 1930 edition there are two additional lines in section 3, following the eleventh line, which lacked its final comma:

> By opposite strivings for entropic peace,
> Retreat to lost home or advance to new,

as well as two additional verse paragraphs in section 4. Following 'Sinks now into a more terrible calm':

> This is the account of growing, of knowing;
> First difference from first innocence
> Is feeling cold and nothing there,
> Continual weeping and oversleeping,
> Is mocking, nudging, and defence of fear;
> Verbal fumbling and muscle mumbling,
> Imagination by mispronunciation:
> Sebaceous belly, swollen skull,
> Exchanging hats and calling dear
> Are rich and silly, poor and dull.

And following 'With organised fear, the articulated skeleton':

> For this is how it ends,
> The account of growing, the history of knowing,
> As more comatose and always in,
> Living together in wretched weather
> In a doorless room in a leaking house,
> Wrong friends at the wrong time.

XXV : Which of you waking early Auden said he tried to remove this poem from the 1930 edition of *Poems* before it was published. Shortly after the book appeared he described it in a letter as 'pompous trash'.

XXIX : Having abdicated Uncollected until 1966; reprinted here from *Cambridge Left*, Summer 1933, where it bore the title 'Interview'.

XXXI : Get there if you can The 1930 edition of *Poems* included two couplets whose omission in 1933 may appear to have been the result of a printer's error (there is a page break at this point in the 1933 text) but was in fact deliberate. The couplets followed the one beginning 'When we asked the way to Heaven';

Ours was a Renaissance, we were going to have lovely fun;
Quite prepared for any lark, until we found it wasn't done.

So we sit at table talking, pornographic as we dine,
Each the good old topic, meaningless as an electric sign.

XXXII : Pick a quarrel These short verses are selected and arranged from a larger number scattered among Auden's notebooks and letters; some were published in 1966, the remainder are printed here for the first time.

XXXV : Who will endure The date of this poem is conjectural. In one marked copy of *Poems* Auden dated it April 1929, which appears in the *Collected Poems* with a qualifying '?'. I now think this date is improbable, partly because the poem does not appear in Auden's notebook from the period, partly because Auden gave the place of composition as Wescoe, his parents' cottage in Cumberland, although Auden was in Berlin in April 1929. A later marked copy of *Poems* gives the date as Wescoe, September 1931; the place is plausible, but the date is unlikely, as Auden told Isherwood he would only use 'pre-Orators work' (i.e. before early 1931) in the 1933 edition of *Poems*, where the poem first appears; and the note to that edition says it adds poems written before 1931. Possibly Auden confused the year, writing 1931 for 1930; a date in the neighbourhood of August 1930 is quite plausible. The poem is similar in manner to 'Doom is dark' which almost certainly dates from this period, and, like the latter poem, it may have served as a chorus in the lost play *The Fronny*.

PART III: THE ORATORS

The present text restores cuts and changes made to avoid libel, obscenity or discourtesy at the time of publication. The dedicatory poem is from the original edition. I have made emendations to the Shetland place names.

Book I The Initiates: ii Argument In the first edition of *The Orators* the penultimate paragraph of this section includes a phrase dropped in the second edition, possibly inadvertently. At the end of the first sentence the word 'rashes' is followed by a comma and the phrase, 'the brakes burnt out'.

    iii Statement In part III, paragraph 3, line 5, the phrase 'The leader shall be a fear' is possibly incorrect; at least Auden thought so when he emended it for the 1967 American edition to 'shall be father'. The original reading is entirely plausible (see *OED*, 'Fear', *sb., 5d.*), but conceivably two words, roughly synonymous with 'preserver against', are missing immediately preceding 'fear'. No manuscript of the prose in *The Orators* survives.

Book II Journal of an Airman Two poems included here in the first edition of *The Orators* in 1932, but dropped in 1934, are reprinted in Appendix IV. Also dropped in 1934 was a prose paragraph, printed with three stars above and below it, immediately preceding the section headed 'Thursday':

A man occupies about 6 ft. in space and 70 years in time. Assuming the velocity of light to be 186,000 miles a second, then geography is just about a hundred thousand million times more important to him than history.

The separate poems in the Journal may be dated as follows: 'After the death of their proud master', September 1931; 'We have brought you, they said, a map of the country', September 1931; 'The airman's alphabet', June 1931; 'Last day but ten', ?1930; 'Beethameer, Beethameer', October 1931; 'There are some birds in these valleys', May 1931; no evidence survives for the remaining verses. The prose sections of the Journal seem to have been written between August and October 1931, and revised through November.

Book III Six Odes: iii What siren zooming In the fourth stanza, the reading 'blistered' in the third line is a restoration from a manuscript; the printed texts all read 'blistering'. The 1934 second edition omits the original stanza 13:

We shall rest without risk, neither ruler with rod
Nor spy with signals for secret agent
    Tasteless for fruit
    Too nervous for feat
    Spending all time
    With the Doc or the Jim.

v Though aware of our ranks The punctuation of stanza 10 is reconstructed from a manuscript.

vi Not, Father, further The convolutions of the last line of the second stanza are present in all manuscripts; I have not adopted Auden's later revision, 'We set our maddened foot.'

PART IV: POEMS 1931–1936

This section corresponds to *Look, Stranger!* (American edition *On This Island*) and retains its dedicatory poem. A few poems are added, as noted. The sequence of poems is partly conjectural.

I: For what as easy Uncollected until 1945; reprinted from *New Signatures* (1932).

III: Enter with him This apparently began its history as a separate poem, then found its way into *The Chase* and *The Dog Beneath the Skin*, whence this text derives.

IV: Now from my window-sill Originally the second part of a longer poem which appeared in *New Country* (1933) as 'A Happy New Year'; the first part is reprinted below in Appendix IV. The *New Country* text of the second part included three stanzas following stanza 10 of the present text:

Permit our town here to continue small,
What city's vast emotional cartel
Could our few acres satisfy
Or rival in intensity
The field of five or six, the English cell?

Preserve our Provost, Piermaster, Police,
Make swimming-bath and tennis-club a place
Where almost any summer day
A visitor is carried away
By unexpected beauty of speech or face.

Well you have watched before, but watch again
The Lindens, Ferntower, Westoe, and this pen,
Remember them especially please,
Throughout the coming year with these
Be very very patient, gentlemen.

V : The chimneys are smoking First published in *New Country* with, among other variants, the following in place of the first three lines of the present text:

Me, March, you do with your movements master and rock
With wing-whirl, whale-wallow, silent budding of cell;
Like a sea-god the communist orator lands at the pier:

And with the following stanza following the seventh:

What we do for each other now must be done alone:
It's not just another case of *laisser-faire*;
It is not necessity but our loving will
    That lets us out of our sight.
    But we are not together and we care;
    Not all the languages it masters
    Can make one heart secure
    Nor summer's moistures.

In stanza 5 of the present text the word 'one' in line 2 is a restoration; it appears in all surviving manuscripts, but not in the printed editions.

VII : The sun shines down The final stanza seems inadvertently to have been omitted in *Look, Stranger!* Auden wrote the version given here in a friend's copy, probably in 1939.

VIII : Brothers, who when the sirens roar The opening line of this poem has an eventful history. In Auden's notebook it reads 'All you who when the sirens roar'. When Auden sent the poem to Isherwood, and when he published it a month after composition with the title 'A Communist to Others', the first line became 'Comrades who when the sirens roar'. The present version first appeared in *Look, Stranger!* The earlier published texts also included six additional stanzas. After the present stanza 5:

    You're thinking us a nasty sight;
    Yes, we are poisoned, you are right,

> Not even clean;
> We do not know how to behave
> We are not beautiful or brave
> You would not pick our sort to save
> Your first fifteen.

After the present stanza 14 (text slightly emended):

> The worst employer's double-dealing
> Is better than their mental healing
> That would assist us.
> The world, they tell us, has no flaws
> There is no need to change the laws
> We're only not content because
> Jealous of sisters.

> Once masters struck with whips; of recent
> Years by being jolly decent
> For these are cuter
> Fostering the heart's self-adulation
> Would dissipate all irritation
> Making a weakened generation
> Completely neuter.

And after the present final stanza:

> Unhappy poet, you whose only
> Real emotion is feeling lonely
> When suns are setting;
> Who fled in horror from all these
> To islands in your private seas
> Where thoughts like castaways find ease
> In endless petting:

> You need us more than you suppose
> And you could help us if you chose.
> In any case
> We are not proud of being poor
> In that of which you claim a store:
> Return, be tender; or are we more
> Than you could face?

> Comrades to whom our thoughts return,
> Brothers for whom our bowels yearn
> When words are over;
> Remember that in each direction
> Love outside our own election
> Holds us in unseen connection:
> O trust that ever.

IX : I have a handsome profile Uncollected; reprinted from *New Verse*,
  January 1933.
XI : The Witnesses Uncollected in this form; reprinted from *The*

Listener, 12 July 1933. The poem first appears in Auden's notebook as an inset in a long, unfinished and unpublished dream-vision poem in Cantos which dates from September 1932 to around January 1933. Auden used a slightly cut version of the third part of the present text in *The Chase* and *The Dog Beneath the Skin*.

XII: The month was April Unpublished. Printed from a notebook, extensively emended by the editor. The apparent nonsense spoken by the Professor is made up from the conventional terms used in describing string figures.

XV: What was the weather Apparently written separately, and published in *Life and Letters*, May 1934, as 'Sermon by an Armament Manufacturer'; incorporated in *The Chase* and *The Dog Beneath the Skin*.

XVI: Here on the cropped grass When first published in *New Oxford Outlook*, November 1933, this poem included an additional stanza after the seventh:

> Guilty, I look towards the Nottinghamshire mines
> Where one we quoted in the restaurants received
> His first perceptions of the human flame
>   Smoky in us.
> We were to follow leaders; well, we have:
> The little runt with Chaplains and a stock
>   Or the loony airman.
> We were to trust our instincts; and they come
> Like corrupt clergymen filthy from their holes
> Deformed and imbecile, randy to shed
>   Real blood at last.

XVIII: Turn not towards me This sonnet sequence is based on a sequence Auden sent Isherwood late in 1934. That sequence included also 'The earth turns over' as the opening poem; 'To settle in this village' following the present sonnet 5; 'That night when joy began' following the present sonnet 6; and 'Easily, my dear' following the present sonnet 11. In the present text, although I have followed Auden's 1934 sequence for the remaining poems, I have used later texts where available. Sonnets 1 (the first line originally 'Sleep on beside me though I wake for you'), 3, and 4 are uncollected; they appeared in *New Verse*, October 1933, together with sonnet 12 and a further sonnet (which Auden seems later to have reworked into the song 'Seen when night was silent', printed elsewhere in the present edition):

> I see it often since you've been away:
> The island, the veranda, and the fruit;
> The tiny steamer breaking from the bay;
> The literary mornings with its hoot;
> Our ugly comic servant; and then you,
> Lovely and willing every afternoon.
> But find myself with my routine to do,
> And knowing that I shall forget you soon.

There is a wound and who shall staunch it up?
Deepening daily, discharging all the time
Power from love. Our loves, our lives, our hope,
Quack remedies that make a three-day's claim
And injure worse; of this we are quite sure,
And that this ends in death, but of no more.

Sonnet 2 appeared in *Rep* (magazine of the Croydon Repertory
Theatre), October 1934, but is uncollected. Sonnets 5 and 10 are
unpublished. Sonnet 6, which first appeared in *New Verse*, July
1933, was poem IV in the proofs of *Look Stranger!*; Auden replaced
it at the last minute, presumably because he wanted to re-use the last
two lines in 'Journey to Iceland'.

XXVI: The Creatures Written for Benjamin Britten's song cycle *Our
Hunting Fathers*.

XXIX: The soldier loves his rifle Uncollected; reprinted from *New
Verse*, April–May 1936. A few lines of this poem appear in *The
Ascent of F6*, but it was written separately, before Auden and
Isherwood began work on the play, and is part of a series of love
poems.

XXXIV: Stop all the clocks A revised version of a song written for *The
Ascent of F6*; the original text included references to characters in
the play.

XXXVI: Casino In stanza 3, line 4, although 'world' may seem a
misprint for 'worldly' (to which Auden later revised it) it is confirmed
both by a manuscript and by a recording Auden made of this poem in
1940.

PART V: LETTER TO LORD BYRON

In Part I, the fourth line of stanza 15 is taken from a proof copy. The
published text, altered to avoid libel, reads 'The help of Boots had
not been sought'.

PART VI: POEMS 1936–39

This section includes most of the poems in *Another Time*, with the
separable poems from *Letters from Iceland* and all the poems from
Journey to a War, and one uncollected and one unpublished poem.
The epigraph to the section is the dedicatory poem (to Benjamin
Britten) from *On the Frontier*. The sequence of poems in this section
is sometimes uncertain; I have inverted the order of the first two
poems, and the poems dated December 1938 are printed in the order
Auden gave them on first publication.

VII: Blues Uncollected; reprinted from *New Verse*, May 1937.

VIII: Spain 1937 Printed from the text in *Another Time*, probably
revised late in 1939. The revised text introduces three major
revisions. In place of the present stanza 17 the 1937 edition of the
poem printed these three stanzas:

On that arid square, that fragment nipped off from hot
Africa, soldered so crudely on to inventive Europe;
    On that tableland scored by rivers,
Our thoughts have bodies; the menacing shapes of our fever

Are precise and alive. For the fears which made us respond
To the medicine ad. and the brochure of winter cruises
    Have become invading battalions;
And our faces, the institute-face, the chain-store, the ruin

Are projecting their greed as the firing squad and the bomb.
Madrid is the heart. Our moments of tenderness blossom
    As the ambulance and the sandbag;
Our hours of friendship into a people's army.

After the present stanza 19, which ended with a comma, this omitted
stanza:

The beautiful roar of the chorus under the dome;
To-morrow the exchanging of tips on the breeding of terriers,
    The eager election of chairmen
By the sudden forest of hands. But to-day the struggle.

And in stanza 21, in 1937 the first line read 'deliberate' for 'inevitable'
and the second line read:

The conscious acceptance of guilt in the necessary murder;

Some readers have assumed that Auden changed this on reading
George Orwell's criticism of the poem in *Inside the Whale*, but
Auden first published his revision a month before Orwell published
his objection.

XVIII: Oxford The version published in *The Listener*, 9 February
1938, had an additional stanza immediately before the final stanza:

And all the lanes of his wish twist down to the grave:
The lovers poisoned in a fabulous embrace,
The doomed comrades riding to their known destruction,
    The flags like a third sex,
    And the music nobilmente.

XXIII: Passenger Shanty Unpublished; from a notebook containing
manuscripts of the poems written during the voyage out to China. In
the notebook the sequence of poems runs: 'Paris' [unpublished and
uninteresting]; 'The Sphinx' [an 80-line poem, ancestor of the
present text, in which the sphinx has 'A vast vacant accusing face /
Peering out towards America, denying Progress'; Auden later
corrected the geography]; 'The Voyage'; 'Liner' [i.e. 'The Ship'];
'Passenger Shanty' [the MS title is 'Passengers Shanty']; and 'The
Traveller'. The order in the present edition is that used in *Journey to
a War*, with the shanty added. The poems 'Macao' and 'Hongkong'
were not part of the sequence when *Journey to a War* was sent to the
publishers; Auden and Isherwood planned to write 'Hongkong-
Macao: A Dialogue' (or two dialogues?), but then rejected the idea,
and Auden wrote the two sonnets instead.

XXXIX : In Memory of W. B. Yeats When first published in *The New Republic*, 8 March 1939, the poem lacked the present part 2 (except for its first line, in third person not second, at the end of the fifth verse-paragraph); when the poem appeared in *The London Mercury* in April 1939, this section had been added.

PART VII: IN TIME OF WAR

The dedicatory poem is that used for *Journey to a War*. The date of the sequence is uncertain. Sonnet XII was written probably in 1936, when it was first published; XVIII was written in China in April 1938; the remaining sonnets were probably written in the late Summer and Autumn of 1938. The first half of the sequence was complete by September 1938, the second half and the Commentary by November. Some of the contents were shuffled in composition: in *The New Republic*, 7 December 1938, Auden published five sonnets of which two survived to the final version only in fragments. The two are:

Press Conference

Officials are always glad to give you information:
We smoke their cigarettes and wonder what they cost;
We're among friends, and warm; tea keeps away the frost;
The dead are news, and news a social occupation.
O lies are sometimes noble but each glib evasion
Seems only to confirm the Yellow River crossed;
And there are truths too gross for cakes and explanation,
Teruel fallen, gay Austria in a week-end lost.

Are there the truly human, or the just, or strong?
Not in this room, this world. Our small star warms to birth
Lives that will never grow. Snow whirls down from the North;
The quick new West is false; and prodigious but wrong
This passive flowerlike people who for so long
In the Eighteen Provinces have constructed the earth.

Air Raid

Our rays investigate the throbbing sky
Till, suddenly, within that brilliant field,
Alone and bad, their bombers are revealed,
The dread bacillus all identify,
The little natures that can make us cry:
Some sad request has sent them to do ill
Who are not sad, but execute the will
Of the intelligent and evil till they die.

Yet not in us the clear unerring blood:
Our fit breed germs, our greatest are not free.

Defective and remote in history
Our average, our talent and our good.
The cured years and the well are yet to be;
Happy their wish and mild to flower and flood.

This second sonnet is an ancestor of Sonnet XIV, which also has another, intermediate ancestor. A typescript of the entire sequence, evidently later than the two sonnets printed above, conforms to the published text in *Journey to a War*, except in the first eight lines of Sonnet XIV. In the typescript these lines read:

It exists, identified like a bacillus;
The searchlights focus on it in the sky;
Those little natures can make cities cry;
There is a power that has the will to kill us.

Resist then; be destructive and as strong:
All killing hurts, but it will always matter
Whose dust the twelve winds lift and scatter;
All people are not equal; some are wrong.

The remaining six lines conform to the present text.

Early in January 1939 Auden returned the proofs of the poems to Faber with a letter which said in part, 'I must say I am a little surprised at the anxiety of your reader to rewrite some of them, but as he seems to be interested in prosody, you might tell him from me that beats and feet are not the same thing.' That proofreader may have decided on the reading 'boist'rous' in the published text of Sonnet XVII, line 11; the typescript reads simply 'boistrous', and as the printed reading is uncharacteristic of Auden, I have spelled the word out in the present text.

In Sonnet XXV the typescript lacks the word 'And' in line 12; its presence in the printed edition *may* be an error.

PART VIII: THEATRE, FILM, RADIO

I: Drama began as the act This manifesto was published in the programme of the Group Theatre production of *Sweeney Agonistes* and *The Dance of Death*, 1 October 1935, as one of a series of theatre-programme statements by various hands under the general title 'I Want the Theatre to Be . . .'

II: Choruses and Songs These are printed in approximate order of composition. Because the plays by Auden alone and in collaboration with Isherwood were constantly rewritten and adapted for stage purposes, I have felt free to choose a version earlier than the latest in some instances.

1 You who have come Concluding speech of *The Enemies of a Bishop*; unpublished.

2 You who return to-night Originally in *The Fronny*, then in *The Chase* and *The Dog Beneath the Skin*, whence this text derives. In 1931 Auden put another version of the poem to use as an epithalamion for a friend.

427

3 Alice is gone The full text is from a notebook; the first two stanzas found their way into *The Chase* and *The Dog Beneath the Skin.*

4 You were a great Cunarder From *The Dance of Death*; possibly written separately.

5 Hail the strange electric writing From *The Dance of Death*; the text here is based in part on copies of the play marked by members of the cast, and in part on an undated MS.

6 Seen when night Possibly rewritten from a sonnet quoted in the note to Part IV, Poem XVIII, above. This song appears in *The Chase* and *The Dog Beneath the Skin.*

7 Love, loath to enter A torso of a longer and duller poem, possibly written separately, which appeared in *New Oxford Outlook*, May 1934. This fragment is all that survived into *The Chase* and *The Dog Beneath the Skin.*

8 A beastly devil came last night From *The Chase*, where it perhaps adapts an earlier version with a name other than Olive. Partly rewritten as the song 'Michael, you shall be renowned' in *The Ascent of F6.* The present version is unpublished.

9 You with shooting-sticks From *The Chase* and *The Dog Beneath the Skin.*

10 So under the local images Partly from *The Chase*, partly written for *The Dog Beneath the Skin* (the source of this text).

11 The Summer holds Written for *The Dog Beneath the Skin.*

12 Happy the hare Written for *The Dog Beneath the Skin.*

13 Now through night's Apparently written for *The Dog Beneath the Skin.*

14 The General Public has no notion Written for *The Dog Beneath the Skin*; sung by the two journalists.

15 Evening. A slick and unctuous Time From *The Ascent of F6.*

16 The chimney sweepers From *The Ascent of F6.*

17 Death like his From *The Ascent of F6.*

18 Let the eye of the traveller From *The Ascent of F6*

19 At last the secret is out From *The Ascent of F6*, and although apparently separable, written for the play.

20 O quick and furtive From an unpublished early draft of Act II, Scene I of *On the Frontier.*

21 Ben was a four foot seven Wop From *On the Frontier.*

22 The biscuits are hard From *On the Frontier.*

23 Roman Wall Blues From the radio script *Hadrian's Wall.*

III : Three Fragments for Films Partly based on a manuscript with this title in the University of Texas Library. Evidently Auden submitted this manuscript to *New Writing*, but withdrew it when he decided to use a few of its lines in *The Ascent of F6.*

2 Night Mail This is an eclectic text, made up from an early working version in the Texas manuscript, and combined with the final text used in the film. The two versions overlap; the final text may be found in *Collected Poems*; the first version consists of the following lines of the present text: 1–20, 23–24, 27–43, 48–49, 52–end.

3 Negroes The project for this film was abandoned, although a film based on it, titled *God's Chillun*, was made some years after Auden left the G.P.O. Film Unit; this latter film seems never to have been released. The present text is excerpted from the Texas manuscript. Another version of the final chorus became part of the final scene of *The Ascent of F6*.

PART IX: ESSAYS AND REVIEWS

For the principles on which this selection is based, see the preface. I have omitted Auden's review of Christopher Caudwell's *Illusion and Reality* (*New Verse*, May 1937) because it consists almost entirely of quotation and summary, but the review's opening and closing are of interest. It begins: 'We have waited a long time for a Marxist book on the aesthetics of poetry. *Axel's Castle* was a beginning but it was about individual matters, not fundamentals. Now at last Mr. Caudwell has given us such a book.' And it ends: 'I shall not attempt to criticise *Illusion and Reality* firstly because I am not competent to do so, and secondly because I agree with it. . . . This is the most important book on poetry since the books of Dr. Richards, and, in my opinion, provides a more satisfactory answer to the many problems which poetry raises.'

I: Journal entries These are compiled and arranged from two notebooks, both dating from 1929. The first group of entries (down to the first three stars) seem to be the latest; they derive from a notebook in the British Library. The remaining entries are from a journal Auden kept during the spring and summer of 1929, found among his papers at his death (this is the only one of his journals—he seems to have kept another around 1939—to have survived). I have followed Auden's later practice in abridging, re-arranging and editing these entries. Groups of entries between stars appear together and in sequence in the notebooks. Otherwise the arrangement is editorial.

V: Problems of Education In the third sentence 'valuable' is an emendation for 'vulnerable'.

VI: How to Be Masters of the Machine Published under the title 'A Poet tells us how to be masters of the machine'.

X: The Liberal Fascist This is the title in the manuscript; for consistency with other essays in the collection *The Old School*, the published title was 'Honour'.

XV: Review of 'Documentary Film' Published anonymously. Attributed to Auden in *The Listener*'s payment records and in a reply printed in *World Film News*, April 1936. The review was written at about the time Auden left the G.P.O. Film Unit.

XXIII A revised version of an essay published in *The Nation* (New York), 24 December 1938.

XXIV: Educational Theory The second chapter, 'Theory', of a pamphlet by Auden and T. C. Worsley, *Education To-day—and To-morrow*; this chapter was written almost entirely by Auden, the other two almost entirely by Worsley.

XXVII: The Prolific and the Devourer This is the title of a book of prose written probably in the Spring or Summer of 1939, and never published during Auden's lifetime. Only the first part is printed here; the remaining three parts, more discursive and less aphoristic, represent early efforts to work out the religious and political ideas later developed in 'New Year Letter'. Auden may have written the book on a tentative commission from his American publisher (although no record of such a commission survives), but he abandoned it when, partly on the advice of friends, he grew dissatisfied with its mandarin style. He also prepared and then abandoned a book of literary essays, based mostly on his reviews. This latter book, possibly titled *Pothooks and Hangers*, seems entirely lost.

This text of *The Prolific and the Devourer* is based on Auden's draft typescript, now in the University of Texas Library.

Appendix III

The Contents of Auden's Books of Poems
1928–1940

POEMS
(Privately printed by Stephen Spender, 1928)

I	*a* The sprinkler on the lawn
	b Bones wrenched, weak whimper, lids wrinkled, first dazzle known
	c We saw in Spring
	d This peace can last no longer than the storm
	e 'Buzzards' I heard you say
	f Consider if you will how lovers stand
	g Amoeba in the running water
	h Upon the ridge the mill-sails glow
II	I chose this lean country
III	No trenchant parting this
IV	Suppose they met, the inevitable procedure
V	On the frontier at dawn getting down
VI	Who stands, the crux left of the watershed
VII	Nor was that final, for about that time
VIII	The crowing of the cock
IX	Because sap fell away
X	The mind to body spoke the whole night through
XI	From the very first coming down
XII	The four sat on in the bare room[1]
XIII	To-night when a full storm surrounds the house[1,2]
XIV	Night [*for* Light] strives with darkness, right with wrong[1,2]
XV	Control of the Passes was, he saw, the key
XVI	Taller to-day, we remember similar evenings
XVII	The spring will come[1,2]
XXVIII	The summer quickens grass[1,2]
XIX	Some say that handsome raider still at large[1,2]
XX	To throw away the key and walk away[2]

---

[1] A version of this poem is included in the early text of 'Paid on Both Sides' (see Appendix I).

[2] A version of this poem is included in the final text of 'Paid on Both Sides'.

POEMS
(Faber & Faber, 1930)

To Christopher Isherwood : Let us honour if we can
Paid on Both Sides

POEMS
(Second edition, Faber & Faber, 1933; reprinted in *Poems*, Random House, 1934)

[The following seven poems replace the corresponding poems in the 1930 edition:]

432

LOOK, STRANGER!
(Faber & Faber, 1936; as *On This Island*, Random House, 1937)

ANOTHER TIME
(Faber & Faber, Random House, 1940)

To Chester Kallman : Every eye must weep alone

[3] Not in this edition; see *Collected Poems.*

Appendix IV

Uncollected Poems 1924–1942

This appendix reprints the separable poems that Auden published in book form but did not preserve for his *Collected Poems* and which do not fall within the boundaries of the main text of the present edition. These poems divide into four groups:

I. The poems in the privately printed 1928 pamphlet *Poems* that did not survive into the published 1930 edition, or were not incorporated into one of the two versions of 'Paid on Both Sides'.

II. Two poems included in 'Journal of an Airman' in the 1932 first edition of *The Orators* but dropped from the 1934 edition.

III. The first part of 'A Happy New Year', published only in the anthology *New Country* (1933), where it was followed by a second part which Auden reprinted separately ('Now from my window-sill I watch the night') and which appears in Part IV of the present volume.

IV. Poems of 1939–42 written after Auden's arrival in America and printed neither elsewhere in this edition nor in the *Collected Poems*. In this group, poems 1 and 2 are from *Another Time*, and 3 is the dedicatory poem of that book; 4 is from the libretto *Paul Bunyan*, and is printed as it appeared in the 1945 *Collected Poetry*; 5 is the prologue to *The Double Man* (published in Britain as *New Year Letter*); 6 is one of about twenty uncollected verses from the notes to 'New Year Letter', and the only one which Auden printed separately in a periodical; 7 and 8 are reprinted from the 1945 *Collected Poetry*.

The texts are taken from the first editions in book form, with revisions Auden marked in friends' copies at the time of publication.

The poems that remain unreprinted from Auden's books are either collaborations or parts of longer works, and are best read in their original context. These include: verse from the plays and libretti; two verse letters and the 'Last Will and Testament' written in collaboration with Louis MacNeice for *Letters from Iceland*; and the remaining uncollected verse scattered among the notes to 'New Year Letter'.

I

(*a*)

The sprinkler on the lawn
Weaves a cool vertigo, and stumps are drawn;
The last boy vanishes,
A blazer half-on, through the rigid trees.

? May 1927

(*b*)

[This is the same as poem I in Part II of the present edition.]

(*c*)

We saw in Spring
The frozen buzzard
Flipped down the weir and carried out to sea.
Before the trees threw shadows down in challenge
To snoring midges.
Before the Autumn came
To focus stars more sharply in the sky
In Spring we saw
The bulb pillow
Raising the skull,
Thrusting a crocus through clenched teeth.

? August 1926

(*d*)

This peace can last no longer than the storm
Which started it; the shower wet and warm,
The careless striding through the clinging grass
Perceiving nothing, these will surely pass
When heart and ear-drums are no longer dinned
By shouting air. As surely as the wind
Will bring a lark song from the cloud, not rain,
Shall I know the meaning of lust again;
Nor sunshine on the weir's unconscious roar
Can change whatever I might be before.
I know it, yet for this brief hour or so
I am content, unthinking and aglow;
Made one with horses and with workmen, all
Who seek for shelter by a dripping wall,
Or labour in the fields with mist and cloud
And slant rain hiding them as in a shroud.

? 1925

'Buzzards' I heard you say,
And both of us stood still
As they swept down the sky
    Behind the hill.

I, though a watcher too,
Saw little where they sped.
Who could have dreamed that you
    Would turn your head?

? October 1924

(f)

Consider if you will how lovers stand
In brief adherence, straining to preserve
Too long the suction of good-bye: others,
Less clinically-minded, will admire
An evening like a coloured photograph,
A music stultified across the water.
The desert opens here, and if, though we
Have ligatured the ends of a farewell,
Sporadic heartburn show in evidence
Of love uneconomically slain,
It is for the last time, the last look back,
The heel upon the finishing blade of grass,
To dazzling cities of the plain where lust
Threatened a sinister rod, and we shall turn
To our study of stones, to split Eve's apple,
Absorbed, content if we can say 'because':
Unanswerable like any other pedant,
Like Solomon and Sheba, wrong for years.

May 1927

(g)

Amoeba in the running water
Lives afresh in son and daughter.
'The sword above the valley'
Said the Worm to the Penny.

? May 1927

(h)

Upon the ridge the mill-sails glow
Irrelevant to Quixote now.

The dew-wet fur of the dead hare
Smokes as light sparkles on the snare.

The grass looks upward at the flower
Through lenses of a fallen shower.

Wind chills the wet uplifted thumb.
'Change seats. The King's come.

'He has the key.' But Chanticleer
Questions the Platonic year.

Snotty Eulenspiegel stands
To snook and smirk behind the hands.

Gargantua—the race is run—
Kicks the view over, pisses at the sun.

? May 1927

2

I chose this lean country
For seven-day content,
To satisfy the want
Of eye and ear, to see
The slow fastidious line
That disciplines the fell,
A curlew's creaking call
From angles unforeseen,
The drumming of a snipe,
Surprise where driven sleet
Had scalded to the bone
And streams were acrid yet
To an unaccustomed lip.

So stepping yesterday
To climb a crooked valley,
I scrambled in a hurry
To twist the bend and see
Sheds crumbling stone by stone,
The awkward waterwheel
Of a deserted mine;
And sitting by the fall
Spoke with a poet there
Of Margaret the brazen leech,
And that severe Christopher,
Of such and such and such
Till talk tripped over love,
And both dropped silent in
The contemplation of

A singular vision
And sceptical beholder,
While a defiant bird
Fell down and scolding stood
Upon a sun-white boulder.

Last night, sucked giddy down
The funnel of my dream,
I saw myself within
A buried engine-room.
Dynamos, boilers, lay
In tickling silence, I
Gripping an oily rail,
Talked feverishly to one
Who puckered mouth and brow
In ecstasy of pain,
'I know, I know, I know'
And reached his hand for mine.

Now in a brown study
At the water-logged quarry,
I think how everyman
Shall strain and be undone,
Sit, querulous and sallow
Under the abject willow,
Turning a stoic shoulder
On a Saint Martin's summer,
Till death shall sponge away
The idiotic sun,
And lead this people to
A mildewed dormitory.
But as I see them go,
A blackbird's sudden scurry
Lets broken treetwigs fall
To shake the torpid pool;
And breaking from the copse,
I climb the hill, my corpse
Already wept, and pass
Alive into the house.

? June 1927

3

On the frontier at dawn getting down,
Hot eyes were soothed with swallows: ploughs began
Upon the stunted ridge behind the town,
And bridles flashed. In the dog days she ran
Indoors to read her letter. He in love,
Too curious for the East, stiffens to a tower;
The jaw-bone juts from the ice; wisdom of
The cooled brain in an irreverent hour.

At the half-close the muted violin
Put cloth and glasses by; the hour deferred
Peculiar idols nodded. Miles away
A horse neighed in the half-light, and a bird
Cried loudly over and over again
Upon the natural ending of a day.

July 1927

4

Because sap fell away
Before cold's night attack, we see
A harried vegetation.
Upon our failure come
Down to the lower changing-room,
Honours on pegs, cast humours, we sit lax,
In close ungenerous intimacy,
Remember
Falling in slush, shaking hands
With a snub-nosed winner;
Open a random locker, sniff with distaste
At a mouldy passion.

Love, is this love, that notable forked-one,
Riding away from the farm, the ill word said,
Fought at the frozen dam? Who prophesied
Such lethal factors, understood
The indolent ulcer? Brought in now,
Love lies at surgical extremity;
Gauze pressed over the mouth, a breathed surrender.

November 1927

5

The mind to body spoke the whole night through:
'Often, equipped and early, you
Traced figures in the dust, eager
To start, but on the edge of snow
As often then refused me further;
Proffered a real object, fresh,
Constant to every loyal wish.

'Never to the Dark Tower we rode,
But, turning on the hill crest, heard,
Catching the breath for the applause,
A tolling disillusioned bell
The leaking of an hour-glass,
Till lightning loosed the frantic skull.

441

'Granted that in a garden once
And a wind blowing, a voice,
Beyond the wall, unbroken, hid
The jabber of the blood, and bred
No fever.'

Cocks crew, and sleeping men turned over.
Rain fell for miles; ghosts went away.
The jaw, long dropped, stopped at reply.

? November 1927

II · FROM THE 1932 EDITION OF 'THE ORATORS'

[Among the passages dropped in the 1934 second edition were two
pems originally printed in 'Journal of an Airman'. The first of these
followed the section headed '*The Enemy as Observer*' and immediately
preceded the section beginning 'We leave to-morrow'; the second
followed the passage headed '*After Victory*' and preceded the section
beginning 'Very little progress this year.' See also Appendix II.]

I

Well, Milder, if that's the way you're feeling—
To give up coughing, honesty and stealing,
To be contented and to look it
To the bluejacket plainness of the wicked.

We have blackheads for squeezing, the cat for torture,
No need on our part for further procedure
To legalise the windmill gesture
Exclude the kitchen from the greenhouse nature.

Acting suspiciously as road-repairers,
Hard riding—drinking—swearing as the devil,
Is not enjoyment to another level;
We symbolise what we appear as.

And here is truly where we arrive at
Supplying all in the way of watches,
Raised little footpaths, waterproof matches,
Plenty of beauty and nothing private:

And courage is courage to those who try it,
To fish the nuisance from the public fountain
And lay it sopping on the hard dry mountain
But technical skill and pleased to be it.

And love calls love with a loving letter,
Remains to tea, has never felt better;

And death avoids the settled wager
With the black clergyman and the decorated major.

February 1931

2

The draw was at five. Did you see the result?
It was up last night in the post-office window.
Abel from Hackwood Lodge, and young Spinney—
I must say I'm glad about him.
He's always so nice and polite when he comes to the door,
Not like that whipper-snapper Fleming.
He'll look the part too. They say his father's so proud.
Can you think of anything else I might have forgotten?
There's cook. I've seen her about the fast.
I'm packing off Helen and Vi. to their grannie's.
I shall hide the house key under the mat.
That ought to be safe, don't you think?
I hope the weather will last; it's looking too clear.
Though the glass is rising it's not a good sign
To be able to see to the wreck like this.
You'll call for me about eight? Good-bye.
And we'll walk up together. The silence begins at nine.

More than before, O steel the will,
Though shops are open, traffic regular,
The piston plunging in the oily cylinder,
The flywheel turning in the sunny room.
Be calmer still,
Keep perfect to the last the long-kept vow,
In very little time from now
That hour is come.

Remember his words 'You must love your life'.
You mustn't believe the fools when they tell you
'The bankers have caused you sorrow, destroy them',
Or 'Strengthen the power of the king and be saved'.
We live as before, apart in our families,
The girl considering her dress, the golfer his swing,
The professors discussing the date of a battle.
The stranger here sees nothing out of the common,
He would scarcely notice our preparations.
The two dance leaders chosen quietly by lot.
The faggots for the beacon carted this morning
Up the Highwayman's Road, the cases of rockets . . .
We have done as he said; we have not forgotten his promise,
'Your desire shall be granted when the time is perfect,
Let the moon be a sign to your eyes of the trust,
Assemble all of you when the moon is full,
The power shall fill you, the touch be restored.'

443

The musicians are having their final rehearsal;
The town seems stiller, our greetings quieter than usual.
O charged-to-the-full-in-secret slow-beating heart,
To-night is full-moon.

November 1931

III · A HAPPY NEW YEAR
(TO GERALD HEARD)

(PART I)

The third week in December frost came at last.
Into a windless morning I stepped and passed
Outside the windows of untidy rooms
Where boys were puzzled by exams,
The ridges cloudless and the day my own.
The Clyde untilted as I climbed;
Boom of a distant siren skimmed
Over the water like a well-shied stone.

Motion reversed, blood to the day had turned,
For justice rather than for love was burned,
Withdrawn from loins into a quickened mind
Its spiritual use to find.
The old old arguments were still as dangerous
As I walked by myself in the sun;
Hands miles away were laid on iron
That rested lately in the dark on us.

No strange sound laid my echo on the road
And when where two little lanes branched off I stood,
On either side the moorland grew away,
Luminous all Glen Fruin lay
And sky was silent as an unstruck bell.
Loch Lomond was below, I saw
Boats on a bay like toys on floor;
Scotland on every quarter touched me still.

But suddenly the unnoticed wire above
Began invisibly to move,
That secret-bearing sensitive taut line
Which south into alluvial England ran;
And though its resonant vibrations were
Unorganised and formed no word,
A voice spoke straightway and was heard
Within the labyrinth of the inner ear.

'Look not at sky through the forelegs of mares,
    The age of migrations is over and gone,
Nor behead a diviner when the rains are scarce;

You who at midnight have whispered to one
　　Sworn comrade your secret distrust of the sun.
I show you a cooled soil, fertile for grain,
A land of rivers, a maternal plain.

'Look down, look down at your promised land:
　　There's Murgatroyd's Folly and Waster's Well,
The dark peninsula shaped like a hand
　　Where the long-headed dance-loving miners dwell;
　　To your left is the quarry where the lovers fell;
The Marsh of Five Churches lies to your right
Where the parsons are credited with powers of flight.

'There on the golf course are the tiny red flags,
　　There's tea being laid on the vicarage lawn,
There's the only factory for carpet bags.
　　Can you hear the echo of the hunting horn?
　　Do you see the one passenger waiting forlorn
At the halt for the narrow-gauge motor train?
Take it. It's yours. Descend to your plain.'

The voice ceased but the wire droned louder still
And more insistent on the sterile hill.
The landscape moved, from East and West I saw
Converging quickly on that moor
The English in all sorts and sizes come
Like an army recruited there
From lake and bush and stone and air
By the unbearable excitement of a drum.

From the East out of Luss a force would appear;
　　Though a road-bend hid them I heard their song
From the West whence I came, I could see and hear
　　A second contingent march singing along.
　　From the distance I guessed them to be thousands strong.
I knew they would presently meet where I stood
Waiting with my back to a little fir wood.

Hugging the curve of the road from the right,
　　His open exhaust like a maxim gun,
A helmeted rider swept into sight,
　　Looked to the left as he passed on and then
　　Skidded towards me with a telemark turn,
Pushed up the triplex goggles he wore
And shut down the throttle on his Matchless-Four.

Anxiously he asked 'Can you tell me the time?'
　　When I showed him my wrist-watch, he said with a smile
'We never changed down the whole of the climb;
　　In fifty-one secs we have covered the mile;
　　Sporty and speedy is the British style;

445

Tempo. Tempo. . . .' I caught no more:
His back wheel juddered; he was off with a roar.

From the left in bathing-dresses, a troupe
    Of boys and girls came laughing and skipping
Hand in hand, a most graceful group
    If only they hadn't had to keep stopping
    Because their drawers were constantly slipping.
They looked rather chilly, but they sat down to rest
For a band was arriving now from the West.

In corduroy trousers and seedy black coats
    A dozen performers had managed to come
With red flannel mufflers pinned at their throats
    Five cornets, three trombones, an harmonium
    A harp, an accordion and a great big drum.
The choir who followed them on ladies' bikes
Were singing a hymn by John Bacchus Dykes.

But just as their drawn-out Amen ceased
    Came a second-hand Thorneycroft lorry bringing
Four saxophone boys to play up the East:
    'Rhythm. Spring. Waggle that thing
    Do Do De O' they were singing.
Each wore tails, had a mascot cat,
And perched on each head was a celluloid hat.

And now at last the main bodies came
    Glancing at each other in suspicious fear.
When eyes met they darted sideways in shame
    Or braved it out in an awkward stare.
    The equipment was curious they had found to wear.
Silk stockings, cigar boxes, covers of sumps,
Newspapers, ham-frills, and bicycle-pumps.

So many bodies looking ashamed,
    So many eyes which expected worse,
So many legs too lanky or lamed,
    So many mouths like a missioner's purse,
    So many cases which needed a nurse,
So many dreading the Arm of the Law
Were never seen in one place before.

So much stammering over easy words,
    So much laughter spasmodic and queer,
So much speech that resembled a bird's,
    So much drawling concealing a fear,
    So much effort to sound sincere,
So much talk which was aimed at the floor
Was never heard in one place before.

A Bristol Fighter which flew overhead
    Swooped down as the pilot leaned out from his seat.
'It's Lawrence of Arabia,' somebody said
    And a typist tittered 'Isn't he sweet!'
    He threw down a paper which fell at my feet:
'I've a devil,' it ran, 'I'm ordered elsewhere.
God what a crew! But your best are there.'

An order was issued to silence the bands:
    Down the long columns ran the cry 'Fall out.'
With spotless wash-leather gloves in their hands
    The section commanders swaggered about,
    And here were the generals, there could be no doubt.
Covered with medals, with flies in their caps,
They unfolded a table and fished out the maps.

Doctors attended behind each chair,
    Behind the men was Sir Thomas Horder,
Behind the women Dr. Norman Haire;
    Maisie Gay and Sir Harry Lauder
    Were told off to keep the ranks in order;
Ramsay MacDonald was rubbing his seat:
At last he'd been invited to a Leicestershire Meet.

Thomas was only demanding fair play,
    Baldwin was wiping his nose on his pipe;
Snowden was for making the landlord pay;
    Limping but keeping a stiff upper lip
    Churchill was speaking of a battleship:
It was some little time before I had guessed
He wasn't describing a woman's breast.

'Just let them wait till the dark nights come,'
    A voice whispered suddenly close at my side.
'Walk ahead till I poke you twice with my thumb
    And don't look round. We shall have to hide.
    Remember how Lord Kitchener died.
A certain person whom I shall not name
Would shoot if he knew that we knew his game.

'Now slip through the gate but don't make a noise.
    Look out. They're after us. Run.' I ran—
Behind the wall I looked at the voice;
    Mopping his hair stood a fat little man.
    'When I saw the semaphore I guessed their plan.'
With field-glasses first he looked all round,
Then plugged a field telephone into the ground.

'In the headmaster's study yesterday morning
    An interesting conversation took place.
I mention the matter just as a warning.

I don't suppose you will be one but in case . . .'
Nearer he came till he breathed in my face:
'Have you ever heard of the Beastly Bard?
Now I want to listen, so you keep guard.'

Expecting the usual delay all ranks
    Were making themselves at home on the moor,
With a railway carriage, some cloth and some planks
    Had rigged up a pub, and a chemist's store,
    A plain tea for sixpence and a dancing floor
With a canvas latrine attached at the side.
Longings were loosened there, very sad.

Soon I saw Mosley, the descendant of Pitt,
    Standing a boxer a small port wine.
Rothermere and Beaverbook were eating bananas,
    Sir Owen Seaman was teaching some swine
    To sneer at a char with a washing-line,
And standing aloof like a blasted tree
Was the gaunt Director of the B.B.C.

Sir Alfred Mond was arranging the seating
    And distributing programmes at a special booth
Where Sir Austen was addressing a mothers' meeting.
    'Send your sons to us. To tell you the truth
    Our managers are very fond of youth.'
Sir Benjamin Drage went round with a tray
Selling them cocktails in the old Drage way.

A colonel from Cheltenham stopped everyone
    To tell them the lost Ten Tribes were there.
The Dolmetsch family, father and son
    Who had driven in a brake from Haslemere,
    Were giving a concert, but no one could hear.
Lord Baden-Powell with a piece of string
Was proving that reef-knots honour the King.

Then Major Douglas got up to preach.
    He held up two pennies for all to see
Then put them down and laid match-stalks on each.
    'Let this be A and let this be B.'
    A boy in kilts went down on one knee
But Sir Montagu Norman so debonair
Walked by without looking, his beard in the air.

Unhappy Eliot choosing his words
    And D'Arcy's beautiful head at a glance
I noticed building a sanctum for birds;
    Pound had just sent them a wire from France.
    The Sitwells were giving a private dance
But Wyndham Lewis disguised as the maid
Was putting cascara in the still lemonade.

A council scholar was shaking his fist,
    'I can't understand it. O, but I see
Dum not an adverb.' A Wykehamist
        Was refuting Joseph under a tree,
        'But Plato and Aristotle were both B.C.'
In the ditch below me sulked Maynard Keynes,
'In Cambridge,' he blubbered, 'they think I have brains.'

On a lorry the centre of a gaping crowd
    A man was eating a hedgehog whole;
Presently he rose and said very loud
        'The colon we know is the seat of the soul
        Keep the colon clean by conscious control.'
In the middle distance a titled whore
Was distributing trusses to the ruptured poor.

'The swine, the swine! He's gone into that wood,'
    My strange companion suddenly cried:
'Excuse me.' He rushed off as hard as he could
        Leaving his phone in my hands: I tried
        To pick out the wool which was stuffed inside,
And listened: at first I could hear no sound,
Then confusing murmurs came up from the ground.

'My next slide, ladies, shows the Amœba.'
    'He admitted at last he'd dreamed of a fort.'
'Meine Liebe ist kein körperliche Liebe.'
        'Look at the peachy ferrets I've brought.'
        'Mumsie, darling, don't cry.' 'You ought
To have seen her taking those hairpin bends.'
'I say, you fellows, can't we be friends.'

'You beastly rotters, you've made me come.'
    'You must follow through, sir, after your ball.'
'Haven't we given you a happy home.'
        'Chilean Nitrates are certain to fall.'
        'I can't understand this poem at all.'
'O but you should have seen her; she was lovely in Wings.'
'Try to let your mind dwell on the beautiful things.'

A cry went through me like a stab of a knife
    And the flex of the telephone gave with a snap,
'Life. Life. Eternal Life.'
        Striking out wildly like a beast in a trap
        A youth charged head down; under his cap
A trickle of blood from a bullet smear showed
As he zig-zagged shrieking down the road.

Orders were shouted, a hubbub arose:
    'Look out. A deserter. We want that man.
Gup Vexer, Bramble, Verse out of Prose!'

Waving rattles the healers ran.
Dr. Ernest Jones was well in the van,
And panting and pounding after the rest
My old headmaster in a little pink vest.

Comments were uttered from every direction.
    'There goes the result of a banker's ramp.'
'He only wants regular sexual connection.'
    'In Germany they'd send him to a summer camp.'
    'The cure for all this is a sunlight lamp.'
'In Russia such cases are unknown now for years,
In Russia they've got some ripping new rears.'

The ranks got unruly and yelled 'Let's be free!'
    Some pulling up saplings were thrashing their wives.
'I can fly,' cried one and fell off a tree.
    'Comrades,' another, 'draw your knives.'
    The secret police had the time of their lives.
Herding hundreds to a long black van
They drove them off to the Government San.

'Never sleep, never sleep, always on the go,'
    The owner of the telephone was back again.
'O the fools, the fools. Why, don't they know
    What I said to Lloyd George in 1918?
    He couldn't answer, his hands weren't clean.
And I gave them lessons in deciphering codes,
I warned them of spies in acrostic odes.'

Something fell on my head. It had started to snow.
    The rioters stopped and fell quietly in,
'You have your orders, you know where to go.'
    The general's voice sounded queer and thin.
    'The Eagles' attack on the North will begin.
The Tigers will occupy the South to-day.'
The bands struck up and they moved away.

Darker grew the sky and my companion's look.
    'The answer, my friend,' he muttered, 'is No.'
From his pocket a water-pistol he took,
    Then, turning to me, 'I'm afraid it's snow.
    You will have to excuse me, but I must go.
This means that Farrel will certain start
Debauching Gibson. I shall keep them apart.'

Wheeling at once one column marched
    Across the Black Bridge for Arrochar,
The Tigers in the old Luss Road I watched
    Head for Dumbarton where the ship cranes are;
    Throbbing of drums came back from far:
A girl reading letters stayed after the rest
Then stumbled away with them held to her breast.

Stillness was total; everyone had gone.
I stared into the road; the snow fell on
Soundlessly closing on the winter day.
All other feelings died away
Absorbed in its enormous slight sensation
Leaving the mind to moralise
Upon these blurring images
Of the dingy difficult life of our generation.[1]

February 1932

IV · UNCOLLECTED POEMS 1939–1942

I · PASCAL

O had his mother, near her time, been praying
Up to her crucifix and prayed too long?
Until exhausted she grew stiff like wood;
The future of herself hung dangerous and heavy
From her uprightness like a malefactor,
And in a trance she re-negotiated
The martyrdom that even in Auvergne
Would be demanded as the price for life.

Knowledge was lifted up on Love but faced
Away from her towards the lives in refuge,
Directed always to the moon-struck jeering neighbours
Who'd grown aware of being watched and come
Uneasily, against their native judgment,
And still were coming up the local paths
From every gate of the protective town
And every crevice of the noon-hot landscape.

None who conceivably could hate him were excluded;
His back was turned on no one but herself
Who had to go on holding him and bear
The terror in their faces as they screamed 'Be Angry,'
The stolid munching of their puzzled animals
Who'd raised their heads from grazing; even ploughs
They'd left behind to see him hurt were noticed;
Nothing in France was disregarded but her worship.

Did then the patient tugging of his will
Not to turn round for comfort shake her faith,
O when she saw the magistrate-in-charge,
The husband who had given him to her look up
Into that fascinating sorrow, and was certain
That even *he* forgot her, did she then deny
The only bond they shared, the right to suffer,
And join the others in a wish to murder?

[1] For Part II see headnote to this appendix.

Whatever happened, he was born deserted
And lonelier than any adult: they at least
Had dwelt in childhoods once where dogs were hopeful
And chairs could fly and doors remove a tyrant;
Even the ablest could recall a day
Of diagnosis when the first stab of his talent
Ran through the beardless boy and spoilt the sadness
Of the closed life the stupid never leave.

However primitive, all others had their ferry
Over the dreadful water to those woods from which,
Irrelevant like flies that win a coward's battle,
The flutes and laughter of the happily diverted
Broke in effectively across his will
To build a life upon original disorder:
How could he doubt the evidence he had
Of Paris and the earth? His misery was real.

All dreams led back into the nightmare garden
Where the great families who should have loved him slept
Loving each other, not a single rose
Dared leave its self-regard, and he alone was kneeling,
Submitting to a night that promised nothing,
Not even punishment, but let him pray;
Prayer bled to death in its abyssal spaces,
Mocked by the silence of their unbelief.

Yet like a lucky orphan he had been discovered
And instantly adopted by a Gift;
And she became the sensible protector
Who found a passage through the caves of accusation,
And even in the canyon of distress was able
To use the echo of his weakness as a proof
That joy was probable, and took the place
Of the poor lust and hunger he had never known.

And never told him he was different from the others,
Too weak to face their innocently brutal questions,
Assured him he was stronger than Descartes,
And let him think it was his own finesse
That promised him a miracle, and doubt by doubt
Restored the ruined chateau of his faith;
Until at last, one Autumn, all was ready:
And in the night the Unexpected came.

The empty was transformed into possession,
The cold burst into flames; creation was on fire
And his weak moment blazing like a bush,
A symptom of the order and the praise;
And he had place like Abraham and Jacob,
And was incapable of evil like a star,

For isolation had been utterly consumed,
And everything that could exist was holy.

All that was really willed would be accomplished:
The crooked custom take its final turning
Into the truth it always meant to reach;
The barrack's filthy oath could not arrest
Its move towards the just, nor flesh annihilate
The love that somewhere every day persuades it,
Brought to a sensual incandescence in the dark,
To do the deed that has made all the saints.

Then it was over. By the morning he was cool,
His faculties for sin restored completely,
And eight years to himself. But round his neck
Now hung a louder cry than the familiar tune
Libido Excellendi whistled as he wrote
The lucid and unfair. And still it rings
Wherever there are children, doubt and deserts,
Or cities that exist for mercy and for judgment.

August 1939

2 · EPITHALAMION
(FOR GIUSEPPE ANTONIO BORGESE AND ELIZABETH MANN,
NOV. 23, 1939)

While explosives blow to dust
Friends and hopes, we cannot pray,
Absolute conviction must
Seem the whole of life to youth,
Battle's stupid gross event
Keep all learning occupied:
Yet the seed becomes the tree;
Happier savants may decide
That this quiet wedding of
A Borgese and a Mann
Planted human unity;
Hostile kingdoms of the truth,
Fighting fragments of content,
Here were reconciled by love,
Modern policy begun
        On this day.

A priori dogmas brought
Into one collective will
All the European thought:
Eagle theologians swept
With an autocratic eye
Hungry for potential foes
The whole territory of truth
Where the great cathedrals rose;

453

Gentle to instinctive crimes,
With a sharp indulgence heard
Paradox-debating youth,
Listened where the injured wept
For the first rebellious sigh,
And unerringly at times
On some small progressive bird
    Swooped to kill.

But beneath them as they flew
Merchants with more prudent gaze
Broke eternity in two:
Unconcerned at the controls
Sat an ascetic engineer
In whose intellectual hand
Worlds of dull material lay,
All that bankers understand;
While elected by the heart
Out of sentiment, a lamb
With haemorrhages night and day
Saved enthusiastic souls;
Sorrow apt to interfere,
Wit that spoils romantic art,
In the social diagram
    Knew their place.

Yet no lie has only friends
Too polite to ask for proof:
Patriots, peering through the lens
Of their special discipline
At the map of knowledge, see
Superstition overcome
As all national frontiers melt
In a true imperium;
Fearing foreign skills no more,
Feel in each conative act
Such a joy as Dante felt
When, a total failure in
An inferior city, he,
Dreaming out his anger, saw
All the scattered leaves of fact
    Bound by love.

May this bed of marriage be
Symbol now of the rebirth
Asked of old humanity:
Let creative limbs explore
All creation's pleasure then;
Laughing horses, rocks that scream,
All the flowers that ever flew
Through the banquet of a dream,

Find in you a common love
Of extravagant sanity;
Till like Leonardo who,
Jostled by the sights of war
And unpleasant greedy men,
At Urbino watched a dove,
Your experience justify
    Life on earth.

Grateful in your happiness,
Let your Ariels fly away
To a gay unconsciousness
And a freely-chosen task:
Shame at our shortcomings makes
Lame magicians of us all,
Forcing our invention to
An illegal miracle
And a theatre of disguise;
Brilliantly your angels took
Every lover's role for you,
Wore seduction like a mask
Or were frigid for your sakes;
Set these shadows, now your eyes
On the whole of substance look,
    Free to-day.

Kindly to each other turn,
Every timid vice forgive
With a quaker's quiet concern
For the uncoercive law,
Till your double wish be one,
Till, as you successful lie,
Begotten possibility,
Censoring the nostalgic sigh
To be nothing or be right,
Form its ethical resolve
Now to suffer and to be:
Though the kingdoms are at war,
All the peoples see the sun,
All the dwellings stand in light,
All the unconquered worlds revolve,
    Life must live.

Vowing to redeem the State,
Now let every girl and boy
To the heaven of the Great
All their prayers and praises lift:
Mozart with ironic breath
Turning poverty to song,
Goethe ignorant of sin
Placing every human wrong,

455

Blake the industrious visionary,
Tolstoi the great animal,
Hellas-loving Hölderlin,
Wagner who obeyed his gift
Organised his wish for death
Into a tremendous cry,
Looking down upon us, all
  Wish us joy.

         September 1939

      3
   (TO CHESTER KALLMAN)

Every eye must weep alone
Till I Will be overthrown.

But I Will can be removed,
Not having sense enough
To guard against I Know,
But I Will can be removed.

Then all I's can meet and grow,
I Am become I Love,
I Have Not I Am Loved,
Then all I's can meet and grow.

Till I Will be overthrown
Every eye must weep alone.

         ? 1939

      4

'Gold in the North,' came the blizzard to say,
I left my sweetheart at the break of day,
The gold ran out and my love turned grey.
You don't know all, sir, you don't know all.

'The West,' said the sun, 'for enterprise,'
A bullet in Frisco put me wise,
My last words were 'God damn your eyes.'
You don't know all, sir, you don't know all.

In the streets of New York I was young and swell,
I rode the market, the market fell,
One morning I woke and found myself in hell,
You don't know all, sir, you don't know all.

In Alabama my heart was full,
Down by the river bank I stole,

The waters of grief went over my soul,
You don't know all, ma'am, you don't know all.

In the saloons I heaved a sigh,
Lost in deserts of alkali I lay down to die;
There's always a sorrow can get you down,
All the world's whiskey won't ever drown.

Some think they're strong, some think they're smart,
Like butterflies they're pulled apart,
America can break your heart.
You don't know all, sir, you don't know all.

? 1939

5

O season of repetition and return,
Of light and the primitive visions of light
   Opened in little ponds, disturbing
    The blind water that conducts excitement.

How lucid the image in your shining well
Of a limpid day, how eloquent your streams
   Of lives without language, the cell ma-
    noeuvres and the molecular bustle.

O hour of images when we sniff the herb
Of childhood and forget who we are and dream
   Like whistling boys of the vast spaces
    Of the Inconsistent racing towards us

With all its appealing private detail; but
Our gestures betray us as, crossing the legs
   Or resting the cheek in the hand, we
    Hide the mouths through which the Disregarded

Will always enter. For we know we're not boys
And never will be: part of us all hates life,
   And some are completely against it.
    Spring leads the truculent sailors into

The parks, and the plump little girls, but none
Are determined like the tiny brains who found
   The great communities of summer:
    Only on battlefields, where the dying

With low voices and not very much to say
Repair the antique silence the insects broke
   In an architectural passion,
    Can night return to our cooling fibres.

O not even war can frighten us enough;
That last attempt to eliminate the Strange
    By uniting us all in a terror
    Of something known, even that's a failure

Which cannot stop us taking our walks alone,
Scared of the unknown unconditional dark,
    Down the avenues of our longing:
    For, however they dream they are scattered,

Our bones cannot help reassembling themselves
Into their philosophic cities to hold
    The knowledge they cannot get out of;
    And neither a Spring nor a War can ever

So condition his ears as to keep the Song
That is not a sorrow from the Double Man:
    O what weeps is the love that hears, an
    Accident occurring in his substance.

Spring 1940

6 · NIETZSCHE

O masterly debunker of our liberal fallacies, how
Well you flayed each low Utilitarian and
All the arid prudence of their so-called Rational Man
That made envy the one basis of all moral acts.

All your life you stormed, like your English forerunner Blake,
Warning, Nietzsche, against that decadent tradition
Which in Luther appeared a fragrant and promising bloom:
Soon Europe swarmed with your clerical followers.

In dim Victorian days you prophesied a reaction,
And how right you've been. But tell us, O tell us, is
This tenement gangster with a sub-machine gun in one hand

Really the Superman your jealous eyes imagined,
That dark Daemonic One whose voice would cleave the rock open
And offer our moribund era the water of life?

1940

7 · CHRISTMAS 1940

The journals give the quantities of wrong,
Where the impatient massacre took place,
How many and what sort it caused to die,
But, O, what finite integers express
The realm of malice where these facts belong?

How can the mind make sense, bombarded by
A stream of incompatible mishaps,
The bloom and buzz of a confessed collapse?

What properties define our person since
This massive vagueness moved in on our lives,
What laws require our substance to exist?
Our strands of private order are dissolved
And lost our routes to self-inheritance,
Position and Relation are dismissed,
An epoch's Providence is quite worn out,
The lion of Nothing chases us about.

'Beware! Beware! The Great Boyg has you down,'
Some deeper instinct in revulsion cries,
'The Void desires to have you for its creature,
A doll through whom It may ventriloquise
Its vast resentment as your very own,
Because Negation has nor form nor feature,
And all Its lust to power is impotent
Unless the actual It hates consent.

'The universe of pure extension where
Nothing except the universe was lonely,
For Promise was occluded in its womb
Where the immortal families had only
To fall to pieces and accept repair,
Their nursery, their commonplace, their tomb,
All acts accessory to their position,
Died when the first plant made its apparition.

'Through a long adolescence, then, the One
Slept in the sadness of its disconnected
Aggressive creatures—as a latent wish
The local genius of the rose protected,
Or an unconscious irony within
The independent structure of the fish;
But Flesh grew weaker, stronger grew the Word,
Until on earth the Great Exchange occurred.

'Now to maturity must crawl that child
In whom the old equations are reversed
For that is cause which was effect before,
Now he must learn for what he has been nursed
That through his self-annulment the real world
Of self-enduring instants may endure
Its final metamorphosis and pass
Into invisibility at last.'

The sacred auras fade from well and wood,
The great geometries enclose our lives

In fields of normal enmity no more,
The definitions and the narratives
Are insufficient for our solitude,
Venus cannot predict our passion, nor
The Dioscuri plant their olive trees
To guide us through the ambiguities.

And winds of terror force us to confess
The settled world of past events has not
A faiblesse any longer for the dull
To swim in like an aqueous habitat;
We are reduced to our true nakedness:
Either we serve the Unconditional,
Or some Hitlerian monster will supply
An iron convention to do evil by.

O beggar, bigwig, mugwump, none but have
Some vision of that holy centre where
All time's occasions are refreshed; the lost
Are met by all the other places there,
The rival errors recognise their love,
Fall weeping on each other's neck at last;
The rich need not confound the Persons, nor
The Substance be divided by the poor.

It is the vision that objectifies:
Only its Roman rigour can bestow
On earth and sea 'la douceur angevine,'
Only its prayer can make the children grow,
Only its trembling can externalise
The bland Horatian life of friends and wine;
It is the tension of its inner dread
That moulds the beautiful patrician head.

Our way remains, our world, our day, our sin;
We may, as always, by our own consent
Be cast away: but neither depth nor height
Nor any other creature can prevent
Our reasonable and lively motions in
This modern void where only Love has weight,
And Fate by Faith is freely understood,
And he who works shall find our Fatherhood.

December 1940

8 · IN WAR TIME
(FOR CAROLINE NEWTON)

Abruptly mounting her ramshackle wheel,
Fortune has pedalled furiously away;
The sobbing mess is on our hands to-day.

460

Those accidental terrors, Famine, Flood,
Were never trained to diagnose or heal
Nightmares that are intentional and real.

Nor lust nor gravity can preach an aim
To minds disordered by a lucid dread
Of seeking peace by going off one's head.

Nor will the living waters whistle; though
Diviners cut their throats to prove their claim,
The desert remains arid all the same.

If augurs take up flying to fulfill
The doom they prophesy, it must be so:
The herons have no modern sign for No.

If nothing can upset but total war

That solitude is something you can kill,

If we are right to choose our suffering
And be tormented by an Either-Or,
The right to fail that is worth dying for,

If so, the sweets of victory are rum:
A pride of earthly cities premising
The Inner Life as socially the thing,

Where, even to the lawyers, Law is what,
For better or for worse, our vows become
When no one whom we need is looking, Home

A sort of honour, not a building site,
Wherever we are, when, if we chose, we might
Be somewhere else, yet trust that we have chosen right.

June 1942

Index of Titles and First Lines

Separable poems in the two versions of 'Paid on Both Sides' and in 'Journal of an Airman' are indexed selectively. Where variant titles or first lines are mentioned in the textual notes in Appendix II, these are indexed with a cross-reference to the version printed in the main text. Of the prose essays in Part IX, only those with titles are indexed.